The Tecumsehs of the International Association

ALSO BY BRIAN MARTIN
AND FROM MCFARLAND

*Baseball's Creation Myth: Adam Ford,
Abner Graves and the Cooperstown Story* (2013)

The Tecumsehs of the International Association

Canada's First Major League Baseball Champions

BRIAN MARTIN

Foreword by William Humber

McFarland & Company, Inc., Publishers
Jefferson, North Carolina

ISBN 978-0-7864-9436-1 (softcover : acid free paper) ♾
ISBN 978-1-4766-1869-2 (ebook)

LIBRARY OF CONGRESS CATALOGUING DATA ARE AVAILABLE

BRITISH LIBRARY CATALOGUING DATA ARE AVAILABLE

© 2015 Brian Martin. All rights reserved

No part of this book may be reproduced or transmitted in any form or by any means, electronic or mechanical, including photocopying or recording, or by any information storage and retrieval system, without permission in writing from the publisher.

On the cover: 1876 London Tecumsehs baseball club (*Canadian Illustrated News,* July 15, 1879)

Printed in the United States of America

*McFarland & Company, Inc., Publishers
Box 611, Jefferson, North Carolina 28640
www.mcfarlandpub.com*

Dedicated to the late Les Bronson,
who for so many years kept alive
the memory of the Tecumsehs.

Table of Contents

Acknowledgments — ix
Foreword — 1
Preface — 7

1. A Newcomer Catches Fever — 11
2. Roots — 25
3. Of Arms Races and Foreign Legions — 40
4. Out with the Old… — 58
5. A New Era — 72
6. Opportunity Knocks — 90
7. Setting the Tables — 104
8. Early 1877—The Magical Run Begins — 116
9. Late 1877—Champions — 129
10. Between Innings — 146
11. Rumblings — 160
12. The Dream Dies — 175
13. Moving On — 190
14. After the Glory Days — 203
15. Pitching the Pitch — 221

Epilogue — 235
Chapter Notes — 241
Bibliography — 257
Index — 261

Acknowledgments

To the many people who were so kind to help this author pull together information from many sources to make this book possible: Thank you.

The first who must be acknowledged is William "Bill" Humber, who was wonderfully supportive and generous in sharing the fruits of his research with the author. He has done what has been impossible in the past—found publishers in Canada willing to consider books about baseball. That is no small feat, as the author of this book can attest from sad experience. The notion of putting a hockey stick in the hands of the Tecumsehs in hopes of drumming up interest among Canadian publishers was considered for precisely a nanosecond. Publishers love hockey books in the Great White North but have little appetite for works about the country's summertime sport. Despite that attitude, Humber has done a wonderful job reminding Canadians that baseball is their game, too, with his several books on the subject.

London historian Dan Brock could always be counted on to confirm a fact or track down a crucial detail, no matter how small. He proved to be an invaluable resource, along with Arthur McClelland at London Public Library's Ivey Room and Theresa Regnier at the Regional Room Collection at Western University in London. Also in London, historian Stephen Harding constantly provided a nugget or two of interesting information. Assistance was also provided by the wonderful staff members at the Lambton Room at the Lambton County Public Library in Wyoming, Ontario. Also in Lambton, Sylvia Fairbank and Tom Martin in Petrolia and Donna McIlmoyle at Petrolia Discovery proved to be great help in understanding the life and times of Jake Englehart in that community.

In Guelph, Ontario, archivist Darcy Hiltz at Guelph Public Library was conscientious and efficient. Also in Guelph, special thanks are extended to Jan Brett, library assistant, and archivist Kathryn Harvey at the University of Guelph Library, keepers of the Sleeman Collection of papers. Lynette Walton, archivist for the Imperial Oil Collection at Glenbow Museum in Calgary, shared some wonderful, hard-to-find images.

At the Canadian Baseball Hall of Fame in St. Marys, Ontario, Scott Crawford was supportive and bent over backwards to help. At the National Baseball Hall of Fame Library in Cooperstown, former research director Tim Wiles was cheerfully helpful. Also there, John Horne deserves a shout-out for locating and sharing some fine images.

In Buffalo, Shane Stephenson at Buffalo History Museum was very helpful. Thanks are also due to Buffalo baseball historian John Boutet. In Pittsburgh, Craig Britcher, curatorial assistant at the Senator John Heinz History Center, was kind and generous while shedding light on the Allegheny club and the city.

John Castle, Jr., the grandson of Tecumseh pitcher Fred Goldsmith, conducted a painstaking amount of research to buttress Goldsmith's claim that he invented the curveball pitch. The body of his work appears in his book, *Goldie's Curve Ball*. I thank him for his interest and support.

David Arcidiacono of East Hampton, Connecticut, again deserves my thanks. A fellow member of the Society for American Baseball Research, he helped me find a publisher for my first book on a baseball topic a few years back. David and I have swapped information about Goldsmith for some time, and he eventually produced an excellent article on Goldsmith's claim that he invented the curve pitch. I was delighted to cite his "closer look" paper on Goldsmith in this book.

Finally, kudos and a medal are deserved by my very patient friend and copy editor, Jane Karchmar, whose eagle-eyed attention to matters of detail, grammar and spelling have helped make this effort immeasurably better.

To anyone I may have overlooked, sincere apologies.

Foreword

Ever notice how often American weather maps stop their forecasting at the Canadian border before resuming their storytelling much farther down the road? It's as if those big storms out of the west are boxed up in Detroit and mysteriously transported east in the manner of witness protection clients before re-emerging somewhere around Buffalo and then marching on to the Atlantic. This analogy could equally apply to a great deal of the history of baseball in Canada and its relationship to the larger story of the game's roots in North America.

Don't believe me? Pick up any of the major works on baseball's early days, starting with that of the venerable populist Al Spalding, through the groundbreaking academic analysis of Harold and Dorothy Seymour, and most recently the deeply researched works of John Thorn and Peter Morris. Check out their Canadian content. It's amazingly thin.

This is not the fault exclusively of American-based historians. Read any standard history of sports and culture written by Canadians. As often as not they'll excuse Canada's predilection for the "Yankee" game as the sadly diminished ability of their countrymen to ward off the continentalist domination of their neighbors to the south. Even Prime Minister Stephen Harper's book about early hockey history in Toronto is the latest to succumb to that canard.

All such perspectives are simply wrong or at least wrong-headed. To put the matter simply, Canadians were among early baseball's regional pioneers, embedding their love of the game and experimentation with its play into local diamonds and "town versus town" rivalries long before the reserve clause, professional ballplayers, and formal leagues were ever imagined. No other baseball-playing country can make that claim.

One reason for this misunderstanding, or at least its limited consideration, is the curse of "presentism"—that tendency to look back on the world and see it only through the eyes of present-day mores and interests, and the success stories of the victors. By the dawn of the twentieth century, Canadian teams were firmly entrenched as members of baseball's disparate minor leagues, and so gave every appearance of being subservient followers of an American overlord. This was a fate, however, shared with most regions of the United States outside the then-dominant northeast.

New sports such as hockey and football had emerged in Canada to trump a one-time fascination with popular nineteenth-century recreations such as cricket, lacrosse, baseball, and even snowshoeing. Indeed, it is significant that of all of those latter fascinations, only baseball has retained a popular affection in all parts of the country to this day.

Baseball-type activity, in its most informal character, has been recorded from Nova Scotia's Dartmouth to Ontario's Beachville (about which Brian Martin has written eloquently and provocatively elsewhere), and from Manitoba's Selkirk Settlement to British Columbia's Victoria in what were the early years of local European settlement. These often primitive games found advocates and rough playing fields comparable to those in the United States, not surprising given the game's overseas roots, and particularly those from "Olde England" to which Canada retains a connection to this day. Historian David Block's rediscovery of this essential origin only confirms the basic connection of Canada's ball playing to, at least in part, a direct British importation, alongside an American influence.

A somewhat distinct Canadian interpretation of baseball play reaches back into a netherworld of unrecorded evolution from the early years of the nineteenth century, while the formalization of club structures had emerged in southwestern Ontario by the 1850s (1854 in Hamilton, and possibly 1855, but definitely 1856, in London). The latter was at the same time—and in some cases earlier—as its organization in nearby American regions.

The Canadian style of play, like other regional experiments in the United States, had largely been abandoned in favor of the "New York game" by the 1860s (the chief change being an end to the "soaking" of a base runner, the tossing of the ball at a runner and hitting him with it while he was between bases in order to "retire" him). Nevertheless, a proudly local realm of control and players dominated until the age of the professional reached fruition in the 1870s. Even then, local rivalries and leagues, and challenge matches on equal terms with the best teams from south of the border, continued well into the 1880s.

The high water mark of this engagement with baseball was the period from 1876 through 1878. By then, baseball had long since surpassed cricket as the dominant bat and ball game in both Canada and the United States, but only in the latter was it described as the national pastime. Canadians, seemingly in a defensive posture, labeled the native game of lacrosse with a similar identity in Canada, despite baseball's greater grass roots appeal. Had the long evolution of baseball in Canada, culminating most particularly in the 1877 season, taken an increasingly upward trajectory, it's possible Canadians would have finally acknowledged that baseball had a similar identity to that in the United States. After all, both the soccer and cricket-loving countries of today have no problem recognizing one, or the other, as their national game despite its British pedigree.

Nowhere was this story of success, and then a kind of failure, more fully played out than in London, Ontario, Canada. English, baseball-type games were played there when the province was still called Upper Canada. It was a place that along with the city of Hamilton (on the shore of Lake Ontario) was the setting for the first organized teams, rules, and organizers. Hamilton's 1850s baseball primacy had been surpassed by Woodstock in the 1860s, and then Guelph in the 1870s. All eventually declined but in so doing laid the groundwork for London's eventual ascendancy within a decade of Canada's 1867 Confederation.

The London Tecumsehs are the storied team of a successful city. Situated halfway between Niagara and Detroit in a rural hinterland with seemingly few natural advantages and the absence of a waterfront location, London was far enough removed from Canadian rivals to create its own mini-business hegemony. Likewise, the arrival of American expatriates and the eventual completion of the Grand Trunk and Great Western railways provided the city with resources, opportunities, and influences that not only staked its local economy to a robust future but found a welcoming place for the emerging baseball enthusiasm of the nineteenth century.

Where in this period, you might ask, was Toronto, the province's metropolis, a mere 150 miles to the east? Its sports picture is more muddled. Cricket dominated the early days, followed by lacrosse; curling was the winter sport of choice. Both baseball and, later, ice hockey were "Johnny-come-latelys" in attracting that city's sporting enthusiasm. London, in other words, had a somewhat clearer path to its baseball supremacy.

The Tecumsehs' route was laid by the Guelph Maple Leafs and their mercurial owner and sponsor, the brewer George Sleeman. They had been Canada's first great professional success story in many contests with American rivals. The 1875 clashes between Guelph and London attracted thousands. In 1876, the two cities entered the first ever, somewhat formal, Canadian league along with teams from Hamilton, Toronto, and Kingston. Even greater crowds of fans flocked to their games.

The problem was that the Maple Leafs and Tecumsehs were too good, largely by being eminently more successful in attracting superior, most often American, talent. There have been few better ballplayers ever to represent a Canadian city than the Tecumsehs' American recruits, Fred Goldsmith and Joe Hornung. In Richard Southam (he of the renowned Canadian publishing family and uncle of a future major league catcher, George "Mooney" Gibson) and Tom Gillean (son an accomplished London business family, later a National League umpire) the Tecs also had two local boys who could play with the best, although they were generally relegated to the city's second team, the Atlantics.

And so Guelph and London entered that great baseball experiment, the International Association of 1877. It was a challenge to the owner-controlled National League, founded one year before. The International Association was open to smaller cities, local civic boosters, and even ballplayer-led teams. In that great endeavor, however, it was already clear that Guelph was slipping from its leadership position. Sleeman's resources could not match those of London's benefactor, Jacob Englehart, an enterprising, American-born financier and oil refiner, nor could Guelph's city size command the larger gates available in London. Baseball clubs, in the era before today's money from media contracts and the sale of sports gear, were gate-money dependent.

London emerged as Canada's top baseball club. Their dominance culminated in the 1877 International Association championship. It was the first accruing to a major rival of the National League, but here "presentism" raises its ugly head. The International Association has been dubbed, long after the fact, a minor league by historians. This may have been caused by confusion with a future unrelated, but actual minor league, the International League, of which many Canadian cities were occasional or long-term members.

The characterization of the International Association as a minor league is absurd in the absence of anything resembling a reserve clause which, as it gradually came into existence in the 1880s, ensured that first rights to a player were held in perpetuity by a League team regardless of the player's contractual status. This allowed the League to control the best players and designate where they might play, thus laying the foundation for the formal dependency implicit in a major/minor league relationship. Secondly, the Association explicitly rejected the League Alliance proposal put forward by the League in which all disputes would be resolved by a League-controlled jurisdictional process. Finally, the Association's teams played League rivals on an equal footing, though this is always a problematic basis for comparison given the hippodroming of the age (losing a game in order to boost the gate at the re-match) and determining the intent of teams involved in what were essentially exhibition matches.

Perhaps the Association's unorthodox structure in light of what emerged in North American sports caused later reviewers to downgrade its status. We should recognize, however, that what the International Association posited, and what it could have become in relation to other leagues, is quite similar to what actually happened with soccer in much of Europe, including England. Even today, complex interpretations of custodial ownership along with upward and even downward movement of teams from one level to another, make for an organizational entity uncommon to the North American viewer.

To his credit, David Pietrusza's *Major Leagues* is one of the few serious histories that acknowledges the Association's major league legitimacy while attempting to account for its later downgrading.

London may or may not have been seriously offered an opportunity to join that National League for the 1878 season, though Harry Gorman, London's managing director, writing to a Buffalo baseball official at the time, says they were. Though it could not have met the League's minimum population requirement, we should remember that in its early years the National League was itself touch-and-go as to whether it might survive and initially included one team from a city below its stipulated minimum population. A flourishing and well-sponsored London team would have been a good catch for the League. The National League restriction on games with teams from outside the League caused Tecumseh management to reject the opportunity. And so, for the want of future games in Guelph and Buffalo, London lost a chance to change Canada's baseball history and perhaps its sport history as well.

Those brief salad days of London baseball, when the summer game reached a peak in Canada not matched until the Toronto Blue Jays' two World Series triumphs, is a story told by Brian Martin with extraordinary depth and understanding in the following pages. If nothing else, it should dispel the dismissal of the game by later commentators as an imposition on a submissive population. Baseball was, has been, and continues to be as much a Canadian as an American sport, and nowhere is this better understood than in the London of Upper Canada, Canada West, and today's Ontario.

I have one last personal reason to recall fondly the London Tecumsehs. As the Canadian league stumbled through its inaugural 1876 season, the high-flying Tecs continued their barnstorming ways, visiting small towns and large, in the manner of Barnum's circus. They drew healthy gates, earned variable amounts of money, and proclaimed the last vestiges of an era in which towns of all sizes could compete on equal terms before being left behind, or consigned to secondary status, by the emerging big business of professional baseball.

That year, they came to my town, Bowmanville, on the shore of Lake Ontario, and played the Royal Oaks, a squad descended from formally organized entities dating back at least as far as 1861. The ball field was on what was then known as the Drill Shed Grounds, a place as well for recreation, visiting circuses, and town fairs. It is just around the corner from where I live today. London beat Bowmanville handily, but what was remarkable was the way they were treated afterwards. A strawberry ice cream social was held in their honor and they stayed as long as possible, joining in a community sing-along, before boarding a westbound train for home.

On warm summer nights, I'll walk down Carlisle Avenue, where the ball field was located. It's been a residential neighborhood for over a hundred years, built by Goodyear for its workers. I like to imagine those Tecumsehs Goldsmith, Hornung, Southam, Gillean, and the others, in the manner, I suppose, of W. P. Kinsella's ghosts of baseball past, lingering in the still of the evening, contemplating the wonder of baseball's grip on Canadians and cherishing the opportunity to share their ball playing gifts with them.

William Humber, an historian and teacher, is the author of five books on Canadian baseball as well as six others. He has taught a Baseball Spring Training for Fans course at Seneca College in Toronto for 36 years and is a tour guide to Cooperstown and a regular participant at its annual Nineteenth Century Baseball History Conference. A Saskatchewan Baseball Hall of Fame member, he is a selector for Canada's Baseball Hall of Fame in St. Marys, Ontario.

Preface

> In 1992, baseball became truly international when the Toronto, Canada, Blue Jays won the World Series...."
> —Narrator John Chancellor, in *Baseball*, the Emmy Award-winning 1994 documentary about the game by Ken Burns

Wrong. Not so. Except, of course, for the fact that the Jays won the World Series.

Baseball did not suddenly vault beyond the borders of the United States in 1992, finally becoming "truly international." Burns' acclaimed documentary about America's national pastime seemed content to perpetuate the myth that the game is purely American and the country's gift to the world. He didn't hold back. Each of its episodes began with a version of "The Star Spangled Banner" as he wrapped the game in Old Glory.

The Toronto Blue Jays had been in existence a mere 15 years when they won the World Series, which, incidentally, took its name from the newspaper *The World*, not the planet itself. They repeated the feat the following year. But this wasn't the first Canadian team to become champions of a major professional baseball league dominated by American teams. The Tecumsehs, of London, Ontario, did that exactly a century before the Blue Jays were born. The Tecumsehs won the inaugural championship of the International Association in 1877. That league was established to challenge the National League, which the previous year was created by a small group of businessmen to wrest control of the game from players and place it on a solid, more businesslike footing. At a time when baseball was exploding in popularity across North America, the founders of the International Association resented the exclusivity a handful of capitalists brought to the game. They rebelled, opening wide the doors of their organization that played baseball as much for the love of the game, and to promote their communities, as for the pursuit of profit. They were inclusive and wanted a "big tent" approach to prevail in the game of baseball. International Association teams paid well and attracted some of the top professionals of the day. Some players launched their professional careers with IA teams. The Tecumsehs weren't the only Canadian entry in the loop that stretched from New York, Connecticut, and Massachusetts to Ohio and Pennsylvania. London's longtime Ontario rival, the Guelph Maple Leafs, also became charter members. The Canadian teams put the "international" in the name of the league. They were the two best teams in Canada, and games between them attracted as many as 10,000 fans. But they sought more competition from American teams than their cross-border barnstorming had been providing.

Baseball's roots lie in England, in the children's game called rounders, and similar bat-and-ball games that have been traced back even further to ancient Egypt. Early settlers in New England, New York, and adjoining states brought with them their customs and games from the old country. So, too, did those who migrated to Britain's other colonies in North America. But in America, the desire to prove that baseball was a completely homegrown sport and not derived from a game played by children in England was powerful. Lingering anti–British sentiment was strong and Albert Goodwill Spalding, a former star pitcher and super-patriot, took it upon himself to prove American paternity for the sport from which he was making a fortune supplying equipment.

When Spalding found a man who said he had witnessed Abner Doubleday invent it one summer's day in 1839 in Cooperstown, New York, he had the proof he needed. Even though the story could not be corroborated, Spalding promoted it widely and it was soon enshrined in American folklore. Cooperstown became home to the National Baseball Hall of Fame, even though the story had already been debunked as impossible. It turns out the tale may have been based on the story of an early game of baseball played in a small Ontario community not far from London in 1838. That game, ironically, was played in a British colony, providing an "international" source for baseball's creation myth.

Baseball has been an "international" game for a long, long time. The Blue Jays can't take credit for that.

This narrative marks the first comprehensive telling of the story of the acclaimed London Tecumsehs baseball club of the 1870s. References to the team often crop up in baseball histories and newspaper accounts of their day, for good reason. The well-financed Tecumsehs attracted some top talent from south of the border, among them early curveball pitcher Fred Goldsmith, outfielder Joe "Dutch" Hornung, catcher Phil Powers, and infielder and famed slugger Ross Barnes. The Tecumsehs played exhibition games against some of the top National League clubs of its day and defeated several of them, including Spalding's Chicago White Stockings. London regularly played throughout the U.S. northeast, making a name for itself as a top baseball city at a pivotal time in baseball history.

This story about the Tecumsehs is also about the International Association, about which little is known and confusion exists. On a visit to the National Baseball Hall of Fame Library, the author found very little about the Association and was dismayed to see that its rather slender file included a great deal of material about the later, but unrelated, International League, a minor loop. The Library staff was unaware of the difference or the years that the Association existed.

The International Association was similar in many respects to the National Association, founded in 1871 as the first professional league. The earlier loop was an unstable organization, with haphazard scheduling, team instability, players jumping from one team to another, and weak leadership that failed to deal with the scourge of gambling. The NA collapsed after its 1875 season, largely because of Chicago businessman William Hulbert, president of the Chicago White Stockings. Hulbert signed several of the National Association's top players and then, to escape sanctions, founded the National League for 1876 with eight charter members. His group wanted to control the game, grant monopolies, and appeal to a more affluent fan in order to make money.

This approach was resented by many of the more than 50 professional baseball teams operating at the time. They felt there was a better way to organize the game. Several of them gathered at a hotel in Pittsburgh and established the International Association for 1877. Teams in the new, less restrictive league would still be able to conduct extensive barnstorming tours but would be left to schedule games among themselves in pursuit of its pennant. And at 25 cents, the admission to their games was half that of the League. The International Association featured some of the best players of its day, including those who had played in the National Association and the National League.

The International Association provided a viable alternative to the League and became a solid competitor. Its founders, teams, and players never considered it as inferior to the League in any way. The concept of "major" and "minor" leagues came later. Historians have relegated the International Association to "minor league" status, the only one of the National League's six rivals to be so dismissed. That is as wrong as saying the game of baseball became "truly international" in 1877 because of the Toronto Blue Jays.

This work shines new light on the International Association and its first champions, the London Tecumsehs. It places credit where credit is due, exposes the discrimination against the rebel league after it was formed, and demonstrates how that situation has short-changed the teams and players who were part of it.

It's time for a fresh look at baseball's third professional league—and its first champions.

1

A Newcomer Catches Fever

When Jake Englehart stepped off the Great Western Railway train in London, Ontario, that day in 1868, he was not yet 21 years of age. Born in Cleveland, one of three children of Joel and Hannah Englehart, he had moved to New York City at the age of 13 when his father relocated the family to pursue business there. Jacob Lewis Englehart has been described as a man of mystery before his arrival in the small but bustling Canadian city of about 14,000 inhabitants.[1] He tended to shy away from publicity, an odd trait for a man whose subsequent activities in Canada would often make headlines, depicting him as a corporate titan, a philanthropist, a rail builder, and a trusted "rainmaker" for the leader of the province of Ontario. His funeral in Toronto would attract even more headlines and draw members of Canada's business and political elite. Today, the Englehart name appears in several places in the country he made his home, saluting his achievements in private and public business and in charitable activities. Not as widely known is the fact that Englehart also played a pivotal role in baseball history in his adopted home.

Englehart was attracted to London because it was an oil refining center, among the first in the world. Crude oil was discovered by James Miller Williams in 1857 about 50 miles to the west of the city, which quickly became the epicenter of the fledgling petroleum refining industry. London was already a metropolis—a prosperous agricultural area that was feeding the growing cities of Canada. Its hometown Labatt and Carling breweries, its foundries, food processors, and manufacturers had been sending their products to a wide hinterland even before the arrival of the railroad in 1853. The discovery of oil in gum beds at Oil Springs in 1857, and soon after in nearby Petrolia, saw crude shipped eastward 50 miles to London for refining into kerosene, an illuminating oil for lamps. The early crude had an unpleasant odor of sulfur, which, by the time Englehart showed up in London, refiners had learned to neutralize with chemicals. The Oil Springs discovery predated the more famous discovery of sweet crude (without the distinctive sulfur smell) at Titusville, Pennsylvania, by a full year.[2]

Members of the tiny Jewish community in London (consisting of 13 individuals by 1869) were involved in business, and several were operating small refineries by the time Englehart arrived. Also a member of the Jewish faith, Englehart appears to have had distant family connections with refiner Isaac Waterman. Born in Bavaria, Waterman had been living in London since 1858 and had entered the oil business with his brother, Herman, owner of a clothing manufacturing business. The Waterman Brothers refinery was one of the earliest in London and made many improvements to the rudimentary refining process, a chronically odoriferous operation plagued by the outbreak of fires.[3] By 1869, a total of 49 small refineries were listed as operating in London and Petrolia and were shipping illuminating oil across Canada and to Europe, Asia, and Africa.[4] The producers were also finding a market for oil as axle grease and as a lubricant for the newly invented machines of industry.

Englehart often visited the oil patch, whose focus shifted from Oil Springs to nearby Petrolia, which lay over a much larger reservoir of oil. With Isaac Waterman's help, Englehart established a refinery in London. It is not known for certain when Englehart first learned of the nascent oil industry that had developed in Canada. He may have seen an edition of the *New York Times* that in 1866 reported on the "celebrated oil fields of Canada West." The reference was to the name of the British Crown colony that the following year would become Ontario within the creation of the independent federation known as Canada. The article provided a lengthy explanation of the rock formation and the extent of the gum beds in the region and concluded: "One thing is very certain, that nature has seldom afforded a more exuberant yield of petroleum than is there indicated." It spoke of an "immense basin" of oil in the area and stated that as early as 1856 a company had been established to exploit it. With the manufacture of kerosene well established by 1857, it said, a new commercial era was under way in Canada.[5]

Jake Englehart and his colleagues were seeking new business opportunities. The oil industry was similar to the successful business in which they were engaged in New York City. There, Englehart worked as a salesman for Sonneborn, Dryfoos & Company and would later become a partner with principals Solomon Sonneborn, Abraham M. Dryfoos, and Leopold Beringer. Sonneborn had originally been in the clothing manufacturing business but the partnership soon turned toward the far more lucrative business of whiskey "rectifying," the bottling of distilled spirits. Rectifying had become a growing and successful economic pursuit as America grew increasingly thirsty. Most rectifiers were reputable wholesalers who bought distilled whiskey from various distillers, then filtered and blended it to produce their own brands. A few operators were quick-buck artists, however, blending small amounts of straight whiskey with flavoring and neutral grain spirits to produce what they called "blended" whiskey.[6]

During the 1800s, the consumption of alcohol was widespread in the United States—and growing. In 1825, for instance, Americans over the age of 15 drank seven gallons of pure alcohol per year. (That was nearly three times as much as they consumed in 1970, almost 150 years later.) By 1860, on a per capita basis, consumption had risen nearly 30 percent from a mere decade earlier, attributable largely to the rise in immigration from countries like England, Ireland, Germany, and Scotland, where drinking was widespread.[7]

With the outbreak of the Civil War, significant consumption of alcohol continued. Aside from providing temporary escape from the horror of war, whiskey was often the only anesthetic available to dull the pain of wounded soldiers and cleanse their wounds. The prolonged fighting also destroyed some distilleries, and prices began to skyrocket. At the same time, advocates of temperance blamed alcohol for some of the losses suffered by their troops, and a push for prohibition was under way. Regardless, by 1863, whiskey was fetching about $35 a gallon on the black market compared to 25 cents a mere three years earlier when 1,193 whiskey distillers and rectifiers were operating.[8] President Abraham Lincoln introduced an excise tax on whiskey in 1862 to help finance the costly Union war effort. It was introduced at 20 cents for each "proof gallon," a move that produced about $3.2 million for the federal treasury in the first year. The levy was increased in annual stages

Cleveland-born Jacob L. Englehart arrived in London in the late 1860s on behalf of a New York firm that had been in the distillery business. He became heavily involved in the new oil refining industry that had been established in London. He stayed at the hotel that was unofficial headquarters of the Tecumseh Base Ball Club (Glenbow Museum Archives IP-26-5-1b).

to two dollars a gallon, where it stayed for several years, producing nearly $30 million tax revenue annually.[9]

The new tax had two side-effects. It virtually killed off the use of alcohol for illumination because of the suddenly higher cost to produce "burning fluids," as they were known. For illumination, petroleum-based kerosene from Pennsylvania and Ontario made far more economic sense. So, indirectly, the tax proved a boost for the new petroleum industry. The tax also stimulated the manufacture of a new style of lamp designed to burn kerosene.[10] A second side-effect was far less positive. It dramatically changed the economics of distilling and rectifying alcohol. Under government rules, the new tax was payable the moment that whiskey was produced. But small distillers didn't have ready pools of cash in hand to pay the taxman. They needed to sell their product to generate that money. And decent whiskey needs to be aged. So, some operators responded by selling their just-distilled product immediately, sacrificing quality. Some went out of business. Still others opted to pay off the inspectors and taxmen to encourage them to look the other way. The practice soon became commonplace, and millions of dollars were diverted from government coffers. The *New York Times* complained in 1866 that "manufacturers have thwarted all these calculations [of tax revenue] by carrying on a system of fraud that has robbed the treasury of millions.... Officials have in many cases connived at these frauds, or have even directly been guilty partners in them."[11]

By 1870, a "Whiskey Ring," as it was called, was in full operation, in which inspectors and tax officials conspired to line their own pockets and those of their political friends. Inspectors told distillers the money collected from them was going into a special fund to re-elect President Ulysses Grant, who returned to office in 1872. It is believed as much as 15 million gallons of alcohol, which would have generated $7.5 million for the federal treasury, went untaxed from 1870 to 1874. The money found its way into the pockets of government officials. The scandal eventually implicated senior officials in Grant's administration.[12]

Englehart's firm was directly impacted by the new tax and, like others, he considered how to respond. Evidence suggests Sonneborn and company joined the tax dodgers like many other rectifiers of their day. About the same time, company principals spotted an opportunity in the new kerosene business that was actually benefitting from the new levy on alcohol. Jake Englehart was assigned the task of looking into it.

Solomon Sonneborn's uncle, Jonas Sonneborn, was an extremely wealthy man from various business interests and he had invested widely in real estate. Jonas' sister Carrie had married Isaac Guggenheim, the millionaire financier and copper magnate, who put some of his money into Sonneborn enterprises, among them some property in Canada's oil field.[13] Credit agency reports of the day shed some light on the operations of whiskey rectifiers Sonneborn, Dryfoos & Company, and the men involved in it. A report was compiled on Englehart as he established himself in Canada by an area agent for the R. G. Dun credit rating agency. In it, Englehart's partners were described as "Jews from NY ... of good character and habits, excellent capacity, capital is said to be large.... They are favorably regarded as reliable and honest, have a capital of $75,000–$80,000 and means outside."[14] Within a year, however, a New York agent for the same credit agency painted a far different picture of Sonneborn, Dryfoos & Company. It reported:

> The concern has the reputation of handling more illicit goods in a given time than any other house in the trade here. Its participants were charged with violating U.S. revenue laws but by management and by some of them leaving the country they were enabled to escape the penalties of the law. Of late, however, many old indictments of this kind have been brought to light, the government being determined to pursue them, and this firm will be likely to suffer if their property can be found.

The same Dun credit report concluded that the associates of Englehart were "shrewd, sharp and unreliable. Their paper will not sell in this market without a satisfactory endorser." It went on:

> The antecedents of the concern are somewhat notorious in the whiskey trade, they having without doubt made more money in illicit whiskey in a given time, than any other house in the trade, which is saying a good deal. They established themselves in Canada in 1869 [sic] and the move was regarded as the establishment of an asylum for the men who had hitherto been employed illicitly here, and for the investment of means which might otherwise [have] been pursued by the U.S. government.[15]

R. G. Dun took some comfort, however, from the fact that Solomon Sonneborn's Uncle Jonas was worth more than one million dollars.

Upon his arrival in London, Jake Englehart connected with the Watermans, and he had money behind him. He moved quickly. Englehart may have done the scouting work that saw the Sonneborn firm become the New York agent for Carbon Oil Works, the pre-eminent producer, refiner, and marketer for the oil patch. Carbon Oil had been organized by the same J. M. Williams who had established the first commercially viable well at Oil Springs.[16] The Carbon Oil operation held vast tracts of land in the area around Petrolia. By 1870, the three firms—Englehart & Company, Waterman Brothers, and Carbon Oil Works—accounted for fully one-third of the

The Tecumseh House Hotel in London was unofficial headquarters for the Tecumsehs, whose meetings were held there. Proprietor of the hotel, Edwin Moore, was a director of the ball club and president Jake Englehart, a successful oil refiner, lived there. Visiting teams stayed at the hotel located beside a rail station and mere blocks from the club's home field (*Illustrated Historical Atlas of the County of Middlesex*, 1878).

production from Ontario's oil field. Aside from their own output, the three firms purchased product from several smaller refiners, which they treated and exported.[17] In a relatively short time, Sonneborn and Englehart were prospering. The next year, Solomon Sonneborn, of Englehart & Company, was recorded by authorities in New York City as the fourth-largest exporter of kerosene from its port, shipping almost exclusively the product of Canadian refiners.[18]

Things would soon change for Sonneborn and others, however. In 1872, Solomon Sonneborn sued Carbon Oil for $100,000 that he claimed he was owed; but the company had suffered disastrous and costly explosions at its "big still" and could not meet Sonneborn's demand. Carbon Oil collapsed, and Englehart, acting as agent for Sonneborn, acquired its assets at auction for a nominal amount and held them in trust for the Sonneborns. Jonas Sonneborn filed for bankruptcy in 1874, a casualty of the widespread financial collapse of 1873, and was accused of hiding assets from a bank creditor, including the Carbon Oil Property.[19]

At the time of the economic setback of 1873, the entire Canadian petroleum industry was facing significant challenges. It struggled to meet quality standards and saw its overseas markets eroded, facing stiff competition from the sweeter and cheaper American product. Although rapid expansion of the Canadian industry had slowed, Englehart, who severed his connection with Sonneborn, had become a major player in it.[20]

Distillation of crude oil creates kerosene and is similar to the process used to create whiskey from grain or corn. Both apply heat to raw material to make their product. As in the whiskey business, the first devices used in the oil fields of Canada and Pennsylvania were known as "stills." When he arrived in London, Jake Englehart had some understanding of the process used to create kerosene and had plenty of money to invest. Given the credit agency reports saying government officials in New York were seeking money from his business partners, it is not a stretch to suggest that Englehart was a front man in what amounted to a cross-border money-laundering operation. No wonder that in later years he tended to shun publicity, hoping his murky past would remain behind him.

Englehart, when he first stepped onto that railway platform in a small foreign city nearly 600 miles from New York City, was carrying far more baggage than most 20-year-olds of his day. Likely the last things on his mind were spare time and baseball.

Just as the Civil War and its taxes had an impact on Englehart and his New York partners, the city of London saw changes during the war that raged south of the border. For London, most of those changes were positive. In 1857, the city was plunged into recession as the effects of a depression in Britain reached its North American colonies. The Crimean War from 1854 to 1856 had provided a boost for the colonies. Britain was at war with Russia for control of the Ottoman Empire and cancelled its traditional wheat shipments from Russia, substituting wheat and other agricultural produce from its far-flung colonies.[21] But with peace, British demand was sharply curtailed, killing business for London merchants and its agricultural community. Compounding that, the first round of railway construction intended to bind the colonies together had been completed, so the economic stimulus it had provided was gone. Then came widespread crop failure and unseasonal frosts that wiped out crops, adding to the region's misery. It was so bad that in 1857–1858, three-quarters of local businesses failed in London.[22]

The one bright spot for London came with the discovery of oil nearby in 1857. That event transformed London into a refinery city for two decades, luring investors and workers into the area along with the unmistakable smell of sulfur that emanated from the refinery district in the city's east end. In trade, the Reciprocity Treaty had been signed with the United States in 1854, an important step toward free trade in raw materials between the republic and the British colonies until it was repealed in 1866. The trade pact increased southbound exports and doubled trade between both parties by 1864.[23]

The outbreak of the Civil War was looked upon with some trepidation north of the border. Would the Northern Army be inclined to march north to acquire the British territory the United States had failed to conquer in the War of 1812? Suppose the North lost territory to the South and was seeking to replace it? As it turned out, the North's preoccupation with the Confederacy was all-consuming, and there was no time or inclination for cross-border military exploits. Instead, the North proved more interested in doing business with its northern neighbor than in waging war against it.

> At the center of British North America's greatest agricultural area, London's merchants were able to make a fortune providing wheat for the Northern armies. In addition, London's manufacturers switched over to wartime production, and its financiers speculated in American paper currency. As a result, when the war ended in 1865, the city's commercial and industrial leaders, far from being in financial difficulties, had reached new heights of affluence.... The financial institutions that were partially founded on the profits of the war and oil refining were to spread the city's influence across the nation.[24]

Canada West (today's Ontario) also saw dramatic increases in exports of horses for the military, cattle for food, and wool for uniforms. Flax, used to manufacture clothing in the absence of Southern cotton, also proved to be in great demand. Human imports and exports also increased. Draft dodgers began to show up in Canada after the middle of 1863, and it was estimated that as many as 40,000 Canadians (many of them already living in Union states) served in the armies of the North.[25]

As neutrals, the British North Americans could also trade with the South, if they chose. And they did, despite their differences about slavery, which Britain had abolished in 1833. Some positive sentiment was directed toward the Confederacy for a variety of reasons. Looking back, today's Central Intelligence Agency has explained the situation this way:

> As a British possession, Canada reflected Britain's brand of neutrality, which tipped toward the South and King Cotton. Many Canadians worried about the possibility that the breakup of the Union might tempt the United States to add territory by attempting to annex Canada. As the war wore on and Canadians' sympathy for the South grew, so did toleration for harboring Confederate agents.[26]

1. A Newcomer Catches Fever

The Tecumseh House Hotel, London's finest establishment, proved popular with Confederate agents, spies, and others. The elegant hotel mere steps west of the rail station, opened in 1856 just before the onset of recession. Conceived in prosperous times, it was the largest hotel in all of British North America. Many of its 150 rooms were occupied by agents conducting business for the Confederacy, clandestine and otherwise. Some guests were also spies from the North keeping an eye on the Confederates and their activities. The Tecumseh became a hotbed of intrigue and a refuge for Southern statesmen and their families. A suite of rooms was occupied by the family of Brigadier-General Pierre Gustave Toutant Beauregard, a wealthy Louisiana plantation owner of French-Creole extraction who had risen to the top ranks of the Southern Army.[27] A defender of Fort Sumter at the outset of the war, Beauregard had commanded armies in the Western Theater. With his wife and daughters safe in faraway London, Beauregard repeatedly defended Charleston, South Carolina, from naval and land attacks and saved the city of Petersburg, Virginia, successfully keeping Union forces out of the Confederate capital of Richmond.[28]

Meanwhile, Union agents and buyers of grain and horses, as well as some families from the Union, preferred the less opulent Arkell's Hotel, just a city block north of the Tecumseh. With large stables, Arkell's played host to American buyers who bought so many horses that they depleted the supply in the region. Their purchases were shipped to Buffalo, Detroit, and Cleveland. By contrast, horses bought by Confederate agents were shipped to Montreal or Quebec, where paperwork was prepared saying they were destined for England or European ports in a bid to deceive Northern spies and hide their true destination in the south. Union agents bought a wide range of products and supplies intended to help the North wage war, putting large amounts of money into the pockets of businessmen in London.[29]

A Union dissident who had run afoul of President Abraham Lincoln made London his home in 1863 and part of 1864. Clement Vallandigham, a staunch opponent of resorting to war to resolve the differences between the North and the South, stayed at one of London's hotels. A Peace Democrat from Ohio, he was a leader of the "Copperhead" movement of northerners who shared his views. At a rally in Ohio in early 1863, Vallandigham denounced a Union military order making it an offense to express sympathy for the enemy. He said it violated freedom of speech. Vallandigham was charged with undermining the Union effort, and a military tribunal convicted him and sentenced him to military prison for the remainder of the war. He appealed and was convicted again, this time sent to a federal prison. Fearing mobilization by dissidents, Lincoln intervened and instead changed Vallandigham's sentence to exile in the Confederacy. Vallandigham went south but stayed there only a few weeks before fleeing to Canada, from which he sought the Democratic nomination for governor of Ohio. Amazingly, he won the nomination from his exile but lost the election to the Union Party's candidate. Vallandigham slipped back into the United States in 1864 but was not punished further by authorities.[30]

Before returning to Ohio, Vallandigham likely participated in an August 7, 1864 conference in London between officials of the Confederacy and representatives of the Knights of the Golden Circle, more commonly known as the "Copperheads." Despite the secretive nature of the organization of Southern sympathizers, some who had traveled from neighboring states, word of the gathering leaked out.[31] Among those vitally interested in such things were the commanders of the British garrison, whose soldiers could also be found on the oh-so-busy streets of London.

Aside from the spies from both foreign belligerents in their midst, Londoners were reminded of the tragedy unfolding south of the border in early July of 1863 when it was said the sun was obscured by smoke emanating from the battle of Gettysburg, a mere 350 miles to the southeast.[32]

Upon the Tecumseh House Hotel's closing in 1929, the daily *London Free Press* recalled some of its more interesting guests during its long history: "Wealthy American landowners from the Southern United States fled with their slaves to Canada at the time of the Civil War and the Tecumseh Hotel became sort of the unofficial headquarters in Canada of the Confederate cause."[33]

While the newspaper may have overstated the Tecumseh Hotel's role somewhat, the Canadian colonies and their cities did provide a convenient base for activity by Confederate agents determined to undermine the Union cause. Toronto, 150 miles east of London, and Windsor, opposite Detroit, 150 miles to the west, were staging centers for campaigns of sabotage against the North. In 1864, the Confederate Congress passed a bill authorizing action against "the enemy's property by land or sea." It created a Secret Service fund of $5 million, of which $1 million was earmarked for agents operating from bases in Canada. By now desperate to win the war, the South sought to encourage large-scale covert actions against its foe.[34]

The most ambitious plan was the Northwest Conspiracy. This campaign targeted what were then known as the "northwestern" states of Ohio, Indiana, and Illinois. Led by Captain Thomas Henry Hines, it was intended to encourage an insurrection in those states, to turn them against the Union side and mobilize the "Copperheads" living there who sympathized with the Southern cause. Confederate President Jefferson Davis sent dispatches to Hines in Toronto as plots were hatched and refined. It is understood that among those with whom Hines plotted was Clement Vallandigham, then living in London. A key scheme devised by Hines and others was to raid two of the Union's prisoner-of-war-camps for thousands of Southern captives and set them free.

One of them, at Johnson's Island near Sandusky, Ohio, held more than 2,500 Confederate officers, including several generals. The other, Fort Douglas at Chicago, held about 9,000 Southern soldiers. Once they were freed, according to the plan, the Southern troops and their leaders would take control of the region and encourage uprisings among citizens sympathetic to their cause and tired of war, thereby forcing the North to seek peace. The complicated missions, involving America's only warship on the Great Lakes, passenger vessels, and daring night-time attacks, were launched but ultimately were foiled by bad luck, double agents, confusion, and treachery.

A later attack on Vermont from a Confederate base in Quebec had only limited success. That plan, to raze St. Albans, saw only a shed burned and a bank robbed. An attempt to set fire to a string of hotels in New York City failed miserably, as well as an effort to derail trains carrying Confederate prisoners near Buffalo and free them. Overall, the conspiracy was an abject failure, and several of its leaders were hanged for their part in it.[35] The daring Hines was lucky. He repeatedly escaped captivity and returned to his native Kentucky, where, after the war, he became a lawyer and then a judge.

Johnson's Island, known as a "prisoner-of-war depot," was similar to many Union facilities where Confederate troops were held far from the battlefields to the south. Many on the Lake Erie island had been captured at Gettysburg and were better fed than their fellow rebels who continued to fight on in a losing cause. At Johnson's Island, prisoners were plagued by boredom, which they fought by writing letters home, making furniture and maps, staging plays, and writing poems. Outdoors, prisoners tended gardens, played chess and checkers, and learned and played a game called "base ball" that was new to many of them.[36]

The Civil War is often credited with spreading the new game of baseball played by men from New England and New York to other states and across the country. While many of the teams in the Northeast lost players to military recruiters, the conflict "proved to be a blessing in disguise" for the game, historian William Ryczek has observed.

Although President Lincoln's army plucked many a player from local teams, the army proved the ultimate melting pot. Small-town lads who had never heard of baseball met city slickers who showed them how to fashion a bat out of a broom handle and how to use it. The newfangled American game helped both Union and Confederate campaigners ease the drudgery of camp life. Bored prisoners often taught the game to their captors.[37]

Aside from spreading the game as played in the northeastern states of the Union, the Civil War helped enshrine baseball as the American pastime as cricket faded in popularity, Ryczek concluded.

Upon his arrival in London, Englehart was likely surprised to discover that the game he had known in New York was extremely popular in this provincial outpost of the British Empire. The Tecumseh House, the city's finest establishment soon to become his home in the city, was a hotbed of baseball enthusiasts.

For military reasons, London was established in 1793 at the forks of the north and south branches of the Thames River in the heavily forested area between Lake Erie and Lake Huron. The British colonial governor of the day felt it would make an ideal capital for the young colony. If American troops were to invade from either Detroit or Buffalo, he felt there would be plenty of time to mobilize troops to defend a capital there. But the location was also remote from the waterways that were still the prime transportation routes of the day. The Thames, while it might appear to be a strategic waterway on maps, was too shallow at London for boats larger than canoes and small craft. With only rudimentary paths through dense forest, London was slow and difficult to develop, and the capital was instead located at York, later renamed Toronto, on the shore of Lake Ontario.[38] Ironically, with its location easily accessible by water, American troops had little difficulty sacking and burning York during the War of 1812, attacking it by ship.

London remained lightly populated and poorly defended during the War of 1812, and the region was repeatedly crisscrossed by invading American troops and militia. American soldiers and militia looted, burned, and terrorized the locals on their way to and from strategic British military installations near Detroit in the west and on the Niagara Peninsula and opposite Buffalo to the east. In 1826, the city at the forks of the Thames was named the administrative center for the District of London, and it began to attract settlers as the town site was formalized and the courthouse and jail established.

After settlers rebelled in 1837 and 1838, seeking more democracy from the ruling political and social elites and were put down, Britain decided to establish an army garrison in London. A military presence would dissuade further unrest, and the distance from the American border was again appealing because some rebels had fled the colony and talked about mobilizing attacks. The town in the bush was transformed with the arrival of the military and became an important outpost in the Empire, distinguishing it from other frontier towns and bringing wealth and a touch of sophistication. British army officers came from the elite and became fixtures at grand balls and other social events in the growing community. Economically, the purchase of supplies to build and supply the barracks and its occupants produced a surge for business and attracted even more settlers and merchants.

Local London industries supplied a vast hinterland between the Great Lakes. The railway arrived in 1853, giving a further boost to the community, which two years later became a city with a population of slightly more than 12,000. The British garrison was pulled out in 1853 to join the British army in the faraway Crimean campaign. In its absence, the dollar replaced the British

The Guelph Maple Leafs became Canadian baseball champions in 1869 and defeated all comers. They hired some American players to ensure their dominance in the early part of the 1870s. This illustration from 1870 is shortly before Guelph brewer George Sleeman took over the club (*Canadian Illustrated News*, November 5, 1870).

pound as currency of the colony at the outset of 1858. The absence of British soldiers was short-lived, however. When the Civil War broke out in 1861, Britain immediately deployed 10,000 troops in North America, of which 2,000 re-established the garrison in London. In mid–1869, two years after Canada became independent, and with the threats from the border no longer a concern, the garrison pulled out for the last time.[39]

The British army was preparing to leave the city when Englehart arrived. The whiskey salesman from New York City may have marveled at how British this small city of London was at the time. It was a new world for him, with new customs and a fledgling industry into which he would pour his talents and the money of his partners.

Despite its Britishness, London was a city that had caught baseball fever, not unlike cities in neighboring New York and New England states. Cricket had been played for decades, but its adherents declined when the last British troops went home. Settlers, an increasing number of whom came from south of the border, had brought baseball with them, and the game had caught the imagination of the clerks, lawyers, merchants, and hoteliers in London. Baseball fever had gripped the city and many others in the former colony, now a province known as Ontario.

It wasn't long before James Conklin and Ed Moore took over as proprietors of the Tecumseh House. Englehart soon discovered that Moore was among the key figures in baseball in London. The oil man and the hotelier saw eye to eye about baseball and agreed on what it could do for the community.

Englehart established himself in London to pursue opportunities in the petroleum industry at a pivotal point in history. He scarcely could have imagined he would find time and energy to pursue opportunities in baseball. But the well-heeled young man was soon to bathe himself and his adopted city in baseball glory.

It was just a matter of time. And timing.

2
Roots

The hunt for the origins of baseball and for the first references to the game has preoccupied researchers for a long time. Millions of words have been written about both. There is something about baseball that leads to such persistent archeological inquisition. Notwithstanding the acknowledgement that games with bats and balls have been played for centuries and gradually evolved into the modern game, the quest continues to find the "eureka" moment for baseball.

Baseball historian John Thorn has noted that games involving bat and ball date back nearly 4,500 years to ancient Egypt. Images depicting important figures holding balls and sticks have been found in shrines in that country, suggesting Egypt is not only the cradle of civilization but perhaps of baseball as well.[1]

Finding written references to a game sometimes referred to as "bass," as "ball," or "base-ball," or to an English game known as "rounders"—now generally accepted as baseball's most recent predecessor—has been a fascinating exercise.

A relatively recent discovery by another baseball historian, David Block, has proven to be illuminating. He unearthed a reference to a game played by members of the English aristocracy in the countryside of Surrey, southwest of London, in 1749. "On Tuesday last, his Royal Highness the Prince of Wales, and Lord Middlesex, played at Bass-Ball at Walton in Surry [*sic*] ..." reported the *Whitehall Evening Post* of September 19, 1749.[2] Block said this reference demonstrates the game was not restricted to children and young people, as had been widely believed. It was further evidence that baseball is connected to games played in eighteenth-century England.

But this isn't the earliest reference to "base-ball." Five years before those gentlemen took to the field in Surrey, a book was published called *A Little Pretty Pocket-Book, Intended for the Instruction and Amusement of Little Master*

Tommy and Pretty Miss Polly. This is thought to be the first book directed at children. Written by John Newberry, it described 32 games and activities for youngsters. A page allocated to "base-ball" had a woodcut illustration and a short poem about the game. The image depicted three players and posts marking three bases. One of the players seems poised to pitch a ball, although a batter cannot be found. Block laments that no copies of the original 1744 edition survive, but subsequent editions can be found in libraries.[3]

For many years, historians believed the first-ever reference to baseball appeared in Jane Austen's 1798 novel *Northanger Abbey,* not published, however, until 20 years after it was written. At one point, Austen described the heroine, Catherine Morland, as a "very good woman" who sought the best for her children. The character fretted that being so preoccupied with her little ones, her older daughters were left to fend for themselves. One of them shared the name Catherine "and it was not very wonderful that Catherine, who had nothing heroic about her, should prefer cricket, base ball, riding on horseback, and running about the country at the age of fourteen, to books—or at least books of information…"[4]

Yet another early English reference caught the attention of baseball historians. In 1828, *The Boy's Own Book* was published in England. It contained descriptions of a wide variety of games and activities of interest to young people and explained how they were played. A section was devoted to "Games with Balls" in which rounders was depicted on a playing surface configured in the shape of a diamond. This is generally acknowledged as the first printed reference to baseball's closest relative.[5] It probably contributed significantly to the belief that rounders was primarily a game for children, something that may have surprised the noblemen of Surrey.

Even older references to baseball or rounders may someday yet be found in some dusty attic, forgotten trunk, or elsewhere. As long as researchers are looking, something is bound to turn up.

Locating ancient references to baseball and its relatives is an easy task, compared to the impossible—and dangerous—effort to establish when the "first" game was played. Or where. Because baseball evolved over a long period of time in a number of places, it's impossible to find definitive answers.

Consensus has emerged, however, that the game, played with different rules in different places, had a watershed moment in 1846 when rules approximating the modern game were codified by the New York Knickerbockers, the first organized baseball club. These gentlemen of New York, including bank clerk and volunteer firefighter Alexander Joy Cartwright, Jr., played across the Hudson River at the Elysian Fields in Hoboken, New Jersey. The Knickerbockers were seen as pioneers because they laid out the playing field in a diamond configuration and established playing rules. They eliminated the traditional practice of "soaking," or "plugging" base runners with a thrown ball to record an out, replacing it with the tag play.⁶ That particular innovation is considered the step that marks the beginning of modern baseball.

Cartwright, after persistent lobbying by his grandson, was inducted into the National Baseball Hall of Fame, long after his death. The inscription on his plaque calls Cartwright "the father of modern baseball" and an influential member of the Knickerbockers, adding: "He played a role in formalizing the first published rules of the game." In her excellent biography of Cartwright, Monica Nucciarone sought hard evidence of the baseball paternity claims made about Cartwright, but found virtually none. "Without primary sources on which to base this theory, it must remain speculation," she wrote.⁷

Nucciarone said his accomplishments appear have been mythologized and she concludes that singling out Cartwright as the "father of baseball" when there are other worthy pioneers "is more than a stretch." She goes on:

> Most likely, Cartwright will continue to be revered and honored more than his fellow teammates, even if the documented evidence for his accomplishments remains weak. Any myth or legend, once embedded in the culture, is difficult to amend. There are a great many people today who still insist that Abner Doubleday invented baseball—after all, baseball's Hall of Fame is in Cooperstown! An established and celebrated location surely signifies legitimacy, doesn't it?⁸

Indeed. Myths can be powerful and lasting. The yearning to find an American origin for the game led at one time to the creation and acceptance of one of the great myths of modern times. So durable is the fable that the game was invented in 1839 in Cooperstown, New York, that many Americans still believe it to this day. Surprisingly, Bud Selig, the commissioner of Major League Baseball, admitted in 2010 that he believes the story of Cooperstown that was once taught in schools.⁹

Baseball's creation myth filled a need at a pivotal time in American history and flourished in the absence of reliable and accurate information. The story that baseball was invented by Abner Doubleday in a farmer's pasture one day in tiny Cooperstown also filled a void and overcame the uncomfortable assertion made to Americans that it was derived from rounders, a game played mainly by children in England. That argument was made eloquently and consistently by Henry Chadwick, a Brit, who became a noted and influential writer about early baseball, most notably in the *New York Clipper* and then as editor of *Beadle's Dime Base-Ball Player* and of *Spalding's Base Ball Guide*. Chadwick became known as the "father of baseball" because of his promotion of the game and his invention of the box score. He was inducted into the Baseball Hall of Fame in 1939, along with another "father," Cartwright, for introducing statistics such as batting averages, for his instructional manuals, and for helping to popularize the game in its infancy. *Spalding's Base Ball Guide* was published by sporting goods mogul Albert Goodwill Spalding, a former star pitcher in the National Association and National League and president of the League's Chicago White Stockings. Spalding grew tired of Chadwick's oft-repeated opinion about the origins of baseball, a game that had made Spalding successful and wealthy. In 1903, Chadwick penned a lengthy article in Spalding's *Guide* outlining "The History of Baseball" and definitively declared: "There is no doubt whatever as to base ball having originated from the two-centuries-old English game of rounders."[10]

For Spalding, his employee Chadwick had gone too far. *The time has come to set the record straight,* felt the Britophobe Spalding, who, by 1903, was retired in California. Spalding took it upon himself to prove that baseball, the game the country had embraced as its national pastime, was quintessentially American, right to its roots. Spalding launched a campaign to find the evidence necessary to support his contention. He delivered public speeches and wrote articles that were published in newspapers, explaining that he was seeking any and all information to help prove baseball was American at its core. In early 1905, he established a "commission" of hand-picked cronies to consider the evidence he expected to shake loose in his cross-country quest. Spalding appointed Abraham G. Mills to chair his Special Base Ball Commission. A personal friend, business executive Mills was a former president of the National League. Years earlier, Mills had made clear his view about the paternity of the game, insisting in a widely reported public speech that "patriotism and research" had proven the game was unquestionably American in origin.[11] If Spalding was determined to find a homegrown source for the game, he couldn't have found a better ally in his quest than Mills.

On April 1, 1905, the *Akron Beacon Journal* carried an article written by Spalding in which he outlined his determination to prove baseball's American pedigree. Spalding appealed to anyone with helpful information to contact the Special Base Ball Commission. "If such an ancestry can be established for base ball," he wrote, "every American friend of the game will be delighted."[12]

A guest at an Akron hotel saw the article and promptly sat down at a typewriter and pecked out 640 words in response. He produced a tale that gave Spalding and America a story that would "delight" both. Abner Graves, a mining engineer from Denver, sent a copy of his letter to the editor of the newspaper and to the Mills Commission. Three days later, with a brief introduction from the editor, his letter was printed in the April 4 edition of the Akron daily. In it, the 71-year-old Graves, who had been born on a farm near Cooperstown, referred to Spalding's appeal and went right to the point, describing a game he had witnessed when he would have been five years of age:

> The American game of base ball was invented by Abner Doubleday of Cooperstown, New York, either the spring prior to or following the "Log Cabin and Hard Cider" campaign of General Harrison for president. The said Abner Doubleday was at that time a boy pupil of Green's Select School in Cooperstown, and who, as General Doubleday, won honor at the battle of Gettysburg in the Civil war.[13]

This story had never before been told. And no corroboration for it could ever be found, despite some cursory effort by Spalding. But this "evidence" was good enough for Spalding and his hand-picked commission. Especially when after three years of receiving submissions, his commission found nothing close to what Spalding had sought. Mills tinkered with Graves's story a bit to remove the reference to runners being "plunked" to retire them, in an apparent effort to make the game seem more modern with tag plays and less like other pre–Knickerbockers contests.

For reasons unknown, Mills settled on 1839 as the birthdate, although Graves might have been referring to 1841 because it was during 1840 that General William Henry Harrison ("Old Tippecanoe") waged his successful presidential campaign. The commission's finding that the game was invented in Cooperstown by Doubleday in 1839 wasn't published, however, until the 1908 edition of the *Spalding Guide*. Spalding himself promoted it in his 1911 book *America's National Pastime*, a 600-page volume widely distributed by his American Sports Publishing Company. In it, Spalding commended the Special Base Ball Commission for the "righteousness of its verdict" by anointing Doubleday as inventor of baseball and Cooperstown as its birthplace.[14]

At a time when America was becoming a major player on the world stage, it could now claim that the game with which it had fallen in love in recent decades was a homegrown invention. A symbiotic relationship had developed between the game and the country that in the early days of the twentieth century was trying to show the world a better way forward. As one observer of the relationship has noted: "As the United States has projected its dominance worldwide, baseball lent a hand—bolstering the military, boosting the nation's global reach, and proselytizing for the American way. As the United States expanded, conquering new frontiers, so did baseball."[15]

Shortly after the Cooperstown tale was promoted by Spalding and others, holes were poked in the old mining engineer's story. Writers and researchers pointed out that Abner Doubleday, who died in 1893, had a long life with numerous speaking engagements and had written extensively, but never once mentioned inventing baseball. Likely because he didn't. Sportswriter Alfred Spink discovered that in 1839, Doubleday was a student at West Point, many miles away from Cooperstown, and took no leaves of absence during 1839 or 1840.[16]

Abner Graves, the spinner of the tale about Cooperstown and baseball's invention there, enjoyed the limelight it created for him in his senior years. He improved his story of that "first game" and his role in it as time went on. At age 78, he told the *Denver Post* he played in the first game in Cooperstown along with the older boys. In his original version, he said he was a mere witness. Graves told the *Post* reporter he expected to play "shortstop or something like that" in an upcoming game between the Denver Chamber of Commerce and the real estate exchange.[17]

Historians have been unkind to Graves for concocting a tale that could not pass scrutiny. In fact, he was a hard-working and reasonably successful businessman, cattle breeder, banker, mining engineer, consultant, and real estate agent. Yet he has been dismissed as a crank or a mental case by many writers. The latter assertion was drawn from the fact that at age 90, in 1924, Graves was found not guilty by reason of insanity for shooting to death his second wife, who he thought was trying to poison him. But this was nearly 20 years after Graves came up with his story, by which time he seems have been suffering from dementia.[18]

Only recently has it come to light that Graves was most likely inspired to tell his story by another Denver resident with whom he must have crossed paths. Adam Ford, a Canadian medical doctor, had moved to Denver a few years before Graves. He had his own story about an early game of baseball, although he never claimed it was the first game. In 1886, Ford described in *Sporting Life* an 1838 game he witnessed as a boy of seven in his hometown of Beachville, Ontario (then known as the British colony of Upper Canada).[19]

Ford was an inveterate storyteller and a near-mirror-image of Graves. Both men liked baseball and no doubt attended professional games in Denver. Both liked their whiskey and were connected through mutual friends in the Freemasons. Graves was a Shriner, and Ford, while not a Mason himself, was one of the first occupants of the new Masonic Building in downtown Denver. Ford had a son who was a mining engineer, the same profession as that of Graves and of Graves' son. Graves and Ford both enjoyed the limelight and writing to newspapers when the mood arose. Most notably, in the three years leading up to Graves spinning his story about Cooperstown, the mining engineer's office was a short block from Ford's medical office in downtown Denver. Their offices were surrounded by saloons in a western city with a well-earned reputation for its love of drink. The similarities of the two men and their stories is remarkable, so it's not a stretch to conclude that Graves's story that "proved" baseball was an American invention—not British—was ironically rooted in the story about an early game in a British Colony.[20]

Ford's account of an 1838 game a few miles west of New York state has stood up to historical scrutiny. Unlike Cooperstown. Canada Post saw fit to issue a postage stamp in 1988, commemorating the 150th anniversary of the event Ford described in Beachville. For his part, Ford never claimed it was the first game of baseball, merely one that resembled the game as it was being played in 1886 when he wrote his letter to *Sporting Life*.[21]

Games like baseball were played in the northeastern United States, brought by settlers from the British Isles. Two major variations of the game developed: the Massachusetts and the New York style of play, the former often known as "town ball," in which plugging runners continued long after the Knickerbockers eliminated it and the New York game prevailed.[22]

Early settlers in British North America came from the same places, some having stopped first in the American republic. Many were United Empire Loyalists following the American Revolution, fearful and persecuted there, and anxious to remain British subjects. More came later as "Late Loyalists," driven by a desire to remain under the British Crown coupled with the desire for inexpensive farmland Britain offered as it made a concerted push to populate Upper Canada. By 1812, the population of Upper Canada stood at a mere 75,000, of whom fully 60 percent were relative newcomers from the United States, prompting concerns about their loyalty to the colony when the War of 1812 broke out.[23] As it turned out, the newer arrivals were more interested in farming than fighting, and after two years of hostilities, the conflict ended in a draw. The new settlers brought with them their customs and games. Adam Ford's family in Beachville was typical of the day. His parents were from Northern Ireland but had met in Pennsylvania, where their families had originally settled. His wife's family was also from the United States, her father born in Vermont and her mother from the Mohawk Valley of central New York. Many of the farmers in the Beachville area of Oxford County, about 120 miles southwest of Toronto, had been lured across the border from similar places with the promise of inexpensive land.

Canadian baseball historian Bill Humber discovered that games played in early Ontario, based on accounts found in New York newspapers, were more akin to the Massachusetts game, with some Canadian wrinkles. Teams fielded from ten to 14 players, but most often 11. Overhand pitching was permitted, unlike the underhand technique in the New York game. The Canadian game included a fourth baseman, and a backstop behind the catcher. The 1838 match in Beachville he described as a "crude game," in which the home team took on the visiting Zorras from the neighboring townships of Zorra and North Oxford. It was played during celebrations to mark the colonial government's victory over rebels seeking greater democracy. As Humber has noted:

> It seems difficult to imagine anyone playing a game so overtly identified by us with American ways as baseball, in the summer following a rebellion based on American ideas of representative government. The explanation quite simply is that baseball had yet to attain a national identity. The Beachville game clearly indicates that Canadians were amongst the earliest regional participants in baseball's evolution in North America.[24]

Regional variations in the game were doomed with the codification of the game in New York and the arrival of the railways in Canada West (formerly Upper Canada) by the early 1850s. Following the introduction of limited free trade with the United States in 1854, greater contact developed between the colonies and neighboring states. Cross-border games, and even those involving teams from different regions, required a clearly agreed-upon set of rules, and those from New York were the logical choice. But interesting local matches continued. *The New York Clipper,* for instance, carried a report of a September 12, 1856, game in which a team from the city of London played a club from the village of Delaware, a few miles west of London. While the box score shows nine players per side, the teams played only two innings, with London prevailing, 34 to 33. "You will perceive that London was declared winner on the second innings without losing a man," said the account, using terminology (along with some rules) apparently borrowed from cricket.[25]

The first city directory for London, which officially became a city in 1855, had an entry for the "Base Ball Club" listing its executive officers and noting the club "consists of 22 members, and days of practice are Tuesday and Thursday in the evening, at the Military Reserve."[26] Historian Humber suggests that with a membership of 22, the London club could easily split itself into two teams of 11, the usual number of players of the day. London was in the heart of southwestern Ontario and less than 30 miles west of Beachville, where Adam Ford's game of 1838 was played. Just as in New York and New England, clerks and entrepreneurs were among those who were most enthusiastic about baseball and competing against other clubs in other cities.

It is hard to pinpoint precisely when baseball became organized in London. A small notice from the "London Base Ball Club" appeared in the May 1, 1856, edition of the *London Free Press*, saying the club "will hold its annual meeting in the Exchange Buildings on Friday Evening 2nd of May, for the purpose of electing officers for the ensuing year, and transacting other business of importance." The use of the term "annual meeting" suggests the organization had been in existence for at least one year. Four days later, the same newspaper noted that the executive officers had been elected and quoted a local weekly publication called the *London Atlas* as saying: "'The Club intends to challenge any other Base Ball Club in the Province as soon as it gets into regular playing order.'"[27]

London may not have been home to the first organized baseball club in Canada, however. The Hamilton Young Canadians (later renamed the Maple Leafs) were playing regularly from 1854 in the city at the western tip of Lake Ontario about 45 miles west of Toronto. Hamilton clerk William Shuttleworth was one of the organizers, and he and the players represented a cross-section of the city's working class. They included clerks, shoemakers, laborers, a broom-maker, a butcher, saloon keeper, tinsmith, boilermaker, teamster, watchmaker, grocer, carpenter, and sailor.[28] Shuttleworth's younger brother, Jim, had helped to organize a team in Woodstock, just a few miles east of Beachville, by 1860. That same year, the first international contest saw the Hamilton Burlingtons lose twice to the Niagaras of Buffalo. In home-and-home games later in 1860, the Niagaras also handily defeated the Hamilton Young Canadians, 87–13 and 45–15.[29] Those games marked the beginning of the end for the Canadian variation of the game in favor of the New York rules, which the Buffalo team had adopted in 1857.[30] The latter rules were in place in July of 1861 when the Maple Leafs (renamed from Young Canadians that year) defeated the neighboring Burlingtons by a score of 33–27 before a crowd of 800 in Hamilton.[31] Such high scores were not uncommon at the time because the game favored batters. Then known as "strikers," batters could wait for pitches of their choosing, specifying high or low ones, and fielders wore no gloves.

The Woodstock Young Canadians established by the younger Shuttleworth became an early powerhouse and in 1861 twice defeated the Hamilton team. As Humber observed: "The best baseball in Ontario had become a place for heated celebration of civic identity in which cheering for the home team was at least part of the purpose of the exercise."[32] Woodstock defeated the

Brother Jonathan Club of Detroit, 29–6, in 1863, and that same year twice prevailed over the Hamilton Maple Leafs, 41–25 and 26–12. Woodstock fans were so excited by the success of the team from their community that they raised money to create a "Silver Ball" to be awarded to the champions of Canada. The following year, Woodstock embarrassed the Hamilton team on its home grounds, 30–2, before a crowd of 1,000.[33] The win marked the passing of the torch from Hamilton to the newcomers. The champion Woodstock team was looking to expand its horizons, and when organizers learned the Brooklyn Atlantics club would be in the vicinity of Rochester at the time of the New York State Fair, they challenged the Atlantics to a game. Both teams had been undefeated, and their contest was touted in some quarters as one for bragging rights for the continent.

The Woodstock–Brooklyn match was a complete rout of the upstart Canadians. Before a crowd of 4,000 fans in Rochester, the Atlantics ran up a score of 75–11.[34] Woodstock returned home and focused on defeating regional rivals, including a strong area team from Ingersoll, just west of Beachville. The Young Canadians retained the Silver Ball as Canadian champions in 1864 and 1865. Woodstock, Hamilton, and Ingersoll competed at an international tournament in 1867 in Detroit, which attracted teams from Detroit, Port Huron, and Jackson, Michigan, and from Pittsburgh. Hamilton lost to Jackson in the final game, picking up a gold-plated ball as runner-up. Woodstock, its pitcher injured, fared poorly. Ingersoll, however, entered the junior, third-class division, sweeping all four games to take home a gold-mounted rosewood bat and $100.[35]

A sign that the game was beginning to be taken more seriously was the formation of the Canadian Association of Base Ball Players at a meeting in 1864 in Hamilton. The name was a bit of a stretch as members were teams strictly from southwestern Ontario, or Canada West, as it was still known. At the time, however, the only nines outside the region were in Victoria, British Columbia, and Montreal. By 1867, two clubs were operating in Halifax, Nova Scotia.[36]

Another noteworthy international match came in 1868 at Niagara Falls, New York, when the Brooklyn Atlantics again played the Young Canadians of Woodstock. The game came at the end the New York State Baseball Tournament and was billed in newspapers as a contest between the "champions of the U.S. and those of Canada."[37] Ten train cars from Woodstock made the trip to the border town, and the 4,000 fans who witnessed the game included many from London and Hamilton and the towns of Ingersoll and Paris. The game had to be called when the skies opened in the sixth inning. The score at the time was 30–17 for the Atlantic club. Afterward, the visitors from Canada were "hospitably entertained" by the host Niagara Falls club and its president, who "won the everlasting gratitude of the Canadian players and their friends."[38]

That same year, 1868, the feeling was growing that the best days of the perennial champion Woodstock team were behind it and they might be toppled. The Young Canadians faced an upstart team from a town about 40 miles to the northeast, the Guelph Maple Leafs, for a game in July to determine the Canadian championship. Guelph had become baseball-crazy, and its mayor declared the Civic Holiday so citizens of the town could take the train to Woodstock to watch the Maple Leafs attempt to wrest the Silver Ball from the Young Canadians. Five hundred citizens and a brass band took the short ride west. A hard-fought game was played before a large crowd, and Woodstock retained its bragging rights and the championship by a score of 36–28. The game was marred by an outbreak of rowdyism, however, as some Woodstock supporters resorted to violence in clashes with Guelph fans, prompting the *Guelph Mercury* to warn afterward: "It will be a long time ere a club from Guelph will go to Woodstock, if a material change does not take place in the way of enforcing order." The paper laid no blame on the Woodstock team, however, criticizing instead the rowdies and the police who failed to curb them.[39]

It was another year before Guelph was able to wrest the baseball crown from Woodstock. At the Provincial Exhibition of 1869 held in London, the Maple Leafs defeated teams from Woodstock, Ingersoll, and London in a three-day tournament to capture the Silver Ball and $150 in gold.[40] The baseball landscape had changed yet again. The Guelph reign as Canadian champions would last for seven years.

For Guelph, the timing of the championship was perfect. The town, whose population stood at 5,800 in 1869, was undergoing an industrial revolution that was improving its fortunes. Optimism about the future was high. Between 1868 and 1871, more than a dozen new manufacturing operations were established to continue its transformation from a mercantile center to an industrial one. New industries included a carriage works, ironworks, stove foundry, tannery, sewing machine company, and makers of steam engines, axles, and springs.[41]

Guelph was founded in 1827 on the fast-flowing Speed River, about 80 miles west of the colonial capital of York, which was about to be renamed Toronto. It was a planned community, and its streets were laid out in a radial pattern that was in fashion at the time and similar to that used in Buffalo.

The name of the place was intended to honor Britain's royal family, the Hanoverians, descendants of the Guelfs. For that reason, the new community's nickname would become the Royal City. It attracted a large number of flour mills anxious to take advantage of the hydraulic power provided by the Speed. A boost to the local economy came in the early 1850s when the railway from Toronto and Hamilton was pushed westward through the town. An economic downturn hit between 1857 and 1860, which inhibited further industrialization, and Guelph's character remained as a retailing and service center for the surrounding farm community. The Civil War stimulated the local economy, as in many Ontario communities, including London. Firms producing machinery began operation, while another factory found it profitable to produce clothing, much of which was shipped south, because cotton was unavailable to northern states during hostilities. The Raymond Sewing Machine Company was established by an American weary of litigation from the Singer Sewing Machine firm in the United States; about the same time, the Bell Organ Company was organized. The technologically innovative sewing machine firm was a particularly successful operation, selling hundreds of thousands of units around the world, including $158,180 worth of the machines it shipped across the border in 1876, despite high tariffs they faced. The organ company produced 100 units each month.[42]

By 1876, Guelph's population had risen to 9,000 and it continued to grow despite the post–Civil War recession that began in 1873 and tough times that continued until 1880. In 1879, when the population had climbed to 10,000, Guelph became a city. All along, Guelph had fought for its place as an industrial center and battled to ensure railways didn't snub it. It was a competitive world among Ontario's towns and cities in Southern Ontario at the time, and Guelph was clamoring for attention. Its men of affairs were adept at civic boosterism, and the success of the Maple Leafs against teams from much larger places was a source of pride.

Alfred Feast, a marble cutter and former member of the Hamilton Maple Leafs, introduced baseball to Guelph in 1861, although some sources say it was not until two years later.[43] He adopted the same Maple Leaf name for his new team, and the New York playing rules were adopted. By 1866, the club operated under formal bylaws and became a contending team in Southern Ontario. Residents of Guelph enthusiastically followed its exploits. William Bookless, owner of the Royal Hotel, was president of the club, and he imbued it with a competitive spirit, setting his sights on nothing less than a Canadian championship. The dream was accomplished in 1869, and after two successful defenses of its title, Guelph was allowed to keep the original Silver Ball.[44]

The new champions of Canada began touring widely and challenged American teams. In 1869, the Cincinnati Red Stockings had become the first purely professional baseball organization, and many of Guelph's opponents south of the border were becoming professional nines, paying some, or all, of their players. In 1870, the Maple Leafs team made its first foray across the border into neighboring New York to play Rochester, Oswego, and Syracuse, losing only to the latter team, a picked nine. Another American tour was undertaken in 1873, as the drift toward professionalism continued. This time, while the Guelph team did well against amateur teams, it lost to professionals: Baltimore, the Philadelphia Nationals, and the New York Mutuals. The Mutuals featured W. A. "Candy" Cummings, later credited as the first curve-ball pitcher, providing Guelph batters with a challenge they hadn't seen before. The Maple Leafs' lone win against professionals came in Ilion, New York, where they stopped on their way home, eking out a 20–19 victory.[45]

By 1873, American professionals George Keerl and Harrison Spence, both infielders, had been added to the Maple Leafs roster, and with their repeated defeat of Canadian challengers, the Guelph team was clearly the best in the country. That summer, the Boston Red Stockings, reigning National Association titleholders since the professional loop of American teams was established in 1871, visited the city on a tour of Southern Ontario. The Boston team prevailed, 28–8, before 4,000 fans, who had traveled to Guelph by train from nearby Brantford, Elora, and Fergus.[46]

The Guelph nine soon realized they needed to step up their game even more to compete with the best in baseball. As early as the end of the 1870 season, management had distributed surplus funds from that season's operations to the players, a first step away from purely amateur status. The trend toward professionalism was under way, and Guelph didn't want to be left out. It has been noted the Maple Leafs began considering other options to make it more competitive: "Repeated contact with American teams over the next few years, and a series of drubbings at the hands of these teams, may have encouraged the club and its management to begin recruiting American players."[47]

Enter George Sleeman. The successful local brewer had been associated with the Maple Leafs since Feast organized the first team in Guelph. Sleeman, who was a pitcher, played on local teams in the 1860s and by 1873 was owner of the Silver Creeks, his brewery-based team. His father, John, had established the Silver Creek brewery in 1851, and by 1867, George was its sole owner. Slee-

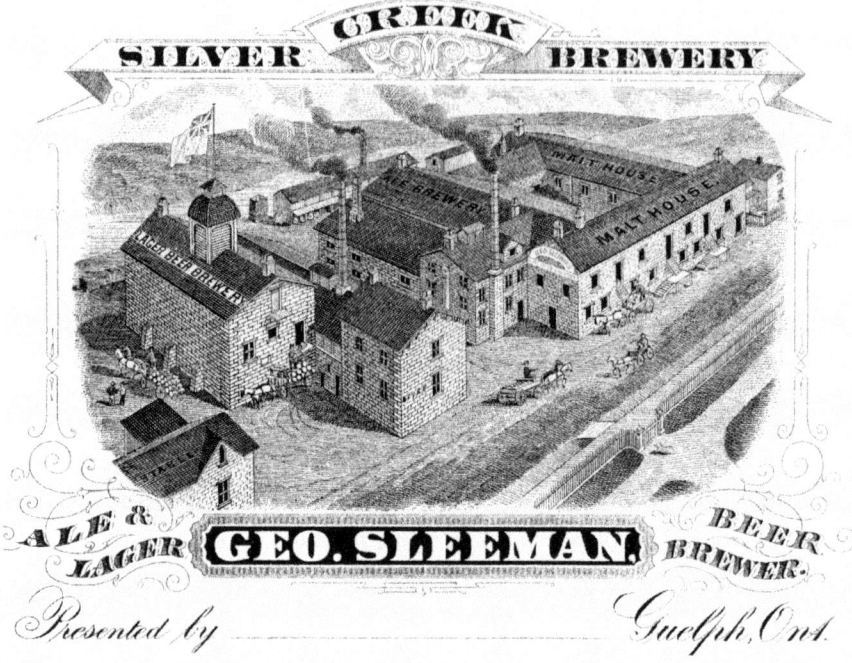

George Sleeman's Silver Creek Brewery had become one of the most successful and innovative breweries in Ontario, but just as important for Sleeman was baseball and promoting his city of Guelph. This is a form of postcard his sales staff would present to prospective customers (Sleeman Collection, Archival and Special Collections, University of Guelph Library, XR1 MS A801).

man proved very adept as a brewer. Between 1871 and 1872, he doubled production, making Sleeman Brewing and Malting one of the more successful breweries at that time in Ontario.[48] Sleeman was elected president of the Maple Leafs in 1874 and immediately ushered in an exciting new era for Guelph and the team. Highly motivated to put his city and baseball team on the map, the brewer was fiercely competitive in business and in sport alike. As a brewer, he introduced innovations based on science such as a special kiln to control the quality of his malt, a cool storage cellar where he could store his sharply ramped-up production, and a device to control the temperature of steam during the brewing process. Such steps saved him money and improved the quality of the product.

Like many entrepreneurs of his day, Sleeman felt promotion of his community would also benefit his business. Success in both was linked, he believed. His hand firmly in control, with another dipping into his wallet, he took the Maple Leafs to nearby Brantford, where he had learned that the Boston Red Stockings were playing. The Red Stockings, a powerhouse team and reigning champions of the National Association of Professional Base Ball Players, featured outstanding pitcher Albert Goodwill Spalding. In Brantford, the Bostons defeated Guelph, 26–6, on June 30 before a crowd of 3,000, and again, 20–4, in a return match the following day in Guelph that attracted at least 8,000 fans, according to the *Guelph Mercury*. Although on the losing end of both games, the Maple Leafs saw the elite Boston nine at work and began to understand what it would take to compete with the top teams. Sleeman later boasted that the game in Guelph drew 10,000 spectators, the largest crowd ever to watch a baseball game in Canada.[49] Regardless of the exact number, it was an impressive turnout of citizenry for a town with a population of 8,000.

Successful brewer George Sleeman had long supported the Guelph Maple Leafs while he managed a team at his brewery. In 1874, he was elected president of the Maple Leaf organization and was determined to make a name for the club he insisted was amateur despite its semi-professional nature (Guelph Public Library Archives, George Sleeman, 190?, F38-0-4-0-02).

With George Sleeman as owner, the Guelph Maple Leafs would soon become a professional team, importing top players from south of the border to compete against—and defeat—some of the top American teams of the day.

The success the Guelph Maple Leafs enjoyed was widely admired. Before long, it would be emulated; and a rivalry develop that would make baseball history in Canada.

3

Of Arms Races and Foreign Legions

George Sleeman was looking for new opportunities to pit his Guelph Maple Leafs against American opponents when he heard about a tournament in Watertown, New York, a small industrial city just east of Lake Ontario and a mere 30 miles south of the Canadian border. Advertised as an all-amateur affair, it was nevertheless attracting semi-professional clubs, and Sleeman felt it would be a good test for his much-improved nine. He had added two more professionals: Hank Myers, a first baseman, and William Jones, a shortstop, to join fellow American infielders George Keerl and Harrison Spence.

The Maple Leafs and some of their supporters left Guelph for Watertown on the night of July 1, 1874, mere hours after losing their second game in two days to the barnstorming Boston Red Stockings. While coming up short on the diamond, the encounters had proven profitable for Guelph, whose share of the gate was $562, as carefully entered in the team's financial records kept by the new team owner. The money helped defray the $1,250 cost of the excursion, miscellaneous travel costs, and Watertown's stiff $900 entry fee. First prize in the tournament was $500.[1] It was a long train trip east to Kingston, followed by a ferry ride and another short hop by train before the weary Guelph players and supporters reached their destination. In all, 14 teams from Canada and the United States were entered, but the Maple Leafs were the only Canadian team to make an appearance.[2] According to press accounts, "immense crowds" witnessed the games.

The number 13 proved to be a lucky one for the Guelph club during their time in Watertown. On July 3, the Maple Leafs played the Ku Klux Klan club of Oneida, New York, defeating them, 13–4. The game was scoreless until the Maple Leafs bats came alive in the third inning for seven runs, followed by a four-run outburst in the fifth. The Oneida team was sponsored by a local chapter of the newly organized white supremacist KKK organization, and its team logo featured a skull and crossbones. Guelph and Oneida were among seven clubs entered in the "first class" division. Others were the Nassaus of Brooklyn, the Flyaways of New York, the Chelseas of Brooklyn, the Eastons of Easton, Pennsylvania, and the Rochesters of Rochester. It was noted the Eastons and Flyaways were largely professional organizations and that betting was heavy on their games.[3] The Easton team was a particularly successful semi-professional club in 1874 when it defeated three National Association teams, the third-place Philadelphia Athletics, the fourth-place Philadelphia Pearls, and the sixth-place Brooklyn Atlantics. The team was led by pitcher George Bradley, a professional, who later became a star in the National League, recording its first no-hitter.[4]

On July 4, the Maple Leafs played the Nassaus and were trailing 9–7 after four and a half innings, when the game was called on account of rain. After a day off on Sunday, the two teams went at it again and the Maple Leafs prevailed, 13–8. Again, the Guelph bats were hot, led by Myers, who scored three runs, while Maddock, Spence, and Sunley picked up two apiece. The Brooklyn nine roared back with four runs in the eighth inning, but it was too little, too late.[5] The following day, Guelph faced the favored Eastons, who it was reported had seven professionals on their roster in the championship game. Betting was heavy on the Pennsylvania team, facing what was perceived to be an amateur club from Canada. Billy Smith pitched for Guelph and held the Eastons scoreless as Guelph got off to a fast start, scoring two runs in the bottom of the first inning and adding three more in each of the third and fourth innings. Easton scored three runs in the fifth, but Guelph replied with another three in the bottom of the inning. The Eastons had a late rally, picking up six runs in the eighth and another in the ninth, but Guelph's lead was too much, and the Maple Leafs rolled to a third straight victory, this one by a score of 13–10. Smith, who had a good fastball, was becoming the successor to William Sunley, the club's long-time hurler who had a much slower, albeit tricky, delivery.[6]

Winning the Watertown tournament was a watershed moment for Sleeman and the Maple Leafs. But they promoted it as much more significant than it really was. In later years, when Sleeman was recalling his tenure with the Maple Leafs, he boasted: "The first year of my presidency we succeeded in winning the semi-professional championship of the United States and Canada, at Watertown."[7] One local newspaper went so far as to state the Maple Leafs were "the only ball team to ever win a baseball

George Sleeman and his Guelph Maple Leafs won a tournament in 1874 in Watertown, New York, against some formidable professional and semi-professional opponents. Sleeman would claim this brought his team the amateur baseball title of the world in his first year as president. This illustration is from the September 12, 1874, edition of *Harper's Weekly* which took note of the team's success (Sleeman Collection, Archival and Special Collections, University of Guelph Library, Acquisition 2010-099).

world series, that the Leafs were the first Canadian ball club to play in the United States, therefore making the competition an international event and to have won the honors in the first world title tournament ever held."[8] The account failed to acknowledge earlier games played across the border by Hamilton, Woodstock, and Ingersoll, dating from as far back as 1860, or their participation in the Detroit tournament of 1867. Or even the Maple Leafs' own tour of New York in 1870.

But there was more. Sleeman was anxious to draw even wider attention to the accomplishment of the Maple Leafs. The tireless self-promoter found some press south of the border. Slightly more than two months after Watertown, *Harper's Weekly*, the influential newspaper of record, carried a large photograph of the Maple Leaf Club with Sleeman seated in the midst of his nine players in their smart white uniforms with large maple leaf insignias on front. The accompanying article read as follows:

3. Of Arms Races and Foreign Legions

BASE-BALL IN CANADA

Every true lover of this invigorating sport will be interested in the group of players printed on page 761. The Maple Leaf Base-ball Club, of Guelph, Ontario, is famous as having for three years past [sic] held the proud distinction of the Champions of Canada; and having defeated some of the best amateur clubs in the United States, at the late tournament at Watertown, New York, they claim also the title of champion amateur club of the world. They are men of splendid physique, as well as of handsome faces—men who richly deserve the professional honors they have won.[9]

An amateur club winning "professional honors"? Such was the confusion of the times when the term "professional" still carried some stigma among lovers of the game who felt that a move from amateur play was bad for it. Sleeman was still passing off his semi-professional group as amateurs, and Guelph papers and the American publication accepted his assertion. Sleeman, no doubt, was the source of the information in *Harper's Weekly*.

Canadian baseball historian Bill Humber suggests the Maple Leafs claimed far too much glory because "the tournament included none of the leading American teams of the day and was little more than a typical exhibition series with an impressive-sounding title."[10] Sleeman and his Maple Leafs were also painting a target on themselves. Their boasting was duly noted in London, no doubt, by Jake Englehart and the Tecumsehs.

On the way home from Watertown, the Maple Leafs picked up a share of gate receipts from games in Cobourg, Newcastle, Bowmanville, and Toronto. They handily won all four contests, arriving home in Guelph on July 11 to a heros' welcome from a brass band. The celebration had barely died down when, five days later, Sleeman took ball in hand like the old days, to pitch for his old Silver Creek brewery team. He scored two runs as his brewery club defeated the Independents, 30–15. The club owner was still a player at heart. The same edition of the *Mercury* reporting that game also noted that the Atlantics of Brooklyn were looking to play the Maple Leafs in Guelph on July 20. The Ontario nine was on the map of the baseball world and would face more challenges from teams anxious to tap their growing fan base for financial gain. The *Mercury* took note of yet another opportunity for the Maple Leafs:

> We learn that a base ball match is likely to come off in Guelph at an early day, between the Flyaways, ex-champions of New York, and the Maple Leaf Club. It is not improbable that the match will be for the Championship of the world; whether for the Championship or not, it will be one of the most interesting games of the season.[11]

Clearly, the *Mercury* had caught the baseball bug and, like Sleeman, had no reservation about making extravagant claims for the ball club. The Maple

Leafs made good copy and brought fame to the community, and boosterism was contagious. The Atlantics quickly brought the Maple Leafs and Guelph down to earth, at least temporarily, pummeling them, 15–1. Outclassed in all aspects of the game, the locals were unable to score their single run until the ninth inning.

The Maple Leafs regained their winning ways in August, defeating the London Tecumsehs, 5–1, on August 14 and again, ten days later, 22–11. In Toronto, Ontario's metropolis, Guelph drubbed the Dauntless club, 25–5, and later accepted complimentary tickets to an evening performance at the Academy of Music. Such entertainment for visiting teams had been prevalent in the days when gentlemen played a purely amateur sport, but the custom was dying out in the trend toward more competitive, professional play.

The game with the Flyaways for the "championship of the world" didn't come off, but that didn't stop Guelph in its pursuit of world supremacy. The Maple Leafs played the touring Staten Island club of New York on September 10 before about 500 spectators, many of them ladies, it was noted in the papers. The Maple Leafs prevailed, 17–7, and the *Mercury's* headline next day proclaimed it the "Amateur Championship of the World," conveniently ignoring the fact that by then nine Maple Leafs were being paid by Sleeman.[12] Soon afterward, Guelph traveled to Brantford, where they again defeated the Staten Islands, 19–7. Aside from its dubious claims of baseball world domination, Guelph did retain its Canadian championship as the 1874 season ended. The Maple Leafs were becoming a business, although not yet very profitable. At the club's annual meeting the following spring, it was learned that total receipts for the 1874 season came to $2,772.67, with $97.98 left in the bank once all disbursements, including money for players, had been paid.[13]

Baseball was becoming a business venture against a backdrop of economic uncertainty across North America. A financial collapse occurred in 1873 in the United States that had many causes. Post–Civil War inflation, overinvestment in railroad construction, a significant trade deficit, and massive property losses in fires in Chicago and Boston all conspired to put a huge strain on bank reserves and reduced the amount of currency available to capitalists. The collapse in September of 1873 of Jay Cooke and Company, which had overextended itself on the Northern Pacific Railroad, created financial panic. Railroad construction had been a major boost to the American economy until that time, but nine out of ten railroads failed. The ripple effect was far-reaching, and the depression that followed was long-lasting. Overall, average wages fell by about one quarter and unemployment rose to double digits in the U.S. and Canada. The situation would not improve until 1879.[14]

3. Of Arms Races and Foreign Legions 45

The game of baseball was growing in popularity despite the bigger economic picture, or perhaps because of it. Teams provided employment for young men and, at the same time, entertainment and escape for those suffering from the worst economic downturn in many years. The Panic of 1873 spilled into Canada and Europe, which was suffering its own economic dislocation following the Franco-Prussian War of 1870–1871. Further currency troubles had been created by Germany's decision to abandon silver in favor of gold to back its currency.

Concerns about the larger economic picture were far from the minds of the baseball community in North America. Baseball was on a roll and had become known as America's national pastime. Southern Ontario was likewise caught up in baseball fever, and the temperature was rising in Guelph and other communities.

Just as George Sleeman was the driving force in what would be considered the halcyon days of baseball in Guelph, the city of London had his counterpart in a competitive, baseball-promoting newspaperman.

Henry Gorman, most often known as "Harry," came to London in 1843 at the age of five. His father, Cornelius, a sergeant-librarian in the 23rd Royal Welsh Fusiliers, was transferred with his regiment from Halifax, Nova Scotia, to the garrison town in Canada West that year. When Cornelius Gorman left the service in 1847, the family opted to stay in London, where young Harry was educated. At the age of 14, he was apprenticed to the *London Free Press,* then a weekly newspaper. The paper had been founded in 1849, and Josiah Blackburn acquired it and became publisher on January 1, 1853. Among his first hires that year were the Gorman boy and apprentice printer William Southam. The latter moved to Hamilton in 1877, where he purchased a half-interest in the *Hamilton Spectator* for $5,000 and went on to establish the Southam newspaper chain.[15]

Years later, Gorman recalled with pride that he helped set type for the first daily edition of the *Free Press* in 1855, the same year that London became a city. With a natural interest in military affairs gleaned from his father, Gorman joined a local artillery battery and in 1858 was one was of the first to enlist in the 100th Regiment, formally known as the Prince of Wales' Royal Canadian Regiment of Foot, in response to the outbreak of hostilities in the Crimea. He attained the rank of sergeant while serving in Canada, England, and Gibraltar during the conflict. Gorman secured his discharge in 1861 and returned to London and the *Free Press.* At the daily, he switched from typesetting to editorial work and, in 1863, moved to the new *London Advertiser.*

The rival daily was founded by John Cameron, another former *Free Press* apprentice. Gorman the printer soon joined the editorial side of the operation, assuming duties as reporter and "local editor."

Although Londoners were playing baseball as early as 1855 (as noted in the first city directory), the city was slower to adopt baseball as enthusiastically as rival centers like Hamilton, Woodstock, and Guelph. It has been suggested that the presence of the British Garrison in London until 1869, with its clear preference for cricket, may have delayed the emergence of baseball in the city.[16] The city's cricket grounds were well established, though baseballists, having no field of their own, were permitted to use the grounds as well.

Cricket played in the city was adapted to local conditions and took a bizarre turn on February 18, 1862, when a match was played on frozen Lake Horn just north of the artillery grounds. It was believed to be the first game of cricket played on skates in Canada. "A number of spectators, including many ladies, were on the ice to see 'the last new thing in cricket,' and everyone seemed to enjoy the fun," reported the *Free Press*. The city team defeated the soldiers from the garrison by a score of 106–88.[17]

Across the border, soldiers were much on the minds of both sides in the Civil War, but not for sporting achievements. The London newspapers were full of stories about the North's celebrating the pivotal capture of Fort Donelson in Tennessee on February 16. Casualties had been heavy in the taking of the key Confederate fort, a development that opened the Cumberland River as an invasion route to the South.

The London Base Ball Club continued dividing itself into two teams for its games, but baseball didn't receive much attention from the local newspapers, which, like others of the day, had no section allocated to sports. Reports of games played and teams becoming organized were mixed in with regular news items. On August 23, 1867, a first "public" game of the newly formed Forest City Base Ball Club drew a large number of spectators for what was described as "this very popular game." Yet again, it was an event that saw club members divide themselves into two teams.[18] About two weeks later, the same Forest City nine played another new club that had adopted an old name: the London Base Ball Club.[19] The Forest Citys won, 59–37. A return match the following week drew another large crowd and the Forest Citys prevailed again, this time 56–41.[20]

The following summer, the Forest City and London Base Ball clubs amalgamated, adopting the name Tecumseh Base Ball Club of London. The name was taken from the fine Tecumseh House Hotel in downtown London. The first president of the Tecumsehs organization was John Brown, soon to become city treasurer. Also involved in the new organization were Harry Gorman of the *Advertiser*; Ed Moore, co-manager of the Tecumseh House; Daniel Perrin, a biscuit manufacturer; and brothers Richard and William Southam. Others included prominent medical doctor Ralph Morden and a young lawyer, William Meredith, who would later become Chief Justice of the Supreme Court of Ontario.[21] One memorable game that first year of 1868 was an 89–46 loss to the Woodstock Young Canadians in a five-hour contest. Woodstock went on to win the Canadian title yet again that year by defeating Guelph, 36–29.[22]

The Tecumseh name (most often pronounced tuh–KUM-see) is one with strong historical connotations in southwestern Ontario and in neighboring states. It is found on community signage, schools, streets, and monuments. It honors Shawnee Indian leader Tecumseh, who was born in 1768 along the Scioto River in Ohio near the present-day city of Springfield. A gifted orator and charismatic leader, the buckskin-clad Tecumseh led the native resistance to settlers from the new American republic who were moving westward into traditional native territory and claiming it as their own. A warrior and chief,

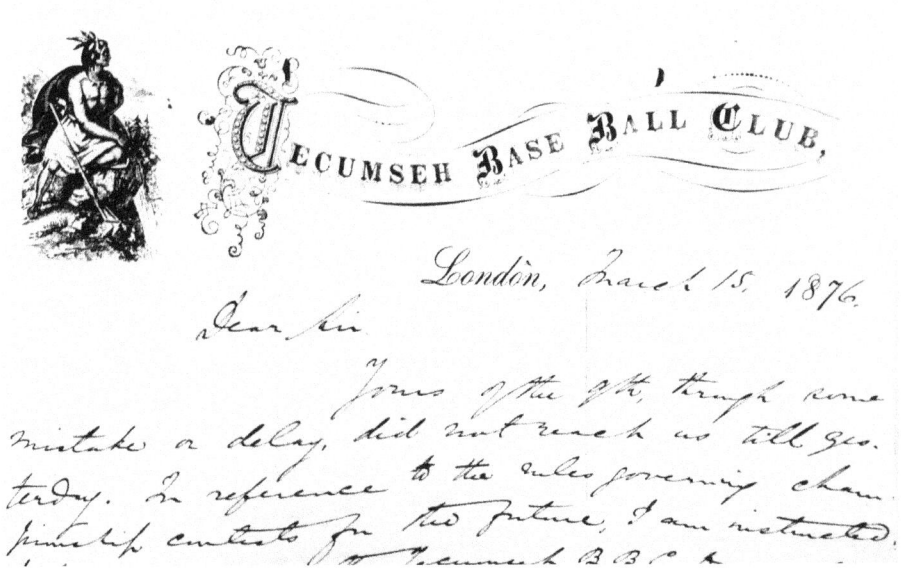

Shawnee warrior Tecumseh, who sided with the British Army and Canadian militia against the Americans in the War of 1812, fell in battle just west of London. His name is revered in Southwestern Ontario and has been adopted by communities and schools. It also adorned the fine hotel built in London in the late 1850s that became unofficial headquarters of the London Tecumsehs.

Tecumseh put together a native confederacy that became allied with the British, who were similarly concerned about American territorial expansion.

The British promised Tecumseh and his confederacy an aboriginal territory, a buffer zone between the British and Americans that native people could call their own. Tecumseh clashed with American troops in Indiana as he and his followers became increasingly drawn into an alliance with the British, ultimately joining them to fight in the War of 1812. Tecumseh and General Isaac Brock respected each other as warriors, and the two men worked well together. They captured the American fort at Detroit early in the war, despite being vastly outnumbered by American defenders. The victory was a setback for the young republic because of Detroit's strategic position controlling access to the upper Great Lakes. Not long afterward, however, Brock was killed in battle far to the east while repelling an American attack across the Niagara River at Queenston Heights.

The American victory in the Battle of Lake Erie in 1813 severed British supply lines by water and led to the recapture of a suddenly vulnerable Detroit. Emboldened, American troops chased Tecumseh, British troops, and colonial militia eastward into Upper Canada along the Thames River. Tecumseh did not respect the British general who had replaced Brock, feeling he was too cowardly. He finally persuaded General Henry Procter to stand and fight near Moraviantown, about 50 miles southwest of London. On October, 5, 1813, Tecumseh was killed in the Battle of the Thames. The natives fled into the bush, marking an end to Tecumseh's confederacy. The British army and settlers accompanying them escaped to the east without further pursuit by American General William Henry Harrison.

To this day, Tecumseh is revered in Canada as a great ally of the British and of the first settlers in Ontario for fighting the Americans. The War of 1812 accomplished little other than to show unexpectedly strong resistance from the Canadians, whose loyalty was doubted because so many of them had come from the United States. After fighting ceased, the borders were returned to those existing before the hostilities. In the peace treaty, the British failed to push for the native buffer area promised to Tecumseh and his followers. A monument near the Thames River marks where Tecumseh fell in battle fighting for his dream of an aboriginal homeland. A massive portrait of him hangs in the Royal Canadian Military Institute, acknowledging his invaluable assistance to Canada.[23] Another portrait was prominently displayed in the London hotel that bore his name.

Other baseball teams besides the Tecumsehs were organizing in London by the early 1870s, among them the Morning Stars, whose members included

3. Of Arms Races and Foreign Legions

the usual clerks and bookkeepers who were being attracted to the game elsewhere in Canada and in the United States. Years later, it was recalled that their favorite practice time was 4 a.m. on the city "common," which had been cleared of trees but on which many stumps remained.[24] Nearby was the site of the British garrison, which had left town in 1869.

The Tecumsehs, the Morning Stars, and the OK Base Ball clubs amalgamated with the Forest City club in 1871 under the name Athletics. That same year, they lost 34–4 to the touring Forest City club from Rockford, Illinois, a member of the new National Association of Professional Base Ball Players. The visitors featured 18-year-old future star Adrian Constantine "Cap" Anson, playing third base, who went on to a long and successful baseball career. The following year, the Athletics were embarrassed, 52–3, by the touring Boston Red Stockings, the best team in the National Association. The powerful Boston squad was led by heavy-hitting Ross Barnes and star pitcher Albert Goodwill Spalding. The best club in baseball showed London how professionals could play the game. The strictly amateur Athletics roster included London lawyer Frank Love and printer Richard Southam, both good local players, but no match for the professionals.[25]

By 1873, it was becoming apparent something had to be done if London hoped to compete with the better teams of the day. That year, the two leading local clubs decided to merge. In late July, Gorman's *Advertiser* reported:

> The best attended base ball meeting seen in this city for years was held in the Tecumseh House last evening for the purpose of permanently organizing the Athletic and Eckford clubs under the old name of Tecumseh. The interest taken in the proceedings by the leading ball players of the city and numerous admirers of the game was exceedingly gratifying, and may be taken as an indication that though the formation of the club comes somewhat late in the year, there is a determination to make up for lost time by earnest work during the balance of the season.[26]

Practices were scheduled for Monday, Wednesday, and Friday evenings at 6:00 p.m. City treasurer John Brown was elected president, the same post he had held with the original Tecumseh club organized in 1868. Among the vice-presidents was Ed Moore, co-manager of the Tecumseh House Hotel. One of the five directors was Harry Gorman, who likely penned the report of the meeting for the *Advertiser*.

The next month, games were played between the first and second nines of the Tecumsehs at the Artillery Barrack Square for possession of a trophy known as the Knowlton Cup. A large number of spectators was noted at the games, including "numerous ladies." The crowd witnessed some "very much admired" fly catches by Bob Emslie, a young man from Guelph who was about to settle in London.[27]

In 1874, the Tecumsehs lost repeatedly to the Guelph Maple Leafs, who the previous year had hired their first professionals and were adding more. One game was a relatively close affair, with Guelph winning, 5–3. "This was undoubtedly the finest game ever played in Canada up to that date," remarked *Bryce's Base Ball Guide* in its recap of the 1874 and 1875 seasons included in its 1876 edition. The *Guide* noted, "the Tecumsehs were composed entirely of local amateurs, while the Guelphs had the advantage of the services of [an all–American infield], all of whom had been induced by the lovers of base ball in Guelph to settle in that town and attach themselves to the Maple Leafs."[28] It wasn't hard to see through that malarkey. The inducements consisted of money, and Sleeman was the source of that. But the *Guide,* approved as it was by Sleeman and Gorman in messages printed in its introduction, chose its words carefully so as not to offend. Sleeman had long asserted that the Maple Leafs were amateur in character, likely because of the lingering sentiment by baseball purists that professionalism brought with it degenerate behavior like gambling and drinking. The publication was similarly careful in its description of a baseball power that was rising to the east, in Kingston. The *Guide* reported that by 1874 the St. Lawrence club in that Eastern Ontario city "called in the aid of foreign players, and made a mad dash for the championship, but they were unequal to the task."

Also in 1874, the Earl of Dufferin, Frederick Temple Blackwood, the governor-general of Canada, christened the 40-acre military reserve vacated by the British garrison five years earlier in London as Victoria Park. He told a large crowd that the city was wise to set aside the property "for the convenience and recreation of the people," as he signed a document inaugurating the park. The ceremony was followed by bands that played "God Save the Queen" and a military salute from Gorman's old artillery battery.[29] Until that time, cricket and baseball teams had shared the old garrison grounds for about 20 years, disturbing animals and humans alike. The ball and the cricket players regularly erected fences to keep out cattle that roamed freely in the area. But area residents repeatedly knocked them down in the dead of night, complaining that the fences interfered with neighborhood shortcuts they were accustomed to taking.[30] It was hoped the new public park would be more suitable for their games.

Guelph's acclaim for winning the Watertown Tournament in 1874, with ever more professionals now that a brewer was in charge of the team, was duly noted in its rival to the west. London, a larger city, was home to two breweries, the Labatt and Carling operations. Brewery principals and employees must have envied Sleeman's success. It stirred the competitive juices of Londoners who cared about boosting their city in an era of optimism when anything seemed possible. At first, London newspapers dismissed the Guelph team as the "Foreign Legion," but the writing was on the wall for London. If the Tecumsehs were to compete with Guelph—and the St. Lawrence team in faraway Kingston—the London team would have to follow suit and hire professionals.[31]

For the 1875 campaign, Sleeman made some further adjustments to the Guelph roster, rendering it nearly all American. Virtually all members of the Kingston club were lured from south of the border; and Toronto hired an American pitcher as it amalgamated its best clubs in a bid to become more competitive.

The games between London and Guelph continued to draw large crowds as the rivalry between the two cities heated up. Directors of both clubs discovered this was good for their coffers, and the newspapers were now providing ample—and highly partisan—coverage. The Tecumsehs and Maple Leafs chose each other for their first game of the season, on May 24, in London. The Tecumsehs got off to a good start with two runs in the bottom of the first inning and another in the third, for a lead of 3–2. The Maple Leafs added five more runs in the top of the fifth, a situation created, the *Free Press* reported, by "two or three questionable decisions by the umpire, Mr. J. T. Nichols (a former captain of the Maple Leafs)."[32] Guelph won the game, 8–3.

The second meeting of the Tecumsehs and Maple Leafs came on June 17 in Guelph, and it was another close game, with a final score of 10–8 for the Maple Leafs. In early August, it was reported that the London Cricket Club had broken up, and the Tecumsehs picked up "several excellent ball players" including young jeweler Tom Gillean. London was becoming a baseball city, and cricket was in decline. The same edition of the newspaper that described the pickups for the Tecumsehs took some potshots at the Maple Leafs.

> The Guelph Foreign Legion feel very touchy over comparisons between them and the Tecumsehs. The Jackson ball players, like those from Detroit, had occasion to remark that their treatment in Guelph was not as courteous and fair as they had a right to expect, and was in marked contrast to that accorded them by the Tecumsehs in London. One of the foreigners, named Spence, undertakes in a column letter to the *Jackson Patriot* to prove that the Legion of which he forms a ninth part are pinks of perfection and so thoroughly devoted to base ball that they had emigrated from distant parts of the States to Guelph out of pure love

for the game, and without any other inducement, pecuniary or otherwise, to tempt them to spend the summer in Canada.³³

The paper went on to complain about Spence's "angry ill-tempered screed" in which he attacked the London club. "We don't for a moment suppose that any of the Tecumseh nine care a straw for Mr. Spence's opinion."

The next contest between Guelph and London came in Guelph on August 16. The much-anticipated event drew a very large crowd, which, the *Free Press* said, "acted very orderly for a Guelph crowd."³⁴ The Tecumseh roster included an American professional named Shevlin, its first, but the newspapers failed to take any special notice of the new fielder who played well. London had a fast start, bringing in five runs in the top of the first inning in what would be a hard-fought contest. After six innings, London was ahead, 9–7. The Maple Leafs erupted for five runs in the bottom of the seventh inning and scored two more in the eighth. The final score was 14–9 for Guelph, which kept its bragging rights over the Tecumsehs.

The following day, proclaimed the annual Civic Holiday in London, saw the return match. Having come so close to finally defeating Guelph, expectations were sky-high for the home team. However, at the scheduled start time of 2:30 p.m. a steady downpour prevented play. An hour later, the rain abated, and an "immense crowd" was on hand at the Exhibition Grounds, where the Tecumsehs awaited the appearance of the Maple Leafs. The Guelph team finally appeared, but not in uniform, the *Advertiser* reported. "The crowd showed their pleasure at the prospects of a game by greeting the Guelph men with a hearty round of applause," a reception that apparently encouraged the Maple Leafs to don their uniforms and begin play.

At the end of the fourth inning, with Guelph leading, 3–0, the Maple Leafs "put on their coats, packed up their bats, and left the field. This movement was met with a storm of hisses and groans from the spectators, who rushed over the ropes and surrounded the Guelph men demanding their return to finish the game." Then things began to get out of hand:

> Outside the gates, the mob assumed a more threatening aspect, the rowdy element predominating, and we regret to say that some of the strangers received rough reminders of their anger. It required the utmost exertions of the few who stood by the Guelph men to save them from serious injury. Nothing approaching such a scene was ever witnessed here before, and we hope will never be again.³⁵

The Guelph club insisted it had been pressured to play, but only four innings, by Tecumseh directors anxious to appease the crowd. A Tecumseh official admitted as much. Besides, the Maple Leafs said the delayed start meant they risked missing their train home if they stayed longer.

The rival *London Free Press* noted that a gang of young persons attacked the Maple Leafs on their way to their hotel, peppering the players with "stones and other missiles." One of the players, Lapham, received a severe blow to the head, it reported. The paper said "such conduct was reprehensible," but expressed some satisfaction that Guelph didn't receive its share of gate proceeds because of the dispute surrounding the early departure. "The crowd were loud in denunciation of the conduct of the visitors, who need not show their faces in this vicinity again if they value good health and sound limbs," it said.[36] The threat from its journalistic competition prompted the *Advertiser* to retort: "Such open encouragement of rowdyism meets with strong condemnation of all hands, and from the feeling evinced on the streets today we are certain that should the Maple Leafs come here to complete their unfinished game they will be as civilly and friendly received as any other club."

The fine hand of Gorman, the Tecumseh secretary and *Advertiser* local news editor, was no doubt behind that reassurance. It wouldn't do for Guelph to refuse to return to London in future for fear of physical violence, even though the final scheduled contest between the two teams that season was to be held in Guelph.

Rival cities were setting a course to topple powerhouse Guelph. The Maple Leafs suffered only one loss in Canada, to Kingston, in a game that went 12 innings before St. Lawrence prevailed, 3–2.[37] That year, Guelph also defeated teams in New York State, while London beat the Michigan champions, the Mutuals of Jackson, and the Detroit Aetnas. This prompted *Bryce's Base Ball Guide* to summarize the situation after it reviewed team records from the 1875 campaign this way:

> Base ball has now reached such a stage of perfection in Canada that its leading clubs are able to cope successfully with the best of the same class in the United States.... The impetus given to base ball by the greatly improved style of play resulting from the introduction of foreign talent, is manifesting itself in the increased patronage bestowed upon the game by the public in all parts of Ontario.[38]

Harry Gorman and the directors of the Tecumsehs belatedly decided to take the London team to a higher level. Likely this was done with the encouragement and promise of backing from Jake Englehart, the oil refiner still residing in the Tecumseh House Hotel and about to assume a leading role in the Tecumseh organization. The club would pursue American professionals but they were venturing into new territory and wanted to catch up as quickly as possible to Guelph and, to a lesser extent, Kingston.

Gorman, the team manager, found a professional named George Warren

"Juice" Latham, who was known in London because his New Haven team had barnstormed through Southern Ontario. That September, the New Havens lost to Guelph by a score of 7–5 but defeated London a few days later, 19–4. Latham, 23, a native of Utica, New York, was an infielder for two teams in the National Association during the 1875 season. He began the year by playing 16 games with the powerful Boston Red Stockings, where he recorded a respectable batting average of .269. On June 14, he was hired by the struggling Elm City team of New Haven, Connecticut, which had a record of two wins against 21 losses. Latham served as player-manager for 20 games as New Haven continued to suffer from defensive weaknesses and poor hitting. Latham was replaced as manager on September 11 when the team record stood at six wins and 35 losses.[39] Latham's nickname was apparently derived from his high-energy approach to the game, although in the era of hard-drinking players, some thought it might have another origin.

The New Haven game in London that September came with some extra-curricular activity that put Latham in an uncomfortable position. The visiting team, as did all who remained overnight in London, stayed at the Tecumseh House Hotel. The visitors had been struggling on the field against their National Association opponents, and financially as well. The late-season tour into Ontario was seen as a means of picking up a badly needed share of gate receipts. But other things were picked up as well. Upon the team's departure from the London train station, the Tecumseh House Hotel managers and several New Haven players noticed that team members Billy Geer, their left fielder, and Henry Luff, the third baseman, seemed to have more luggage than when they arrived. At the hotel, it was discovered that an expensive coat was missing from a room next to that occupied by Geer and Luff. Ed Moore, a Tecumseh club director and manager of the Tecumseh House, sent a telegram outlining his suspicions to the Elm City directors, who in turn relayed it to the chief of police in New Haven. On September 13—two days after Latham left the team—police arrested Geer and Luff in a bar and searched their rooming house. The officers found a large selection of coats, including a fine broadcloth one bearing the identification tag, "D. MacKenzie—Sarnia, Ontario." This coat matched the description provided by Moore about a coat reported missing by a hotel guest from Sarnia, a community about 60 miles west of London. The two New Haven players were jailed on suspicion of theft. Also found in their quarters were other items reported missing from a hotel in Pennsylvania. Luff and Geer were later acquitted of the charges, although Luff gave a statement insisting he was innocent and pointing the finger at Geer.[40] The New Haven team disbanded shortly after Latham left, ending a miserable season but freeing up players, some of whom, like Latham, were picked up by other teams.

The legacy of the New Haven visit was still on the minds of Londoners, and the 1875 ball season was drawing to a close, when Latham agreed to the offer from London to become captain of the Tecumsehs. He became the team's second professional player and he also assumed the post of manager to attract professional talent for next year's campaign.[41] Latham joined the London team for its tour of Michigan later in September for games against the Aetnas of Detroit, the Mutuals of Jackson, and the Unas of Kalamazoo.

Rumors were rampant that London had hired three New Haven players to buttress its lineup for its late-season match against rival Guelph. A final Canadian championship series game was scheduled between the teams for September 24. Editorial comment in the *Guelph Herald* based on the rumors was too much for the *London Free Press*, which repeated the *Herald* story and then fired back with its own salvo:

> The London fellows must be getting desperate, indeed, when it is necessary to import professionals for the game. But when the 24th arrives they will find out that their imported beauties will be debarred from playing. Being an "unauthorized" organ of the club, we [the *Free Press*] are not in a position to deny the statement, but fancy the services of only one man of the New Haven nine has been sought after and secured. But, granted that such is the case, surely the Guelph players will accord the Tecumsehs the same privilege as other clubs have extended them in the matter of "imported beauties." Wonder how many of their nine are natives of Guelph? Eh! It makes all the difference in the world whose ox is being gored.[42]

The rivalry between the Maple Leafs and Tecumsehs was heating up, and the daily newspapers played it for all it was worth—and more. Whether the Tecumsehs actually approached three New Haven players is not known, but Latham was soon sporting the big "T" on the front of his Tecumseh uniform.

"Juice" Latham later became known in a long professional career as "Jumbo" when his weight rose to 250 pounds (from 164) on his five-foot-eight frame. He had extensive connections in the baseball fraternity, particularly in Boston and New Haven, the latter of which the Tecumsehs would build upon.

Latham helped his new London team to easy victories over the Detroit and Jackson clubs, but on September 22 in Kalamazoo, he and the other new professional, Shevlin, were hurt.

Before the game, during warm-up, Latham injured his left thumb, but played in the game anyway. Able only to use one hand, he found batting difficult for him. In the fifth inning, with a 1–1 tie, infielder Shevlin took a ball in the face and was forced to retire from the field. The Tecumsehs were badly outplayed the rest of the way and lost, 12–2. The London papers urged Tecumseh fans against being disappointed by the result in the final Michigan game, noting that five of the Kalamazoo players were professionals earning from $75 to $125 a month. The papers were likely softening up followers of the London team to understand the need for professional players like Latham and Shevlin.[43] In reporting the loss earlier that month to New Haven, the *Advertiser* had sounded a similar note, saying: "As a purely local amateur organization, the Tecumsehs have no equal in Canada." It stressed that Tecumseh players always worked hard, but had to take time away from their paying jobs, so it was "unfair" to criticize their play "against professional players who have done nothing but play ball every day during the season."[44]

The injuries to its new professionals prompted the Tecumseh management to ask Guelph to delay the final game in their Canadian championship series beyond September 24, but Guelph refused. "How magnanimous!" grumped the *Advertiser* in response to that position. The daily took aim at the assertion by Guelph newspapers that Latham and Shevlin would have been

CHAMPIONSHIP BASE BALL MATCH

TECUMSEHS, OF LONDON
vs.
MAPLE LEAF, OF GUELPH

A MATCH WILL BE PLAYED FOR THE CHAMPIONSHIP OF CANADA, ON

FRIDAY, 24th SEPTEMBER

on the Maple Leaf grounds, near the Great Western Railway Station. This match promises to be the most exciting game played in Canada this Season.
The Game will be called at 2 o'clock p.m.   ADMISSION TWENTY CENTS.   LADIES FREE.
GEO. SLEEMAN, President.   Mercury Steam Job Press   **A. WEIR, Secretary**

After losing to London for the first time ever in 1876, Guelph was hoping this last match of the season between the two great rivals would see it retain its Canadian championship. This advertisement is from the *Guelph Mercury*.

ruled unable to play against Guelph anyway. "From this it would appear that the Guelphites assumed to themselves the sole right to employ professionals in Canada," the paper harrumphed. And it reminded readers that it was the Maple Leafs club that had insisted the word "amateur" be removed from the rules governing the Canadian championship.[45]

The final Guelph-London game was never played, and Guelph claimed the title of national champions for the seventh straight year. Guelph management had reason to be concerned that its continued dominance was at risk. With the moves toward professionalism in Kingston, Toronto, and, more recently, in London, Guelph knew the playing field would become more level in the near future.

In London, Juice Latham began tapping his many contacts in the baseball world to convert the Tecumsehs to a professional nine for the 1876 season. He had the full support of a determined group of team directors who had seen how well attended its games were, as the team had captivated the imagination of the city.

After trashing the "foreign legions" in Guelph and elsewhere, London was now actively assembling its own. An arms race was under way, and the enemy was the Guelph Maple Leafs.

4

Out with the Old...

Mother Nature seemed almost as anxious as London and the Tecumsehs to get the 1876 ball season under way. New Year's Day was on a Saturday and it was remarkably warm, prompting the *London Free Press* to describe it "as genial and mild as a May morning."[1] The hint of spring prompted someone to suggest a ball game was in order. More than a thousand people descended on the fairgrounds to see the Tecumsehs play a team known as the Field, consisting of former Tecumseh players. The new Tecumsehs were missing most of their imports, however, because of the short notice of the game and the fact that many of them were at their homes in the United States. Their places on the roster were ably filled by top local players. The New Year started with promise, as the Tecumsehs held the purely local opposition scoreless until the ninth inning for a 10–4 win. The game marked the first opportunity for fans to see first baseman Juice Latham in action for the London club, and he didn't disappoint. The newspaper reported his play was "much admired. He is without a doubt the best ball tosser in Canada, and has few equals in the States."

London was joining the ranks of professional baseball during a time of seismic change for the sport in North America. The 1875 season had been a dismal one for the National Association of Professional Base Ball Players, and some powerful forces were at work in late 1875 and early 1876 to bring about change.

The National Association was founded in 1871 by players who saw and admired the success of the Cincinnati Red Stockings, which in 1869 had become the first purely professional baseball organization, and openly so. Its players earned from $600 to $1,200 for the season.[2] The NA initially consisted of nine contending clubs from places as small as Rockford, Illinois (population 11,000), to the large cities of Philadelphia, Boston, and New York. The other teams were from Chicago, Troy, Cleveland, Washington, and Fort Wayne, Indiana.

4. Out with the Old... 59

As its name implied, the National Association was organized by players, for players. To underline that premise, in 1872 a rule was enacted to ensure that the president of the Association was a ball player. Bob Ferguson, the manager and third baseman for the Atlantic Club of Brooklyn, was elected president and stayed in that post until this first league of professionals was dissolved.[3] Players soon found themselves in the sometimes uncomfortable position of managing the business that baseball was becoming. Their skill sets involved catching, throwing, and hitting balls; not bookkeeping, managing, and human resources. So their decisions occasionally weren't the best for the long-term health of their teams or the Association.

The loop attracted most of the major teams of the day, many established as cooperatives, which relied heavily on extended barnstorming tours to pay themselves and their bills. Chicago was a rarity. It was organized as a stock company, one of the first teams to take that route. Centralized scheduling was not attempted, and it was up to team managers to work out playing dates and arrangements among themselves. Each team contending for the Association championship had to pay a $10 entry fee and play a best three-out-of-five series with every other entrant before November 1. Home teams were required to supply umpires, who were not paid.

The NA was marked by instability, with many of its clubs disbanding mid-season amidst financial turmoil their player-managers could not turn around. Few teams were profitable. Even the Boston Red Stockings club, wildly successful on the field, was only modestly successful as a business operation.

Season returns for Boston ranged from a meager $767 to about $4,000, partly attributable to its high payrolls, which by 1875 had reached $20,685.[4] Keeping track of standings by teams competing for the championship pennant was also a nightmare and the subject of constant controversy, as wins earned and losses incurred from teams that disbanded meant constant adjustments to the records of remaining teams. In some years, as few as five teams even bothered to submit their statistics to Association secretary Nick Young.[5]

Gambling on games was prevalent, and accusations flew that players had "tossed" games on which they had placed bets in an effort to fatten their wallets. Newspaper accounts took note of betting, especially when it was heavy, and gamblers made their presence known at the ballpark, where sometimes large amounts of money changed hands. The practice of throwing games was known as "hippodroming," and some teams like the Mutuals of New York were believed to be controlled by gamblers. Pool selling was a practice in vogue before bookmaking became popular. Based in poolrooms near local ballparks, the complicated schemes involved a third party holding cash and auctioning off the right to bet on upcoming games. The pool seller kept records, paid those who won their wagers, and then skimmed a percentage of each bet.[6] Chicago and Philadelphia were also involved in questionable games that led to rumors of fixes. Drinking and loutish behavior, accompanied by bad language, was common among players, who often jumped teams mid-season when offered more money by rival nines, in a practice known as "revolving." The wealthier clubs were able to attract the top talent available, so the Association proved to be less competitive than was healthy, with Boston winning four of the five championship pennants. In 1875, for instance, the dominant Bostons compiled a record of 71 wins against eight losses. The second-place Athletics were 15 games back. At the bottom of the standings when the season ended were the Brooklyn Atlantics, with a record of two wins and 42 losses. That same year, Boston's best, six of the 13 teams in the Association dropped out, including the Westerns of tiny Keokuk, Iowa, population 12,000, which scored a single win against twelve losses before disbanding in June.

Clubs arose and disappeared as their financial situations waxed and waned. Such was the turnover that only three teams competed for all five NA pennants: the Athletics of Philadelphia, the Mutuals of New York and Boston.[7] Some players were doing very well for themselves, however, even without the proceeds from gamblers and gambling. In 1871, for instance, future Hall of Famer Cap Anson, then 19, was earning $66.67 a month at Rockford, or a bit less than $500 for the season. By comparison, fully nine years later, the average factory worker was bringing home only $347 for a full year's work, while a teacher earned $71.40 for the entire 1879–1880 school year.[8] Published salary schedules for the Boston, Chicago, Philadelphia, and Philadelphia Athletic clubs in 1874 showed how the practice of "revolving" had boosted player pay. All were earning at least $1,000 apiece, with three White Stockings earning more than $2,000.[9] The NA made little serious effort to discipline teams that disbanded before completing the season, much less steps to curb "revolving," gambling, or drinking.

By late 1875, it had become apparent the National Association was in trouble. Pay for players on better-financed stock company teams had risen to an average of $1,200 a year, while those on the weaker cooperatives earned $300, a huge disparity.[10] Fan support was in decline because of the widespread belief that fair competition was being undermined by questionable on-field performance tied to gambling. As one historian has put it: "The integrity of the games was so low that on occasion law enforcement officials were compelled to post signs at ballparks announcing that games played between competing teams should not be trusted. These problems caused attendance to decline each year of the league's existence."[11]

Despite all its problems, instability, and relatively short history, the National Association is considered a major league by baseball historians. Records of its players can be found in sources like *Total Baseball* and Baseball-reference.com. Many of the Association players moved on to other professional leagues and associations in their careers, indicating their skill sets were among the best of the day. However, not all professional leagues in the early years of professional baseball would receive the same treatment from historians.

During the 1875 season, William Hulbert, a coal dealer who had become secretary of the Chicago White Stockings, was advised by his board that Boston's star pitcher Albert Goodwill Spalding had offered his services to Chicago as manager for the next season. Spalding was on his way to recording 57 wins for the dominant Red Stockings in 1875. The board was keenly interested. So Hulbert was directed to go to Boston to sign Spalding, the Illinois native who began his career with the Forest City team in Rockford, not far from his hometown of Byron. The club secretary was also authorized to sign any other players he could.

Hulbert exceeded expectations. He picked up an impressive battery and most of an infield from two teams. He signed pitcher Spalding for $4,000 for the next season, plus 25 percent of net profits from gate receipts, along with a secret sub-deal promising 30 percent of net profits from club business.[12]

Also signed by Hulbert was Boston catcher James "Deacon" White for $2,400 in salary and a $100 signing fee. Hulbert picked up heavy-hitting second baseman Ross Barnes for $1,500 in salary, and first baseman Cal McVey for $2,000 a season in a two-year pact. Hulbert didn't stop with Boston, however. From the Philadelphia Athletics, he signed talented utility player Adrian "Cap" Anson for $2,000 for the upcoming season and a signing fee of $200. Third-baseman Ezra Sutton was offered the same money as his teammate Anson but he later reneged on the deal.[13]

The coup by Hulbert no doubt pleased him hugely because he'd been frustrated for years by wealthy Eastern NA clubs who stole his better players with lucrative contracts. In 1874, for instance, Hulbert signed Davy Force, the White Stockings' star shortstop and pitcher, to a contract renewal for 1875. Force did so in September, but three months later, he signed a contract for 1875 with the Athletics. The Chicago contract was ruled invalid by the Association's rarely activated judicial committee, because it was signed before the playing season had ended. The Philadelphia contract was upheld. Hulbert tried back-dating the Force contract, but that, too, was rejected by the Association, whose control rested with its powerful Eastern clubs. He was still fuming about the loss of Force a year later and was determined to bring the Association to its knees. Some historians have pointed to Force's signing of two contracts in 1874 as marking the beginning of the end for the National Association because of the fire it put into the belly of the determined coal dealer from Chicago.[14]

Hulbert's action prompted rumors that the Eastern clubs were preparing to expel all six players involved. National Association rules, of which Hulbert had already run afoul with Force, still stipulated it was not permitted to negotiate with players or clubs during the season. Critics of Hulbert's move referred to the "Big Four" players from Boston as "seceders," one of the worst things that could be said of any American in the years following the Civil War.[15]

Hulbert was not the least bit worried about the National Association, its rules, or any rumors. He was working on a plan that would shake up the professional baseball world. Upset at the behavior of Association teams and players, by gambling, thrown games, drinking, games played on Sundays, and soaring player pay that left too little for shareholders, Hulbert felt strong measures were needed to bring the integrity to America's pastime. Nothing less was called for, he felt, than an entirely new league, free of player control, for the good of the game—and for businessmen like himself.

As Hulbert saw it, the Association was beyond saving, so an entirely new model must replace it. His action was calculated. And dramatic.

He devised a plan for a new league to clear up the evils he felt were threatening to destroy baseball. With the help of the newly recruited Spalding, Hulbert drew up a constitution for what would become the National League of Professional Base Ball Clubs. It was an organization of clubs, not of players, reflecting that critical change. The new organization was established along business principles by managers and businessmen—not by players. Henceforth, players would be limited to doing what they did best: playing the game. Managers would manage. Observers had trouble understanding how significant the changes were. Spalding, during a honeymoon visit to Rockford, was buttonholed by a *Chicago Tribune* reporter who wanted to know what this new league was all about. The new White Stockings executive was succinct. The transfer of power from players to management, Spalding said, was part of "the irrepressible conflict between labor and capital."[16]

To prevent fragmentation of metropolitan markets, under the new plan only one team was allowed to represent each city, a monopolistic move intended to fatten gate receipts for each club. The entry fee would be increased tenfold to $100 from the old NA, and the money used to create administration for the League. To attract larger audiences, no city smaller than 75,000 population would be accepted for membership (Hartford, Connecticut, was made exempt from that rule) and admission to games would be 50 cents, double that charged by many NA clubs. (The admission fee for Association clubs was not set in stone and had proved to be yet another contentious issue when it came to splitting gate proceeds with visiting teams. Many charged 25 cents; others, 50.) The League idea was to reduce attendance by a lower class of fan, the rowdier element inclined to bad language and gambling; or, as Ted Vincent put it so colorfully in *Mudville's Revenge*, "a desire to flush out from the grandstand the allegedly foul-mouthed, odorous, and tacky-looking working class and replace them with a higher class of people willing and able to pay double the standard ticket price."[17]

Hulbert's constitution clearly decreed that players were not permitted to negotiate with other clubs while they were still playing during the season— notwithstanding his own treachery in Boston and Philadelphia. In another key rule, gambling and pool selling were prohibited in all ballparks, and a ban for life would be imposed on any player found guilty of dishonesty. No games could be played on Sundays, and the selling of beer was banned. The latter rules were promoted by Hulbert in a bid to promote a higher degree of morality than had been exhibited by the teams in the Association.

At a meeting in Louisville in December 1875, Hulbert laid out his plan before representatives of the Cincinnati, Louisville, and St. Louis Clubs. They bought in. All he needed was four more Eastern clubs to establish his dreamed-of first-class league. To accomplish that, Hulbert called a secret meeting February 2, 1876, at Manhattan's Grand Central Hotel with representatives of the Philadelphia Athletics, Boston, Hartford, and the Mutuals of New York. Hulbert was at his persuasive best. Some stories were spread that he locked the doors to the meeting room in a bid to encourage consensus from the teams. In the end, his sales job worked. The four teams signed on and the National League was born. Morgan Bulkeley, of the Hartford Dark Blues, was elected president of the new, eight-team loop. The founding teams agreed to withdraw immediately from the NA, which had been planning to have an 1876 season for which 17 teams had already indicated they would pursue the championship.[18]

Chief among the critics of the move by Hulbert and the other teams was Henry Chadwick, the baseball writer for the *New York Clipper*, the only national sporting publication that gave comprehensive coverage to baseball (along with another popular form of entertainment, the theater). Chadwick, a Brit by birth, witnessed his first baseball game in 1856 and immediately embraced it, saying it was perfect for his adopted land. He promoted the game, invented the box score and became baseball's great proponent, authority, and arbiter of disputes. As soon as he got wind of it, he blasted Hulbert's handiwork as a "coup d'etat." Chadwick insisted that Hulbert's concerns should have been addressed within the framework of the Association, the 1871 creation of which Chadwick had applauded. Chadwick himself had been calling for the need to curb fraudulent play for a year or two, but he took issue with the drastic steps taken by Hulbert and company. He didn't mince words.

> Our baseball friends have taken a new departure—gone secretly to work, as it were, and made a break in the professional arena. Eight clubs have organized themselves into a union league for the avowed purpose of bringing about a reform on the ball-field, and preventing a repetition of those fraudulent transactions which have brought our national game into such disrepute. The object sought to be attained meets our hearty approval and support; but the means by which this end is to be reached cannot be viewed in a favorable light by the great body of ball-players. The whole movement toward the formation of this league has been conducted in secrecy, as if to anticipate action of the National [Association] Convention, if not utterly destroy that body. Reform should not fear the light of day, nor should clubs charged with offenses be denied an opportunity to be heard in their own defense. Neither do we see upon what ground the league decides that but one club shall represent a city. Surely, such an arbitrary measure, if persisted in, cannot increase the popularity of the game, nor can it tend to add to the number of first-class players; on the contrary, it will have a tendency to injure "the best interests of the game," by inculcating a feeling of opposition, of distrust, and of general dissatisfaction. Another error is the rule which refuses to admit a club from any city of less than seventy-five thousand population. This looks as if the league had an eye to the profits, and not the interests of baseball.[19]

It has been suggested that Chadwick's nose was out of joint because Hulbert and his fellow conspirators had not confided in him. To the "Father of Baseball"—as he had become known—Hulbert's National League was an illegitimate child. Clearly, the vision of baseball promoted by Hulbert and his capitalist associates was decidedly at odds with that of Chadwick and the populists he felt he represented. Chadwick wanted the game he loved and nourished to be broadly based, "owned," so to speak, by Americans, rather than by narrow business interests.

The obituary was soon written for the National Association, which couldn't continue after losing four of its strongest teams. Club representatives met on March 1, but the gathering attracted only a handful of teams from Pennsylvania, Ohio, and Maryland. A subsequent gathering in April accomplished little, and the Association was essentially finished. Baseball's first professional league was consigned to history.

Meanwhile, on April 22, 1876, the inaugural National League game was played in Philadelphia between the Athletics and the Boston Red Stockings. Boston won the contest, 6–5 before a crowd estimated at 3,000.[20] A new era was under way, the implications of which may not have been readily apparent to fans of the game, or even the players themselves who had pioneered the professional game. In recent times, historian William J. Ryczek opined that the rise of the National League meant that players lost control of their destinies but, in exchange, the new organization brought much-needed stability to their workplace. He concluded:

> Efficiency is not entertaining. Accounting is not a popular spectator sport. The National Association had its warts, was poorly run, and generated only one worthwhile pennant race in five years. But it was the first major league, a noble experiment that served a necessary function in baseball's awkward transition from an amateur to a professional sport.[21]

The 1876 season was a pivotal one for baseball. A new vision of what the game could be had emerged in the United States. In Canada, the Tecumsehs had chosen an interesting time to enter the competitive ranks of professional baseball.

As the National League hurried to put together plans for its inaugural season with a founding convention in March, the two leading teams in Canada were looking to put the game north of the border on a more formal footing. At the urging of George Sleeman in Guelph, representatives of baseball clubs in Canada were invited to a meeting in Toronto on April 7, 1876, at the Walker House Hotel. Attending the founding meeting of the Canadian Association of Base Ball Players were teams from Toronto, Guelph, London, Hamilton, and the town of Dunnville. Notable for its absence was the St. Lawrence Club of Kingston, which the previous season had been adding professional players in a bid to wrest Canadian bragging rights from Sleeman's Maple Leafs. The name of the new "national" organization mirrored the soon-to-be defunct National Association, placing an emphasis on "players," despite the fact most of the men representing the teams were owners, managers, and businessmen. And all members of the new association were a few miles apart in Southern Ontario, despite the rather pretentious "Canadian" label. A coast-to-coast organization it was not.

The Canadian Association was formed on the eve of the playing season, so time was short. There was no desire to reinvent the wheel and spend months in so doing. The organization adopted a constitution, bylaws, and playing rules based on those of the National Association. The entrance fee was set at $2 for each club and an additional $10 charged to any team wishing to contend

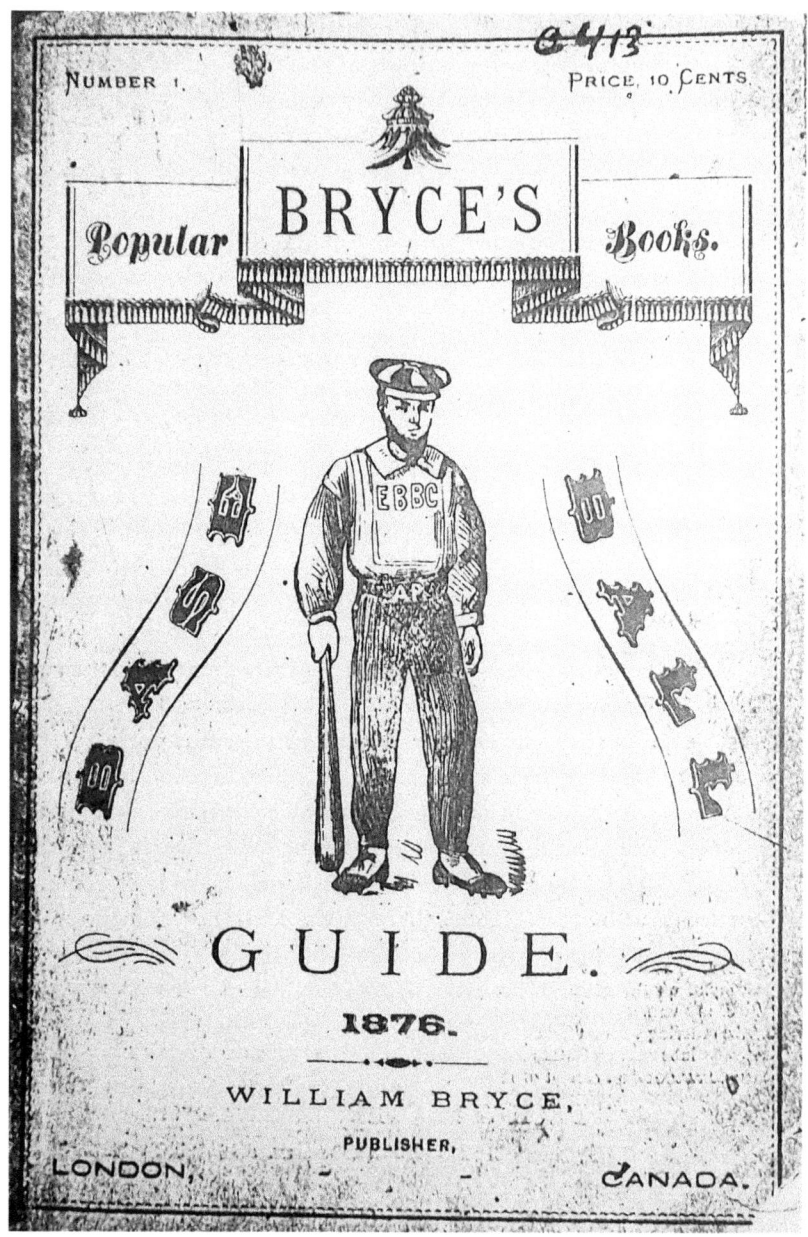

To serve the growing legion of baseball players and fans in Southwestern Ontario, bookseller William Bryce produced baseball guides for the 1876 and 1877 seasons. Like the later *Spalding Guides,* his publication was intended to showcase the selection of baseball equipment he carried in his London store (Western University microfilm collection, London, Ontario).

for the Canadian Association championship. To compete for the association pennant, teams were required to play four games against every other paid-up contender during the course of the season.²² The founding meeting adopted a rule that no Association team could play any other Canadian club that was not also a member. To no one's surprise, George Sleeman of the Guelph Maple Leafs, Canadian baseball's driving force, was elected president. A man named Spalding, from the Tecumseh club of Dunnville, was chosen vice-president. Secretary was Harry Gorman of the London Tecumsehs, while the treasurer was W. F. Mountain of the Toronto Base Ball Association. At the close of its inaugural meeting, the Association executive promised it would soon publish its constitution, bylaws, and playing rules.

Later that same month, William Bryce, a shareholder in the Tecumsehs, a London bookseller, news agent, and retailer of baseball and other sporting goods, published *Bryce's Base Ball Guide*. The 78-page book was authorized by Gorman and Sleeman of the new Canadian Association, as indicated in its introduction. The ambitious *Guide* contained not only the constitution, bylaws, and playing rules but also diagrams of the baseball diamond and explanations of how to play the various positions, and even outlined the duties of the umpire. The *Guide* recounted a brief history of the game in Canada and the play of leading teams and their records from 1875. At the end of the publication, which sold for ten cents, were advertisements for baseball gear available from Bryce's Ontario Games Emporium such as stockings, caps, and belts.²³ In the preface to the new publication, Bryce announced he would award a silver ball to the team in the new Canadian Association that won the greatest number of games during 1876.

Bryce's Guide was not the first such publication for baseball, but it predated by two years the better-known *Spalding's Official Base Ball Guide*. The first baseball guide ever, *Beadle's Dime Base-Ball Player*, appeared in 1860 and was edited by Henry Chadwick. In 1868, *DeWitt's Base-Ball Guide* was first published and by its second year it was also edited by Chadwick.²⁴ Sometime in the early 1880s, Chadwick became editor of *Spalding's Guide,* published by Albert G. Spalding to promote baseball and, just as important, his fledgling sporting goods empire. The latter part of each annual edition was a catalog for the firm's baseball uniforms, equipment, and other gear. *Spalding's Guide* became the official publication of the National League and prevailed as the baseball guide of choice, outlasting its rivals.

The arrival of warmer temperatures in London by April was accompanied by the appearance of newly signed professionals. Early in the month, a new third baseman named Joe Hornung, 18, from Utica, New York, stepped off the train to embark on a professional career that would continue until 1890, during which time he earned a reputation as one of the top defensive outfielders in baseball. His talent had attracted the attention of Latham, another native of Utica, and the player-manager opted to take a chance on the talented youngster. Hornung preferred to play his position without a glove until late in his career, during which he picked up the nickname "Ubbo Ubbo," because of his odd habit of chirping that whenever he made a good hit or nice fielding play.

Within days, yet another Utica man, Mike Dinnen, the new second baseman, arrived. Not much is known about his background, and he failed to move on to the National League, unlike many on the Tecumseh roster. His career later took him to Rochester, Albany, and Utica. During his time in London, the light-hitting Dinnen became a fan favorite for his dazzling fielding. Phil Powers, 21, a catcher from New York, detrained a few days later, and the *Advertiser* predicted, "he will have plenty to do to hold [Hugh] McLean's pitching which is very swift this year."[25] Powers would pick up the nickname "Grandmother," sometimes "Grandma," during a long and successful professional career that included later stints with Chicago, Boston, and Cincinnati.

Another American, Mike (Buck) Ledwith, joined the team at third base. Ledwith and Dinnen had played with the St. Lawrence club of Kingston at the end of the previous season as the Eastern Ontario club made a run for the Canadian championship.[26] Ledwith, likely a native of Brooklyn, appeared in a game with his hometown

Young curveballer Fred Goldsmith was making a name for himself in his hometown of New Haven, Connecticut, when Tecumseh manager Harry Gorman paid him a visit and persuaded him to join the London club for the 1876 season. Goldsmith's father didn't want him to play baseball (John R. Castle, Jr.).

Atlantics late in the 1874 season. But the existence of another Ledwith with the same home town has created some headaches for baseball historians.[27] Regardless, his would be a short professional career.

A player referred to only as "Leary" in the papers appeared in several early-season games. This was likely Jack Leary, 18, of New Haven, found through Latham's connections to that city. A utility player, Leary made little impact with the Tecumsehs, but had a professional career that saw him flit between teams in the National League, the American, and the Union Association. Hugh McLean, a local businessman, was a good pitcher, but Latham believed he could find better. The new manager was trying to land bigger fish to take the pitcher's box—and to occupy other positions. Billy Hunter was also on the roster along with outfielder and fellow Londoner Tom Gillean. Local brothers Tom and Jim Brown appeared in some games as did another local named Chisholm.

Before the opening of the Canadian Association season on May 1, both London and the Maple Leafs contented themselves with games against their amateur clubs, the Atlantics and the Silver Creeks, respectively. One game, on May 4 between the Maple Leafs and a picked team bolstered by two of its professionals, saw George Sleeman pitch the Maple Leafs to a 7–5 victory.[28]

London opened its season by embarrassing the Woodstock Excelsiors, 34–4. Aside from sharp play, the Tecumsehs looked good in their smart new uniforms consisting of red stockings, white knickerbockers, caps, and a large red letter "T" on the bib-like shield attached to the front of their white jerseys. Reports out of Kingston to the east that professional players were arriving in that city indicated that the St. Lawrence club was planning to enter the fray, having fallen short in its championship bid in 1875. As the Tecumsehs prepared for their second game of the season against its amateur Atlantics, it was announced that Fred Goldsmith was joining the professional team. The *Advertiser*, not surprisingly, broke the news on May 17. Its city editor and Tecumseh team manager Harry Gorman had traveled to New Haven and, armed with gold bars as inducement, persuaded Goldsmith to come to London to pitch for the Tecumsehs for $100 a month.[29] The newspaper said that until two weeks earlier, Goldsmith had been playing for New Haven, Connecticut, adding: "He is a splendid specimen of a base ball athlete and will be a great acquisition to the Tecumsehs."[30]

Goldsmith, often known simply as "Goldie," was a gangly 19-year-old native of New Haven. In 1875, he pitched for a team in Bridgeport, Connecticut, before switching to his hometown Elm City team, for which he appeared in a single game, at second base. It was an inauspicious start for a man who would have a successful career as one of the first curve ball pitchers. Among the other players on that 1875 New Haven club that finished tenth in the National Association was Juice Latham. The new Tecumseh manager remembered the six-foot-one Goldsmith and his previously untapped ability to throw his "deceiver."

Goldsmith started the 1876 season with New Haven, which had applied to join the new National League. The bid was rejected, however, perhaps because the city had a population of 51,000, well below the League's mandatory minimum of 75,000 thousand (except for Hartford), or because of its well-known financial struggles the previous year. New Haven failed to overturn the League decision, so it opted to continue the season as an independent nine.[31] About the time New Haven learned its fate for 1876, players including Goldsmith decided to pursue greener pastures. Latham likely played a big role in landing Goldsmith for the Tecumsehs.

On May 17, the Tecumsehs played the Atlantics, and despite threatening skies, a good crowd showed up, curious to the see the newly acquired pitcher and hoping Goldsmith might demonstrate the curve pitch novelty he was said to have mastered.

> Interest was centered on the new pitcher of the Tecumsehs, Mr. Goldsmith, and it is satisfactory to know that he at once won the good opinion and confidence of the spectators. Owing to fatigue through traveling he did not pitch through the entire game.... The new man showed himself to be a very skillful pitcher, a splendid batter, and a fine general player, possessing coolness and nerve and good judgment in critical positions.[32]

The Tecumsehs played a "perfect" game according to the news account of the 16–0 mismatch in their favor. Meanwhile, miles away, Guelph and Kingston continued to add American professionals as they learned London had landed a young curve-baller.

The Tecumseh Base Ball Association held its general business meeting on May 19, chaired by Harry Gorman. Directors were provided a financial statement indicating the club was operating on a sound footing, and members were told about the founding of the Canadian Association and the role club directors had played in bringing it about. Gorman reported negotiations were under way to bring the Boston and Chicago National League clubs to London in June and July. Then an election of officers took place. Longstanding president John Brown, the city treasurer, stepped aside to assume the title of honorary president. Refiner and ball fan Jake Englehart was elected president. Despite his busy days in the oil business, Englehart agreed to emerge from a background role to assume leadership of the ball organization at a crucial time in its history. Harry Gorman was named a managing director along with Ed Moore of the Tecumseh House. The latter also assumed the role of treasurer.[33] The Tecumsehs now had a man at the helm of the association just as determined to bring glory to his city as was brewer George Sleeman over in Guelph.

It was hoped the move to a more professional model along the lines of that already adopted by the Maple Leafs would produce a change of fortunes and see London emerge as a top-flight baseball team, if not the best.

The first test was mere days away.

5
A New Era

Holidays in nineteenth-century Ontario were traditionally a time for civic celebrations, often including baseball games. One of them, Militia Day, marked in 1838 in the tiny community of Beachville east of London, saw the playing of what is considered to be the first recorded game of baseball anywhere.[1]

The May 24 holiday to mark the birthday of Queen Victoria was no exception and invariably saw the first meeting of the year between the London and Guelph baseball clubs. For 1876, however, the approach of the Victoria Day game was marked by concern about a repeat of the violence and rowdyism that had marred the last meeting of the teams the previous August.

The day before the game, Gorman's *Advertiser* reported that Police Chief Richard Wigmore "with a strong staff of police, will preserve order among the large crowd of spectators expected on the grounds during the progress of the match.... We hope to see the game played in an amicable spirit, and that it may be one of its merits."[2] The same item noted that while the Tecumseh roster was not fully set, Guelph's was. The Maple Leafs had the returning battery of speedball hurler Billy Smith and reliable catcher Charlie Maddock. Also back was first baseman William Lapham, who had been injured by London fans during the rowdyism in August. George Keerl, who played six games for Chicago in 1875, was at shortstop, while Harry Myers of Ilion, New York, would play third. Mike Brannock, an outfielder, was brought in from Chicago where he had seen spot duty for the NA club there in 1871 and 1875.

The rail trip from Guelph to London on May 24 took its usual four hours, and upon reaching the train station at 2 p.m. the Maple Leafs were met by a large, friendly crowd at the Tecumseh House Hotel. The team and their supporters made their way north several blocks to the Exhibition Grounds, where the Tecumsehs were warming up. Reporters from as far afield as Montreal were said to be on hand for the match. The *Guelph Mercury* reporter estimated the crowd at almost 9,000, while the *Advertiser* suggested it was closer to 6,000. Regardless, it was the typically large turnout for London-Guelph games. Apprehension was replaced with relief when the visitors entered the park to "cheers and welcomes from thousands of tongues."[3] In the tradition of the day, a flip of a coin determined home team, and Guelph won the toss. After a scoreless first inning, London scored four runs in the top of the second as Guelph struggled and made several crucial errors. The *Mercury* recorded that as the Maple Leafs continued to record "goose eggs," on the score sheet, betting on the home team increased, with "enough bank notes to feed the poor of the city chang[ing] hands." Guelph finally got on the board in the fourth inning with two runs and added two more in the fifth when the Tecumsehs plated three to make the score 7–4. London was unable to add any more tallies, while Guelph picked up three. After nine innings, the score was tied 7–7. "The excitement was intense, and the crowd watched with breathless anxiety every movement of the players."[4]

In the top of the tenth, the Tecumsehs' Hornung knocked a ball to right center field for a single, then took advantage of passed balls to advance to second and to third base. He was stranded there as Gillean was thrown out at first and Brown struck out. Powers came to the plate and connected with a solid hit to centerfield that sailed beyond the outstretched arms of Lapham. Hornung scampered home to a deafening roar from the crowd. The bottom of the inning saw Guelph blanked, and the Tecumseh celebration erupted. This marked the first time the vaunted Guelph Maple Leafs had lost to London, and the city rejoiced. Tecumseh players were hoisted upon broad shoulders in the crowd. The *Advertiser* exulted: "Thus ended one of the best contested and most exciting games of base ball ever played in Canada."[5] It took pains to praise fans for their orderly behavior. The *Mercury* agreed it had been an exciting contest but complained it had been an "unnecessarily long game," forcing Guelph supporters to race to the station to catch the train home. That evening, the Tecumsehs and Maple Leafs enjoyed a meal and fellowship at the Tecumseh House. The ill-will from the previous summer had clearly dissipated, and the London management was determined to relegate it to history. The Tecumsehs had accomplished a long-cherished goal and were as magnanimous in victory as Guelph proved gracious in defeat. Gorman and Englehart, no doubt, enjoyed the evening more than anyone.

Gorman's newspaper tried to restrain itself from too much hyperbole and contented itself with reprinting snippets about the contest from the *Hamilton Spectator* and *Hamilton Times*. It quoted the *Spectator*, saying Guelph would be disappointed at the defeat of "the boys ... and the consequent loss of that empty supremacy which it has cost Guelph so much money to conquer and to maintain." The *Times*, meanwhile, focused on the play of pitcher Goldsmith and his catcher Powers. "Goldsmith's pitching was very effective in the first few innings, the 'nasty curve' bothering the Guelph team very much."[6]

After the loss to London and a night of rest, the Maple Leafs traveled west to Michigan, where they lost to both the Detroit Aetnas and the Jackson Mutuals. On their return home, the Guelph nine stopped in London to change trains and were met by Tecumseh players and fans who expressed sympathy for their string of defeats. It was learned by the Londoners that Myers had decided to leave Sleeman's team and return home to Ilion.[7]

In early June, the Tecumsehs went to Hamilton to play the Standards, but a crowd of 1,000 was disappointed when it was rained out. A second game was quickly scheduled, and on June 10, before a similar-sized gathering, the Tecumsehs prevailed, 27–1. Three days later in Detroit, the Tecumsehs defeated the Aetnas, 25–4. In that game, Goldsmith was hurt at the plate when a wild pitch struck his pitching arm, but he was able to continue.

As excitement grew for the upcoming Tecumsehs game against the touring Chicago White Stockings, boarders at the Tecumseh House Hotel played an exhibition game, pitting one table against another with proceeds from the 25-cent admission charge donated to a home for orphans. Among those taking the field for the "Carty" nine was a shortstop named Englehart.[8]

More than 4,000 spectators, half of them women, were at the ball field for the much-anticipated Chicago game on June 19. The White Stockings were leading the National League at the time, on their way to capturing the pennant in the League's inaugural season. Chicago never lost more than two games in a row that year, riding the strong arm of Albert Goodwill Spalding and the .429 batting average of second baseman Ross Barnes. The Tecumsehs knew in advance they would have their hands full with the Windy City powerhouse. How well they fared against one of the top teams on the continent would be a useful measuring stick to see how far London had come and still needed to go. The London fans quickly saw any hopes for a close game dashed in the first inning. The home team committed many uncharacteristic errors, and Goldsmith threw six wild pitches, his sub-par performance attributed to lingering soreness in his arm from the injury in the Detroit game. The impressive visitors put six runs across the plate in the first inning, and after three innings, the score stood at 10–0. Chicago displayed flawless fielding, and Spalding threw only one wild pitch. As the game went on, the Tecumsehs shed some early nervousness and rallied with three runs in both the sixth and eighth innings. But the Chicago lead was insurmountable and they won, 16–

5. A New Era   75

The barnstorming Chicago White Stockings team played in London in the summer of 1876, the last season the Tecumsehs used the exhibition grounds. This illustration from the July 15 edition of the *Canadian Illustrated News* depicts the game that Chicago won by a score of 16–6.

6. The game attracted wide press interest, including the attention of the *Canadian Illustrated News*, which carried an artist's rendering of the game in its July 15 issue. The previous month, the same publication carried a similar illustration of the Hamilton Standards playing on its Crystal Palace grounds.

In late June, the Tecumsehs took to the road again for a tour of Michigan, Indiana, and Ohio. The London nine downed the Aetnas of Detroit, 12–3, the Mutuals of Jackson, 14–5, and blanked Wabash, Indiana, 8–0, before moving on to Indianapolis to play the Indiana state champions. Back home, a large crowd gathered outside the *London Advertiser* office to see telegraphed reports from the tightly contested Indianapolis game and let out "ringing cheers" when the Tecumsehs held onto an early lead to win, 3–2. The paper noted that the four games in the American tour saw London score thirty-seven runs and surrender only ten. The team's success had exceeded expectations "and places the Tecumsehs in the front rankings as expert ball players."[9] Goldsmith made significant contributions with his bat in the June 22 game against the Mutuals, said the *Jackson Citizen*. Goldie broke a bat as he made a base hit, an event common in baseball in the twenty-first century, but rare enough to warrant reporting it in 1876. It was Goldsmith's pitching, however, that bewildered the Mutuals. He recorded ten strikeouts, with "Goldsmith's ball proving very deceiving and hard to hit."[10] A game scheduled with Columbus failed to come off, attributed to a misunderstanding between the respective team managers about dates. The Tecumsehs instead played Mansfield before leaving Ohio, blanking them, 8–0. The London team returned to Ontario by steamer from Cleveland across Lake Erie to Port Stanley and, after a short rail hop home, was met by a large crowd and the band of the Seventh Battalion, which played "Conquering Heroes."

After a few days' rest, it was time for the Tecumsehs to meet the Michigan champion Jackson Mutuals again, in London. The July 1 Dominion Day holiday contest proved to be a soggy affair. A rainstorm kept attendance to about 1,000 and the game might have been rescheduled, but the visitors were keen to play on, and the decision to proceed came during a lull in the downpour. After four innings, the Mutuals found themselves trailing, 8–0, and they had failed to reach first base. The visitors suggested calling it a game then, but the Tecumseh managers disagreed, fearing a repeat of the Guelph game the previous year when the visitors left before completing their game, agitating the local fans so much. Despite the heavy rain, the Mutuals agreed to continue, and at the end of nine innings, the score was 12–0. The Mutuals remained in London to play a second game on Monday, only to lose again, this time 11–0. Latham was replaced for the game by Bob Emslie, a talented local player who had played with the Tecumsehs on occasion, but more often with the Atlantics. An amateur, he filled in ably, recording two solid hits.[11]

The Detroit Aetnas were having financial troubles when London played them on its tour in late June, and London failed to receive its share of gate proceeds. Not long afterward, the Aetnas reverted to amateur status, and the Cass Club emerged as the pre-eminent professional team in Detroit. Cass traveled to London for a game on July 8, only to suffer the same fate as Jackson, failing to score any runs against the powerful home team. In intense heat and before a large crowd, the Tecumsehs recorded only one error as they romped over the Detroiters, 13–0.[12]

Yet more games with American teams were on tap as the Tecumsehs headed east for a tournament in Syracuse. With no game scheduled on the first day of the tournament, London visited nearby Utica and defeated their club, 24–1. The high-flying Tecumsehs soon fell to earth with a resounding thud. They lost the first two games in the Syracuse tournament, plagued by poor fielding. The first loss was to the hometown nine and the second was a humiliating 15–1 drubbing by Ithaca. London bounced back to take the Binghamton Crickets, 12–2. Back on track, the Tecumsehs downed Ithaca, 13–1, Ilion, 6–2, and Ilion again, 11–3, to take second place behind Syracuse and collect $400 in prize money.[13]

On their way home, they played the second game of the season against

Guelph, the only team in Canada that could compete at the same level as the Tecumsehs. Special trains and fares from the London area took 600–800 fans to Guelph for the much-anticipated return engagement. No less than 6,000 fans witnessed the game in Guelph, most anxious to see if the Maple Leafs could regain their usual form against London. Betting was heavy on the home team. The *Advertiser* was ready with excuses in the event of a loss, noting in its account that the London team appeared weary from the Syracuse tournament, from which it had traveled directly. The paper also said umpire W. F. Mountain, of Toronto, did Goldsmith no favors with his work, "it being the general remark that he did not understand curve balls."[14]

Guelph got off to a strong start in the game, while the Tecumseh bats remained silent. After three innings, Guelph was ahead 3–0, and the local supporters were loud and happy. Goldsmith doubled in the fourth inning to bring home Powers, while Hunter hit a hard shot to left field that scored Goldsmith. London blanked Guelph, and after four, Guelph led, 3–2. London batters went to work and capitalized on Guelph errors to lead 7–4 after five innings and silence the crowd. The sixth inning was scoreless; in the seventh, Goldsmith knocked one over the outfield fence, "toppling an able-bodied man over." But he was awarded a double, by agreement of both teams under ground rules established due to the shallowness of the field. Guelph picked up a single run that same inning. London scored two more runs while holding Guelph scoreless in the eighth. In the ninth, Goldsmith had another big hit to left and ran home on a wild throw. In the bottom of the inning, Lapham and Tuells took advantage of Tecumseh errors and wild throws to cross the plate. At the end of play, Tecumsehs had again defeated their great rivals, this time by a score of 10–7. In London, interest in the outcome was so strong that 200–300 Tecumseh supporters waited outside the office of the *Advertiser* and cheered at the results telegraphed from Guelph. Word spread quickly and Londoners made their way to the Grand Trunk railway station to welcome home their heroes.

> An immense crowd was at the depot, and the players were greeted with hearty cheers, as they were also at stations along the line. This is the first time, so far as we know, that Guelph has been beaten by a Canadian club on their own ground, and it is good deal to the credit of Londoners that they have stuck to it till this result was accomplished, no other club making such a determined effort.

It didn't take long for the *Guelph Mercury* to come up with some excuses for the turning of the baseball tables. One of them was completely unexpected from the city that first hired a Foreign Legion.

> The Tecumsehs, who are a fine, athletic and gentlemanly lot of fellows, were in excellent practice, consequent on their recent participation in the Syracuse tour-

nament and on the superior advantages they have for consistent practice, their whole time being occupied in the game, while the Guelph team can only practice after its members have finished their day's work.[15]

This assertion, picked up and printed by the *London Advertiser*, prompted it to retort: "Isn't it about time the Guelph papers quit their efforts to hoodwink outsiders in regard to the standing of their imported players?"

On July 22, the Tecumsehs journeyed to Toronto, where they spanked the local team, 11–3, showing yet again that London and Guelph were basically in a league of their own. Everyone else, even the team in the largest city in Ontario, was playing baseball at a less competitive level.

In early August, London paid another visit to Detroit, where they lost, 6–3, to a revived Aetna club, after sorting out the money owed from the last trip. In Ontario, the papers said Kingston had decided to abandon the professional model for its St. Lawrence club and in future would be composed of mostly local players.[16] The Kingston nine had been the only other Canadian club to make a serious effort to hire professionals in a bid to challenge London and Guelph.

Thousands of area ball fans descended on the Exhibition Grounds in London for the Civic Holiday in early August. In anticipation of a large crowd, the home team installed several temporary stands. It proved a wise decision, because the crowd that showed up was estimated at from 9,000–10,000. They were anxious to see if London could achieve its third victory from the longtime Canadian champions. Among them was a *Guelph Mercury* reporter, who wrote: "Arriving on the principle streets we hear little else talked of but 'baseball,' 'pools,' and 'bets,' and bets on everything that can possibly be thought of until we wish the game was over and we were home again."[17]

Shortly before 2:30, when the game was about to begin, a section of temporary seats erected alongside the Horticultural Hall collapsed. In short order, two more sections came down, along with the reporters' stand. "The great wonder was that no one was killed," the *Advertiser* remarked.[18] As it turned out, several spectators sustained scrapes and bruises, and several men and women suffered broken bones and other injuries, but nothing of a serious nature. The *Mercury* reporter estimated 400–500 spectators fell a distance of five to ten feet in the collapse, many of them scrambling to the adjacent seating only to see it also fall, producing "less serious results."[19] The *Advertiser* complained that "the flimsy construction of the seats is to be severely condemned." After rescue efforts, the injured were quickly tended to, and team officials delayed the start of the game, rather than cancel it and risk offending the large number of patrons on hand. Chosen to umpire the game was Ed Moore, the hotelier and Tecumsehs director, with the ready acceptance of the Maple Leafs, who were familiar with his work from earlier occasions.

The Tecumsehs were in fine form and many of their players performed flawlessly. "Goldsmith and Powers worked into each other's hands like clockwork," the *Advertiser* noted, while Latham's bat and the fielding of Dinnen, Ledwith, and Gillean drew praise. Of concern was Hornung, who collapsed at third base after driving a ball into the outfield crowd. "Before the game was over, he seemed to revive, but a second attack came on, and during the night it was feared he would die." Hornung revived and the following day was sent to his parents' home in Carthage, New York, to recuperate. Later in the game, a dispute arose about whether Guelph runner Tommy Smith had touched second base on his way to third. Dinnen believed Smith missed it and threw the ball to Ledwith, who tagged Smith. The runner was declared out by umpire Moore. The Guelph players immediately directed some unpleasantries at Dinnen "which it required a good deal of self-control not to forcibly resent." Smith insisted Moore had it wrong; he had failed to touch first base, not second. The gambit failed, it was noted, "so in any case he was out." The Tecumsehs, overall, were too much for Guelph, who were held scoreless as London won, 5–0, in what was then known as a "whitewash," sending the crowd home happy. This marked the third victory in a row over the reigning Canadian champions, a feat thought impossible not long before.

Juice Latham, the man partially responsible for the newfound strength of the Tecumsehs and likely the reason London hired Fred Goldsmith, quietly left the Tecumsehs without fanfare. The last time he appeared on a roster carried in the papers was August 9, when he played first base in the Guelph game. He recorded 14 put-outs and one error but was hitless in four appearances at the plate. Latham soon turned up playing first base for the National League team in Louisville. He played professional ball for three more seasons before hanging up his cleats. The circumstances of his departure from London are lost to history, but Latham had been a key figure in the difficult transition from amateur to professional status for the Tecumsehs.

Within days of London's third victory over Guelph, it was reported that George Sleeman had filed a protest about the umpiring of Ed Moore. The London papers laughed it off and said the game was decided by the superior play of the Tecumsehs, not by any of Moore's decisions. In the meantime, Guelph played a championship match in Toronto, beating them, 10–0. Soon after, London also visited Toronto and ran up the score on the hapless Torontos, 17–0. London's trip to Hamilton for another game to count toward the championship saw them find a much tougher opponent. They edged the pesky

Standards, 5–4. The Tecumsehs started Leary as pitcher, but when they saw the battle put up by the home squad, Goldsmith was brought in to finish the game and ensure victory. The Tecumsehs then made the long rail trip to Kingston at the other end of Lake Ontario, where they easily handled the St. Lawrence club, 12–1. On August 23, in a second game there, the London nine embarrassed the St. Lawrence team, 40–0. In Kingston, the Tecumsehs

> **NEW ADVERTISEMENTS.**
>
> **Amusements.**
>
> **BASE BALL.**
>
> TWO GREAT GAMES NEXT WEEK.
>
> **St. Louis Browns vs. Tecumsehs,**
> MONDAY, AUGUST 28th.
>
> **CHICAGOS vs. TECUMSEHS**
> WEDNESDAY, AUGUST 30th.
>
> These will undoubtedly be the most interesting base ball events of the season, the above-mentioned clubs being the best in the American professional arena, and containing the finest ball players on the continent. This will be the only opportunity given for seeing the American professionals in Canada this season.
>
> Game begins each day at 3 p.m. Admission to grounds, 25c.; boys, 10c.; extra charge for seats.
>
> J. L. ENGLEHART,   J. T. LAWRIE,
> m,th,f,s biw   President,   Sec. Tec. B.B.C.

American teams barnstormed into Ontario because they knew large crowds could be expected. Guelph and London were located between Buffalo and Detroit so they could be easily accommodated. This advertisement from the *London Advertiser* promotes upcoming games with St. Louis and Chicago.

attended an Irish picnic, where Goldsmith picked up a prize of $4 for throwing a baseball the longest distance, while a new player, Favel Wordsworth, won a prize for his rendition of an Irish ballad. On their way home, the team stopped in Bowmanville, where they easily handled the local team and took part in a promenade concert and ice cream festival.

London's record now stood at 9–0 in games played for the Canadian championship. Guelph's record was four wins and three losses, the latter all suffered against London. The remainder of the pack in the Canadian championship—Toronto, Hamilton, and Kingston—each had solitary wins. Returning from the long trek to Kingston, the Tecumsehs played Toronto yet again, defeating them 19–3 this time.

Back home, excitement was building for an August 28 game against the barnstorming St. Louis Browns, at the time second to Chicago in the National League standings. Tecumseh supporters were hopeful, but not optimistic, that the local team could beat the high-flying St. Louis team, especially in light of the defeat at the hands of Chicago. But the St. Louis game proved far more exciting than anyone could have been expected. Goldsmith was up against Joe Blong in the pitcher's box. Blong, a native of St. Louis, had signed with the club as an outfielder and played 62 games in that position before the season ended. The Browns' ace, George Bradley, had won 45 of his 64 starts that season but did not appear in the London game. It is unclear if he was injured or just needed a rest, coming off a 23–3 pasting at the hands of the White Stockings in Chicago on August 26. Bradley would not pitch again for St. Louis until early September. Until then, with Blong replacing him, the Browns lost 9–8 to Guelph 9 on August 29 and 7–0 to Syracuse on August 31.

For his part, Blong had pitched only four innings for the Browns in League games, without a decision, during the entire season and his appearance in London came as a surprise. A light hitter, he demonstrated a good eye at the plate, however, scoring three runs against the home team despite going hitless. He struck out one Tecumseh batter while Goldsmith fanned seven. The battery of Goldsmith and Powers was also impressive with their bats, each recording three of the 17 hits made by the Tecumsehs. Umpiring the game was St. Louis manager Mase Graffen whose work was generally commended, although the *Advertiser* grumbled he tended to favor the visitors on close calls.

The fielding of Hornung, Dinnen, Wordsworth and Ledwith drew praise from the local newspapers, while errors in the field by the visitors contributed to the result. St. Louis scored a single run in the first inning and held London scoreless. Neither club crossed the plate in the second inning. In the third,

London scored once while holding St. Louis off the scoreboard to tie it 1–1. In the next inning, the bats of the Brown Stockings erupted for four runs while the Tecumsehs replied with one. During the next three innings, St. Louis scored once more while holding London in check.

Suddenly, the home team woke up and found their bats. London scored seven runs in the next three innings, easily solving Blong, and showing some of their most powerful batting of the season as they kept St. Louis from crossing the plate again. After eight innings, London led 9–6, much to the delight of spectators who had been warned in advance they faced a tough foe and likely defeat.

The Brown Stockings roared back to plate three runs in the ninth to tie the game, while holding London scoreless. The crowd of about 4,000 held its collective breath as the closely matched teams headed into extra innings. In the top of the tenth, Goldsmith didn't allow a St. Louis runner to reach first base. In the bottom of the inning, Powers singled with his third hit of the day and with two out was driven home for the winning run. Spectators cheered lustily at the 10–9 victory for the home nine against a formidable opponent which was battling with Hartford for second place in the National League standings.

> To find the Tecumsehs beat such a strong club as the Browns was an unexpected surprise and the delight could not be restrained. As soon as the last man was put out, the crowd rushed in and carried some of the men off the ground on their shoulders.... This places the Tecumsehs ahead of many of the clubs outside of the League, and is a big feather in their cap.[20]

The following day in Guelph, the St. Louis club fell 9–8 to the Maple Leafs in nine innings. The loss prompted the *Advertiser* to snort, "The St. Louis Browns will leave Canada perfectly cured of any impression they may have had that they could easily dispose of their Canadian opponents."[21]

On August 30, the Chicago White Stockings again visited London. Memories of the 16–6 loss in June were still strong, and even the most optimistic of Tecumseh supporters were careful in their predictions and bets. About 3,000 fans showed up for the game that was umpired by William Lapham, the Guelph player. Some new faces appeared in the Tecumseh lineup, to which Hornung had returned, but from which Latham was gone. Playing shortstop was Favel Wordsworth, who had played for the Resolutes of Elizabeth, New Jersey, in 1873 when it made a brief appearance in the National Association. A chap named Whalen occupied left field and scored London's only run, as Spalding and the Chicagos were again too much for the Tecumsehs. Spalding struck out 11 men to the three recorded by Goldsmith. The batting of the visitors was impressive, but after the first two innings, both teams were held scoreless. Spalding outmatched London batters until the ninth inning, when the home team scored Whalen's run. In the meantime, Chicago plated two runs in the third, two in the fourth, three in the fifth, and single runs in the sixth, seventh, and ninth innings for a final tally of 10–1. The *Advertiser* praised the play of Chicago, noting, "they played as well as they could," but it complained that Tecumsehs' Wordsworth and Ledwith had played poorly.[22] Hulbert's acquisitions from Boston and Philadelphia, infielders Barnes, McVey, and Anson, had little trouble with Goldsmith, hitting him well. The two losses to Chicago were among the few setbacks suffered by the Tecumsehs in the 1876 season that had exceeded expectations by a wide margin.

The next day, it was learned that Sleeman's protest of the last game with London was filed because he said umpire Ed Moore had bet a box of cigars on the result with a gentleman from Montreal, thereby rendering his decisions suspect. The London papers ridiculed the complaint, but the judicial committee of the Canadian association upheld it and ordered the game to be replayed. Gorman's *Advertiser* was clearly angry at Sleeman for the protest and warned that his Guelph team would likely not be invited back to London as long as Sleeman was involved with them—except when necessary for Canadian championship games. "The Tecumsehs can have no friendly dealings with dishonorable opponents," it said.[23] The good feelings demonstrated on Victoria Day had evaporated.

Of Sleeman's protest, the hometown *Guelph Mercury* said: "This step should be taken. No club on the continent could have defeated the Tecumseh with the unjust decisions of such an umpire as this man Moore."[24] Just as the London *Advertiser* had become the mouthpiece for Tecumsehs management, Sleeman had a friend in the *Mercury*.

The antagonism of the *Advertiser* continued unabated for days. Upon learning that Sleeman claimed he never approved of Ed Moore as umpire for the Civic Holiday game, the paper noted that Sleeman wasn't even in London that day. "Further discussion with an individual so regardless of the truth as Mr. Sleeman would be a waste of time and words."[25] The following day, the paper reported that the Tecumsehs' amateur club, the Atlantics, had traveled to Guelph and defeated the Silver Creeks, the Maple Leaf amateur nine, by a score of 13–12 to take the Canadian junior championship for 1876. It expressed no small amount of joy in the Atlantics retaining its amateur title. "This is the last straw that breaks the Guelph camel's back. To see its pet clubs beaten on their native heath twice in one season by London is enough to drive the base ball maniacs of that town into a frenzy of despair."[26]

Meanwhile, to further strengthen his team for the final game of the season against London, Sleeman found a pitcher named James Sullivan—likely the same Sullivan who played for the Elm Citys of New Haven in 1875. Also new was a catcher named Brown, in an apparent bid to upgrade the Maple Leafs battery of Smith and Maddock, or, as the *Advertiser* put it: "to displace two of the beaten team—a confession of weakness." On September 6, the Tecumsehs played host to the Cass club of Detroit, which they again defeated, this time 5–1. A feature of the game was a bases-loaded home run by Goldsmith. The following day, London won in a rematch, 10–3. The *Advertiser* noted that Guelph had added two more players to its roster but still lost 11–6 to the Cass club, which had stopped by to play the Maple Leafs after its losses in London.

The rematch of the London–Guelph game, on which umpire Moore had bet a box of cigars, was set for September 12 in London. The day beforehand,

After years of trying to dethrone the Canadian champion Guelph Maple Leafs, the London Tecumsehs finally accomplished that goal in 1876. The London club took a page from Guelph's playbook and began hiring American players in an arms race for baseball glory. Curveball pitcher Fred Goldsmith is second from left, front row; catcher Phil Powers is second from right, first row, and shortstop and outfielder Joe Hornung is back left (*Canadian Illustrated News*, July 15, 1879).

the *Advertiser* said Guelph would have to work hard to prevent "a complete wiping out by their old-time rivals" on the season. Guelph, it said, had been adding players all season "in the hope of recovering their lost prestige." A hard-fought game was expected. Then, after having spent weeks trashing Sleeman and his club, the newspaper urged Londoners to behave at the game. "Though the feelings of indignation against the slippery president of the Maple Leafs runs high here, and is very generally diffused, it is to be hoped that no outward demonstration of hostility will be indulged in."[27]

The final London–Guelph clash of the season brought excursion trains packed with fans to London on September 12. A crowd of 4,000–5,000 was on hand to witness the contest. Sleeman was absent, so his players Nichols and Keerl tended to business arrangements. Those details included selecting an umpire, a step which proved difficult for two teams who no longer trusted each other. Guelph wanted a man named McCarthy, whom, it was said, was from Erie, Pennsylvania. But London objected, saying it was known he'd been in Guelph for about a week and suspected he was tied in with the Maple Leafs. The Tecumsehs suggested a Mr. Scully from Windsor or a Mr. Seesing of Detroit. Both were presented as impartial arbiters. Eventually, Seesing was agreed upon. Guelph's four new players since its last trip to London were duly noted, the battery of Sullivan and Brown, and outfielders Walsh and Ely. Spence, who once had so many unflattering things to say about the Tecumsehs, was back, playing third base. Plenty of errors were committed by both teams— London with ten and Guelph with eight—but the home team had superior bats. A feature of the game was a triple play. Guelph had two runners on base with none out when catcher Powers dropped a called third strike. He fired the ball to Ledwith at third, who relayed it to Dinnen at second, who threw to Hornung at first. The side was retired. "It was accomplished so quickly that many on the field did not understand it and some Guelph men objected on the ground that Powers should have caught the ball," the *Advertiser* said. The umpire knew his business, the paper asserted, so the play stood. "Guelph played about as usual, which merely means that they don't usually play well enough to win a game from London."[28] The Tecumsehs scored single runs in each of the first two innings before Guelph notched two in the third. London added a run in the fourth, three in the fifth, and two in the sixth, while Guelph scored three times. The final tally was 8–5 for London, ensuring the Canadian championship would be theirs. The sweep of four games was complete, and the Tecumsehs were triumphant. To sweeten the news was an account reprinted from the *New York Herald* saying that Goldsmith and Powers had agreed to terms with London team management to return for the 1877 campaign.[29]

Jubilation had barely died down in London when it was learned that a visit planned by Indianapolis for games on September 15–16 was canceled. The team manager wired from Erie, Pennsylvania, saying his players were hurt and they were heading home. Meanwhile, from Guelph, George Sleeman wired Harry Gorman seeking a date for yet another game in their championship series with London. If Sleeman was unaware of the depth of feeling against him, Gorman replied in a letter that would leave no doubt in the brewer's mind.

> I received today a telegram over your signature asking for date of our next game in Guelph. Having complied with the championship rules by playing the maximum number of four games with your club, the Tecumsehs have no present intention of departing from their previously expressed determination to having nothing more to do with the Maple Leafs while under your management. The date of our next game in Guelph is therefore a problem that I am not in a position to solve at present.
> Very truly yours,
> H. Gorman[30]

Needless to say, another game between London and Guelph did not occur. The Tecumsehs announced they would try to arrange another game or two with other teams before being forced to vacate the Exhibition Grounds the following week for the annual Western Fair. A game was arranged for September 22 with the Detroit Aetnas, which was expected to be the last home game of the season. The Tecumsehs wanted to extend their successful campaign but were unable to schedule more games without a home field, the *Advertiser* noted.

> The want of grounds is a serious loss to the Tecumsehs at present, as offers from the Mutuals, Hartfords, Syracuse Stars, Auburns and other first-class have been rejected owing to the lack of accommodation. It is to be hoped that for next year the Tecumsehs will have a field that they can occupy as long as the weather will permit.[31]

The paper also reported that George Wright of the Boston Red Stockings had made an offer to Powers to catch for his team for the balance of the season. "This is complimentary to Phil," it observed. The London game planned for September 22 against the Aetnas of Detroit was widely promoted, but it failed to come off when, fearing rain, the Detroiters opted against taking the train to London, "causing considerable loss to the Tecumsehs." Four days later, in Detroit, the Tecumsehs were unable to play the Aetnas, again because of rain.

On September 30, the baseball season in Canada came to an end. Shortly before that, Guelph had scrambled to play four games in Kingston in two days to save face and boost its season record to ten championship game wins to the 11 for London (reduced to ten with the cancellation of the protested Guelph game). London had defeated Guelph in all four head-to-head contests, so there

5. *A New Era* 87

was no doubt London could claim the Canadian championship, the *Advertiser* reasoned. Beyond that, it crowed, the Tecumsehs had shown themselves to be one of the best baseball organizations on the continent.

> Their success on the ball field has been almost unprecedented. Out of nearly forty games played in Canada they only met with two defeats—both at the hands of the Chicagos, who are without doubt the strongest base ball combination in

The Silver Ball Trophy was emblematic of baseball supremacy in Canada. The Guelph Maple Leafs won the Canadian championship in 1869 from Woodstock and held it until the London Tecumsehs won it in 1876 after years of trying (Sleeman Collection, Archival and Special Collections, University of Guelph Library, XR1 MS A801).

the world. Twelve games were played in the States, of which the Tecumsehs won nine and lost three—one each to the Syracuse Stars, Ithacas and Detroit Aetnas, the latter two sustaining defeats from the Tecumsehs that more than counterbalanced their victories.[32]

The Tecumseh season record also attracted the attention of the *New York Clipper* and Henry Chadwick. The journal noted that London and Guelph were much stronger than any other teams contesting the championship of Canada. "The Tecumsehs were completely successful in establishing their superiority, they winning every game, while the Maple Leafs, though too much for any of the other competitors, lost the entire series of four games to their London rivals—one of which, however, was cancelled for breach of playing rules."[33]

Subtracting the game that had to be replayed at that point, the *Clipper* noted that London's record against Guelph was a commanding three wins to none.

The same edition of the *Clipper* reported that Chicago had won the first pennant race of the National League, and it credited the success of Spalding and his club to following its advice to emulate the model of the Boston Red Stockings. It noted, however, that the League was not without its teething problems in its first year of operation. The cash-strapped Mutuals and Athletics had failed to complete the season. Chadwick also complained that players with backgrounds of crooked play had been allowed on League teams. That was despite its stringent rules against gambling, which meant more players than ever before were connected to gambling.

As the leaves turned color and the winds began to blow cold, Tecumseh directors and players alike could reflect on a successful season. The club had made a name for itself by defeating some of the top teams in baseball and could easily claim the Canadian championship, ousting Guelph from a perch London felt the Maple Leafs had occupied for too long. The team gave the city some substantial bragging rights in an era of rampant civic boosterism. The Tecumsehs and the city felt they had taken their small city carved out of a forest into the major leagues and the public consciousness.

Before the American players packed their bags for home, a benefit game between the Tecumsehs stockholders, directors, and players was arranged. On a chilly early October afternoon, with rules modified to help the club investors and officials, a large crowd took in the event. It was their last opportunity to see their heroes in action until spring. Among those playing for the stockholders were president Jake Englehart and directors Harry Gorman and Ed Moore. The *Advertiser* noted, "some very good play," with the professionals winning by a surprisingly close score of 26–24. Donald Harold, the umpire, drew complaints amid suggestions he had placed a wager on the outcome.

"Mr. Harold admitted that he had a box of matches bet on the game, and a protest was accordingly entered. The match will not, therefore, count in the championship series,"³⁴ the paper noted, tongue planted firmly in cheek. Guelph was still on the minds of the Tecumsehs and the newspaper couldn't resist a parting shot at the enemy. Meanwhile, two days later, it was reported, "Mr. Spalding, manager of the Chicago White Stockings, in a letter to the secretary of the Tecumseh B.B.C., sends the congratulations of the champions of the United States to the champions of Canada."³⁵

Henry Chadwick took note of the baseball landscape in America's neighbor in the *Clipper*, saying it "has made rapid progress in Canada this season.... The baseball rivalry in the Dominion this season has been greater than ever before, and it has resulted in the importation of American professionals to assist in settling the local championship." He went on:

> This, of course, is not quite desirable; but as it may be regarded as the stepping-stone to the growth of local skill. Up to 1870 [sic] the Maple Leaf Club of Guelph stood unrivaled as the leading club of Canada; but this season the Tecumseh [sic], London, under the auspices of an enterprising and spirited management, has obliged the hitherto conquering Maple Leafs to take up a secondary position.³⁶

The article went on to hope the Canadian clubs would be "encouraging the growth of a school of native players," so at some time in the future, "picked nines" of Canadians and Americans could play "in a series of international contests." The *Clipper* recounted the winning record of the Tecumsehs, which it found "to be as credible a one as any other that will be furnished by clubs outside the League...."

"Baseball has been very popular in London the past season, and large crowds invariably attend first-class games. Next season the managers intend to put a nine in the field that, it is hoped, will keep up the high reputation already won by the Tecumsehs," it said.

The judiciary committee of the Canadian Association of Base Ball Players ruled on October 27 that London was indeed its champion for 1876, as it overruled objections from Guelph.

On November 18, the *Clipper* published a list of 34 teams and their professional players who took part in the 1876 campaign. Included were London and Guelph.

As the snow began to fly in London and Guelph and blanketed their respective home fields, plans were afoot to top the past season. Optimism reigned in both cities, and anything, it seemed, was possible.

6

Opportunity Knocks

The last of winter's snow had barely melted away, and Londoners were looking ahead to the 1877 campaign of their hometown Canadian champions. After months of controversy, the team finally acquired a new park to replace its old temporary home at the Exhibition Grounds. The city had offered land immediately to the north of the old grounds, a parcel still known locally as the Artillery Block, an area once occupied by the British garrison that left town in 1869. But the directors of the club felt it was too narrow in configuration for their purposes, so they began to scout other potential sites. This move alarmed owners of taverns and other businesses near the old grounds. They protested, worried they'd lose the hordes of thirsty clients they were accustomed to welcoming before and after Tecumseh games.[1]

Finding new quarters was essential to the team, whose popularity was soaring. Contests with the archrival Guelph Maple Leafs, for instance, had drawn as many as 10,000 spectators. After the collapse of temporary stands during a Guelph game the previous year, Tecumseh directors were determined to create something more permanent to meet team needs and those of its growing legion of fans. Besides, every September, late in their season, the team lost their field, which was needed for the annual Western Fair. Properties to the north and east were inspected, but nothing was deemed suitable for a home park without straying too far from the station that served the Great Western and Grand Trunk railways. The team, its supporters across the region, and opponents all relied heavily on trains, so a park couldn't be too far removed from either depot. The search for a new home took several months and proved somewhat controversial, sparking complaints from residents living near other potential downtown sites worried about noise, traffic, and the flight of errant balls.

W. J. Reid, a successful china merchant and team backer, found a chunk of land across the Thames River from downtown at the confluence of the

For 1877, the London Tecumsehs were among the founding members of the International Association, a professional baseball league established to challenge the National League, founded in 1876. The Tecumsehs went on to take the pennant of the league that attracted some of the top professionals of the day. In this photograph, Joe "Dutch" Hornung is in the back row, second from left, while curve ball pitcher Fred Goldsmith is front row left and his catcher, Phil "Grandmother" Powers is front row, center (*Illustrated London,* 1900).

waterway's northern and southern branches. The low-lying field at the river forks was susceptible to flooding, but when dry, animals grazed there. Impromptu games, including baseball, had been played for at least two decades on the grassy meadow where natives had once grown corn. The six-acre site, located in a small settlement known as Petersville, had great potential. A ballpark at that location would be an easy five-minute walk across Kensington Bridge from downtown shops, businesses, and homes. It was even closer than the Exhibition Grounds to downtown streetcars and the Grand Trunk railway station on York Street.

In mid–April, the *London Advertiser* reported that the Tecumseh club had acquired the meadow at the forks, thereby ending the "vexatious delays" of many months. The paper noted the recent bad feelings demonstrated by tavern keepers near the old grounds and "the threatening attitude of certain parties who appear determined to have the ball grounds at their own doors, so as to benefit from the custom which large crowds invariably draw to people in their line of business."[2]

The *Advertiser*, still tapping into the happy fact that its local editor was a Tecumseh director and manager, produced regular updates on the feverish activity that began immediately to prepare the new grounds for the upcoming season. The field was named Tecumseh Park. Sprinkled amid stories about work at the park were reports of ballplayers returning to town, ready to christen it. Of the playing field, it said:

> There is a strong force at work leveling and preparing the new grounds for the Tecumsehs, and numbers visit the place during the day to view the location and watch proceedings. Every friend of the club appears pleased with the pluck and enterprise displayed by the Tecumseh managers in grappling so successfully with the difficulties thrown in their way by certain citizens who opposed the granting of a ball field off the Park grounds. Property in the immediate neighborhood of the new ball grounds has increased in value a hundred per cent, since Saturday.[3]

A contract for 2,000 yards of sod was let to a Mr. Murdoch, and fencing and construction of stands for spectators proceeded quickly, along with a "brisk competition" for the lease of the refreshment stands. The city helped the effort by providing road shavings as fill to help raise and level the land.

Construction of the grandstand and bleacher seating was well under way by contractors Broadbent and Overall. Work was delayed somewhat by bad weather, but it was expected the park would be ready for play by early May. A former manager of the Great Western Railway named Kitchen was overseeing the work, which included installation of a telegraph wire from the downtown office of the Montreal Telegraph Company so game scores could be relayed promptly to and from other ballparks.[4] Meanwhile, Dick Southam, an apprentice printer at the *Advertiser*'s smaller rival, the *London Free Press*, was hired by the Tecumseh directors as team manager and was added to the roster as a substitute player.[5]

A 600-seat grandstand, described as "a large commodious building," arose in short order as well as a separate structure for reporters, scorers, and telegraph operators, and a large section of open seats. The playing surface featured the innovation of an in-ground watering system. A "director's pavilion" was also erected, paid for by new Tecumseh president Jake Englehart. Tickets for all seats in the grandstand were snapped up for the entire season by excited team supporters even before work on it was completed.

On April 30, the *Advertiser* reported:

> The Tecumseh ball grounds are beginning to look as pretty as a picture....
> Though the grounds will be ready for playing on next Saturday, when the Hartfords open the season with the Tecumsehs, they will not be in their best condition for some weeks to come. The progress made during the past two weeks is something wonderful.[6]

The new ballpark caught the attention of the *Canadian Illustrated News* a few months later. The publication featured an illustration of Tecumseh Park during a game between London and Guelph. "The baseball grounds and buildings," it said, "have been fitted up at an expense of upwards of $3,000 and without doubt are the best for the purpose in the Dominion."[7]

An exhibition game was played at the new park on May 3 when the Tecumsehs defeated the city's premier amateur team, the Atlantics, 5–1, before a crowd of 1,000.[8] The stage was set for a serious campaign in a fine new home in 1877, and Londoners couldn't wait for it to get under way.

London and area had embraced the Tecumsehs. The 1876 season had marked a sea change in team fortunes. The London nine had soundly defeated the Guelph Maple Leafs in all four of their contests before thousands of rabid fans, many of whom wagered heavily on the outcome of the games, as was the custom of the day. The decision by Englehart and his fellow Tecumseh directors to lure professionals from south of the border was in direct response to Guelph's hiring what London papers had derisively called its "foreign legion" in previous years.[9] To beat the Maple Leafs at their own game, the Tecumsehs adopted the same tactics, gradually adding more Americans to their roster. The escalation of diamond warfare had risen to new heights. The Tecumsehs captured and mirrored the young city of London's hopes and aspirations, just

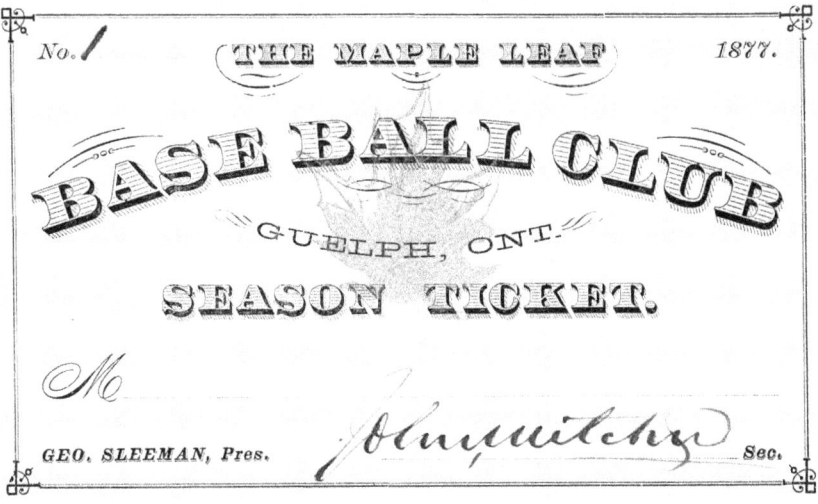

Maple Leaf president George Sleeman was a packrat and kept much of his baseball memorabilia, correspondence and records. Here is the first season ticket for the 1877 campaign. It was unused and is likely his (Sleeman Collection, Archival and Special Collections, University of Guelph Library, XR1 MS A801).

as the Maple Leafs had done for Guelph. The Tecumsehs weren't about to accept defeat, certainly not at the hands of a team from a town half its size.

London and its team wanted to flex their newfound muscles by competing with other cities and teams in a world growing ever more competitive and interconnected along the iron rail. If it took foreigners to get an edge, the Tecumseh directors had concluded, so be it.

With their ascendancy as the premier baseball club in Canada, the Tecumsehs looked toward the border with the United States, a mere 150 miles away at Buffalo to the east, and the same distance to Detroit in the west. Having dethroned Guelph at home, the London club sought even greater challenges. An unexpected opportunity arose in late 1876 when Harry Gorman learned some American clubs were considering a new organization of professional clubs to rival the National League, a struggling loop that had just concluded its first season with six teams after two were expelled. The timing was perfect, and the Tecumseh directors didn't hesitate to seek more information. They suggested to George Sleeman, despite their oftentimes rocky relationship with him, that he and his Guelph club might also want to explore the notion. It meant the two teams could take their epic battles to another, more competitive forum to stay sharp. And both would continue to compete for the Canadian championship.

It wasn't far-fetched for either team to want to play some of the best teams in the United States on a regular basis. Topnotch competition in Canada was hard to find. The Tecumsehs and Maple Leafs were accustomed to making short hops south of the border for games and the all-important share of gate proceeds to help cover their growing expenses. Barnstorming American teams often included Southern Ontario in road trips and regularly sought games with London and Guelph because of the good crowds they drew. For them, it was easy to fit the Ontario teams into any tour that included places like Rochester, Buffalo, and Detroit. Despite their relatively small size compared to many American cities, London and Guelph felt that the strong attendance at their games was a factor that might help gain them entry into any U.S.-based professional loop. National League teams had drawn 343,750 spectators in 1876, that organization's inaugural year. That averaged out to a bit more than 1,300 fans per game.[10] By comparison, London and Guelph easily drew crowds of that size, swelling to 10,000 fans for games against each other. When it came to attendance, the Ontario cities were already in the big leagues.

London and Guelph were not alone in their thinking. Many cities, of all sizes, felt their teams deserved a chance to show what they could do. There were dozens of communities beyond the handful that the National League felt were worthy competitors. Also anxious to compete with the top teams of the day were teams in St. Louis and Pittsburgh, for instance. Their principals were L. C. Waite, secretary of the St. Louis Red Stockings, and Pittsburgh businessman Harmar Denny McKnight, both of whom saw their clubs shut out of the National League. Waite's team was excluded from membership, but its in-city rival, the St. Louis Brown Stockings, was a charter member of the League and was returning for 1877. The League had its rule about allowing only one team in each city. McKnight had failed to get Pittsburgh into the League in its first season and was operating his Allegheny club as an independent nine. Both Waite and McKnight were concerned that the National League was trying to monopolize professional baseball and restrict it to only the largest and most important cities. The League had become an instant old boys' club, and the two men, who became allies, resented it from their perspective on the outside.

McKnight was the son of prominent Pittsburgh lawyer Robert McKnight, a city councilor and member of Congress from 1859 to 1863. His mother was Elizabeth Denny, a member of a wealthy landowning family. For his part, he felt he had to do something for his city. The young civic booster began to voice the growing sentiment that the National League and its vision was too narrow and its practices discriminatory. He reached out to other clubs and offered to host an organizing meeting for professional teams willing to consider another option.

Born in 1847, McKnight had played baseball in his teenage years and, while he loved the game, he realized he didn't have the skills to play at the professional level. So he contented himself with being a manager, organizer, club owner and executive. He obtained a graduate degree in mining and metallurgy from Lafayette College in Easton, Pennsylvania, and upon returning home became president of the Pittsburgh Base Ball Association. After a stint as a bookkeeper for the Third National Bank in Pittsburgh, McKnight became director of an iron smelting company, the Eclipse Steam Pump Works, by the mid–1870s.[11] In 1876, he helped organize the Allegheny team on a professional basis. The club played its home games in Allegheny City, immediately across the Allegheny River from Pittsburgh. Upset when his club was rejected by the League, McKnight became angry when its teams lured away several of his top players.

McKnight decided something must be done to provide opportunities for his city and team along with 50 other professional clubs outside the National League. So he and Waite invited many of them to a meeting to see if there was sufficient interest to form a rival league.[12]

In a letter sent to clubs in many cities, Waite laid out the plans he and McKnight were formulating for a "big tent" approach to professional baseball:

> Dear Sir: Let me give you a little idea of what kind of an association we ought to form. It would take in all clubs in the United States and Canada who hire part or all of their players on the broad ground of protection to clubs and players alike, and allow them a full representation in the convention, say, about two votes each, all of whom should be governed by the constitution and by-laws of the Association. Then have a ring within the ring, composed of clubs who desire to compete for the championship, who should be governed by a code of rules something like the League's. This would allow and bring under some kind of restraint and responsibility the vast number of clubs who play as they please, under such rules as they please, with what men they can get, and a new nine every game. This peculiar kind of play and club tactics has a demoralizing influence on the rising players, upon whom we here hope to depend in the future. It would also be beneficial to fostering good nines at various points who would be able to keep up, knowing they could not be broken up every day by secession of players, inveigled away by weaker clubs.[13]

The letter found its way north to London. At a meeting of Tecumseh directors on February 14, 1877, when plans for the upcoming season were approved, directors considered the notion of sending a delegate to the Pittsburgh gathering. "The idea of joining the International Association was favorably received," and it was decided to send manager Gorman, reported the *Advertiser*.[14] Club management was praised for the quality of players engaged for the season and concluded, "the nine as constituted would be a hard one to beat." Finances had never been better, with citizens generously supporting the team. "Several subscriptions of $100 each have been received and additional sums are promised."[15]

In Pittsburgh, McKnight enjoyed support from influential quarters for his contention that the National League needed competition. The *New York Clipper* had noted with approval the talk of forming an international organization from among the large number of teams playing professional or semi-professional baseball.

> The probability is that over forty professional clubs—stock-company, cooperative, gate-money, amateur and semi-professional—will enter the arena in 1877, and to accommodate these clubs with the necessary controlling legislation there is at present time of writing but one Association governing professional clubs practically in existence, and that is the League association.[16]

The newspaper's baseball writer, Henry Chadwick, had opposed the formation of the League in the first place and felt its scope was too narrow and monopolistic. The *Clipper* noted the League would likely operate with only six teams for the 1877 campaign because two of its members from 1876 were expelled for failure to complete their schedules. But many, many more professional nines were organizing for the upcoming season:

> [T]here must necessarily be a number, if not a majority, who are not circumstanced so as to enter the League under the rules they have provided. The question is, are these clubs to be deprived of the protection the membership of a Professional Association affords by their inability to enter the League, or by their desire to belong to some differently organized Association? We incline to the belief that the interests of the professional class as a whole will be best served by the organization of the International Association of Professional Clubs, as proposed in the call for the convention at Pittsburgh in February. It is, of course, not desirable that there should be two or three professional associations in existence, when one institution should suffice to control every professional club in the country; but it will, perhaps, result in the organization of a regular permanent association of the kind, if the proposed experiment is tried.[17]

The National League was unhappy at the prospect of competition, claiming it alone should be the final arbiter of disputes in the professional game, and there were hints that League nines would be barred from playing members of the International Association. Games with non–League teams had been important to its members to help pay their bills, so any threat to prevent games with non–League teams was likely a hollow one—at least for the time being. Again, Chadwick at the *Clipper* weighed in, saying, "There is no need for any spirit of ill-will or unfriendly rivalry existing between the two Associations."[18] The *Clipper* dismissed the idea of preventing games between League and Association teams as "nonsense" and insisted harmony was needed between the two organizations, because the League alone cannot do battle "against the army of crooked players, revolvers and others, which invest the national game."

Representatives of 17 professional baseball clubs gathered at the St. Clair Hotel in Pittsburgh on February 20 for a two-day convention to consider forming a new league. They were unhappy at the attempt to control the professional game by the fledgling, businessmen-led National League, which sought to minimize the role of players in league affairs and maximize profits for owners. League teams operated as stock companies, and the League's leaders were determined to develop baseball into a business. In so doing, they had assigned territorial monopolies to teams, sought to eradicate gambling, appealed to a higher class of fan by instituting a 50-cent admission charge (double the norm), and excluded baseball cooperatives in which players earned part or all of their pay from gate proceeds. Many teams outside the league were cooperatives, in which gate money was simply split among the players.

In his perceptive analysis of what was transpiring from a sociological and cultural perspective, Ted Vincent, in *Mudville's Revenge: The Rise and Fall of American Sport,* noted that the National League was an attempt by business to wrest control of baseball from players and re-establish the game on business principles. The players, merchants, small business owners, and local politicians who had controlled the game in its early days and during the National Association years were to be pushed aside. In response, those same interests rebelled, spearheaded by McKnight, Waite, Gorman, Sleeman, and others to organize on a model similar to the old National Association. As Vincent put it, a showdown was coming, as "one organization, run strictly for financial profit, was pitted against another run not only for the money, but also for the social and political profit to be gained from hometown glory."[19] It was a battle of Labor versus Capital, as Albert Goodwill Spalding had explained it not long before.

The League also sought to limit its membership to cities of 75,000 or larger on the assumption more money could be made in larger markets. This caused bitter feelings in the smaller centers in New York and New England,

The cities of London and Guelph were just west of the baseball hotbeds of New York, Massachusetts and Connecticut. The Tecumsehs and Maple Leafs joined many of the cities depicted here to form the International Association of Base Ball Players in 1877 (author's collection).

where the professional game was thriving and drawing good crowds. For them, the Association was more reflective of their interests. Vincent noted that while the IA had its metropolitan clubs, "what it really represented was the organized expression of an immense popularity of baseball in the smaller industrial city."[20] Association membership was sought and extended to teams in places like Worcester, Lynn, New Manchester, Bedford, Lowell, and Fall River, Massachusetts, and to Binghamton and Rochester. The team organizations included seven mayors, five future mayors (including Sleeman in Guelph), and the son of a mayor, Vincent wrote, adding, "rallying the populace for some scheme to boost the old hometown is a specialty of the politicians." Some team organizers believed team success could produce hometown pride and lead to electoral success.

There were some points of agreement between the Association and the League. In a bid to introduce some stability to team rosters, the rebels shared the League's desire to eliminate the practice of players jumping from one team to another while under contract. They also wanted to curb the gambling and crooked play that had sullied the professional game. Delegates and proxies were present at the Pittsburgh hotel from the following U.S. clubs: Resolutes, New Jersey; Fairbanks, Chicago; Brown Stockings, Erie, Pennsylvania; Chelseas, Brooklyn, New York; Live Oaks, Lynn, Massachusetts; Manchesters, New Hampshire; Alaskas, New York; Buckeyes, Columbus, Ohio; San Franciscos, San Francisco; Mountain City, Altoona, Pennsylvania; St. Louis Red Stockings, St. Louis, Missouri; Rochesters, Rochester, New York; Reading, Reading, Pennsylvania; Allegheny, Pittsburgh; and Essex, Buffalo, New York. Harry Gorman of the London Tecumsehs did double duty, representing his club and also acting as proxy for the Guelph Maple Leafs and president George Sleeman.[21]

Both Canadian clubs agreed to affiliate, and a constitution was hammered out for the International Association of Professional Base Ball Players. Playing rules of the National League were adopted, with minor exceptions, because Association clubs wanted to continue playing League teams to boost their bottom lines. At the close of proceedings, William A. "Candy" Cummings of the Live Oaks was elected president, a fitting figurehead for a league in which players would play key roles. It was another way in which the International Association mirrored the National Association. A pitcher many years later credited by the National Baseball Hall of Fame with developing the curveball, Cummings had played for the League's Dark Blues in Hartford during the 1876 season. He then jumped to the Live Oaks, the independent club in Lynn, Massachusetts. Elected vice-president of the IA was Tecumseh manager Harry

Gorman, while the absent Maple Leafs owner, George Sleeman, was appointed to the judiciary committee to sit alongside Denny McKnight of Allegheny.

A key decision made by delegates was to ban "revolving," the practice of players jumping from one team to another while still under contract. It was the same rule adopted by the National League. The entry fee for the Association was set at $10 for the season. If a team wanted to compete for the International Association championship, a further fee of $15 was due by April 1. Competing teams had to play four games against each other, two on home grounds, two as visitors. The title of IA champion would be bestowed on the team winning the most designated championship games by season's end.

The practice of self-scheduling was not unusual. A firm schedule of games was not introduced to baseball until the National League did so in 1877. The National Association adopted a championship race when it was founded in 1871, requiring each of its nine teams to play each rival five times during the season. Dates for such games were established by club secretaries and were often sandwiched among exhibition games with local clubs and those played during barnstorming tours. Sometimes it was unclear to spectators and reporters alike which contests were considered "championship" games and which were merely exhibition contests. Disputes arose that had to be settled by judiciary or championship committees of the leagues. In its inaugural year, the National League required each of its eight teams to play their rivals ten times, but to work out dates between teams. The National Association required its members to play the required games before having any exhibition with any championship rival, but that wasn't always followed. Opportunities for non-championship games often arose that could be easily arranged to further pad a team's bottom line if the rival was willing to play on an exhibition basis, especially on or near public holidays when good crowds were assured.[22] Until a set schedule was adopted by the League in 1877 – and by the International Association in 1878 – disputes inevitably arose and spectators were sometimes disappointed when a game believed to be for the pennant turned out to be an exhibition contest with no impact on the standings. The latter situation did little for public relations or to provide clarity to those who followed pennant races in the newspapers.

The admission fee was set at 25 cents for International Association games. That was half the levy charged for League games.[23] By late April, it was announced that seven teams had paid to compete for the Association pennant: the Tecumsehs, Maple Leafs, Allegheny, Live Oaks, Manchesters (New Hampshire), Buckeyes (Columbus, Ohio), and the Rochesters.[24]

The new optimism in baseball cities across North America stood in sharp relief to the continued effects of the 1873 economic collapse. Unemployment was increasing, reaching 14 percent in the United States—and about the same in Canada—at a time when jobless measurements were imprecise. It was estimated, however, that one of every four inhabitants of New York City was without work. Historians have described the situation as the worst depression endured by the U.S. until that of the 1930s.[25] While millions were unemployed, many of those still working faced cuts to their pay packets. Police were called upon to disperse angry crowds of workers as families went hungry. Some workers, angry at the concentration of wealth in so few hands, began calling for a second American Revolution as the nation celebrated its Centennial.[26] A much larger conflict of labor versus capital was well under way.

On the surface, these would seem to be strange times to launch new baseball teams and leagues and think they'd succeed. But baseball provided escape for those who were suffering economically, for the hordes who had joined the industrial revolution, exchanging country life for the grit, grime, and hard work of cities and their factories. Baseball was becoming increasingly popular among urban dwellers because it provided respite, however brief, from bleak times. The game harkened back to a simpler, more pastoral era and created a bond among people struggling to adapt to life in increasingly congested cities. Its appeal was widespread, not restricted by borders.

The same economic pressures were faced in Canada. Baseball offered players in both countries the prospect of an attractive paycheck. At a time when the average factory or railroad worker was bringing home $2 a day or less for a 60-hour, six-day work week, professional ballplayers were earning $800 or $1,000 or more for a season of seven or eight months, and could still pursue off-season employment if they so chose.[27] In 1874, as a heavy-hitting infielder with the Boston team in the National Association, Roscoe "Ross" Barnes earned $2,000, making him the highest-paid player in the game. That was more than twice the amount earned by the average American worker—$864—for an entire year.

In London, the picture was similar. Upholsterers earned $9–$10 a week, while factory workers received from $12 to $15 for their six days of work. Teachers in the London area earned from $245 to $445 annually.[28]

By 1876 and 1877, the National League was treating baseball as a business and began pinching pennies as it reduced the pay and influence of players. In 1874, Fergus Malone of Chicago was the top-paid player at $2,800. By 1875, it was Dick Higham of Chicago at $2,200. In 1876, Al Spalding earned $4,000, but by 1877 that had been cut to $2,900. Both years, Chicago's star pitcher led the pay parade.[29] By 1878, Barnes, whose skill had begun to decline, turned up in London to manage and play second base, suggesting the Tecumseh pay scale had become sufficiently competitive to attract first-rate players.

Allegheny, it was reported at the outset of the 1877 season, was paying two of its players $1,200, with the rest earning from $800 to $1,000 apiece.[30] Paying like that, the team was able to attract top talent, some who might otherwise consider a League team.

The Tecumsehs couldn't have known it early on, but the Alleghenys would become a key adversary for them in the inaugural season of the International Association. Few residents of London had likely heard of Allegheny City. It was a separate political entity from Pittsburgh and its inhabitants liked it that way. When Allegheny City was eventually annexed to Pittsburgh in 1907, it was done so against local wishes, but its inhabitants were outvoted by the larger city. It became known as Pittsburgh's North Side. Allegheny City had roughly half the population of its better-known neighbor across the river. Pittsburgh counted 86,000 residents in 1870 and 156,389 by 1880.[31]

"Allegheny" is a Delaware Indian word for "fair water." The first recorded inhabitants settled in 1740 at the junction where the westward-flowing Allegheny and Monongahela Rivers become the Ohio River. By 1800, a tavern, glass factory, rope maker, and plow-making firm had been established there. The first bridge from Pittsburgh was erected in 1820, and in 1840, when it was incorporated as a city, Allegheny City had reached a population of 10,000.[32]

Noteworthy immigrants included a Scottish family named Carnegie who settled in an area at the base of Monument Hill in 1848. Their boy, Andrew, 13, took a job paying $1.50 a week at a cotton mill in the city.[33] He would go on to great things as a railroad and steel mogul, but Carnegie never forgot his formative years in Allegheny City. Years later, the wealthy philanthropist established the first Carnegie Free Public Library in his American hometown.

It wasn't until 1857 that rail service to Philadelphia began with the arrival of the Pennsylvania Railroad. The coal that was in abundance in the region powered rail locomotives and was the fuel of choice to power the boilers of the burgeoning industries of both Allegheny City and Pittsburgh. This reliance on coal created poor air quality in the valley, however, and led to Pittsburgh's earning the nickname "Smoky City." Other industries that arose in both places included steam engine manufacturing, as the cities became railroad hubs, with extensive rail yards and roundhouses. Large mills turned out lumber, paper, iron, and later, steel.[34] Pittsburgh was described as "the very cockpit of industrialism in the iron and steel industry" and in 1874 was the home of 29 independently owned wrought-iron works and eight crucible steel mills.[35] By

1870, Allegheny City itself had 15 foundries and machine-and-engine-building shops that employed nearly 400 workers.[36] After the Civil War, Pittsburgh's blast furnaces turned out nearly half of America's iron. Workers on both sides of the river played baseball and began to follow it closely, making this fertile ground for the game.

Aside from being a regional manufacturing center keen on baseball like London, 400 miles away by rail, the Pittsburgh area had something else in common with the smaller city to the north: oil. Both were early refining centers in the fledgling petroleum industry because of their proximity to the first oil discoveries made in North America.

In 1859, oil was discovered at Titusville, 100 miles north of Allegheny City. A small refinery to process its output was established in downtown Pittsburgh, where its qualities for lubrication and illumination were studied. The Titusville well is often considered the first producing oil well in North America. But Drake's drilled well came a year after oil first flowed in quantity from a well dug by hand in gum beds west of London. By 1861, 400 wells in those beds were producing from 50 to 400 barrels a day of sour crude, oil with a distinctive odor of sulfur that required chemicals to neutralize it.[37] The Titusville operation produced sweet crude, without the unpleasant smell, and it quickly surpassed the oil patch up north, which in 1866 relocated a few miles northwest to a community called Petrolia.

The oil from Canada's oil patch was refined in London, the reason Jake Englehart settled there. By the 1870s, Englehart had become a key player in the Ontario refining industry. He was surviving, if not thriving. Englehart and a handful of London refiners produced seven out of every eight barrels of oil that was being shipped to Canadian customers by 1877.[38] Englehart was a fierce and respected competitor in what was becoming a cutthroat business.

Englehart hoped he could replicate his success in another growing new business—baseball. As in anything he tackled, Englehart spared no expense or energy to get what he wanted.

With a brand-new ballpark, some top-flight professionals, a determined president heading an organization with deep pockets and a strong fan base, the Tecumsehs were poised to soar to new heights.

7

Setting the Tables

The directors of the Tecumseh Club were determined to put on a good showing in the International Association. The American professionals they hired to achieve that goal in the 1877 season were a mix of players beginning their careers and those who had already proven themselves in the National Association and the League. For some, it was their first trip to the small Canadian city, which they soon discovered had contracted baseball fever.

It was an interesting collection of characters that stepped off Great Western and Grand Trunk railway trains as finishing touches were put on Tecumseh Park and plans were coming together for the upcoming campaign.

George H. "Foghorn" Bradley, 22, was among the newcomers, a backup pitcher for Goldsmith. The right-hander was born in Medford, Massachusetts, and in 1876 played with the Boston Red Caps (the renamed Red Stockings) of the National League. In Boston, he pitched in 22 games, winning nine and losing ten as his team finished in fourth place behind Chicago, Hartford, and St. Louis.

Also new to London was Ed Somerville, 24, a shortstop born in Philadelphia, who lived in New Haven. He may have been encouraged to travel north by Goldsmith, who also called the Connecticut port city his home. The previous season, Somerville played 64 games for the Louisville Grays, which placed fifth in the National League standings. A second baseman for the Grays, he had a batting average of .188, but fielding was really where his strength lay. Somerville led the League in assists and he was second in putouts. In 1875, Somerville played in the NA with the Philadelphia Centennials until they disbanded and he moved to New Haven's Elm City team. He would have met Goldsmith, who was playing for New Haven.

Other newcomers were reasonably experienced. Jake Knowdell, 22, a Brooklyn native, was a catcher expected to back up Powers. He played for the Atlantics of Brooklyn in the National Association in 1874 and 1875. John

Henry "Herm" Doscher, 24, born in New York City, was solid in both the infield and outfield. He appeared in a handful of games for the Atlantics of Brooklyn in 1872–1873 and joined Washington of the National Association for 22 games in 1875. Fred Waterman, 32, born in New York City, was a member of the Cincinnati Red Stockings of 1869–1870, the first truly professional team. He saw spot duty totaling 61 games for the Olympic, Washington, and Chicago clubs of the National Association between 1871 and 1875. He had a strong bat, boasting a .300 average in 1875. A third baseman, he was set to play center field for the Tecumsehs. A bit of a nomad, however, Waterman left London after appearing in only a few early-season games.

Along with Goldsmith, Powers, and Hornung, back for another campaign was Mike Dinnen, the sometimes flashy, but light-hitting second baseman.

At the outset of the season, the ninth man on the roster was W. Spencer, a forgettable right fielder who couldn't hit. His first name, rather appropriately, is lost to history. He was still with the team for its official 1877 photo, in which his last name appears as "Spence." He batted at the bottom of the order for obvious reasons and by early June found himself replaced by John Magner. A St. Louis native, Magner, 22, played left field for the St. Louis Red Stockings the previous season and for the Buckeyes of Columbus in the International Association to start the 1877 season.[1] He was a much stronger presence at the plate than Spencer. Late in the summer, Magner, too, was gone, replaced for short stints by local amateurs Billy Reid, Tom Gillean, and Billy Mountjoy. Two other professionals joined the team before the season was over, jumping from the Maple Leafs. Tommy Smith, 26, a native of Guelph, signed on to patrol the outfield. Also signed was Marshall Quinton, 25, a Philadelphia native, who was a catcher, outfielder, and infielder. At the very end of the season, a player named Burke joined the team at shortstop. Likely this was Mike Burke, a Cincinnati native who returned to the Tecumsehs in 1878 and went on to play for Cincinnati in the National League in 1879.

It was a solid lineup for the Tecumsehs, still basking in the success of 1876 and looking forward to its brand-new home for the coming campaign. London was upbeat about its chances in a new league, bolstered as it was by additional top-flight professionals.

In Guelph, George Sleeman had let it be known he was looking to strengthen his lineup with more American imports. He received plenty of responses and did his best to choose wisely, using his well-developed contacts south of the border.

One newcomer was Mike Lawlor, 23, a relatively untested catcher from Troy, New York. He would go on to play for Troy of the National League in

1880, and the 1884 Washington team in the short-lived Union League. Marshall Quinton, 25, a versatile competitor who could catch and play outfield or infield as needed, signed on but left the Maple Leafs later in the season to play for the Tecumsehs. After his time in Guelph and London, Quinton bounced around a bit before landing with the Richmond and Philadelphia teams in the American Association in 1884 and 1885, respectively. Tommy Smith, 26, the Guelph native and outfielder, was back for another year, but like Quinton, he would jump to the Tecumsehs to finish the 1877 season. Back again was pitcher Bill Smith, another Guelph native. He became the preferred pitcher for the hotly contested games against London. Another pitcher named Sullivan, whose background is not known, also joined the team. He may have been a local, because like London, the Maple Leafs used local players to fill gaps in their lineup, especially later in the season.

Clearly, the Tecumsehs had out-recruited their long-time rivals in Guelph. Englehart, the Tecumseh president and London booster, had no less desire than Sleeman to take his team to the top ranks of baseball. But the oilman's pockets were so much deeper than the brewer's. A credit rating book from 1879 estimated Englehart's worth at from $75,000 to $150,000, while Sleeman's stood at from $40,000 to $75,000. The credit rating for both businessmen, however, was considered high.[2]

There was no lack of effort on Sleeman's part as he readied the Maple Leafs for the 1877 campaign based again at Exhibition Park, the team's home since 1871. Beginning late the previous year, he'd been seeking skilled professionals willing to come to Guelph. He had corresponded with several of the top players of the day, eager young men anxious to become professional players and willing to consider a team just beyond the U.S. border.

Sleeman kept meticulous records and apparently was loath to throw anything out. He kept the letters he received from prospective players as well as detailed team ledgers showing everything from payments to players to the amount spent for rail fares and hotel accommodation. Today, they are preserved in the Sleeman Collection of documents at the University of Guelph library. They produce a fascinating snapshot of the early days of professional baseball and of what was on the minds of those who played it. The letters from players suggest that some were merely trying to see what sort of money the Maple Leafs were willing to pay. Others seemed more sincere. Regardless, for a variety of reasons, many went elsewhere for the 1877 season. The letters also reveal the poor level of literacy some had achieved. Manager Harry Gorman of the London Tecumsehs no doubt had similar correspondence, but unlike Gorman didn't see fit to keep them, at least none have been unearthed.

7. Setting the Tables

A minute book for early meetings of the Tecumseh club has survived, but it is an incomplete record, its contents a haphazard collection of discussions and decisions.

The Sleeman letters featuring penmanship that can be deciphered provide glimpses into another time and place. Among the top players who corresponded with the Guelph brewer were Chick Fulmer, George "Charmer" Zettlein, Pete Hotaling, and Scott Hastings. Only the latter eventually reached a deal with Sleeman, and he became a pipeline to other players. Others who wrote Sleeman were taking early, tentative steps in their professional careers.

Fulmer, 24, a Philadelphia native and solid infielder with a reliable bat, began his career in 1871 with Rockford in the National Association. He moved to the Mutuals and Philadelphia before joining Louisville for the inaugural season of the National League in 1876. He later joined the roster of Buffalo's National League team for 1879 and 1880. He moved to Cincinnati and St. Louis of the American Association before ending his playing days after the 1884 season.

In a letter from Philadelphia, dated February 12, 1877, Fulmer went straight to the point: "I will take $900 and board. The Athletic [sic] make me as good as I ask you to stay here in Phila. [sic] but I would like play with Hastings. Send me an answer as soon as possible."[3]

Fulmer apparently didn't like the answer provided by Sleeman and showed up with another International Association team that season.

George "Charmer" Zettlein was a veteran who was entering the twilight of a long and distinguished career. He, too, sought work from Sleeman. At age 32, he had won only four games for Philadelphia Athletics of the National League in 1876, but his resume was impressive. A pitcher, he started his career with the Brooklyn Eckfords in 1865, then moved on to the Atlantics. He was the winning pitcher of the extra-inning game in 1870 that ended the two-year, 89-game winning streak of the Cincinnati Red Stockings. A year later, with the Chicagos, he had the lowest earned-run average in the new National Association. Zettlein pitched all but ten innings and recorded 18 wins against nine losses as the White Stockings finished in second place despite the Great Fire that destroyed their ball grounds and much of Chicago late in their season. He moved on to the National Association teams of Troy, Eckfords (of Brooklyn), Philadelphia, Chicago, and back to Philadelphia for 1875 and 1876. The Athletics were expelled from the National League at the end of the League's inaugural season (along with the cash-strapped New York Mutuals) for failing to complete their schedule.[4] So Zettlein was looking for work.

In his November 16, 1876, letter from Brooklyn, Zettlein wrote:

> I see by the newspapers that you are going to organize a joint stock company out of a good nine next season in Guelph, if you want a pitcher to play in your nine I would go out and pitch for you if we can make satisfactory arrangements. I would like to go to Canada for to live there for a season. Answer this note as soon as possible.[5]

Zettlein and Sleeman couldn't agree to terms, and Zettlein ended his professional playing days not long afterward.

Pete Hotaling was on the cusp of a fine career as an outfielder, catcher, and infielder. About to turn 20 when he wrote Sleeman from his home in Ilion, New York, Hotaling would go on to play nine seasons in professional baseball, beginning in 1879 with Cincinnati; then Cleveland, Worcester, Boston, and Cleveland again, all of the National League. A speedster on the base paths, the diminutive Hotaling then joined Brooklyn and Cleveland of the American Association, ending his playing career after the 1888 season. He appeared in 840 games and registered 931 hits with a batting average of .267.

In a letter dated December 14, 1876, Hotaling wasted no time asking about money and hinted that he was considering offers.

> I would be very glad to play with you this coming season but I would like to have you state what you will pay me per month to come and play with you. If you can pay me a reasonable sum I will come. I need you to make me an offer and then I will tell you if I will come or not. Please answer as soon as possible as I have some letters to answer as soon as I hear from you.

The money offered by Sleeman was insufficient to meet Hotaling's expectations, because at the end of the same month, the player advised, "I cannot come and play with you this next season for that salary.... I am going to play this next season where I can get the most money. Give my regards to the boys."

Sleeman must have enhanced his offer somewhat to the plain-speaking Hotaling, who responded in another letter dated January 8, 1877:

> I received your letter of the 6th and was glad to hear from you. And what you offer is enough for me and I think that I will join you. But—I cannot give you a deffinate [sic] answer inside of a week if you will wait that long you will oblige me very much. In a week I will let you know for sure if I will come or not. I am not afraid of not getting my money at all. I know that I will get it if I play with you.

Hotaling sent a final letter in mid–February saying he had signed with another club because he wanted to remain near his father, who was ill. He said he was enclosing contracts Sleeman had sent him.[6] Hotaling signed with the Syracuse Stars of the International Association for 1877–1878, a team much closer to home, and found himself playing against Guelph. In 1879, he moved to the League club in Cincinnati.

Yet another veteran who wrote Sleeman was Scott Hastings, 29, an Ohio native who began his career with Rockford in 1871. A versatile player, Hastings had played for Louisville in the National League in 1876 after appearing with Cleveland, Baltimore, Hartford, and Chicago in the National Association. In an unexpectedly neat hand, Hastings made promises in his several letters to the brewer that he could enlist other professionals to come with him to Guelph. In a November 16, 1876, message from Baltimore, Hastings said he understood Sleeman paid his players in gold and that he'd play for $150 a month, or $900 for the entire season. A month later, Hastings again wrote Sleeman from Baltimore, but this time on the letterhead of the Louisville Base Ball Club. He said he had reconsidered his offer to play and would now do so for $125 a month in gold, amounting to $750 for the season. Hastings advised Sleeman, however, that because of the short six-month season for the Maple Leafs, he needed an advance before the season started in May.[7] In even later correspondence, Hastings outlined his work history away from the ball field.

> In regard to what I have done in the way of work, I am like the majority of our profession without a trade. I have worked at railroading for over five years—and when I quit it was as conductor on freight running between Chicago and St. Louis. Have also clerked in a hotel and worked in a drug store. But my experience in the latter won't do to bet on.[8]

Hastings eventually signed with the Maple Leafs, but before the season ended, he showed up with Cincinnati of the National League, where he played in 20 games.

On the letterhead of Whitney's Piano, Organ and Musical Warerooms of Brockton, Massachusetts, dated November 8, 1876, Arthur Whitney, an 18-year-old third baseman, advised Sleeman he'd play for $100 a month plus traveling expenses to and from Guelph. He and Sleeman failed to reach a deal, but that didn't end Whitney's plans to become a professional. In 1880, he landed with Worcester of the National League to begin an 11-year professional career that included making the roster of the Detroit, Providence, Pittsburgh, and New York teams of the National League and the American Association clubs of Pittsburgh, Cincinnati, and St. Louis. In all, he played in 978 games and registered 820 hits.

On a postcard from Philadelphia dated March 19, 1877, Marshall Quinton suggested terms that even the mail carrier could see. "I have an offer of $90 a month from Providence, but have not yet signed there. Will play with you on same terms, and my expenses to Guelph. Can refer to Al Wright or Al Reach of this city. Will hold the matter open until I hear from you, which I hope will be soon."[9]

Letters also appeared from two players who within months would be key figures in one of the first great scandals of professional baseball. When they put their hands to pen and paper, however, the two were among the top players of the day.

A short note from William H. "Bill" Craver is dated February 11 (presumably 1877, when Sleeman was most active recruiting players in the United States). "Having been informed that your intentions the coming season are to have Canada well represented with a strong base ball nine and wishing to become one of your players, I ask you if my services are required. I play any position with the exception of pitcher."[10]

The message was from Troy, New York, where the 32-year-old began his professional career in 1871. Craver played with American Association teams in Baltimore, Philadelphia, and Brooklyn. In 1876, he had been a member of the New York Mutuals nine in the National League, which was later expelled for failing to complete its schedule. A versatile player, he was sometimes also a manager. Craver was strong at the plate and recorded a batting average of .343 in 1874, although that fell off to .224 two years later.

Another letter was a three-pager from James A. Devlin, an accomplished 27-year-old pitcher who also played first base and outfield. Neatly penned, it was riddled with errors of grammar and punctuation. Dated February 28, 1877, it was from Devlin's hometown of Philadelphia.

Devlin was a rising star. He began playing for the Easton, Pennsylvania, team in 1872 at third base. The next year, he moved to Philadelphia's club in the National Association. A year later, he was a first baseman and outfielder for the Chicago White Stockings in the Association. Still with Chicago in 1875, he played mainly at first and began pitching, recording seven wins against 16 losses. Moving to Louisville of the National League for 1876, his pitching was much improved as he threw in nearly every one of the Grays games, winning 30 and losing 35. Most impressively, Devlin pitched 622 innings and recorded 122 strikeouts, both league-leading numbers. He had an earned run average of 1.56, among the League's best. Devlin helped his cause with his work at the plate. His batting average that same year was a more-than-respectable .315.

Devlin wondered if Sleeman could use his services:

> As the Louisville club has broken contract with me and have acted the meanest of ways towards me I have come to the conclusion not to return to that city on the way I now stand with them. This is the way it commences. The Louisville club contracted to pay me 5 five hundred [*sic*] dollars advance. The 1st 250 was to be paid July 1st wich [*sic*] I got and the other 250 I was to get Nov. 15th. I

never got that amount not one cent of it. So I made my appeal to the League and by not beaing [sic] there my self I got no show. So I have written to Louisville 20 times and got one letter saying if I would answer [sic] I would get my money right away. I done so and I have never heard from them. Since 2 months ago I have a standing offer in Pittsburgh. But I don't like the nine they have. If you want a man what will you give me to play with your nine. You know my reputation as an honest ballplayer 1st baseman and pitcher if you have no chance in your club I wish you would make known the facts to Mr. Gorman. State your price to me as pitcher if you want one. Is Hastings in your club he can tell you what I am. Hoping to hear from you soon.[11]

Devlin was naïve in thinking Sleeman would mention his availability to Sleeman's nemesis, Harry Gorman, manager of the Tecumsehs.

Devlin's "reputation as an honest ballplayer" would soon take a serious beating. For the 1877 season, Devlin returned to Louisville, and Craver joined him there. Scandal erupted within months, and Devlin and Craver were in the midst of it. The Grays had a successful start to the season and grew stronger, eventually holding a comfortable lead in the eight-team National League loop largely because of Devlin's pitching, which relied on an effective drop ball. For the season, he won 35 games and was second in the League in strikeouts with 141. But a sudden losing streak of eight games late in the season during a road trip led to suspicions that Louisville players were throwing games for gamblers. The Boston Red Caps (renamed from Red Stockings) edged past Louisville to win the pennant by seven games. Immediately suspicious, Louisville team officials demanded to see telegrams to and from four players, including Devlin and Craver. Devlin admitted his involvement, but Craver refused to cooperate. Devlin and Craver and the two others were banned for life from the League, whose president, William Hulbert, was determined to stamp out gambling. Later appeals by the players proved fruitless.

For his part, Craver's entire career had raised suspicions about his ethics. His first team, the Troy Haymakers, had been controlled by New York City gamblers. Unable to play for leading professional teams after being banned by the League, both Devlin and Craver eventually became police officers in Troy and Philadelphia, respectively.[12] Had they reached deals with a baseball-loving brewer to play the season in Canada, the fates of Devlin and Craver—and the Grays—would have been different in 1877. Possibly for the Guelph Maple Leafs, as well.

Meanwhile, many miles to the south, Denny McKnight was also busy, loading up his team for the inaugural season of the International Association. He was looking for talent and found it with a combination of veterans and newcomers who would go on to successful careers.

The money McKnight was prepared to commit to make Allegheny a contender was sufficient to attract James "Pud" Galvin, an outstanding 20-year-old pitcher. A St. Louis native, the five-foot-eight Galvin made his major league debut in 1875 with the St. Louis Red Stockings in the final year of the National Association. Unaffiliated for the 1876 season when they couldn't get into the National League, the Red Stockings played and defeated the Philadelphia League team in an exhibition game on July 4 when Galvin tossed a no-hitter.[13] He did even better a month later against the Cass Club of Detroit, when he threw a perfect game.[14] The acquisition of the fastballer with a good changeup and wicked pickoff move would make Allegheny competitive with teams like London and Lynn and their curveballers Goldsmith and Cummings. Galvin was at the outset of an outstanding 18-year professional career that would eventually propel him into the National Baseball Hall of Fame and Museum.

Chick Fulmer, after corresponding with Sleeman and demanding $900 from him, agreed to join McKnight's team. A steady infielder with a solid bat, he had played for Louisville's entry in the National League during 1876, his fifth year as a professional with a topflight club. His career began in Rockford, Illinois, in 1871 and continued until 1884 with Cincinnati and St. Louis.

One of the most experienced players to throw his lot in with Allegheny for the season was Candy Nelson, a first baseman and outfielder. The 28-year-old from Portland, Maine, had already played four years on the professional circuit with Troy, the Eckfords, and the Mutuals. From 1878 to 1881, he would go on to play with National League clubs in Indianapolis, Troy, and Worcester. He ended his career with Brooklyn in 1890 after suiting up for New York's American Association and League teams. His career batting average was .253.

George Creamer, also 22, an infielder from Philadelphia, was just beginning a career that would see him move on to the Milwaukee Grays of the National League in 1878, followed by four more seasons with League teams Syracuse and Worcester and then two more back in Pittsburgh with its American Association nines of 1883 and 1884. Another rookie about to embark on a successful career was 18-year-old Tom Dolan of New York City. Primarily a catcher and outfielder, he moved on to Chicago of the National League in 1879. His career ended in 1888 after stints with Buffalo, St. Louis, and Baltimore in the National League, American Association, and the Union Association.

Another newcomer was Jake Goodman, 23, from Lancaster, Pennsylvania. The first baseman later played for Milwaukee's 1878 National League team and the 1882 Pittsburgh American Association nine.

Bill Holbert, 22, a catcher and outfielder from Baltimore, had played 12 games for the 1876 Louisville Club with Fulmer. In 1878, he began a decade of play with National League and American Association teams in Milwaukee, Syracuse, Troy, New York, and Brooklyn, playing in 623 games and registering 486 hits.

Yet another rookie was 19-year-old Ned Williamson of Philadelphia, a versatile infielder who the next year would begin a 12-year career in the National League, 11 of them with Chicago after one with Indianapolis. He ended his career in 1890 after playing with Chicago's entry in the Players League. He played 1,201 games over which his batting average stood at .255.

Al Nichols, 25, a third baseman from Brooklyn with a weak bat, played only nine games with Allegheny before defecting to Louisville, where he joined Devlin and Craver in fixing games and, along with them and center fielder George Hall, earned a lifetime ban from playing in the National League. Previously, Nichols had played for the Atlantics in 1875, before joining New York for the 1876 League campaign.

Joining the team as a backup pitcher was 22-year-old northern Pennsylvanian Russ McKelvy, who would pitch and win only one game, seeing limited duty because of Galvin's dominance. In 1878, he moved to Indianapolis of the National League.

Denny McKnight had assembled an impressive roster to pursue civic glory on the stage provided by the new professional league he was instrumental in forging.

The Alleghenys were set to play their games at Recreation Park, formerly known as Union Park, a field alongside the Pittsburgh, Fort Wayne, and Chicago Railroad in Allegheny City south of Pennsylvania Avenue. The park was also used for fairs, football games, and other community events. Best of all for McKnight, it was owned by a member of his mother's wealthy family, the Dennys, who had extensive landholdings in Allegheny City.[15] So he enjoyed a convenient venue for his team with low overhead and a reasonable landlord. As in faraway London, his home park was just across a river from downtown.

The London, Guelph, and Allegheny clubs were ready to play with the new International Association, and they ignored the decision by other teams, including some IA members, to join an "alliance" proposed by the National League.

In January 1877, Chicago manager Albert Goodwill Spalding issued a circular proposing that all independent (non–National League) teams sign an agreement with the League, which would have the effect of ensuring mutual respect for player contracts. Independent teams needed merely to advise the League secretary of the existence of contracts, and they would be recorded by him. The proposal seemed reasonable on its surface, but additional details suggested there was more to it and that the League was attempting to impose its will far beyond its narrow membership. The same teams would be required to play by the rules of the National League and abide by League decisions in resolving disputes. Such provisions, in effect, acknowledged the supremacy of the League and was an attempt to subjugate the Association.

The National League's new president, William Hulbert, Spalding, and their cohorts came up with the plan in the self-serving belief that "theirs was the lone true 'major' operation" in the game.[16] Spalding had learned of the plans to create a rival league and was concerned because, in its first year, the NL was far from successful. Only his team had made any money. He discovered that at least 13 teams unhappy with the League were gathering the next month in Pittsburgh at the invitation of Denny McKnight.[17] Meanwhile, things were somewhat bleak for the League as it looked ahead to 1877. Two of its teams were expelled for failure to complete their schedules, and it faced the prospect of continuing with six teams, with only two from the East.

London, Guelph, and Allegheny were among the founding members of the IA and weren't the least bit interested in the move by Spalding and the League. They rejected any notion of entering an arrangement that became known as the League Alliance. Particularly offensive was the requirement that disputes would be adjudicated by the League, a measure which implicitly gave the final say in baseball matters to Spalding's organization.

Some charter members of the International Association against whom London, Guelph, and Allegheny would play were among the 13 clubs who opted to enter the League Alliance. They included the Crickets of Binghamton, the Stars of Syracuse, and Lowell and Fall River, both in Massachusetts. By April, more had signed on, including the Hornells of Hornellsville and the Haymakers of Troy, both in New York. These latter teams may have signed on after the *New York Clipper* noted in March that there was nothing in the League Alliance agreement to prevent teams from being members of both the League and the Association.[18] After all, one key part of the deal was mutual respect for player contracts, and that was a positive step. Nearly 30 clubs eventually signed the Alliance agreement, but by as early as June those numbers began to dwindle as members disbanded because of internal financial turmoil. The Syracuse and Indianapolis clubs conducted regular barnstorming tours and were quite successful, but the remainder of the League Alliance teams tended to remain closer to home.

Little more was heard of the Alliance until late in 1877 as the National League continued to struggle through a second season. Its Cincinnati club foundered, released its players, then reorganized and returned. St. Louis resigned, Hartford was ruled no longer a member, and the "Louisville Four," including Devlin and Craver, were banned from baseball for throwing games.

That December, a League Alliance championship was announced by the NL for the following season, and the affiliated members were extended non-voting status at League meetings.[19] The promised Alliance championship never materialized. Meanwhile, two months later, at the second meeting of the International Association held in Buffalo, members agreed they would not play any member of the League Alliance until a $100 game guarantee demanded from non–League teams was rescinded. The IA declared: "each club, a member of this Association, may make such arrangements with any other clubs as are extended to them by such clubs."[20] The Association teams were unwilling to declare war on League clubs, upon whom they relied heavily for games with healthy gate receipts. But the Association continued to chafe at the League, with so few teams, trying to impose its will on the large number of teams it had shunned, and on the game itself.

Politics of baseball aside, for London, Guelph, and Allegheny City, their rosters were set and their hopes were high for themselves and the new organization. After all their careful preparations for the inaugural 1877 International Association season, all they wanted to hear now was the umpire call for the first pitch.

8

Early 1877—The Magical Run Begins

The businessmen who established the National League were looking for a better season in 1877 than the loop's inaugural one, though the economic downturn lingered. Having expelled the cash-strapped Mutuals of New York and the Athletics of Philadelphia for failing to complete their 1876 schedules, the League entered its second season with only six teams. It would soldier on with the Chicago White Stockings, Boston Red Caps (renamed in 1876 to avoid confusion with the Cincinnati Red Stockings), Louisville Grays, St. Louis Brown Stockings, Hartford Dark Blues, and the aforementioned Cincinnati Red Stockings. The loss of teams in the major markets of New York and Philadelphia was a blow to the League, financially and from a public relations perspective. The major cities of Baltimore and Washington were also without franchises in what purported to be a "national" league. In 1876, only pennant-winning Chicago had been profitable, and only mildly so. That same year, Boston lost money after ringing up five profitable seasons in the old National Association, the most successful being 1875, when it earned $3,933.[1] The struggling Hartford club decided to play its home games in 1877 at Brooklyn's Union Grounds, hoping to attract larger crowds and find profitability.

Founding president Morgan Bulkeley, of the Hartfords, left his post to pursue a political career, and William Hulbert, the driving force behind the League, took over and began making changes. He introduced a centralized schedule to relieve each team of the task. This was also a means of keeping better track of its member teams, to avoid a repeat of the arguments of 1876 with the Mutuals and Athletics about the failure to complete their schedules. Anxious to contain costs, the League tightened its belt at the expense of its employees. Henceforth, each player had to pay a deposit of $30 for his uniform and also repair and launder it at his own expense. While on road trips, players were required to contribute 50 cents per day toward the cost of room and board.²

Overall, the early years of the National League were a financial flop. Boston, for instance, recorded losses of $777 in 1876, $2,230 in 1877, $1,433 in 1878, $3,346 in 1879 and $3,315 in 1880. Estimated losses for 1877 alone came to $8,000 for St. Louis, $6,000 for Chicago, $2,230 for Hartford, and $2,000 for Louisville.³ Especially in its first two or three years, the very survival of the League was in doubt, and some observers felt it was no improvement on the old National Association. "Although managerial austerity, salary cuts, and new stock issues lightened the burden somewhat, it was a discouraging picture," historian David Voigt said of the early days of the League. "Ranged alongside the modestly profitable Association era, it goes far to debunk the myth of League superiority."⁴

By 1877, there were 54 professional baseball clubs in operation. Many of the best teams and players of the day remained outside the National League, however, by their choice—or the League's. Some stayed away because of the perceived elitist attitude of the new organization, which saw itself as pre-eminent in baseball, and which treated players as its employees. Others simply couldn't meet the requirement of a minimum population of 75,000 for member cities. At the time, professional baseball was hugely popular in many cities with far fewer inhabitants.

By contrast to the gloom permeating the National League, the upstart International Association was buoyed by optimism in 1877. Its nearly two dozen clubs, most of them cooperatives, were better able to weather the economic downturn than business-oriented teams reliant on the profits needed to please stockholders. For them, making money was not the primary goal, or the reason for their existence, as sports historian Ted Vincent has explained. "The season provided the first among a number of cases in the history of American pro sport where one organization, run strictly for financial profit, was pitted against another run not only for the money but also for the social and political profit to be gained from hometown glory."⁵

The International Association was attractive to smaller industrial cities seeking fame on the baseball field, and many of their directors were from the retail sector or local government, including some current or future civic leaders. Several were mayors or future mayors, or other political "wannabes," anxious to tap baseball and civic boosterism for their own purposes. Being associated with a winning team that drew thousands of spectators, they felt, would prove helpful at the ballot box. George Sleeman, for instance, the man responsible for the Guelph Maple Leafs and their triumphs, was elected mayor in 1880 when Guelph reached city status—and five more times over the years up to and including 1906.[6]

Seven of the IA clubs paid the extra $15 fee to vie for the association's championship pennant: London Tecumsehs; Guelph Maple Leafs; Pittsburgh Allegheny; Columbus Buckeyes; Lynn Live Oaks; Rochester; and Manchester. Sixteen more clubs had signed with the Association but were not interested in the pennant race.

Henry Chadwick at the *Clipper* was sounding as optimistic about the new direction in baseball as were Denny McKnight, L. C. Waite, Harry Gorman, and George Sleeman. Even before its late February founding meeting in Pittsburgh, Chadwick was solidly behind the IA movement. He suggested that the League and Association could work together for the betterment of the sport, to rid baseball of its "evils ... the army of crooked players, revolvers, and others that infest the national game." He said he could not see any reasonable objection to a new group willing to "embrace every professional club in the country not connected with the League.... We advocate the organization of the International Association."[7] He argued it would be "nonsense" for the League and Association not to get along, or to boycott each other. In early March, Chadwick wrote approvingly of a key decision made by the IA's founding fathers, that the Association was not interested in the League's offer to adjudicate baseball disputes through the League Alliance. Its own judiciary committee would handle that job. Chadwick noted that with the men who were in charge of the new organization, "the Association should meet with success."[8]

By April, the teams of the Association and the League were practicing hard and playing exhibition games as they prepared for the first pitches in each loop. During one such game between the Lynn Live Oaks and Harvard College on April 12, the college's catcher, James Tyng, wore the first-ever catcher's mask. It had been designed by team manager Fred Thayer and crafted by a local tinsmith. Thayer received a patent for it the following year. Technology was belatedly coming to the aid of catchers, in recognition of the battering they took behind the plate. Billy McGunnity of the Fall River, Massachusetts, team had worn the first catcher's mitt in a game in 1875.[9] But two years later, that improvement had yet to catch on. The protective devices were intended to reduce the incidence of mangled fingers, broken noses, and other injuries that were sidelining catchers.

Two weeks later, on April 26, the opening pitch for the International Association was thrown in Lynn, where the hometown Live Oaks played host to the Manchester club. The visitors hammered the Live Oaks and the pitching of Candy Cummings, the IA player-president. Infielder Louis Say of the Manchesters proved a handful for Cummings that day, scoring four runs as his team won, 14–3.[10] It was a blowout and a precursor to what would be a difficult season for Lynn.

April 30 was historic on two counts. The National League opened its season that day with a game between the Hartford Dark Blues and the Boston Red Caps in Hartford's new home park in Brooklyn. After 11 innings, the game was called, the score standing at an unsatisfying 1–1. The same day, Jim "Pud" Galvin, the young new pitcher for the Pittsburgh Allegheny, threw a shutout, the International Association's first, as his team downed Columbus, 2–0. Two days later, Galvin was again brilliant. He pitched a one-hit shutout at the Boston Red Caps and helped himself and his club by hitting a home run over the outfield fence at Union Park in Allegheny City, a first for the park.[11]

In London, the Tecumsehs took to their new grounds for the first time on May 3, for a game with its amateur club, the Atlantics. About 1,000 spectators showed up for the contest from which Tecumseh catcher Phil Powers was missing because of a broken finger sustained in practice. The pitching of Goldsmith, it was noted, featured some "new wrinkles," as Jake Knowdell filled in as catcher. The final score was 6–1 for the professionals against the city's best amateurs.[12] The game was a warmup for the first professional game on May 5 when the National League's Hartford Dark Blues (of Brooklyn) came to town. Powers remained out of action, and while Goldsmith blanked the visitors in the first two innings, by the third they "got the hang of [his] 'larboard twisters.'" Goldsmith was pulled after five innings for Foghorn Bradley, but the Hartfords were already well ahead at the time, having capitalized on fielding errors. The final score was 6–2 for the visitors. The next day, Hartford won again, this time 8–4, as they again took advantage of Tecumseh fielding errors, Knowdell making seven of the home team's 13 miscues.[13] While there was no crowd count mentioned for the first game, 1,500 spectators saw the rematch. It hadn't been a crowd-pleasing start for the London team in its new league, dropping its first two contests. Things would not get easier for the Tecumsehs as they awaited the arrival of the powerful Allegheny team, coming off wins against the National League's Boston and Louisville clubs.

On May 9, Pud Galvin and the Alleghenys came to town. The Pittsburgh nine was feeling upbeat, having blanked Boston with the throwing arm and bat of Galvin. Soon to be nicknamed "The Little Steam Engine," the short, stocky Galvin's hard-driving style was beginning to attract attention. In London, Tecumseh catcher Powers remained on the sidelines, still nursing his broken digit, while local amateur Richard Southam played center field. The umpire was Scott Hastings, the newly signed professional from the Guelph Maple Leafs, and its captain, who brought along some of his teammates to see the game. The fielding of both teams was first-rate, and only four base hits were recorded. The Tecumsehs played better than in the Hartford games, but the locals made three of the game's four errors. In the end, the Allegheny shut out the Tecumsehs, 2–0, in their first IA championship contest.

The Tecumsehs next welcomed the Syracuse Stars for games May 11 and 12. Powers returned to the roster for the first game but was restricted to batting, his hand still too sore for catching. Powers was greeted with "a warm round of applause" when he first came to the plate and immediately responded with a base hit that he converted into a run. Tecumseh bats made life miserable for the Stars' pitcher, Harry McCormick, with 14 hits. Meanwhile, Goldsmith's pitching proved difficult for the visitors. The final score was 7–2 for London. In the second game, before a crowd of 2,000, the Stars and the Tecumsehs each put up six runs in the first inning in a game marked by errors on both sides. The teams settled down defensively, and after seven innings, the score was tied at 8–8. A ninth-inning hit and aggressive base running by Ed Somerville for the home team was the difference as London won, 9–8.[14]

After Allegheny took both games from London, they traveled east to Guelph, where they earned a split from the Maple Leafs. On May 10, Guelph's new pitcher, Sullivan, used his curveball to good effect, while newcomer C. J. Dixon made some dazzling plays at shortstop as the Maple Leafs overcame a slew of their own errors to prevail, 3–2. The next day, in wet conditions, the Alleghenys roared back, blanking the home team, 5–0, before 600 fans. Sullivan struggled for control of his curve with a wet ball, but that didn't seem to bother Galvin with his fastball. In all, Allegheny had eight base hits while Guelph could manage only two.[15] Meanwhile, it was reported that games played to date between League and Association teams had produced eight victories for teams representing each loop. League clubs were Chicago, Louisville, Cincinnati, St. Louis, and Boston, while the Association nines were from Syracuse, Indianapolis, and Allegheny City.[16]

The Tecumsehs traveled to Detroit, where they played the local professionals, with Powers finally back behind the plate where he caught an effective Bradley; Goldsmith was having a day off. The Tecumsehs won, 15–0.

The first game of the season against Guelph was eagerly anticipated. On May 17, before a "very large crowd" at the Maple Leaf home grounds, both teams put on a display of impeccable fielding in a rain-delayed game, their first matchup in the championship race. First baseman Bradley and shortstop

Somerville of the Tecumsehs were particularly sharp, and the outfielders for both teams found they had little to do. Goldsmith and Billy Smith pitched well for their respective clubs. Both teams scored single runs in the first inning, and the Tecumsehs added another in the fourth for the only other score in the game. At one point, umpire A. P. Crooks of Guelph, upset at abuse from the crowd and an argument with the Maple Leafs scorekeeper, threatened to walk off the field but was persuaded to stay. Guelph and London were held to two hits apiece, with no runs earned. Billy Smith struck out ten Tecumsehs while Goldsmith fanned five Maple Leafs. The final score was 2–1 for London as the Tecumsehs picked up where they left off the previous season.[17]

The exploits of the Guelph and London teams in the new International Association had drawn attention in Hamilton, whose Standards were a notch below the Maple Leafs and the Tecumsehs in the annual pursuit of the Silver Ball for the Canadian championship. The *Spectator* in that city expressed mock despair that Hamilton couldn't compete with the successful teams to the north and west. It opined: "That important industry, base ball, is showing great activity both in London and in Guelph, the only places in Canada which have sufficient spare capital to carry it on successfully."[18]

The Philadelphia Athletics, unaffiliated since being cut free by the National League at the end of the 1876 season, rolled through Southern Ontario on a road trip. On May 21, in Guelph, the hometown bats got to Athletics pitcher Sam Weaver early for a 3–0 lead after four innings in a game marked by the constant carping and umpire-baiting by Athletics players. Tired of yet another heaping of abuse on the Guelph grounds, four days after the London game, umpire A.P. Crooks left the game in the sixth inning, and a replacement had to be found for him. Philadelphia picked up two runs that inning to tie the game, 3–3. Guelph added two more in the eighth, and the Athletics responded with a single score at the bottom of the ninth, to fall short of the home team. The final score was 5–4 for the Maple Leafs.[19] The Athletics moved on to London to play the next day. A cold drizzle kept the crowd there at about 600 spectators, and the contest was called after three innings with London ahead, 1–0. The score might have been higher for the home nine, but, after making a fine hit, Goldsmith stumbled on the base paths and fell down, unable to advance past third base. Left-fielder Joe Hornung drew applause for a spectacular running catch, as did a double play on throws from Powers to Bradley to Dinnen.

Victoria Day, May 24, was the first big holiday of the summer and, for some time, playing the Guelph Maple Leafs had been a featured part of activities for the Tecumsehs. Not this year. The Boston Red Caps were the opposition for a heavily promoted game that was to be followed by fireworks at Tecumseh Park. More than 6,000 fans, perhaps as many as 8,000 by some counts, crammed the park to see the famous Boston nine who were vying with Louisville for the top spot in the League. It was the largest crowd of the season so far. The game pitted Goldsmith against pitcher Tommy Bond, formerly with Hartford and the Atlantics, who was on his way to a League-leading 40 wins. Bond replaced a trio of Chicago pitchers from 1876 who included Foghorn Bradley. A strong wind from the northwest was blamed for a large number of errors committed by both teams. The umpire was London jeweler Tom Gillean, a member of the amateur Atlantics who occasionally played with the Tecumsehs. Boston scored a single run in the second inning and three more in the third before London plated a run in the fourth. The Red Caps were winning, 7–3, by the ninth inning when the home team's bats came alive and London scored four runs to tie the game and send it to extra innings. The big crowd was on the edge of their seats as the Tecumsehs rallied and forced the game on. In the top of the tenth, Dinnen fouled out to the catcher while Hornung and Bradley were thrown out at first. (In the custom of the day and pursuant to Association rules, the home team batted in the top of the inning.) In the bottom of the tenth inning, hard-hitting Boston first-baseman Deacon White drove home the winning run with a hit over the head of Tecumseh center fielder Spencer, whose days were numbered on the team roster. The final was an 8–7 Boston victory.[20] It wasn't a win, and the opposition hadn't been Guelph, but the crowd was treated to an exciting game against the team that went on to win the National League championship that year.

Meanwhile, in Guelph, the Maple Leafs celebrated the Queen's birthday by defeating the Syracuse Stars, 5–4, before a crowd of nearly 2,000. Sullivan held the Stars to five hits while the home team made seven off McCormick. The game was a nail-biter for the crowd, with the score tied 4–4 after nine innings. In the 11th, Guelph put one run across the plate, while blanking Syracuse, for the win.[21] Guelph fans, too, had been treated to an exciting game, although one with a happier result than that in London.

The Tecumsehs packed their bags for a tour of the U.S. northeast, playing Lowell, Massachusetts, on May 28, where they won, 6–5, before heading to Boston for a Decoration Day game on May 30. In Lowell, the London team was tired after an all-night train ride from Albany and eked out the win, much to the displeasure of hometown supporters, who lustily booed and hissed at the visitors. In Boston, there would be no close, extra-inning game in the return match with the Red Caps. The Tecumsehs put two runs across the plate in the ninth inning but it was too little, too late, and Boston won, 6–2, before a crowd of 1,000.

During their time in Boston, Tecumseh catchers Powers and Knowdell traveled to Harvard College to inspect the new catcher's mask developed there. "They liked it so well that they have ordered one and expect to be able to wear it in the first game in London on their return," noted the *Advertiser*.[22] The Tecumsehs took two games to count in the championship series with Manchester, by scores of 3–0 and 5–0, before moving on to Fall River for a June 1 exhibition game, which they lost, 1–0. In that contest, Powers appeared to break another finger on his catching hand, still not wearing a glove and apparently not interested in getting one.

A championship game against Candy Cummings and his Lynn Live Oaks was next up. The Live Oaks scored a run off Goldsmith in the first inning, and it wasn't until the seventh that the Tecumsehs were able to put one of their own across the plate. In the top of the ninth, with two out, the umpire ruled that a batter failed to get to first base ahead of the throw and called him out. A Lynn runner was stranded at third as a result. The Live Oaks complained bitterly about the decision and urged the umpire to reverse himself so their man at third still had a chance to score. The crowd hissed its displeasure, and the argument became prolonged. With no end in sight, and a train to catch, Tecumseh captain Phil Powers agreed with the home team to call it a draw, so the final score was recorded as 1–1.[23]

In Brooklyn on June 4, for a game at the Union Grounds against the Chelseas, four former Tecumsehs—Ledwith, Wordsworth, Whalen, and Shevlin—showed up in the small crowd to renew acquaintances with the London players. Player fatigue from travel and loss of sleep, unfair decisions by the umpire, and yet another finger injured by Powers were blamed as the London club lost, 2–1, to the Chelseas. The following day, the Tecumsehs bounced back with a 4–2 victory in Binghamton over the Crickets in what the *Advertiser* called "the most exciting game of the trip." Hornung had a pivotal role in the game, the left fielder throwing a ball to home for a tag out within a foot of the plate. He also doubled in the seventh inning to drive-in a run and then took advantage of a wild throw to score. Hornung singled in the ninth and tallied along with Bradley when Somerville cleared the bases with a hard hit to the outfield. Doscher then connected for a hit to bring home Somerville, and the Tecumsehs had a three-run ninth inning for the come-from-behind victory.[24]

The light-hitting Spencer was dropped from the London lineup at about this time and was replaced in the outfield by John Magner, who had started the season in Columbus. Magner made an immediate impact in strengthening the Tecumseh offense. In a championship game played in Rochester on June 7, Magner hit two doubles and a single to bring in four of the six runs as London shut out the home team, 6–0. The following day, in an error-filled contest on a wet field in Syracuse, none of the Tecumseh bats showed up as the Stars won, 4–0.[25] The Stars were still riding high from shutting out the League nine of Hartford, 2–0, the previous day in Brooklyn. After a rest day on Sunday, the two teams went at it again on June 11 before a crowd of 1,200 spectators. The game was delayed when Stars pitcher McCormick failed to show. After a frantic search, he was found asleep in his room at a local hotel and was rushed onto the field. He might have wished he had stayed in bed, however, as the Tecumseh bats were lively, driving two runs across the plate in the first inning while McCormick was still rubbing sleep from his eyes. Despite poor fielding, the Tecumsehs had Goldsmith in fine form, largely baffling the hometown batters. With some aggressive running, the Stars scored a single run in the seventh inning, but the game ended with a 2–1 victory for London. McCormick not only lost the game, but was fined $20 for his untimely nap.[26]

The Tecumsehs ended their two-week tour of the northeast with a record of six wins, four losses, and a tie. In games to count toward the IA championship, they had three wins, no losses, and a tie. Before leaving home, they'd lost one championship game to Allegheny, but had won one from Guelph; so overall, they were 4–1–1 and in the thick of the pennant race.

The Chicago White Stockings came to town for a game on June 13 that drew 1,200 spectators to Tecumseh Park. This was the first meeting of the clubs since Chicago twice defeated the Tecumsehs in 1876, the season it captured the first League pennant. But it was a different Chicago team this year than the one that dominated London, 16–6 and 10–1, in those earlier contests. Batting leader Ross Barnes had been ill, and a change in League rules that no longer allowed batters to hit "fair-foul" hits didn't help him. They would now be called foul if they first landed fair and then rolled foul. Barnes had become accomplished at "fair-foul" hits. Likely ill, he was not in the lineup for the London game.

Even worse for the White Stockings was the decision by its star pitcher to quit his position. Eight days before playing the Tecumsehs, Albert Goodwill Spalding made his last appearance as a pitcher against Cincinnati on June 5 when he gave up five runs in one inning. The player-manager, who had won a League-leading 47 games in 1876, realized his talent was in decline and he moved to first base, where his play was considered barely adequate. As a pitcher in 1877, he had recorded only a single win by June. In this new position, he

8. Early 1877—The Magical Run Begins

would soon be wearing a black leather catching glove, a product his fledgling sporting goods business would soon introduce.[27] He was replaced in the pitching box by George Washington Bradley, the St. Louis hurler from 1876 that Spalding had urged team president William Hulbert to bring on board during the off-season.[28]

Chicago, overall, was no longer the force it had been in 1876 and would finish fifth in the six-team NL loop in 1877. Despite their change in fortunes, the Chicagos remained one of the leading teams in professional baseball, and London fans approached the rematch with apprehension.

For a time, it looked like another easy win for the White Stockings as the visitors put three runs across the plate in the first inning, while London managed only one. London picked up another run in the second followed by three scoreless innings for both teams. Chicago tallied again in the sixth to put the score at 4–2, but London replied with a single run in the top of the next inning. The crowd gasped and held its breath as Powers was bowled over by a Chicago player running home. He lay on the ground motionless for several minutes amid fears he was seriously injured in what was considered an unfortunate accident. Powers eventually gathered his senses and resumed his place behind home plate to a "hearty cheer" from the crowd. Another incident occurred when Chicago pitcher Bradley teamed up with shortstop John Peters and third baseman Cap Anson to demand that umpire Thomas Gillean reverse a call. A pitched ball had been missed by the Chicago catcher Joe Quinn and glanced off Gillean behind him. The Chicago players insisted the ball should have been called "dead" at that point, but Gillean would not budge. The *Advertiser* said it was clear the threesome was trying to "bull-doze" Gillean, thinking he didn't know the rules of the game. The paper was offended, in particular, by the behavior of Bradley, saying: "The 'phenomenal pitcher' of the 'Chicagos' does not seem quite so phenomenal, and could enhance his reputation as a gentleman by using a trifle more choice in the selection of the language he uses."[29]

London brought home two more runs in the top of the ninth inning. Final score: Tecumsehs 5, White Stockings 4. The crowd was jubilant as the outcome was taken as a reflection of the giant strides made by the home team. But it was also a sign of the decline under way in Chicago.

On June 18, the National League's last-place Cincinnati Red Stockings announced they had no funds for a planned eastern tour and disbanded after playing only five games on their schedule. Their players were released from their contracts. Several days later, stockholders reorganized club affairs and tried to retain players who had been released. In the interim, William Hulbert, the White Stockings president, swooped in to hire three of them. But after denunciation of the actions of the League president, Hulbert returned one of the three. Rather than do what he could as League president to help salvage the struggling team, whose loss would have reduced the League to a mere five teams, Hulbert had acted in the same self-interest that prompted him to create the League in the first place.

The Red Stockings limped on to finish the season as debate raged about whether its results should be included in the National League standings. Some papers chose to report them, others didn't. Five days later, Pud Galvin led Allegheny to a 6–0 shutout of Chicago, allowing only three hits. Galvin was becoming a dominant force for his team as it compiled one of the best records in the International Association. On June 30, Candy Cummings, a pitcher expected to be a star attraction in the Association, suddenly left Lynn, jumping to the reorganized Cincinnati club. Cummings and the Live Oaks had struggled, and the much-traveled curveballer sought a change. In the pitching box for the League's cellar-dwelling Red Stockings for the rest of the season, he won five games and lost 14. In a move that would seem strange, Cummings remained as president of the International Association, a post he had occupied for barely four months.[30] League president Hulbert must have smiled at the irony that one of the players now toiling in his organization was head of the rival association against which he was determined to prevail.

London's next game for the IA championship was against Guelph, on June 21 in London. Compared to other games between the two rivals, this was lightly attended, with only about 1,500 spectators on hand. Perhaps London followers of the game had become less passionate about the old rivalry now that London was so dominant. Or, more likely, it was because their games were no longer played on public holidays, which had always guaranteed a good turnout. This particular game was on a Thursday afternoon, when it was difficult for some Londoners to get away from work. The weather didn't help, with a strong wind sweeping clouds of dust across the diamond. Tecumseh batters had little trouble with the pitching of Billy Smith as he struggled with his control. Goldsmith proved effective again, and Powers, his finger injuries from weeks earlier nearly healed, caught a good game. London led throughout the game for a 5–2 victory.[31]

The Tecumsehs traveled to Hamilton the following day, where they defeated the Eries of Erie, Pennsylvania, 15–5. The next day, in London, the Tecumsehs won again, this time 12–1. Magner continued his hot batting with two triples, while Foghorn Bradley, who pitched, clobbered one into the outfield seats. Bradley also hit a double, a feat matched by Somerville and Doscher.

London entertained Guelph in brand-new Tecumseh Park on June 21, 1877. The Tecumseh mastery of the former Canadian champions continued as London won the game, 5–2. In this view, looking east, the Middlesex County courthouse and jail can be seen in the distance on the right. Home plate was later changed to what in this illustration is center field (*Canadian Illustrated News,* July 14, 1877).

The St. Louis Brown Stockings came through London on its eastern tour on June 25 for a game that had been promoted for some time. Fielding and pitching were strong for both teams, and no runners crossed home plate for eight innings. In the ninth inning, Tecumseh shortstop Somerville hit a double just inside the foul flag in left field to score base runners Dinnen and Bradley. In the bottom of the inning, the Brown Stockings scored an unearned run to come within one of the home team. Joe Blong, the St. Louis right fielder, hammered a big hit to center field with a runner on first and two out. Jake Knowdell ran for it and, jumping high, made a spectacular one-handed catch to win the game for the Tecumsehs.[32] The final score was 2–1, the second such victory for the London team over a League nine in the month of June.

The Eries were back, looking for more games against the London club, this time to be played in Toronto and Buffalo. In Toronto, the Tecumsehs sat Goldsmith and Powers, playing with two amateurs, and lost to the Pennsylvania visitors, 6–4. The next day, June 27, in Buffalo, the Tecumsehs won, 4–0.

On June 30, a double header to count in the championship series was played in London against the Buckeyes of Columbus. Before a crowd of about 700, the home team came from behind to defeat the visitors, 4–3, in a contest that featured sharp fielding by both sides. In the second game, the score was tied 4–4 in the tenth inning when the game was called on account of darkness.[33]

Dominion Day, July 1, was another holiday that had traditionally featured clashes between London and Guelph. The Hartford Dark Blues were visitors this time, and there was little celebration in London as the League visitors triumphed, 13–3, capitalizing on Tecumseh errors and their general sloppiness. After six innings, the score was tied at 3–3, but the Hartfords added three runs in the next inning and Goldsmith was pulled in favor of Bradley. He was no challenge for the League team and he allowed seven more runs in the ninth inning. The *Advertiser* grumped about the play before an "immense" crowd, saying it "was about the poorest we have seen the home team play this season."[34] The *Free Press* put the crowd at from 3,000–3,500 spectators, who, it said, fully expected the Tecumsehs to give the visitors "a hard tussle.... The home team in the last inning were not equal to many amateur teams—and the fault was the pitching." The latter paper didn't stop there, noting five Hartford runners crossed home plate in the ninth inning "on some of the worst muffing and fumbling that ever was seen on the Tecumseh grounds, the majority of the Tecumseh players seeming to vie with each other in dropping balls, throwing wild, and cutting up antics in the field." It suggested the Tecumseh directors should warn their players "to fulfill their engagements" if they wanted to enjoy continued support from the public.[35] The *Free Press*, as usual, was inclined to be more critical of the home team than its rival, the *Advertiser*, where team manager Gorman was local editor.

After all the successes of the Tecumsehs, the newspapers and fans were unwilling to accept defeat without feeling their team had played at the top of its game. The suspicion of fixes and thrown games was still widespread in baseball, on whose games betting was still prevalent. The criticism of the home team was not the first and would not be the last. It was, however, an ominous foreshadowing of developments that lay in the future.

But for now, the London professionals were still on the upswing and knew they had to buckle down for the next three months and play with purpose if they were to entertain any hopes of reaching the top and making baseball history.

9

Late 1877—Champions

A reorganized Cincinnati Red Stockings club was back in the National League by early July. Hulbert of the White Stockings had kept second baseman Jimmy Hallinan and substitute player Harry Smith, but returned left fielder Charley Jones. The National League president otherwise blithely ignored widespread outcry at his actions. Joseph Medill, publisher of the *Chicago Tribune*, was so incensed at the act of piracy by Hulbert that he decided to boycott the hometown team. The *Tribune*, which had the most widely read sports section in the entire Midwest, carried no stories or scores of White Stockings games until after Hulbert died in 1882.[1] The businessman who had founded the League on business principles, it turned out, was made to pay a price for his monkey business. Meanwhile, the Red Stockings, whose baseball pavilion was nearly blown down in a late June windstorm, were back in uniform on July 3 when they lost, 6–3, to the Louisville Grays. Their brief absence from the League and subsequent return would prove controversial. The question about what to do with the Cincinnati record was not resolved until December, when directors at a National League meeting discovered the Red Stockings had never paid their membership dues for the season, so all their games were thrown out of the championship race.[2] Boston remained League champions.

The Tecumsehs embarked on a western tour, making a first stop in Detroit on July 3, where they played Boston and lost, 10–2. On Independence Day, in Indianapolis, a doubleheader was scheduled to take advantage of large holiday crowds. The first game produced a 1–1 tie, and the second took 11 innings before the hometown Blues prevailed, 3–2. In the latter game, Bradley came in to pitch in the second inning after Goldsmith complained of severe pain in his side and withdrew. About 1,900 fans attended the second game, about which the hometown *Sentinel* said, "never has a finer game been played in this city than the one yesterday afternoon."[3] It noted that the Tecumsehs' fine hitting was undermined by a series of errors they committed. In a third game the following day, the Blues defeated London, 4–2, with Bradley again pitching for the still-disabled Goldsmith.

The Tecumsehs moved on to Columbus for a pair of games against the Buckeyes to count for the IA championship. On July 7, with Goldsmith back in the pitching circle, the visitors defeated the Buckeyes, 7–2, a report of which the *Sunday News* headlined, curiously: "The British Lion Claws the Eagle in a Frightful Manner."[4] Two days later, after Sunday off, a titanic struggle took place between the same two teams. Columbus pitcher Jim McCormick largely silenced the heavy-hitting Tecumsehs. He had a no-hitter going for seven innings, but surrendered four runs late in the game. Fielding was sharp by both sides as Columbus's second baseman, George Strief, scored a single run in the second inning. London replied with a single run scored by shortstop Ed Somerville in the eighth. Both sides were blanked in the ninth, forcing the 1–1 game into extra innings. Inning after inning went by without further scoring, and, after 18 were completed, the game was called on account of darkness, the result recorded as a tie.[5] The Tecumsehs traveled to Wheeling, West Virginia, where they played three games, losing the first, 9–1, but recovering to post 10–5 and 12–3 victories over the Standards. Next up for the Tecumsehs were two championship games against the Allegheny club, the only IA team to defeat London in the race for the pennant. On July 14, with Goldsmith reported as feeling "unwell," the Tecumsehs lost, 6–2. Two days later, Allegheny won again, this time 5–1. Allegheny now led the championship race for the Association with 13 wins, followed by Rochester with eight and London with seven. Hopes were still high for the Tecumsehs at home, however, where the *Advertiser* noted the team still faced 12 championship games on its own field and only two away. "Having the smallest number of defeats and the largest number of games to play at home, the chances are still in their favor for winning the pennant, notwithstanding their defeats in Pittsburgh," it reported.[6] Before leaving Pennsylvania, the Tecumsehs played two games in Erie, losing the first, 4–1, and bouncing back to take the second, 7–3.

The London team left Pittsburgh and Pennsylvania just in time to avoid being caught up in labor violence that swept the United States, shut down rail lines, and crippled commerce. The general strike had a particular flashpoint in Pittsburgh. The Great Railroad Strike of 1877 had its roots in the economic collapse of 1873, from which the United States was still suffering. Three million Americans were out of work, about one quarter of the country's labor force, when in May 1877, the Pennsylvania Railroad imposed its second 10 percent wage cut in two years. Railroads were determined to cut costs and had already been running fewer trains and doubling the size of the trains they did run, but without increasing the size of their crews. They laid off hundreds of crewmen. On July 13, the Baltimore and Ohio Railroad cut wages by 10 percent for anyone earning more than a $1 a day and reduced the work week to two or three days.

At the same time, the B&O increased shareholder dividends by 10 percent, sparking charges that the railroads were profiting at the expense of their workers. At the time, a wage of $1 a day was considered "absolute poverty" in Ohio.[7] Workers, angry and frustrated, decided the time had come to act. On July 16, in Baltimore, workers and sympathizers blocked trains. So, too, did rail workers in West Virginia. Strike action soon spread to Reading, Scranton, Harrisburg, Washington, Erie, and Pittsburgh, among other cities. All commercial train traffic was halted. Strike organizers held rallies in Pittsburgh and elsewhere to explain the situation to the public and the goals of workers. Violence flared in Baltimore, Chicago, Kansas City, San Francisco, St. Louis, and Pittsburgh amidst rumors the troublemakers were foreign agitators.

In Pittsburgh, resentment already existed about the Philadelphia-headquartered Pennsylvania Railroad, which the Smoky City felt had been squeezing it for profits for years. The authorities were alarmed at the mobs that disrupted rail operations and occupied railroad property on July 19. City police, reduced to a force of 11 men due to budget cuts, were ineffective even when augmented by 10 laid-off officers.[8] The local militia in Pittsburgh, of which Denny McKnight of the Allegheny club was a member, was called in to disperse strikers and their supporters, but they refused to act against their fellow citizens, for whom many in the city had great sympathy. They lay down their arms. Railroad officials demanded action, so Pennsylvania Governor John F. Hartranft called upon National Guard troops in Philadelphia to restore order. Arriving by rail, nearly 1,000 guardsmen approached the mob with fixed bayonets. They were taunted by strikers who set fire to railway cars and buildings. The troops fired into an unarmed crowd on a nearby embankment at one point, killing 20 including a woman and three children, and leaving many more wounded in a bloodbath that unleashed even more violence. Workers at nearby shops and iron mills joined the mayhem in the rail yards.

On the nights of July 21 and 22, strikers and their supporters exchanged gunfire with troops who had found refuge in a railway roundhouse. Another 20 residents and five guardsmen were killed in the standoff, and the mob set fire to the roundhouse in a bid to flush them out—or roast them alive. The troops escaped incineration by storming out of the structure and brandishing Gatling guns, panicking the crowd. The Philadelphians attempted to find shelter at the Allegheny Arsenal, but the local commandant in charge refused them entry, and they were forced to flee the burning city. A legislative report later said the troops were fired at from second-floor windows and from a police station where eight or 10 policemen were seen in uniform.[9] Union Station and 38 other buildings were set ablaze by a crowd variously estimated at from 10,000 to 30,000 men. Also damaged or burned were 104 locomotives, 46 passenger rail cars, and 506 rail cars.[10] The Pennsylvania Railroad later claimed that damage reached $4 million in Pittsburgh. Violence also characterized striking mobs in Buffalo, Harrisburg, and Chicago; but Pittsburgh was by far the bloodiest and most deadly confrontation. Governor Hartranft arrived in Pittsburgh on July 28 with thousands of National Guard troops, but by then, order had been restored. Railroad officials met with strikers, and many of their grievances were eventually resolved, with few charges laid. America's first general strike highlighted the growing divide between labor and capital wrought by industrialization. For a time, baseball, engaged in its own struggle between labor and capital, was forgotten.

Across the river from Pittsburgh, Allegheny City escaped the rioting, fires, and bloodshed, a fact attributed to the high regard rail workers there had for the Pennsylvania Railroad's general manager.[11] Things remained unsettled for a time, however. Many miles away, the *Guelph Mercury*, connected to many of the cities involved in the strike only because of baseball, carried this item:

> The *New York World*, speaking of the probable bad effect of the existing railroad troubles upon the interest in baseball says: All the games appointed to be played in Western Pennsylvania will have to be indefinitely postponed or played in another State. The condition of things in Pittsburgh almost leaves the noted Allegheny Club without a home, and the consequence is that the club's games on their own grounds may be set down as all off for the present. This includes the grand tournament arranged to take place on Aug. 20th, and the probability is that the scene of the tourney will be transferred to the Union Grounds, Brooklyn, that metropolis being about the only railroad centre, where law and order reign supreme, of course, excepting Boston.[12]

In the midst of all the confusion created by the rail strike on the regular flow of news, Pud Galvin was credited with pitching a perfect game on July 21 against the Champion City club in Springfield, Ohio. The Alleghenys defeated Springfield, 1–0, and Galvin faced the minimum 27 batters. Only later was it determined that Galvin had actually allowed a single hit in the contest.[13]

Guelph, which had secured only three wins toward the championship, was generating some unsettling news of its own. The Maple Leafs defeated Rochester, 7–3, on June 30, and again, 8–3, on July 2. In Rochester on July 4, before 6,000 Independence Day spectators, the Guelph nine lost, 7–2. After that game, rumors began to circulate that the Maple Leafs had disbanded. The *Guelph Mercury* saw fit to deny the story, asserting, rather weakly: "the Leafs will, in all probability, continue playing until the end of the season."[14] The lack of a spirited and categorical denial left the impression that something was afoot. On July 18, a meeting of Maple Leafs shareholders was called, for which full attendance was requested. Afterward, it was reported "the only business of importance done was the refusal of the management to accept the proposition from some parties in Buffalo to transfer the headquarters of the nine from Guelph to Buffalo."[15] It's hard to conceive that Guelph president George Sleeman, a diehard booster of his hometown, would consider leaving—or letting his team go—even if his team was struggling financially. Such a move would have gone against his grain.

It was becoming apparent that Buffalo was very anxious to get into the professional game, and the city was exploring opportunities. A few days earlier, a story had circulated that the Erie, Pennsylvania, team was considering a move to Buffalo because of poor fan support.[16] That effort had apparently failed, and the western New York city was still considering its options. The *Advertiser* in London gleefully picked up on a report from the *Buffalo Sunday Courier* about the overture to Guelph. The *Courier*, it noted, was "indignant at the idea of importing to that city a club that has been so badly beaten and occupies so poor a position as the Maple Leafs, of Guelph. It [the *Courier*] says better abandon the idea of putting a nine on the field this year and concentrate their means and energies to procuring a first-class team for next."[17]

As it turned out, Buffalo baseball promoters weren't prepared to wait long. On August 3, a professional team freshly organized in that city played its first game, a ten-inning scoreless tie with Rochester at the Rhode Island Street grounds.[18] Buffalo was anxious to make up for lost time, and the following season, as a member of the International Association, it would find great success.

Back home in London, the Tecumsehs had played host to Rochester on August 1 in another championship contest. In a game marked by flawless fielding and strong bats wielded by both teams, the Tecumsehs notched an 8–4 win. For right fielder John Magner, this was his last appearance for London before he left to join the Red Caps team in St. Paul, Minnesota. The following day, in a non-championship match, Rochester beat London, 4–2. The loss was particularly upsetting to the Tecumsehs because the visitors were held scoreless until the ninth inning when they finally solved Goldsmith, batting across four runs. On August 4 and 6, London welcomed the Manchesters to Tecumseh

Park for two championship games. The first game, described as one of the best played on the new ball field, saw London pull off two double plays, a triple by Bradley and "a difficult foul caught by Hornung, who injured himself by colliding with a buggy in the attempt." Also noted was a fine throw from center field by Bill Reid, a player from the amateur Atlantics who replaced Magner for the game. The final score was 4–1 for London. In the second game, Manchester was held hitless for five innings. London had no such problem, romping to a 12–4 win. The next day, Guelph arrived for a championship game with London and yet again came up short, losing 7–3 to the Tecumsehs. The win put London in second place in the IA standings behind Allegheny.

Back in Guelph, the Maple Leafs played the Manchesters on August 7 and 8, winning the first game, 6–5, but dropping the second, 5–4. London played its fourth and final championship game of the season against Guelph on August 10 in London and again defeated the Leafs, this time 6–2, solidifying its hold on second place in the pennant race. In its account of the game under the headline, "The Old, Old Story," the *Guelph Mercury* acknowledged London had earned bragging rights by downing the Maple Leafs yet again. "Guelph owns up to have been squarely beaten by the Tecumsehs, four games for the International championship, and it would please the Leafs to see their old rivals come out at the head of the list."[19] Followers of London must have rubbed their eyes in disbelief. Graciousness in defeat had not been the hallmark of either the Guelph or London newspapers, poison appearing in their accounts more often than praise.

More exhibition games were played between the two great rivals at the upcoming Civic Holidays, observed as they were on different dates in London, Guelph, Toronto, and Hamilton. In the well-attended game in Toronto which London won 6–0, London catcher Phil Powers wore his catcher's mask for the first time "and it saved him from a broken face, a sharp foul tip striking it and rebounding without doing any injury."[20] He wasn't the first IA catcher to don a mask, however. On July 11, Pete Hotaling of Syracuse wore a wire one, having been struck in the eye by a foul tip a month earlier and seeking some protection from a repeat. Hotaling and teammate Al Hall used the team mask often during the rest of the season. St. Louis replacement catcher Mike Dorgan was the first National Leaguer to wear a mask on August 8 when he entered a game to replace catcher John Clapp, whose cheek had just been smashed by a foul tip.[21] The device was beginning to catch on.

On August 15, during London's Civic Holiday game, Guelph tied the Tecumsehs before a crowd of about 2,000. The ten-inning game was called with the score at 7–7 because the visitors had to catch their train home. It wasn't a win for Guelph, but it was enough to make Maple Leafs supporters happy after so many recent defeats at the hands of London. Powers was again sporting his mask.[22] The following day, as the Tecumsehs departed for the holiday game in Hamilton, the *Advertiser* calculated that London had already played 52 games against professional clubs, winning 29, losing 18, and recording five ties. In Hamilton, London defeated Guelph, 15–4, one of the worst drubbings the Maple Leafs ever suffered at the hands of their rivals, sending their fans back into a funk.

The Tecumsehs still had another championship game to play against the Rochesters, who were nipping at London's heels for second place. So an Eastern tour to accommodate it began after the exhibition game in Hamilton. On August 18 in Rochester, Tommy Smith of the Guelph team played outfield for London as it took 13 innings to defeat the home team, 4–3. Noteworthy were injuries to the hands of Powers and Knowdell, the latter having replaced Powers behind the plate, only to dislocate a finger. Two days later, in a non-championship game, London again won, this time, 6–3. In the next several days, the Tecumsehs lost to Auburn, 3–0, bounced back to defeat them, 6–3, then downed Hornellsville, 4–0 and 16–2, before rolling into the new hotbed of baseball, Buffalo, on August 25. Many of the Tecumsehs were nursing injuries but they still managed to overcome the home team, 9–4. Buffalo unveiled a 17-year-old Brooklyn lad named Larry Corcoran as its newly signed pitcher. He featured a curveball and surprisingly good control in the pitcher's box for someone his age. The slightly built Corcoran was embarking on a decade-long professional career that would see him amass 30 or more victories in four seasons with Chicago. There, in 1881, manager Cap Anson teamed him up with Fred Goldsmith, in his post–Tecumseh days, in what is generally accepted as the first use of a formal pitching rotation by a team. As early as the 1877 season, some teams in the International Association had already decided not to rely on one pitcher to pitch every inning of every game. They handed off one in five starts to their secondary pitchers.[23]

While the Tecumsehs were out of the country, the *Guelph Mercury* noted some changes with the Maple Leafs. Tommy Smith had signed with the Tecumsehs, Dixon left to become shortstop for Rochester, and Sullivan joined him there as a pitcher. Despite allowing his professionals to disperse, president George Sleeman announced the team was building a new ball field adjacent to its home at Exhibition Grounds. His motivation was not clear. Perhaps Sleeman felt Guelph had to keep pace with London. Or maybe he was hatching some grand plan. Regardless, the paper said this venture was undertaken "so that Guelph will be able to boast of the largest, best, and most convenient grounds in Canada or the United States."[24] Several days later, the same paper said Maple Leafs catcher Marshall Quinton was joining the Tecumsehs, where receivers Powers and Knowdell "had their fingers completely spoiled."[25] Guelph was winding down from a disappointing season in which it had battled with the lowly Live Oaks of Lynn for last place in the seven-team Association pennant race.

By August, questions about the integrity of games and players were being raised in the National League, where Cincinnati had struggled and the League president had poached its players. The impact of gamblers and gambling on the game had continued despite the expressed desire of the League and the Association to stamp it out. But such entrenched practices as gambling in poolrooms, called "pool-selling," did not disappear overnight. Much was at stake. It was said that wagering on a single game in larger New York poolrooms could reach as much as $70,000. Boston had eight poolrooms operating.[26]

In Boston, the Red Caps had started the season strongly, its roster still including several members of the four-time National Association champions. Tommy Bond, the new pitcher, had come from Hartford and proved to be effective, racking up a League-leading 40 wins. Louisville was also strong, led by pitcher Jim Devlin on his way to winning 35 games. Devlin pitched every game and was also one of the Grays' best hitters. Louisville passed Boston in the standings in early August and appeared headed for the pennant. By August 13, Louisville's record stood at 27–13, with only 15 more games to play. To win the pennant, the Grays needed to win about half those games. But they collapsed, losing eight in a row. Louisville dropped four to Boston, then suffered three losses and managed to tie the Hartfords in Brooklyn.

Observers became suspicious, especially when they noted that four Grays were suddenly wearing expensive diamond stickpins and rings. They were Devlin, who threw poorly during that stretch of games; veteran shortstop and catcher William Craver, the team captain (who had been tossed from Chicago in 1870 for gambling and insubordination); outfielder George Hall, whose career in the old National Association produced rumors of corruption; and newcomer Alfred Nichols, a former member of the New York Mutuals, a team long associated with gambling and with whom he retained some connections.

During their final road trip, Grays vice-president Charles E. Chase received an anonymous telegram advising him that gamblers were betting heavily against his team. A second message, repeating the assertion, arrived before a game in Brooklyn, where Devlin, Nichols, and Hall all made costly errors. Confronted by Chase with his suspicions, Devlin and Hall cracked and admitted they had been dealing with gamblers. They implicated Nichols and Craver, the latter of whom refused Chase's request to obtain telegrams received and sent to him during the season. Nichols and Craver admitted nothing. An investigation later showed that telegrams to and from Devlin and Hall revealed that all four players had been communicating with gamblers and had agreed to "fix" games. In late October, Louisville formally expelled Devlin, Hall, and Nichols for "selling" games and Craver for disobeying orders. In December, League president William Hulbert expelled all four players from baseball for life.[27] The episode gave him the perfect opportunity to put some concrete action behind his pious words about the need to clean up the game.

The Chicago White Stockings, among the weaker teams during the National League's 1877 season, made their second appearance in London at the end of August. It marked the beginning of a lengthy tour for the club. About 2,000 spectators turned out to see the still-battered Tecumsehs face the visitors on August 27. Powers and Knowdell, the catchers, were still nursing sore hands, as was shortstop Ed Somerville. Filling in was local amateur Tom Gillean, along with Marshall Quinton, newly acquired from the Guelph Maple Leafs, and earlier Leafs acquisition Tommy Smith. Chicago pitcher George Washington Bradley struggled against the Tecumseh bats, giving up 11 base hits. Meanwhile, Goldsmith surrendered only seven hits for London. Chicago scored its first run in the second inning, but the home team put up two in the fourth before Chicago responded with its own run to tie the game. Goldsmith's delivery kept the visitors largely at bay, and London added two more tallies in the sixth. In the ninth inning, Chicago scored one run and thought it had scored another when Cap Anson ran home on a double by shortstop John Peters. But Anson was called out when, in the opinion of umpire C. W. Andrus, the ball thrown by Dutch Hornung from left field reached home plate before the runner. Anson vociferously disputed the call and created a scene, prompting the crowd to get on him. The *Free Press* noted that the player's outburst marred the game for the crowd, "who had all along testified their appreciation of good play on both sides by unstinted applause, yelled 'out' as vociferously and as their lungs could." The journal also complained that the umpire wasted time as he "conversed too much entirely with the 'big man' of the Chicagos after giving his decision."[28] Regardless, the call stood, and London took the game, 4–3.

In Guelph, to help the Maple Leafs celebrate the town's Civic Holiday on August 29, the Tecumsehs gave their longtime rivals something to celebrate: a 6–6 tie in a game called after nine innings because London had to catch a train home. Foghorn Bradley pitched for the visitors and proved no mystery for Maple Leafs batters. He was replaced in the fifth inning by Goldsmith, who fared little better. Billy Smith of the Leafs allowed only three base hits to the normally heavy-hitting visitors. Guelph was comfortably ahead, 6–1, after five innings. In the following inning, the Tecumsehs capitalized on Maple Leafs errors to score three runs. Going into the bottom of the ninth inning, the score remained at 6–4 when the visiting team came to bat as was the custom, and rule, of the day. London picked up two runs to tie the game and snatch away the chance of Guelph ending a winless streak with London that had extended to 12 games over two seasons.[29] The game marked the end of Guelph's season and prompted the *Advertiser* to take a cheap shot. "The Guelph club managers are entitled to every praise for the favors bestowed upon the Tecumsehs in not allowing their team to win a game off them in two years. Such generosity is seldom witnessed."[30] The dig was probably a reply to a similar one contained in the *Mercury's* report of the same Civic Holiday contest that ended with the 6–6 tie.

> The game, up to the last three innings, was a very pleasant one. It was then, however, marred by the totally unnecessary "kicking" of the Tecumsehs. It ill became them to indulge in their penchant at Guelph, after the favors they have received at the hands of the Guelph managers, but it just shows what they would do, when they are in a tight place. Goldsmith and Gillean showed themselves closely related to—well, by no means to gentlemen.

The on-again, off-again good feelings between the Canadian baseball rivals was definitely off again, contributed to significantly by their hometown newspapers, which had returned to their usual hawkish form.

In early September, it was learned that Buffalo had formally applied for entry into the International Association for the 1878 season. But if they failed to discharge shortstop Louis Say, who had been expelled by the Association, it would undermine their chances of acceptance. In other news, it was reported that Candy Cummings, the former IA president who had started the season with the Live Oaks of Lynn in the Association, then had jumped to Cincinnati in the League, was on the move again. He had left the Red Stockings, where he pitched in 19 games and won five of them. The *Advertiser* printed an item that appeared in the *Chicago Sunday Tribune* of September 2 suggesting Cincinnati had looked north to London to replace Cummings. It also shed light on the impact Tecumsehs pitcher Fred Goldsmith was having on the game and how his fame was spreading. The tidbit was particularly interesting in light of the departure of Cummings from Cincinnati, and revealing about the Tecumsehs, from an apparent insider.

> A note from a member of the Tecumseh Club of London, Ont., gives a rather amusing account of the pilgrimage of a brother of J. Wayne Neff, the gentle-

manly and courteous president of the new Cincinnati Club. It seems from the letter that the brother went up to London to secure the services of Goldsmith to pitch for next year's Cincinnati; and that the visit was timed to cut off the arrival of the Chicago Club, who were due two days later. The writer adds: Neff wanted to cut off Spalding, whom he suspected of also wanting Goldsmith, and he had about two days' start, but made no encouraging progress. I am not sure whether Spalding wanted Goldsmith or not, but I suppose he did. It is said that he went to the managers and asked about the matter, and they told him that both Goldsmith and Phil Powers were under contract. Unlike the Cincinnati man, Spalding wasted no more words about the matter, but went his way. The fact is, Goldsmith has been cleverly treated here and likes the people, the managers, the team, and the city. He has always had his money and always will. I don't mind adding that we are proud of our Tecumseh Club, and propose to keep them going further. I may say that it takes money to do it. We expect to have a deficiency of about $3,000 this season, and hardly less next season, unless times improve; but we can and will raise this sum to support an amusement which we fancy more than any other. Nobody can get any player we want to keep.[31]

Alarmed at the interest League teams had shown in one of its players, and to ensure its contracts were honored by them, London decided to join the League Alliance.[32] The Tecumsehs furnished NL secretary Nick Young with a list of players they had under contract so other teams could not poach them.

A game scheduled for September 7 in London was canceled when Indianapolis failed to show. Two games planned with Hornellsville in London were also canceled when the Hornells refused to release a player named Baker who had been blacklisted by the International Association. To fill the void, and for an interesting diversion, the Tecumsehs played a match of cricket against the London club and administered what was described as a "severe defeat" on the cricketers by relying on superior fielding.[33] In Guelph, unwilling to quit playing ball while the sun was still warm, the Maple Leafs played an exhibition game against its amateur Maple Leaf club. George Sleeman pitched for the "professionals," whose ranks were thin, so amateurs were called upon to fill out the roster. The amateurs won by a score of 16–10.[34] Fierce competitor that he was, Sleeman couldn't take the loss, and two days later, a rematch was held. This time, he pitched the professionals to a 25–17 victory. Likewise, in London, a return match was played between the Tecumsehs and the cricket club. The baseball team was handily defeated in this contest largely because of its poor work with the cricket bat.[35]

In Pittsburgh, a three-team tournament among Allegheny, Syracuse, and Indianapolis took place in mid–September. The city was trying to get back to normal after the violence and destruction wrought by the rail strike of late July. The tournament ended in a tie, with each team recording two wins and two losses. The event was moved to Chicago, where Syracuse won it. On September 23, the tournament was denounced as a "swindle" by the *Chicago Times*, the paper claiming the outcome of games was determined by gamblers. The following day, two Allegheny players confirmed that games in Chicago were "sold" by two of their fellow players and that three of the Allegheny directors had bet on the winners from Syracuse.[36] More news of corruption still plaguing the game soon appeared when the Louisville newspaper charged Devlin and Hall of the hometown Grays with throwing the previous day's game to Indianapolis.

Baseball still had a long way to go to rid itself of the scourge of gambling, in both the Association and the League. Meanwhile, the *Chicago Post* reported that it appeared likely that Louisville and Hartford would drop out of the struggling National League, leaving it with only four teams for the 1878 season. If that occurred, it opined, Chicago might drop out, too, adding mysteriously: "President Hurlburt [sic] has, however, gone east, and it is suspected that he may transact some startling business that will throw the base ball world into commotion."[37]

The Tecumsehs left for a week's tour of New York State amid reports

This is a game between the London Tecumsehs and Syracuse Stars, in a championship match for the International Association pennant, during 1877, or possibly 1878. The Middlesex County courthouse can be seen in the distance in this composite image that also shows the stands for scorers, reporters and other officials (Western Archives, Western University, London, Ontario, AFC49.1.20131).

that Candy Cummings, curveball pitcher and former IA president (replaced by Allegheny president Denny McKnight), had landed in Buffalo, where he was playing shortstop.[38] The Tecumsehs played four exhibition games, two in Danville and two in Binghamton, the only loss a 17–4 rout at the hands of the latter team on September 20. While they were on the road, it was learned that the Live Oaks of Lynn and the Buckeyes in Columbus had disbanded, and the likelihood was that the championship of the IA would be decided by a game in London between the Tecumsehs and Allegheny.[39] London's only championship game on the eastern trip was a September 21 contest it lost, 3–1, to Rochester, which didn't alter the nature or importance of the upcoming Tecumseh–Allegheny game. A non-championship game the following day saw Rochester shut out the London visitors, 1–0.[40]

The same day, J. A. Williams, secretary of the International Association, sent a letter to George Sleeman in Guelph: "I am very much pleased to receive your letter of the 20th informing me that your club had not disbanded. It was so reported in all the papers and no contradiction appearing, I took it for granted it must be true, though I wrote you but a day or two since inquiring about it."[41] Rumors that the Maple Leafs had disbanded had been circulating for weeks, and letting several of its professionals leave before the season was over had only fed into that perception.

Back in London, London tied a game with the touring Fall River, Massachusetts, team, 4–4. The next day, the plucky visitors handed London a 15–9 defeat, one of the worst drubbings for the home team all season. The exhibition matches did not affect the IA standings; London had reached the top. The Tecumsehs recovered to eke out a 6–5 win on September 26 and were no doubt glad when the New Englanders left town.[42]

Next to appear on the Tecumseh grounds was the Milwaukee club for three exhibition games that attracted large crowds. The first game saw both teams wield their lumber, with London prevailing, 11–8. Milwaukee turned the tables in the second game, embarrassing the home team 11–1. In the third game, before "a large number of spectators" on Saturday afternoon, London was leading 10–8 when manager Richard Southam "unfortunately" agreed to give the visitors their share of gate proceeds, as the *Free Press* put it. The manager of the Milwaukees appeared unwilling to complete the game, in which his team was trailing, and in the eighth inning led his players from the field, amidst complaints about the pitching of Goldsmith. After 15 minutes, with the refusal of Milwaukee to return to the field, the game was declared a 9–0 victory for London.[43] The Milwaukees continued east to Buffalo, where on October 1 they defeated the new professional nine, 3–2.

Ed Somerville, the reliable shortstop for the Tecumsehs, had taken ill and missed the Milwaukee games. Mike Dinnen, the second baseman, was hurt. It was doubtful they would be back in action for the pennant-deciding game against Allegheny on October 2 in London. This caused concern among team followers, because the Tecumsehs had lost all three of their previous games against the Pittsburgh club and needed to play at their best. On October 1, the same day Allegheny arrived in London, Somerville died, a victim of pneumonia, or, as the *New York Times* put it, "hemorrhage of the lungs."[44] His death was a shock and was keenly felt. A funeral was held at his home on Clarence Street, attended by stockholders of the Tecumseh club and players from local amateur teams. His teammates acted as pallbearers as his casket was placed on an eastbound express train destined for his home in New Haven, Connecticut, where interment would take place.[45] The loss of the 24-year-old shortstop with good hands on the eve of the biggest game of the season was a major distraction for the Tecumsehs. Somehow, Harry Gorman quickly found Cincinnati native Mike Burke to replace Somerville. The move paid off for a team in mourning, as Burke would soon demonstrate.

The championship game had been arranged on relatively short notice for Tuesday afternoon, October 2. It wasn't an ideal day of the week to draw a large crowd, despite the Great Western Railway's offer of a special fare for baseball followers from neighboring communities and its offer to hold trains at the London station if the game ran late.[46] The *Advertiser* estimated the crowd at Tecumseh Park that day at from 1,500–1,600 spectators, while the *Free Press* reported as many as 2,000 were on hand. Umpire was Mike Dinnen, hurt and unable to play his position at second base, but recommended to Allegheny as a fair arbiter by the captain of the departing Milwaukees.

The game itself was described as the most exciting contest ever witnessed on the new ball grounds, as sharp fielding and strong pitching kept both teams scoreless for six innings. Sparkling catches were made by both teams, starting with John McKelvey, for Allegheny, a one-hander in center field on a hard hit by Burke in the top of the first inning. He also made a line-drive hit in the bottom of the same inning. Tecumsehs catcher Phil Powers collected a particularly difficult foul pop-up at one point. Burke was aggressive, stealing bases, and Goldsmith pitched as fine a game as had been witnessed by the hometown crowd.

Controversy erupted in the bottom of the fifth inning, however, when Allegheny veteran second baseman Chick Fulmer stepped outside the lines marking the batter's position at the plate as a pitch was delivered. Powers was familiar with Fulmer's habit and had drawn umpire Dinnen's attention to it.

Dinnen called Fulmer out, sparking an uproar that took some time to die down, but Dinnen would not change his mind. At another point in the game, an irate Allegheny pitcher, Pud Galvin, unleashed a barrage of bad language, directing it at the crowd, a display that prompted the *Advertiser* to note: "he may thank the forbearance of Londoners for not receiving some physical reminder that such insolence is not appreciated."

In the bottom of the sixth inning, Allegheny recorded hits by first baseman Goodman and shortstop Nelson, with two men out. Galvin came to bat with a chance to put the visitors on the scoreboard. But for the third time in the game, Goldsmith struck him out. The crowd responded "vociferously," as the *Free Press* put it. In the top of the seventh, Galvin returned the favor by fanning leadoff batter Goldsmith. Burke reached first on a fielding error by Fulmer, and he advanced to second on a hit by Dutch Hornung. Burke then stole third. Foghorn Bradley connected for a triple that scored Burke and Hornung. Marshall Quinton's sacrifice single brought Bradley home, and the Tecumsehs led, 3–0. Allegheny players failed to get a hit in the bottom of the inning. The eighth inning was scoreless. Center fielder Tommy Smith was struck out by Galvin to start the ninth inning for the home team. Powers was next up and he doubled, prompting cheers from a crowd that was anxious for insurance runs. Goldsmith singled, and Powers made it home, helped by a "muff" near the plate by Allegheny catcher Dolan. As that happened at home, an alert Goldsmith raced to third. Burke again proved his worth, with a timely hit to right field that scored Goldsmith to "deafening applause" from the stands. Hornung then singled, advancing Burke to second, who continued on to third on a wild throw to first. Hornung advanced to second on the play but was hung up there when Quinton flew out to Galvin, and Bradley popped up to Dolan, to retire the side.

Going into the bottom of the ninth inning, the Tecumsehs had played errorless ball and Goldsmith had baffled the Allegheny batters. Things soon changed. Leadoff batter McKelvey fouled out to Powers. Next up, Nelson connected for a single and advanced to second on a wild pitch by Goldsmith, the home team's first error. Galvin struck out but third baseman Williamson connected for a hit. Powers tried to pick off Williamson at second base but overthrew Quinton, and the ball continued to the outfield, where Smith bobbled it. The two errors allowed both Nelson and Williamson to cross the plate, and it looked like the visitors suddenly had some momentum with two outs. Fulmer, however, popped up a foul that was caught by Powers, ending Allegheny's hopes. The Tecumsehs won, 5–2, for their first-ever victory against Allegheny. After the game and on-field celebrations, the victors were entertained at the Tecumseh House Hotel by Tecumseh vice-president W. H. Birrell and his wife. Players received flowers and praise for bringing glory to the city. The joy was tempered by the loss of Ed Somerville, in whose memory the Tecumsehs wore black crepe on their uniforms. An exhibition game the following day between the two teams was anti-climactic. Goldsmith's arm was sore, and he retired from the pitching box to be replaced by Bradley. Galvin and Quinton each homered for their teams in what was a lackluster, error-filled game before a small crowd. The final score was 22–6 for Allegheny as their batters easily solved Bradley.

London had won the International Association pennant, through its claim would not be made official until the Association met several months later. However, it was immediately acknowledged by most observers, including Henry Chadwick and the *New York Clipper*, that there was no question it was London's:

> Nothing better could have happened for the advancement of the popularity of baseball in Canada, for one thing, or to give a new impetus to the International Association pennant race of 1878 for another, than the success of the Canada Tecumsehs in winning the International championship, as they have done. It will not hurt us on this side of the lakes much, but it will do the Canadian baseballists a heap of good. The Tecumsehs by their victory last week over the Alleghenies [sic] won a double triumph, they having previously won the Canadian championship with ease.[47]

The Tecumsehs' triumph was an amazing accomplishment for a city of 18,000 that had competed with teams from large American cities—and defeated many of them. The Tecumsehs, along with Guelph, had put the "international" in the International Association, and had proven to be among the top teams in all of professional baseball. And for the second straight year, London also claimed the Silver Ball as national champions.

The London club had played 80 games in the 1877 season, winning 47, losing 26, and tying seven. They won all their games for the International Association championship except three against Allegheny and one against Rochester. The final standings saw London with 14 wins against four losses. Allegheny was second, with 11 wins and five losses. Rochester finished third with eight wins and eight losses, followed by Manchester (7–9), Guelph (4–12), and Columbus (2–8). The Maple Leafs recorded 17 wins and 16 losses in their season, noteworthy victories having been recorded against Allegheny, Rochester (two), and Syracuse (two).[48] The Tecumsehs played nine games against League clubs, winning three—two from Chicago and one from St. Louis. *The Free Press* recounted the team record and remarked: "This record is a very creditable one, and the friends of the team have reason to feel proud of their success. The best of feeling prevailed amongst the members during the five months they played together, and to this happy condition of affairs most of their success is attributable."[49]

Phil Powers and Ed Somerville, the captain and co-captain, were credited with keeping the good feelings alive during the long season. Within days, it was reported that all of players, except Jake Knowdell, had signed on for the 1878 season. Knowdell was off to play for Milwaukee, which would become a member of the National League.

On October 6, the final day of the League season, Chicago relied on local 18-year-old Lawrence Reis to shut out Louisville, 4–0. Boston claimed the League championship with a record of 42 wins and 18 losses, followed by Louisville, seven games back at 35–25. Hartford was third, then St. Louis, Chicago, and Cincinnati. Syracuse was considered champion of the League Alliance by virtue of having won a dozen games against League teams, including two over Boston.[50]

Independent Buffalo closed its short season with a 3–0 loss to Rochester on October 16. It had been a winner at the box office, recording a profit of $490, the only professional baseball team to end the year in the black.[51] Optimism was high about the future of baseball in the western New York city. The NL champion Boston Red Caps, meanwhile, lost an estimated $1,500; Chicago, $6,000; St. Louis, $8,000; Louisville, $2,000; and Hartford, $2,230, despite moving its home games to the baseball hotbed of Brooklyn specifically to improve its finances. In the International Association, Allegheny finished the season $8,000 in the red, and the Tecumseh loss was estimated at $3,000.[52]

Even with the attempts by William Hulbert and the National League to put baseball on a businesslike footing, the game remained a risky business at best. The future of his organization was not assured, and he and the other powers behind the League were likely having sleepless nights as they looked ahead.

10

Between Innings

The Allegheny Club disagreed with Henry Chadwick's assertion in the *New York Clipper* that the Tecumsehs had carried off the honors in the International Association. In a letter from the Allegheny secretary dated October 10, the club laid out its argument to the *Clipper* that it deserved the championship pennant. Allegheny had won 15 games to 14 for the London team, the secretary insisted. The Tecumsehs, he claimed, had been awarded one win too many against Columbus. And it was argued that the games played by the Maple Leafs should not have been counted in the standings "as that organization has no nine other than some local players, the original nine having been disbanded long since, some of their players today being in the Tecumseh and Rochester nines." If the *Clipper* wasn't prepared to count the Live Oaks games because that team disbanded, it wasn't appropriate to count the Maple Leaf games in calculating the standings, Allegheny said. The *Clipper* dutifully published the claim, but Chadwick seemed to hold his nose in so doing. In a preamble, he wrote:

> We give place below to a statistical statement from the secretary of the Allegheny Club, in which is claimed the International championship on the grounds that the Maple Leaf club disbanded when they gave up their professional players, or most of them. While any club which originally enters the arena stands ready to play its series of games with a legal club team, it matters not whether it is the original team or a new nine. The Maple Leaf Club has not disbanded, and by the secretary's own showing the Tecumsehs tie [Allegheny] in won games on a legal count, and win by fewest defeats.[1]

Just a couple of days later, it was reported that the Allegheny club had "gone by the board with upward of $8,000 in debt."[2] Henry Gorman couldn't let the Allegheny claim go unchallenged, however, notwithstanding the clear support for London from Chadwick. In his own letter published in the *Clipper*, Gorman said: "Much amusement has been created here over the charming innocence displayed by the secretary of the Alleghenys in his claim to the championship." Gorman said the Allegheny secretary did not understand the rules, especially as it related to two games London tied with Columbus that Allegheny claimed had been credited as London wins. The Tecumsehs had two other victories over the Buckeyes, but the Allegheny club insisted only one should have been recorded. Gorman suggested the Allegheny secretary should "study up the rules before he ventures to air his knowledge again in print." For good measure, he noted that the Pittsburgh club had refused to play a championship game that had been arranged with Guelph on the Allegheny grounds. Gorman suggested Allegheny should have their winning record reduced by two games, leaving the club in fourth place.[3]

Entering the fray, it appears, was George Sleeman. In a letter to the *Clipper*, signed simply as "Canadian," he sought to set the record straight and defend the Maple Leafs from the claim that Guelph had refused to play those two games in Allegheny City. "Allow me to say, as one who writes with full knowledge of the facts, that the Maple Leafs kept together a good nine up to the end of the season," it read. "Canadian" noted that two games had been played with Allegheny in Guelph early in the season.

In June, the Maple Leafs had planned a road trip to the United States, specifically to accommodate championship games in Pittsburgh and Columbus. At first, the writer said, the games against Allegheny were scheduled for June 18 and 19.

> But on May 20 Mr. McKnight, for the Alleghenys, telegraphed that he couldn't give those days they had offered to him, and which had been accepted, to Indianapolis. Correspondence ensued, Mr. McKnight admitting that there had been a blunder, and suggesting that the Maple Leafs alter their arrangements to suit him. This Mr. Sleeman was unable to do. The Maple Leafs do not deserve to be taunted with lack of desire or inability to meet their engagements, at least by the Alleghenys, at whose hands not only they, but other International clubs have been treated so badly.[4]

No more was heard of the matter until the International Association's annual meeting held in Buffalo in February, when a report on the dispute was filed by the judiciary committee.

Over in the National League, the situation was looking grim and unstable as it looked back on its second season. Because of their financial losses, Louisville, St. Louis, and Hartford were stepping away from the six-team loop. On the field, the League hadn't been particularly successful either. During 1877, League teams lost seventy-two times to non–League teams in fewer than 200 meetings. Once games were set aside that had been played against amateur teams and "picked" nines, their record against other professional clubs was only slightly better than .500. And the League certainly had no monopoly on the top players of the day, it has been observed. "Despite its high-priced tickets and other classy features, the League was no more than the equal of the 1877 International Association in playing talent, with the players in the top six IA clubs having more past and future years of 'big league' baseball among them than had the six clubs of the NL."[5]

By contrast, the International Association, a worthy successor to the old National Association in the eyes of many fans and players, had enjoyed a modestly successful start. The rather loosely knit organization appealed to players who wanted a say in the affairs of their loop and wished to stay closer to their roots, playing for hometown pride, often in cooperatives. It certainly had no intention of subjugating itself to the National League, and there were no reasons, in terms of player talent or financial success, to do so. In his detailed history of 18 professional baseball organizations since 1871, David Pietrusza put the situation this way:

> From a modern perspective, it would be tempting to term the association a "minor league." Yet at the time, it could not be so easily pigeonholed. Despite a rather miserable form of organization, a good caliber of ball was played by these nines. International Association and National League players were equally named to nationally recognized all-star teams. Additionally, of course, the very idea of a minor league simply did not yet exist.[6]

Others, years later, would relegate the International Association to minor league status. Yet the National Association, upon which it was largely modeled, with similar flaws, is today considered a major league.

The annual convention of the National League was scheduled for the Kennard House Hotel in Cleveland beginning December 5. There was plenty on the agenda. The record of the Cincinnati club was thrown out in its entirety when it was learned that the team had failed to pay its fee to enter the League championship. Hartford was expelled, St. Louis resigned, and the lifetime bans imposed on Louisville's Devlin, Craver, Hall, and Nichols were confirmed. Louisville, although represented at the convention, was expected to withdraw from the organization. That move would leave only three teams—Chicago, Cincinnati, and Boston, the latter being the only team in the populous east. If he was to ensure survival of his shaky venture, League president William Hulbert knew he needed to find more teams, especially successful ones, in the east. Indianapolis Blues and Milwaukee Cream Citys were admitted for membership; and it was known that Hulbert had been pursuing the Providence (Rhode Island) Grays of the International Association, which was

10. Between Innings

also a member of the League Alliance.[7] His efforts would eventually prove successful.

The Tecumsehs were invited to attend the convention in Cleveland, which was a pivotal event for the League. Harry Gorman was authorized by his board of directors to take notes but not make any commitments about joining the League. As local editor and reporter for the *Advertiser*, he was able to provide fulsome accounts of proceedings for readers back home. He wrote:

> The League, at present, is not in a flourishing condition. Of the six club members last year, two have disappeared—Brooklyn [Hartford, which played its home games there] and St. Louis—[and] a third, Louisville, though represented at the Convention, is as good as gone. It was an open secret among the delegates that Louisville will not have a nine for '78.

Gorman noted that with the addition of Milwaukee and Indianapolis, the National League would still have only one team in the east—Boston—and that moves were afoot to address that. Continuing, he wrote about himself in the third person:

> To make the League campaign a success, it is necessary to secure three new eastern clubs as members, and the choice lies between the Tecumsehs, Buffalo, Rochester and Hartford, with the feeling decidedly in favor of the three former. In response to an invitation, the Secretary of the Tecumsehs attended the League Convention in Cleveland, heard all that was to be said in favor of entering the League, but did not commit the Tecumsehs in any way, as his instructions were to obtain the fullest information and report to the Directors. The time for making applications for admission was extended, so as to give an opportunity to outside clubs to join before the opening of the season.... There are a great many reasons to urge in favor of the new proposition and there are some weights for and against it, all of which will no doubt have due consideration when the Tecumseh directors come to discuss the subject. The admission of three more clubs to the League is of vital importance to that body and it may be taken for granted that whether the Tecumsehs is one of the three or not, the requisite number will be secured.[8]

In its own account, without the benefit of an on-the-scene reporter, the *London Free Press* noted that Gorman was at the convention "and stated that he was not empowered to make an application, but he hoped he could arrange matters so that his club could enter the League hereafter." It reminded readers that the League rule that member cities must have a population of 75,000 would have to be suspended to admit London.[9]

The convention reiterated the League ban on Sunday games and rescinded the rule requiring home teams to bat first, reverting to a coin toss beforehand to determine the order. But more ominous business was transacted, spearheaded by Hulbert, who was determined to squeeze the lifeblood out of

International Association teams he felt were impeding success for the League. He and his fellow directors were prepared to take the gloves off as they faced an uncertain future. The convention endorsed his plan to ban non-League clubs from playing in the generally larger parks of League teams. The idea was to place a limit on the revenues that independents and IA teams could earn from playing in National League venues. This would hurt the bottom lines of non-League teams more than League teams with their deeper pockets, it was reasoned.

Boston was unhappy with this change and their directors protested. The Red Caps would still be able to play at the 2,000-seat ball yard that was home to the IA team in Lowell, but Lowell was barred from playing in Boston's South End Grounds, which could seat 10,000. Games against New England teams had drawn quite well in Boston during 1877, when every fee from admission was important, with mutual financial benefit. The League also insisted that a League ball and League umpire be used in all games with outside clubs, and it reserved the right to cancel games arranged with outside nines, if necessary, to play rained-out League games. Non-League teams were required to put up a $50 guarantee to play League teams, which would be lost if a game was not be played for any reason—including because of rain.[10]

To further tighten the screws on the IA, the convention voted to amend the constitution of the League Alliance to ban any member of the Alliance from also being a member of any other association.[11] This was potentially ominous for teams like London that had joined the Alliance only to protect their players and contracts from predation by League teams. Alliance members were assured they were the only team in their area that could play against the local League team, but the League retained the right to hold "neutral court" games in the same area between two League teams, a practice that was somewhat common in the day. Some non-League teams liked the opportunity to play League teams and signed up. Others refused.

As Ted Vincent observed in *Mudville's Revenge*, "The prime function of the Alliance was in helping the League divide and conquer the small-town competition." But there was a lot of competition out there, with a dozen teams expected to compete for the IA championship in 1878, a dozen more nominal IA members, and a large number of independent clubs in existence on the eve of the National League's third season. The *Chicago Tribune*, whose city housed a League team and the League president, was blunt in its assessment of the purpose of the Alliance and the new rules making life more difficult for non-League teams. Its baseball writer, Lewis Meacham, seemed to be under the sway of his source, Hulbert, and often channeled the thoughts of the League president in his stories.¹² According to Meacham: "The truth is, gentlemen of the smaller cities, the League ... finds it doesn't want you on their grounds.... The League can make more money off thirty first-class games than they can off sixty ... and they are going to play the thirty with the clubs they think most likely to interest their patrons."¹³

As time went on, some teams grudgingly decided to join the Alliance. But others remained steadfastly opposed, especially those in smaller centers that sensed they would never be allowed into Hulbert's club of gentleman capitalists. They urged solidarity in the face of the actions taken by the League. In New York state, for instance, a circular was sent to every club by the secretary of the Auburn club, urging them to "stick together and kick together." When Davy Force, the new shortstop for the Buffalo Bisons, heard rumors his team might leave the IA, he reportedly said: "I heard that we was going to join the League. I hope and pray not for if we do we are gone financially ... for there is nothing in it."¹⁴ Some players, upset at the League and its approach, jumped to the International Association. Among them was Ross Barnes, the heavy-hitting former White Stocking, who in 1877 missed many games because of illness and clashed with Hulbert about his pay. In December, the *London Advertiser* reported that the second baseman had signed on with the Tecumsehs to be their captain for 1878.¹⁵

The convention in Cleveland gave Gorman much to think about as he headed home to London for his report to the Tecumseh directors and a decision about the 1878 season. On Gorman's desk at the newspaper, he found a letter from the Buffalo Bisons baseball club that had arrived in his absence. In it, Buffalo was proposing a share of gate receipts for games planned for public holidays during the upcoming season. Buffalo was following up on an exchange of proposals with London. In a letter dated December 10, Gorman responded to a club official named Sprague, saying the Tecumsehs were inclined toward the invitation from the League:

> Since my last writing to you circumstances have arisen than may interfere with our proposed arrangements. I refer to the fact that proposals have been made for the Tecumsehs entering the League. The object of my visit to Cleveland was to hear what the League directors had to offer in support of their request to have the Tecumsehs join the League, and to report the same to our directors here. While there I was informed that your club was also to be taken into the League, and also the Rochesters, or Hartfords, or both, in case that Buffalo or ourselves should decline. Of course, if you should join the League, and we did not, or vice versa, our scheme would collapse; should both join, or both remain out, it might be carried into effect. Pending the settlement of those points, we have not taken into consideration your last offer [for gate receipt share]. We would like to hear

from you in regard to the League. What are your intentions? The inclinations of our directors here are in favor of the League proposition, but so far they have not committed themselves by any notice of acceptance. We are desirous of learning your views and intentions, as it would be desirable to have both clubs adopt the same course. Have you had any communication with Rochester on the subject, or are you aware of what their intentions are?[16]

Sprague replied promptly, indicating that Buffalo had no plans to join the League. Gorman then sent back a brief note saying Tecumseh directors had been unable to meet to consider the gate-sharing plan (or presumably, the League option), and he would bring it to their attention when they did gather. Gorman sought assurances that Buffalo planned to stick with the International Association and asked whether it would be competing for the IA championship.[17]

It is not known exactly what happened next, but soon afterward, the idea of London's joining the League was dead. Tecumseh directors, wary of the travel costs they would face as the only Canadian entry in the geographically dispersed League, may have decided against pursuing the notion. After all, they were coming off a season in which the team had lost $3,000 and they were likely concerned about their financial prospects as the economy continued to sputter. Perhaps, once Hulbert had persuaded Providence to jump from the International Association to the League for 1878, his interest in London—and other eastern cities—evaporated. Providence formally applied for League membership on January 21, but Hulbert would have known this well in advance because he'd been wooing them. The Tecumsehs were simply denied membership, according to one historian. David Pietrusza says the Tecumsehs were voted down when the required unanimous vote of member clubs to waive the minimum population requirement was not achieved. Why they did so is unclear. London had a population less than one-third of the 75,000 minimum.[18] An exception had been made for Hartford. Providence, approaching a population of 100,000, faced no such barrier to entry.

Regardless, by the time Gorman wrote another letter to Sprague on January 2, 1878, London was no longer talking about the League, other than in negative terms. Gorman began by expressing his regrets that the International Association convention had been postponed until February and that he would be unable to attend it.

> I have received several letters from non–League clubs in regard to the unjust legislation of the League in regard to interchange of games, as there is, as you say, a strong feeling of resentment and inclination to see the International retaliate. My position in regard to this matter is this: that a retaliatory policy, pure and simple, would look spiteful and ill-natured and leave the International open to

the same charge of lack of liberality that is now laid against the League. The better way would be, I think, for the International clubs to unite in a special agreement to give guarantees only to clubs that give guarantees in return, and only to the same extent. In other words we would be willing to give outsiders the same terms, and no better than, we give to each other. The result would be the same. [The] League could not avail themselves of our offer without violating their own compact, and we would stand before the public in the position of extending to all clubs, irrespective of associations, the same terms and privileges that we give each other. Should the League come down from their high horse, they ought not to look for, nor receive, more than that.[19]

Gorman realized the futility of war with the National League, in which everyone would suffer. He took the high road and wanted the public to see that the IA supported inclusiveness and a "big tent" approach to the professional game. If Gorman was hoping to shame the League into fair dealing with its rival, however, he was sadly mistaken.

Gorman's restrained approach was not universal. A member of the judiciary committee of the Association, A. B. Rankin of Brooklyn, was incensed at the paternalistic attitude of Hulbert and the League. On January 7, he sent a letter to all IA clubs complaining that "the high hand with which the League undertakes to control the baseball fraternity, for 1878, is so unreasonably absurd.... Are we to submit to a clique or ring? Or, are we to assert our own independence?" He called it the "height of presumption" for the League to dictate terms to organizations "that have shown equality in playing, and in some cases, superiority." He noted that the Association had been formed a year earlier "to protect non–League teams from being imposed upon." So he urged non–League clubs to stand united now and encouraged a strong turnout for the upcoming Association convention in Buffalo.[20]

At the end of January, the *Advertiser* praised a writer for the *Boston Herald* for his assessment of the League–Association situation, saying it displayed "more accuracy and sound judgment than any of the base ball critics have been able to do so far." It quoted the *Herald* as suggesting the two organizations ought to find a way to work together, for the good of the game. The *Herald* said the League had looked at Lowell, Syracuse, and London as potential members, but they were highly regarded, and needed, by the Association, where they enjoyed good relations with IA clubs. Representatives of the three nines, it said, were all expected to attend the Association convention. The *Herald* went on:

> The New York State clubs appear to be almost a unit in supporting the International movement. The existing condition of affairs is deplorable. Where harmony and universal goodwill should exist, strife and discord dwell. There is need

of but one association in the country. Each club should have a voice in legislation, and the interest of each should be the interest of the whole. [If that could be accomplished,] [t]here would be no selfish grasping to gain any advantage over a certain club or class of clubs."[21]

Twenty-five team delegates attended the annual meeting of the International Association in Buffalo on February 19–20, 1878. Attending for the Tecumsehs, in the absence of Harry Gorman, was president Jake Englehart. He chaired a committee appointed to revise the association's constitution and took an active role in business proceedings. Guelph did not appear, having decided against rejoining the loop. There was no sign of Allegheny, as the club was apparently in the throes of reorganizing as a cooperative for the season. As it turned out, Allegheny mailed its entry fee to the Association just two days before the entry deadline of March 15.[22]

One of the first pieces of business the judiciary committee considered was the written claim of Allegheny for the pennant. It found the record of games to be complete and ruled against the Allegheny contention that it should have been awarded a game against Rochester, because Rochester had used ineligible players. Allegheny argued that Dixon and Sullivan had not been released by the Maple Leafs at the time of the contest. The committee ruled, however, that the pair had been properly released and were entitled to play in that game. The committee then turned its mind to the Allegheny argument that the record had to be adjusted to reflect the impact of teams disbanding before the season was over. All games played by the Live Oaks were thrown out, it was agreed. The situation with Columbus was a bit more tricky, it having withdrawn late in the season. Only its first two games against each of its opponents were to be counted. The championship record was then confirmed, showing London with 14 wins and four losses, compared to Allegheny with 11 wins and five losses. London was then formally awarded the International Association's first pennant. The convention voted to extend membership to eight new clubs, including Troy Haymakers; New Bedford, Connecticut; Alaskas of Brooklyn; and Springfield, Holyoke, and Lowell of Massachusetts. The entrants further enhanced the character of the organization as being largely centered in New York and Massachusetts. A dozen more clubs indicated they expected to enter the championship race, and an equal number said they would not.

A key amendment to the constitution, as recommended by Englehart, was a rule that "each club belonging to the Association shall have the right to regulate its own affairs; to make its own contracts; to establish its own rules, and to discipline and punish its own players." This was in stark contrast to the centralized approach by the League and one of the reasons players found it a preferable work environment. The disciplinary committee, it was promised, would promptly adjudicate disputes between players and their clubs or between players and other clubs.

Considerable discussion surrounded the League's proposed treatment of non–League teams and organizations as second-class. But a desire for equity was the preferred response, not a declaration of war. The following motion was adopted: "Each club, a member of the Association, may make such arrangements with any other clubs as are extended to them by such clubs." That would suggest that if the League held fast to its superiority complex, few exhibition games with their nines were likely. A new executive was elected to lead the organization into the troubled waters of 1878. J. W. Whitney of Rochester was elected president; Hamilton White of Syracuse became vice-president; and J. A. Williams of Columbus returned as secretary treasurer.[23]

On March 8, Louisville officially tendered its resignation from the National League, which left the loop with six teams for the upcoming season. Only Boston, Chicago, and Cincinnati remained from its inaugural campaign of 1876. Newcomers were Providence, Milwaukee, and Indianapolis. By contrast, about two dozen teams were signed with the International Association and another 20 or so professional teams barnstormed as independents.

That same month, reports came out of Guelph that it was planning to create a new playing field for its "first-class amateur team." Seating was planned for 1,000 spectators in stands configured as an amphitheater, making the field "one of the most complete on the continent." But only amateur nines would use it. Meanwhile, in London, directors of the Tecumsehs were planning to reconfigure Tecumseh Park to remove seating at the west end of the field and move it to the south side of the park, providing spectators a new view from left field.[24]

At Prospect Park in Brooklyn, a baseball game was played between picked nines of professional players. Tecumsehs third baseman Herm Doscher was honored as the best player in any position during the game and was awarded a special ball by Henry Chadwick. Doscher was going to have impressive company in London's infield for 1878. The *Advertiser* shared an opinion about that company in the upcoming season that appeared in the *Clipper*.

> The Buffalos are going for the scalps of [Ross] Barnes' Tecumseh champions the first thing. Don't be too sanguine, boys. Barnes is the captain of the Canadians now, and that means a great deal. If we mistake not, Ross will show some of the finest second-base play this season ever witnessed. He will have no one to cramp his action as he did in 1877.[25]

Late in March, the International Association closed off entries for the championship race. Ten teams had signed up: London, Buffalo, Rochester,

Binghamton, Syracuse, Utica, Hornellsville (population about 8,000), Lowell, Manchester, and New Bedford. Lynn and Allegheny were late entries. The Tecumsehs, it was noted, would have their hands full if they hoped to repeat as champions.

> They are very much stronger, however, this year than last, inasmuch as they have the noted Ross Barnes to captain the nine and to play second base for them. In the new Buffalo team the Tecumsehs will find the pitcher and catcher of the Allegheny nine of 1877 to oppose them, and that, too, with a better support in the field than they had last season, for in 1877 they defeated the Tecumsehs in three out of four games.[26]

March was not yet over when the new president of the International Association, James Whitney, became embroiled in a controversy that agitated some of its members. It would have severe repercussions for the Tecumsehs. Following the lead of the National League the previous season, the Association had decided to introduce some structure to its scheduling of games for its championship. By March 15, Whitney was required to select a four-member committee to devise a schedule, consisting of two members from Eastern teams and two from Western clubs from among the 12 contending entries. He chose representatives from Rochester and Hornellsville in the West, and from newcomers New Bedford and Springfield in the East. The *Buffalo Express* noted widespread "displeasure" at Whitney's first official act.

> As will be seen, the strongest teams in the Association have been entirely ignored, and those gentlemen who have been instrumental in bringing the Association to its present standing were entirely disregarded. Not doubting the ability of the gentlemen appointed, and believing that the smaller clubs should be recognized, we should still prefer to have seen Ross Barnes, of the Tecumsehs, one of the best-known base-ballists in the country, on that committee.[27]

The exclusion of a representative from London led to a schedule that would see the Tecumsehs on the road for four out of the first five weeks of the new season. That schedule, designed to accommodate championship games, would prove hard on its fans anxious to see the home team, and even harder on club finances.

In the lead-up to the season, many baseball writers were assessing the professional clubs in both the National League and the International Association, beginning a tradition that continues every spring. The *New York Mercury*, provided its thoughts about the upcoming season, noting that 12 clubs were pursuing the pennant of the International Association "which, this season, for the first time, assumes an importance fully equal to that of the League. For two years the clubs of the country have been 'even up,' until there are a dozen nines which vary little in playing skill." The *Mercury* also considered the prospects of the IA contenders and it concluded that the race for the championship would be among Buffalo, Syracuse, London, Lowell, and Rochester, which it found were "evenly matched." Its overview noted Buffalo had hired pitcher Pud Galvin and Tom Dolan, his catcher from the 1877 Allegheny club, plus top players like veterans Davy Force at shortstop and Chick Fulmer at second base, along with outfielder Dave Eggler. The Rochesters, considered "among the best of clubs," featured the solid battery of Isaac Van Burkalow and Doc Kennedy, while the Springfields featured Larry Corcoran, the promising teenaged hurler, described as "very swift and hard to hit." The Syracuse Stars, the roundup continued, "are selected by many people as the club most likely to win the chief honors," because of the solid all-around lineup of last

The Buffalo Bisons joined the International Association in 1878 and took their second pennant, largely due to the pitching of Jim "Pud" Galvin, right rear. Galvin relied on a fastball and deceptive pick-off, never able to master the curve because of small hands (courtesy of Buffalo History Museum).

year's Alliance champions. For the Tecumsehs, it noted Goldsmith and Powers made an excellent duo, backed up by Barnes, Bradley, Doscher, Dinnen, Burke, Hornung, and Smith. Utica had former Tecumsehs captain Juice Latham on its roster. Lowell was described as bringing back to the field the surprisingly strong team of the previous season, including the strong pitcher-catcher tandem of Foley and Sullivan. The *Mercury* said it expected the Live Oaks of Lynn would be admitted to the pennant race despite missing the entry deadline. There, Lapham and Gillespie, formerly of the Guelph Maple Leafs, were part of what was considered a hard-hitting lineup.[28]

Buffalo was a special case. The city had become excited about baseball and was anxious to make up for lost time. Partway through the summer of 1877, it established its first professional team, an independent nine. Overall, the team that became known as the Bisons won 20 games and lost 30. Their opponents that short season were members of the National League, the International Association, and other independents. Buffalo had signed on early to join the IA for its second season. Among its players were Larry Corcoran, signed to pitch when he was just 16, and John Montgomery Ward, a versatile player, good at stealing bases, who was embarking on what would be an 18-year professional career.

Buffalo directors had expected more from their 1877 campaign, so they built a new roster from scratch, opening their coffers to attract talent from both the League and Association. Corcoran, surprisingly, despite his promise, was among those released. The young man apparently needed more maturity, criticized because he was "a poor team player and showed no sympathy for his catcher."[29] It wasn't an auspicious start for someone who would come to be considered one of the era's great pitchers. Buffalo directors were prepared to spend what they felt was necessary to make their club a contender. Player pay ranged from $700 for the season for centerfielder Dave Eggler, outfielder Bill McGunnigle, and substitute John "Trick" McSorley, and up to $1,200 for shortstop Davy Force. Force had eight years' experience with National Association and National League clubs, most recently with St. Louis. Chick Fulmer, the captain, had been a professional for seven years. Like the young battery of Galvin and Dolan, Fulmer had played for Allegheny in 1877. The Bisons roster was an interesting blend of rookies and veterans.[30] Aside from assembling what appeared to be a strong contender, directors scrambled to lease and upgrade grounds in the city's west end at Niagara and Rhode Island Streets. Despite another snowy winter in Buffalo, the park was ready for practice by mid–April.

Guelph had reverted to amateur status for the 1878 season, although pitcher Billy Smith was back with the team as it looked forward to its new ballpark. Others returning from last year's roster were Maddock, Reid, and Hewer. Professionals Lapham, Tommy Smith, Quinton, Gillespie, Dixon, Sullivan, and Walsh had left for other teams late in the previous season after being released by George Sleeman.

The Maple Leafs that spring of 1878 figured, however, in a story told late in the season about the serious financial troubles of Indianapolis owner William Merritt. He attributed most of his money woes to a pre-season raid of the Maple Leafs while pursuing professional talent. Merritt, it was said, felt it necessary to flee Indiana to get away from his many creditors. But a review of his Indianapolis National League roster shows none of the names of professionals—or even amateurs—who had plied their trade in Guelph. If he went to Guelph at all, Merritt didn't lose his money on ballplayers. It may simply have been a story he used to cover his poor management. Merritt's efforts running the team that year were not entirely in vain, however, as three of the professionals he did sign—third baseman Ned Williamson, catcher Silver Flint, and pitcher Jim McCormick—went on to become stars of the game.[31]

With all the arrangements for the 1878 season in place, along with attendant expectations, it was time to play ball. Despite the flagging economy and the prospect of fewer spectators because of reduced competition expected between League and Association teams, the two organizations looked forward to successful campaigns. The International Association had proven it was an equal for the older loop but it could sense storm clouds on the horizon because of the League's growing antagonism toward it. For its part, the National League, under William Hulbert, was determined to see better financial results and vindication for its dogged insistence that baseball was a business best conducted by businessmen.

11

Rumblings

For 1878, Ross Barnes had something to prove. As newly appointed captain of the Tecumsehs, he was hoping to get back on track with what had been an impressive career. One of the best players of the era, he left the Chicago White Stockings in 1877 on bad terms, and the veteran second baseman was looking for a fresh start.

Charles Roscoe Barnes was born in 1850 in Mt. Morris, in western New York, but his family moved to Rockford, Illinois, when he was young. There, Barnes played baseball, working his way onto the roster of the successful Forest City club alongside promising young pitcher Albert Goodwill Spalding. Only five-foot-eight, Barnes played mostly shortstop, where he attracted attention in his three years there. In 1871, Harry Wright hired Barnes and Spalding, both turning 21, for his Boston Red Stockings of the new National Association, where he moved Barnes to second base. Barnes demonstrated great hands and a talent for stealing bases with the Red Stockings as they dominated the NA, winning its championship every year from 1872 through its final 1875 season. But it was with the bat that Barnes truly excelled. He led the Association in 18 offensive categories, recording 459 runs and 531 hits with an overall batting average of .391. In 1871, he batted .401; in 1872, .430; and in 1873, .431. Aside from hitting for power, Barnes had mastered the tricky "fair-foul" hit to get on base. In those days, a ball was considered fair as long as it first struck the ground in fair territory, even if it then rolled outside the baselines and into foul territory. Barnes, a right-handed batter, would go after low pitches and pull them so they'd land fair and then continue into foul territory. With such a large area to patrol for opponents at first and third bases, the "fair-foul" was almost impossible to defend. For Barnes, it was an effective tool.[1]

Barnes was one of the "Big Four," along with Spalding, Cal McVey, and Deacon White, lured from Boston by William Hulbert to join the Chicago

One of the top hitters of his day, Ross Barnes became playing manager for the London Tecumsehs for the 1878 season. Ill during 1877 while with Chicago, Barnes lost much of his strength and never really regained his form. He was one of the "Big Four" players from Boston, along with pitcher Albert Goodwill Spalding who jumped from Boston to Chicago after the 1875 season, a move that led to the founding of the National League (National Baseball Hall of Fame Library, Cooperstown, N.Y. Roscoe Barnes 387-56_FL_PD).

White Stockings for the first National League campaign of 1876. Chicago captured the League title that year behind the pitching of Spalding, with 47 wins, and the stellar performance at the plate and at second base by Barnes. On May 2, in Cincinnati, Barnes hit the first home run in National League history off Cherokee Fisher of the Red Stockings, but power was not his forte. Consistency was his hallmark, averaging more than two hits per game.[2] He led the League in 1876 with 126 runs scored, 138 hits, and a batting average of .429. He also had the top fielding average, at .910. No wonder Barnes was one of the best-paid players in baseball. He had been earning $2,000 a year in Boston.[3] By 1877, Chicago signed him to a deal paying $2,500 for the season.[4]

Things were soon to change for Barnes, however. Before the League's second season, it banned the "fair-foul" hit. If the ball skipped from fair territory into foul, it was to be declared a foul. It has been speculated the rule was changed because of the number of arguments they generated that "fair-foul" hits slowed the game down. One of the best weapons in Barnes's arsenal was gone.[5] The season dealt him another blow, one considered far more serious by modern historians. In May, Barnes came down with what was then known as "the ague," an illness similar to malaria, which sapped his strength. Plagued by alternating high fevers and chills, he was ill from mid–May until early September. As a result, he appeared in only 22 games that 1877 season, compared to 66 the previous year. His stamina was gone and he had permanently lost some of his strength. His batting average plunged to .272. Club management withheld $1,000 of his salary while he was ill, so Barnes took the White Stockings to court to force them to pay up. A year later, a county court judge ruled in favor of the Chicago management.[6] Subsequent events would show that Barnes never reclaimed his form or his strength, and his days in the game were numbered. But he wasn't going to give up without a fight, and the Tecumsehs were willing to gamble on him.

It's likely Barnes took less money to captain and manage the Tecumsehs than he'd been earning in Chicago, where Hulbert felt salaries were too high. In a day when player salaries amounted to two-thirds of a professional club's expenses, Hulbert fulminated famously: "It is ridiculous to pay ballplayers $2,000 a year when the $800 boys often do just as well."[7] In London, Barnes was paid the same as top earner Fred Goldsmith, who received more than $100 a month. Aside from Barnes, two other new faces were on hand as players arrived in early April. Joe Dunnigan, a New Yorker, was to be a substitute at several positions, and Albert Hall came from Syracuse to play outfield. The three were replacements for Marshall Quinton, Jake Knowdell, and Mike Dinnen, who had moved on to other teams. Knowdell became catcher for the Allegheny club, while Dinnen showed up in London at one point, playing second base for Rochester.

As was the tradition in London, the Tecumsehs played their first game of the new year against the top local amateur team, the Atlantics, from whose ranks the professional club often borrowed players. The Atlantics, three-time amateur champions of Canada, invariably gave a good account of themselves. The April 13 game attracted a large crowd to newly upgraded Tecumseh Park, where it witnessed a sparkling display of fielding despite very windy conditions. The *Advertiser* reported Goldsmith's "old-time deceivers" were working well. And it took special note of the Atlantics pitcher, 19-year-old Bob Emslie, a curveballer who had filled in with the Tecumsehs from time to time. "Emslie made his debut as pitcher for the Atlantics, and he gave every promise of being a good one. He throws a very swift, deceptive ball, and if he continues to practice hard, and is not spoiled by overdue flattery, will make a name for himself on the ball-field."[8]

The newspaper prediction proved accurate, in the fullness of time. Emslie, a native of Guelph, had moved to London because of baseball and became a regular with the Atlantics. On occasion, he also played for the Tecumsehs as a substitute. His major league career began in 1883, when he joined Baltimore of the American Association. During a three-year span, he pitched in 91 games, winning 44 and losing 44. He played all but four of those games with Baltimore. In 1891, Emslie turned to umpiring in the National League, where he became a fixture. He picked up the nickname "Blind Bob" and is best remembered for his role in the famous "Merkle's Boner" play in 1908, one of the most controversial episodes in the annals of baseball.

On September 23, the hometown New York Giants were in a struggle for first place in the National League with the Chicago Cubs they faced that day. Emslie was the base umpire and missed seeing Giants runner Fred Merkle fail to touch second base in a crucial play in the bottom of the ninth inning with the game tied, 1–1. Merkle was at first base with two outs, when Giants shortstop Al Bridwell singled to center field, knocking Emslie off his feet, to bring in what everyone in the park believed was the winning run from third. Fans swarmed the field, and Merkle, seeing the commotion, headed for the clubhouse without bothering to touch second. Cubs second baseman Johnny Evers saw Merkle depart, hollered to the outfield for the ball, then touched second with it, demanding Merkle be called out. Under the rules of the day, a run could not score on a force play where a base runner was the third out. Emslie admitted he didn't know whether Merkle had touched second and he called upon the only other official on the field, home plate umpire Hank O'Day, to make the call. O'Day declared Merkle had missed the bag and was therefore out, so the run didn't count. Jubilant fans turned angry and could not be cleared from the field. The Cubs had to be given a police escort from the field for their protection. The next day, the game was declared a 1-1 tie and it was ordered to be replayed. In that rematch, Chicago won 4-2, a victory that allowed it to claim the National League pennant by a single game over the Giants.[9] Merkle, an otherwise good player and intelligent man, wore the baserunning error for the rest of his life, but Emslie seemed to weather the controversy. During his long career, however, Emslie wore a wig while on the field because his nerves were completely frazzled by his job and his hair had fallen out. Despite his eccentricities, Emslie was considered competent. He umpired in the major leagues for 33 years and then served as National League chief of umpires before retiring in 1924.[10]

The Tecumsehs won the Atlantics game, 11-4, with Barnes, Hall, Doscher, and Smith all scoring twice, capitalizing on seven errors by the amateurs. A return match six days later saw Emslie again pitching well, and the Atlantics led, 3-2, until the Tecumsehs came up with two runs off him in the ninth inning for a 4-3 win.

The International Association season opened, and the schedule for championship games was released. Each of the 13 contending teams was required to play each other team four times—twice at home, twice away. In all, 312 such games had been scheduled by president Whitney's committee. The Tecumsehs faced a particularly challenging start to their season. Their first championship game was May 6 in Rochester. To prepare, they agreed to exhibition games in Buffalo on May 1 and in Auburn on May 3. This kicked off a lengthy road trip through New York and Massachusetts that would conclude May 23 in Syracuse. The team would get back home just in time for the May 24 Victoria Day holiday to welcome Buffalo. On May 30, they would hit the road again, starting with a championship game in Buffalo. This second, shorter tour would conclude on June 7 with an exhibition game in Cleveland after a pair of championship games with Allegheny.[11]

So, beginning May 1, the Tecumsehs were away for 32 of 38 days. Theirs was a brutal schedule. Aside from the wear and tear on the players bouncing around for hundreds of miles in railroad cars, it meant London fans could attend only a few games at Tecumseh Park before June 10. The schedule made it difficult to get local fans into the swing of baseball early in the season and behind their local heroes. Reading newspaper accounts or waiting for telegraphed updates were poor substitutes for the ballpark experience. The schedule's early emphasis on touring also meant the team incurred major expenses for travel and accommodation before playing what traditionally had been more lucrative home games. It's hard to speculate what the Association schedulers had in mind. Perhaps they wanted to keep the reigning International Association champions on the road to attract fans, especially in newer IA cities. Other teams and their supporters could then use the Tecumsehs as a benchmark to measure their clubs' prospects. It's doubtful, however, that had London been represented on the committee drawing up the schedule, it would have agreed to such an onerous calendar. Geographically, the Ontario city was out in left field, so to speak, with nearly all its competition centered in New York and Massachusetts, so extra travel had to be expected to some degree. Today's equivalent would be the Seattle Mariners and Seahawks or the Vancouver Canucks in the American League, the National Football League, and the National Hockey League respectively. Travel is accepted as a costly fact of life in far-flung franchises.

Buffalo came to town for an exhibition game April 26, and despite threatening weather, it was described as one of the finest games seen on the London grounds. Pud Galvin pitched effectively for the visitors, as did Goldsmith for the home nine. The Bisons led, 3–2, after seven innings when the Tecumseh bats finally woke up. They scored five runs in the ninth when Smith, Hall, Burke, Goldsmith, Powers, Burke, and Doscher all connected for hits. Earlier in the game, Barnes distinguished himself with a running catch of a difficult foul ball that landed between first base and right field. He also recorded a hit. Galvin, it was reported, "pitched all he knew, which is not a little, but the Tecumsehs were too much for him, as they were on a memorable occasion last fall, when off his pitching they earned the International Championship."[12] Galvin, Dolan, and Fulmer no doubt didn't appreciate the reminder of their loss as Alleghenys in their first trip back to London. On May 1, the Tecumsehs left on the 6:00 a.m. train for Buffalo to begin their three-week road trip. That night, a general meeting of the Tecumseh directors and shareholders convened to close the business of the old organization and place its affairs in the hands of a new stock company.[13]

Game day in Buffalo, May 1, had been much anticipated in that city of 150,000, with placards everywhere announcing the exhibition game on the newly leased Rhode Island Street grounds. About 3,000 fans filled the park to overflowing, braving a chilly Lake Erie wind that blew across the damp grounds. The Bisons were as cool as the weather, again succumbing to the powerful Tecumseh bats. London led the entire game for a final score of 5–2, prompting keen local disappointment. "The Tecumsehs outplayed us and out-batted us, and won the game by dint of hard hits, though neither side scored an earned run," the *Buffalo Courier* reported. It lamented that the large turnout hadn't motivated the home nine to play better. On the bright side, it was reported that game receipts amounted to a healthy $710.[14] In the game, Barnes had a base hit and Burke and Hornung each recorded two.

On May 3, the Tecumsehs defeated Auburn, 2–1, in an exhibition contest. London played its first game for the IA championship on May 6 and easily defeated Rochester, 4–0. The following day, before a large crowd in Syracuse, London scored two runs in the first inning and held a 2–1 lead until the fifth inning, when Syracuse brought in a run to tie the score. The Syracuse bats were stronger than those of the Tecumsehs for the day and they scored two more runs in the ninth inning to take the win, 4–2, in the exhibition match, marking London's first loss of the season. Wins were recorded in exhibition games with Troy and New Bedford, by scores of 10–4 and 17–4, respectively, before the Tecumsehs rolled into Lowell on May 11.

In the first of two championship games, the Lowells scored four runs in the 14th inning to win an epic struggle, 11–8. Two days later, the Tecumsehs blanked the Lowells, 6–0, with newcomer Albert Hall garnering half the London runs, while Barnes had two base hits. A championship game on May 14 at Manchester saw London score three runs in the tenth inning to defeat the home team, 3–0. May 15 was cold and so were Tecumseh bats for the second Manchester game, which London lost, 2–0. Goldsmith sprained his ankle in Manchester, so Foghorn Bradley replaced him in the pitching box for a championship game on May 16 in Lynn, Massachusetts, that the Tecumsehs won, 14–0.

On May 17, history was made when a black man named Bud Fowler pitched for Lynn in another championship game. He had been called up from the amateur team in Chelsea to replace a Live Oak hurler named Prince, described as "lame." In so doing, Fowler became the first African American to play in professional, organized baseball.[15] Fowler overpowered the reigning International Association champions. He allowed two hits and no runs as he recorded three strikeouts and threw only one wild pitch. A Boston newspaper said: "Fowler's pitching was so effective, and the general play of the Live Oaks so sharp...."[16]

Lynn was leading the Tecumsehs, 3–0, in the seventh inning when London refused to play further after a close call at home plate that favored Lynn. Ross Barnes had been complaining about the umpiring since the second inning and demanded umpire Henry Murphy be removed. Barnes drew abuse from the home crowd for his kicking up a fuss, but Murphy was replaced by James Tuft. In the bottom of the ninth, Barnes hit a fly ball that was caught, and

Hornung was called out at home on a close play. This re-ignited Barnes and the Tecumsehs. When they walked off the field, Tuft declared the Live Oaks default 9–0 winners.[17] Barnes was known for his disdain of black players, likely picked up from Cap Anson, his former White Stockings teammate who was outspoken on the subject.[18] His prejudice might have been a factor in his behavior. Of the game, the *Boston Daily Globe* said: "Fowler's effective pitching and the handsome manner in which he was backed up fairly earned the game for the Oaks."[19]

Fowler was hired by the Oaks and pitched two more games for them before moving on in a career that saw him constantly changing teams. In 1881, he was lured north to the Guelph Maple Leafs by George Sleeman. The brewer was still running the Leafs, now a semi-professional club. Just as south of the border, Fowler suffered racism at the hands of his teammates, some of whom Sleeman was still hiring from south of the border. Fowler was released to play a few games with the Petrolia Imperials.[20] Former Tecumsehs president Jake Englehart had relocated to Petrolia by 1881 from London and was a principal in Imperial Oil, so it is tempting to think Englehart played some role in Fowler's moving there and playing for a team that shared the name of his refinery. Teammates and the press, however, continued their racist taunts, and the talented pitcher again moved on.

Because baseball historians decided to consider the International Association a minor league, Fowler's accomplishment of being the first black to play professional baseball has been largely ignored. The credit has gone to Moses Fleetwood Walker, a catcher for Toledo of the American Association in 1884. The American Association was a successor to the International Association and was founded in 1881 by, among others, Denny McKnight, who had established the IA in 1877.[21] So it is difficult to understand why the importance of the International Association, and players like Fowler, continues to be suppressed.

During the Tecumsehs' road trip that included Lynn, the *Advertiser* reported that Tommy Smith had sprained his ankle, and Bradley had injured his leg, making it difficult to run the bases with his customary speed. The newspaper took special note of the play of the new captain:

> Barnes has been making wonderful play at second base for the Tecumsehs. In fifteen games played, of which scores have been received to date, he put out 48 men and assisted in retiring 76, or a total of 124 who fell by his hands—an average of over eight to a game. This is unequalled as a second base record. His error column shows a total of 12, which is light when the number of chances offered and taken is considered.[22]

It was also noted that Barnes had 16 hits in 61 at-bats for an average of .262. His batting, it would appear, was not nearly as strong as his defensive play.

In Guelph, the Maple Leafs opened their season on May 16 and defeated the Iroquois of Markham, a small town north of Toronto, 13–0. Despite the mismatch, the *Mercury* pronounced Sleeman's warriors as "very little inferior to last year" and predicted they would resume their old position as amateur champions of Canada.[23]

London's next championship game in the IA was played on May 18 in New Haven, Goldsmith's hometown. London won, 5–0. Goldsmith was still sidelined by his ankle injury and his place was taken by Bradley. New Haven's pitcher, the much-traveled curve-tosser Candy Cummings, was also disabled by injury and unable to play. The home team's shortstop, Lynch, filled in for the former IA president. A second match, scheduled for two days later, was rained out.

Back home in London, the rivals *Advertiser* and *Free Press* were engaged in a war of words about the Tecumsehs. The former complained the latter was too negative in its coverage of the home team and tended to pounce too forcefully on bad play, yet fawn over players when they did well. The dispute had its roots in their arrangements to cover out-of-town games, and the long tour was bringing it to a head. The *Advertiser* said it relied on reports filed to it by team captain and manager Ross Barnes (which may explain the glowing report of his fielding acumen from a few days earlier). The *Free Press*, meanwhile, had arranged with Goldsmith to file reports, but claimed manager Barnes denied him access to the information he needed for his accounts. So the *Free Press* had taken some shots at the Tecumsehs manager, who may simply have been attempting to control the flow of information. It seems he had already filed a glowing report about himself and may not have wanted to lose editorial control over what went out for public consumption. Regardless, the *Advertiser* replied with ridicule for its competitor:

> Our dismal friend had first choice, selected its man, and told him what to do. If it picked the wrong man, or failed to instruct him properly, why seek to throw the blame on other shoulders? The trouble about the whole affair is, it was badly beaten and everybody knows it. As for the aspersions sought to be cast upon the Tecumseh Secretary, they meet with no sympathy from the Directors of the club and are treated with absolute indifference by the party against whom they are directed.[24]

The rivalry between the newspapers was somewhat entertaining, but it had a serious side. The *Free Press*, the smaller paper, generally didn't cover the

Tecumsehs as well as its competitor, but in the tough times that lay ahead, any ill feelings it harbored about the team would not prove helpful.

On May 21, the Tecumsehs rolled over Springfield, Massachusetts, 13–3, before a crowd of 600. Twice that number witnessed another exhibition game the following day in Utica that the Tecumsehs won, 3–2. In that game, a foul tip struck catcher Phil Powers in the face and he had to retire. Outfielder Dutch Hornung, playing in his hometown, put on a fine display for his friends and family, scoring all three London runs. The last date on the trip was May 23 at Syracuse, an exhibition game, where London notched another win, 7–4, as Syracuse pitcher Harry McCormick sat out with a sore arm. Ross Barnes hit three doubles for the visitors, and Hornung, Hall, and Doscher each scored twice.[25] As the Tecumsehs headed home, they could derive some satisfaction from the successful road trip in which they had played 16 games and won 12 of them. Barnes was likely pleased with his personal performance. He hadn't regained his old form but he was still proving to be one of the strongest players on his new team. Statistics published in the *Advertiser* showed he was tied for top batting average with Hall at .270, and his fielding percentage was tied for second with Bradley at .916.

On the eve of the May 24 holiday game, and while the tired Tecumsehs took the long train ride home from Syracuse, the newly incorporated Tecumseh Base Ball Club met at the Tecumseh House Hotel. Several provisional directors stepped down and were replaced. Among the directors appointed was Jake Englehart, who was also elected president, the same post he'd held in the previous organization. Other directors included Ed Moore and Harry Gorman. To the regret of his fellow directors, Gorman tendered his resignation as club secretary and was thanked for his services. Gorman was replaced by director P. Mulkern. Ross Barnes was confirmed as manager of the club by the new officers. It was reported that the just-concluding Eastern tour of the team had been very successful, with estimated receipts exceeding expenditures by about $600.[26]

The Buffalo Bisons showed up for the big game to mark the Queen's birthday, Victoria Day, on May 24. The Tecumsehs didn't. More than 3,500 London fans, starved of professional baseball for more than three weeks, were on hand to see the game. The papers warned that Buffalo was a strong team and predicted a close contest. But, in what was described as "one of the most wretched exhibitions of the uncertainties of the sport ever witnessed in London," the visitors took advantage of the home team, hammering them, 7–1. The Tecumsehs had traveled all night and returned home on the 6:00 a.m. train that same day. So they did have an excuse. "In fact the whole nine appeared to be fagged out, and unfit to do the work required of them. The result was a great disappointment to our citizens," the *Advertiser* said. The Tecumseh bats were easily silenced by Galvin, and their errors were plentiful. Buffalo's fifth run, for instance, scored when Powers failed to catch a third strike and the runner made it to first, then capitalized on a wild throw and scampered all the way home to score. For his part, Powers, with one eye almost completely closed from the injury he had suffered in Utica, wore a mask to prevent further injury. It was remarked that the result was not so much a testament to the abilities of Buffalo as to the poor play of London. "It appears to be the misfortune of the Tecumsehs to play their worst games on holidays, when the largest crowds turn out to witness their efforts," the newspaper grumped.[27]

The Tecumsehs had a few days to rest up and heal from their injuries as they awaited the first visit of the Allegheny club since the one the previous October that had decided the International Association championship. A familiar face, Jake Knowdell, from last year's London club, was catcher for Allegheny and renewed acquaintances. The games on May 27–28 were to count toward the championship, and a revived London won them both. The two games proved to be thinly attended contests. In the first encounter, Tecumseh bats pounded pitcher Henry Luff for 12 base hits on their way to a 10–0 shellacking of the visitors. Barnes led the Tecumsehs with three of their 13 base hits. The second game London took by a 6–2 score, with Goldsmith described as "brilliant." Goldsmith had two men on base with none out in the first inning and retired the side without allowing the runners to advance.

The Tecumsehs left London for another road trip on the morning of May 30 as the unofficial standings in the International Association pennant race were published. Syracuse was in the lead with 12 wins and one loss; Hornell second with 14 wins and six losses; Buffalo third with 11 wins and six losses; and Rochester fourth with ten wins and seven losses. London was sixth with six wins and five losses. Allegheny was mired in 11th with two wins and 17 losses. Over in the National League, Cincinnati led with ten wins and two losses, followed by Indianapolis (6–6), Boston (5–3), Chicago (4–8), Milwaukee (4–8–1), and Providence (3–5).[28]

The crowd at Buffalo was immense, estimated at more than 6,000 for the May 30 championship game. The Tecumsehs hadn't seen such a crowd since 1876 in games against Guelph. Many Londoners had also made the trip with their team. The play of both teams was sharp, and after a scoreless first inning, Buffalo got its first run, to loud cheers from the enthusiastic throng. McGunnigle pitched for the home team but when the Tecumsehs hit him hard in the third inning to score two runs, Galvin was brought in from right field to take his usual position in the pitcher's box. The move was loudly cheered because the team's success so far in the season had relied heavily on his arm. Goldsmith kept the Bisons batters in check, helped by a plucky Powers, who continued to play even after a foul tip disjointed the little finger on his left hand. Hornung tracked down a long fly to left field to snuff out Buffalo's hopes to end the game with the final score, 2–1, for London. The *Advertiser* had a reporter at the game who was impressed with the good-natured throng on hand:

> London is looked upon as a "base ball town," and with some reason too, but it can't touch Buffalo. The epidemic rages there—everybody has the base ball fever! Even the ladies examine the score cards critically, know what a base hit is, and dispute the umpire's decision, when necessary, with all the readiness of professional ball-tossers.[29]

The reporter noticed an unusual spectacle every few innings when a "good-looking, middle-aged man in the grandstand rose gravely to his feet, extended his hands to heaven and in the most yawny voice ejaculated 'Stretch!'" His fellow fans rose, "laughing and stretching their stiffness away." The reporter said it "was so apparent that only blessings could be showered at the man who struck upon the novel idea of a 'stretching time.'" One is left to wonder today if Buffalo, the city that later gave chicken wings to the world, also originated the seventh-inning stretch.

On May 31, the Tecumsehs took on Rochester and displayed flawless fielding to take the championship game, 2–1. Barnes and Powers scored London's only runs. The following day, Rochester bounced back to win, 7–3, in an exhibition game that Doscher pitched for the visitors with a delivery described as "very wild." Barnes led the hitting parade for London with two base hits and scored one of their three runs.[30] In Binghamton on June 3, the Tecumsehs defeated the Crickets, 9–0, in a championship game. On June 4, the Tecumsehs were in the small "southern tier" of New York community of Hornellsville for a championship match. They defeated the Hornells, 2–1, before boarding a train for an overnight trip to Allegheny City for two more championship meetings. The Tecumsehs arrived at Recreation Park just in time for the Allegheny game. They didn't seem to suffer from the trip and defeated the home team, 7–1. The following day, with more rest, they won again, with a score of 6–1. It meant that in four games for the pennant, they had beaten their former great rivals from Pennsylvania all four times.[31] More important, it gave London six consecutive wins toward the pennant while on the road. The Tecumsehs closed their tour on June 7 with an exhibition game against the Forest Citys of Cleveland, winning 6–1, before crossing Lake Erie by overnight steamer to Port Stanley and the short rail hop home.

Rochester arrived in London for a pair of championship games on June 10 and 11. The Tecumsehs played poorly, and their bats were little help in the first encounter, which the Rochesters won, 6–5. Dinnen, of last year's London team, played second base for the visitors and was warmly greeted by the fans. Powers, still nursing a sore hand from the road trip, was replaced behind the plate by Hall, who made several costly errors. Powers was called in to replace him but by then it was too late to change the outcome. The *Advertiser* noted that the Tecumsehs had lost two of the four championship games played at its home field, both times when Powers was hurt. "These losses are very disheartening to the friends of the team in the city, who expect to see their favorites win every time, and will make no allowances for accidents or the ordinary chances of the game." London was proving a tough crowd to please. Perhaps they had been spoiled by the long string of successes of the home team and expected that to continue.

That night, Foghorn Bradley's resignation was accepted at a meeting of the Tecumseh directors, without public comment or explanation, although the *Guelph Mercury* soon reported that his departure was "owing to some unpleasantness."[32] Concerns were being expressed by newspapers about their ability to report the championship race accurately with so many exhibition games sandwiched between championship contests. Sometimes the latter were confused with the former. Meanwhile, a rumor was floating that Allegheny was disbanding, a move that, if true, would further complicate the race and require adjustments in the standings to reflect its departure.[33] In Buffalo, the same day, the Bisons were pummeled by Chicago, 7–1, in what was described as their worst game of the season.

The Tecumsehs, in their second game with Rochester, won by a score of 5–3. The home team fielding was exceptionally sharp, with the combination of Burke, Barnes, and Dunnigan pulling off two double plays. Turnout at the ballpark was light, attributed to the poor game of the previous day. The *Guelph Mercury* reported on June 12 that the Allegheny club had indeed disbanded on June 8, shortly after its two losses to London. Allegheny had played 27 games in the championship series but had won only two, both against cellar-dwelling Hartford. Because Allegheny had played just one game against first-place Syracuse, it was decided that only the first games Allegheny played against other contenders would be counted in the standings. That meant the Tecumsehs lost credit for three of their four victories.[34]

Two championship games were held in London on June 13–14, with Hornellsville. London won the first contest, 4–3, but the Hornells came back for a 6–3 victory in a clash with so many bad calls that the umpire was replaced partway through the game. Meanwhile, Bradley was back with the Tecumsehs, it being reported: "His promises of amendment have been accepted by the Directors and other means adopted to mark their disapprobation of his conduct than those resolved upon at a previous meeting." That explanation in the *Advertiser* was about as clear as mud, but it did indicate some tension existed within the same club that had drawn praise the previous season for its togetherness. Too much travel may have frayed nerves. The paper also published unofficial standings for the championship, showing the Tecumsehs had climbed to second place behind Syracuse, but it was conceded that the three wins against Allegheny had not yet been subtracted.

Aside from the issue with Bradley, it seemed something else might be afoot behind the scenes. The same edition of the *Advertiser* carried an intriguing item from the *Pittsburgh Leader* that suggested as much. The *Leader* reported that movement was under way to transfer London's financially troubled franchise to that city, at least partly because London was "too far away" from other IA cities. It said Pittsburgh parties had contacted the Tecumsehs, suggesting the move, but no response had yet been received. "If the 'Tecumsehs of Pittsburgh' becomes a fact, the base ball furor of last year will be revived at once," the *Leader* predicted, sounding hopeful. The *Advertiser* replied:

> Similar rumors to the above have cropped up in various places during the past three years—Buffalo, Cleveland and Pittsburgh claiming that they were going to buy up the Tecumseh nine and transfer them to their respective cities. No thought of the kind was ever entertained here, and the report that letters had been sent to the Tecumseh directors here, urging the transfer, is entirely foundationless. So also is the assertion that the Tecumseh club is in financial difficulties. Notwithstanding the large outlay occasioned by fitting up the new grounds, and the heavy expense of keeping up a team of first-class players, the club has never failed to meet its engagements with its players. In fact, so far from being embarrassed, the rule has been that the players have to a large extent received there [*sic*] salaries in advance. There is some truth in the remark that London does not give enough patronage to support a first-class club out of the gate receipts, but those who have been managing the affairs of the Tecumsehs know that the club does not depend entirely on gate receipts for its support.[35]

The hints of problems with player discipline, rumors of financial troubles, and a possible move out of town, along with an admission that fan support was inadequate, all tended to suggest the Tecumsehs of 1878 were a far different club from the popular champions of just a year earlier. Jake Englehart and his fellow directors of the ball club had their hands full.

Against this backdrop, London traveled to Guelph for a game on June 18 that attracted only 400–500 spectators. Games against Guelph in recent years had drawn 10 or 20 times that number of fans and filled the cashboxes of both clubs to overflowing. It was yet another reminder that the old rivalry that prompted both cities to take baseball to new levels was gone. In the game, both clubs made numerous fielding errors, a situation attributed to the rough and unfinished condition of the new park. The Tecumsehs batted well against Billy Smith, the longtime Leafs hurler, who complained of a weak arm. In the second inning, Smith helped himself by hitting a bases-clearing triple to score three runs. Goldsmith pitched well and also had a good day at the plate, hitting two triples and a single. The game was called after eight innings because the Tecumsehs had to catch the train for home, the score standing at 9–8 for London.[36]

As they took that train home, Goldsmith, Powers, and Hornung may have reflected on how times had changed. The three were in their third season with the Tecumsehs and were the senior members of the professional club. If they began to wonder about the future of the game in London, they were not alone.

12

The Dream Dies

Barely two months into the 1878 season, the Tecumsehs captain and manager had reason to feel much better about himself and his decision to join London. He likely saw the brief item in the *Advertiser* gleaned from the *New York World* that said: "Ross Barnes, captain of the Tecumsehs, has recently received two or three offers from United States clubs, but says he'll stop in Canada this season."[1] His play had been noticed, and he was still in demand. Barnes wasn't batting .400 as in previous seasons, but he was still making a major contribution to one of the top teams of the day. He had no intention of abandoning a team that had placed its confidence in him.

The Binghamton Crickets were in London for exhibition contests on June 20–21, the first one left as a scoreless tie when rain halted play in the seventh inning. The next day, the Tecumsehs again battled rain as they rode roughshod over the visitors by a 9–1 score. Marshall Quinton was back in a Tecumsehs uniform, replacing the still-battered receiver Powers, who moved to right field.

The Guelph Maple Leafs came to London for a game on June 24. The visitors had high hopes because they had lost to their old rival only by a single run six days earlier in Guelph. They were hoping to return to their winning ways. Game day, Monday, was not conducive to drawing a large crowd, but London had a busy schedule and had to find gaps between its International Association and touring commitments to shoehorn in games against its old rival. Billy Smith, Guelph's longtime and reliable pitcher, surprised everyone by withdrawing from the game after facing the first Tecumsehs batter. The *Mercury* said Smith had been suffering from chronic pain in his pitching arm and had been planning to retire from that position. He wanted to pitch one more game against Guelph's old rivals before doing so, but the pain overwhelmed him. Smith switched positions with second baseman James Hewer, who had little experience pitching and immediately allowed six London runs.

London showed no mercy, and after eight innings the score was 20–2 when Guelph had to catch its train home.[2]

As the Tecumsehs left town for a five-day tour of New York state, Gorman's *Advertiser* took the *Buffalo Express* to task for unspecified assertions it had made about Quinton and his eligibility to return to the Tecumsehs. Whatever the *Express* had reported was "uncalled for and maliciously mean. The Tecumseh Directors are perfectly competent to manage the affairs of the club and to determine who to retain in their service." The paper said the directors acted with full knowledge of the facts about Quinton (whatever they were).[3] The Buffalo paper likely suggested Quinton was under contract elsewhere and his signing by London was improper. Quinton had not appeared on Buffalo's roster that year but may have been with another New York team where he caught the attention of the *Express*. Regardless, Quinton remained with London for the rest of the season. In the same column, the *Advertiser* noted Guelph's Billy Smith had decided to end his pitching career after the game against the Tecumsehs:

> Old time Canadian ball players will regret to hear of Billy's retirement. He was without exception the best pitcher Canada has up to the present produced, and if he had been as ably supported behind the bat and in the field as he deserved he would have ranked still higher in the profession. He has done his duty well for Guelph, and he is entitled to an honorable rest.

In Syracuse on June 26 for a championship game, the Tecumsehs' bats were lively, led by Dutch Hornung, who made three hits in four at-bats. London won, 6–2. The following day in Utica, in another game for the championship, the Tecumsehs lost, 4–2. Championship losses were recorded in Binghamton and Hornellsville on June 28 and 29, by scores of 9–7 and 3–2, respectively. The Tecumsehs headed home after losing three out of four games to count for the IA pennant, making it harder to defend their crown. The only thing to bring cheer to London and its supporters was the fact that the club was scheduled to play all but one of its remaining championship games at home.[4] Anticipation was great for the July 1 Dominion Day game, for which the visitors would again be Buffalo. On the previous public holiday in London, Victoria Day, Buffalo had won, 7–1, and the Tecumsehs and their supporters were anxious to avenge that loss. Games on public holidays invariably drew the best crowds, and the directors of the club were hoping to cash in.

The July 1 meeting drew 2,000 spectators and featured a pitching duel between Fred Goldsmith and Pud Galvin. Defensively, errorless ball kept the teams close. Ross Barnes connected for a hit in the third inning and "by the exercise of pure unadulterated nerve in base running, got in a run" for the first score of the game. London held a 1–0 lead until the ninth inning, when Buffalo replied with a single score to tie it. In the tenth inning, the visitors scored twice to take the win, 3–1.[5] Tecumsehs supporters were disappointed by yet another loss in a big holiday game. Meanwhile, over in Guelph, Syracuse defeated the now-amateur Maple Leafs, 10–6, before 1,000 holiday fans. Guelph featured a newcomer named Bailey, replacing Smith in the pitcher's box, and he seemed to win the approval of the crowd.[6]

An exhibition game played on July 3 in Lockport, New York, saw Buffalo beat the Tecumsehs, 11–3, as the Bisons continued their winning ways against London. The next day, a large crowd of at least 6,000 attended the July 4 holiday game in Buffalo for the championship, double the number that witnessed the May 30 game in Buffalo when London won, 2–1. Umpiring the game was C. W. Nicholls, a train brakeman in the winter, who relied on his earnings as umpire for Buffalo games in the summer. He was developing a reputation among other teams as a homer for the Bisons, who used him regularly.[7] His calls this day were not challenged, however. A hit by Ross Barnes to right field in the top of the first inning scored center fielder Albert Hall to put the visitors ahead. London added another run in the fourth inning. The following inning, Galvin hit a long fly to Dutch Hornung in left field. Hornung made a spectacular one-handed catch while running backward to record an out, "making the audience applaud until their hands were sore." Meanwhile, alert base runner Dave Eggler scored on the play for Buffalo's only run. The game ended 2–1 for the Tecumsehs.[8] Buffalo had ruined the Dominion Day game for London, and now London had returned the favor on Independence Day. Two days later, in Cleveland, the Tecumsehs were blanked, 8–0, by the Forest Citys before a large crowd. Goldsmith was reported to have taken ill after the first inning and had retired from the field.[9]

The Tecumsehs returned home to disturbing reports about the future of the club as they awaited the arrival of Syracuse for a championship game on July 9. The *Advertiser* pulled no punches as it outlined the problems it saw facing the nine:

> Tomorrow the Tecumsehs meet the Stars of Syracuse on these grounds, the first time this season, and it is to be hoped that there will be a large turnout of citizens to see the game. The sparse attendance which has been the rule this season has a discouraging effect upon the players and managers, and if our people desire to keep up a first class ball nine to supply amusements and recreation during the summer season, they should patronize the games more liberally than they have done in the past. Tomorrow's game between the great rivals for the championship ought to draw a large crowd. Owing to the fact that no less than twelve championship games are set down on the schedule to be played in this city dur-

ing the present month, an effort is being made by the Tecumseh managers to have about half of them played in outside cities. If satisfactory arrangements can be made games will be played in Hamilton, Toronto, Guelph and Detroit, affording the citizens of those places an opportunity of seeing contests between first-class clubs.[10]

The latest standings in the International Association pennant race were included, showing Buffalo in the lead, with 19 wins and ten losses, followed by Syracuse with 18 wins and six losses. London stood third with 18 wins and 11 losses, followed by Utica.

The troubles facing baseball in London were noted by the *Guelph Mercury*, and it was apparent the paper had a source for information about the financial affairs of the Tecumsehs. "London citizens are weakening on base ball," the paper reported on July 9. "The patronage bestowed on games played this year is nothing like it was formerly. On the Queen's Birthday the Buffalos played in London and took away with them only $75, and on Dominion Day $124."[11]

Fans in London had begun to question the integrity of baseball. With all the money being wagered on the outcome of games, temptation still remained for players and officials. The National League's expulsions of Devlin, Craver, Hall, and Nicholls for selling out to gamblers in 1877 hadn't ended questionable conduct of players. They were still around. Craver, it was reported, had signed a contract with the Troy Haymakers and was playing second base for the International Association club. Some controversy was raging there about whether Craver's appearance might negatively impact the outcomes of games played by Troy if the IA ruled he was ineligible.[12] Devlin was soon to surface in London. During that season of 1878, evidence of crookedness continued to emerge. In June, followers of the game in London saw an account in the *Advertiser* alleging that the Syracuse newspapers claimed the Stars lost a game to Worcester because a gambler umpired the game. Later that same month, a Syracuse umpire was accused of having "sold" a game for $200 to gamblers. At the end of June, Indianapolis suspended their star pitcher, Ed "The Only" Nolan, while they investigated him for "crooked play."[13] It was noteworthy that two of the allegations of dishonest conduct involved Syracuse, against whom London had played three times, losing a championship game in Syracuse in May and splitting two exhibition contests.

Syracuse appeared at Tecumseh Park before what the *Free Press* described as "a fair crowd." It was an important showdown between two of the top teams in the pennant race, and it was umpired by the seldom-challenged Tom Gillean.

London was hoping to rebound from three consecutive championship losses in Utica, Binghamton, and Hornellsville. London supporters were hungry for a win. In its unusually brief account, the *Advertiser* reported:

> Up till the eight innings [sic] the game between the Stars and the Tecumsehs yesterday was about as fine a display of the beauties of base ball as one would wish to see. The home team then led by four to nothing, and the prospects were that the game would end that way. But it did not, and as to why those who saw the game will have little trouble in guessing.... The people were very much disappointed at the result of the contest after it appeared to be in the hands of the Tecumsehs.[14]

The comment "as to why those who saw the game will have little trouble in guessing" is more than a little puzzling. The contempt, however, is obvious. But why? Did London "sell" the game?

London surrendered three runs in each of the eighth and ninth innings to lose, 6–5. Yet the Stars had been "outplayed at every point," the paper said. Goldsmith had "weakened" in the eighth inning and was replaced by Bradley. That did not improve Tecumseh fortunes, and Goldsmith returned to his position only to have the home team commit errors that gave the Stars a victory. The *Free Press* account was much more detailed and shed some light on what its journalistic competitor might have been hinting. It noted that in the eighth inning, with two Stars already retired, "Goldsmith left his position, stating that a pain in his side necessitated his withdrawal from pitching the remaining innings." Foghorn Bradley replaced the big right-hander, but: "The change was not acceptable to the audience by any means and great dissatisfaction was expressed in consequence." It continued:

> Of course the visitors could not have wished for a better move, as it is no trouble to experienced batters like them to bat Brad's pitching. Before the third man was retired, no fewer than five base hits were made, and three runs scored, two of them being procured, in part, by an error of Doscher at third base. Goldsmith's conduct was inexplicable to the crowd, and many did not hesitate to state that he left his position without the slightest excuse or reason. On the other hand Goldie contended that he had been ailing with a pain in his left side, in the region of the heart, for weeks past, and that it had troubled him terribly during the progress of the match.[15]

London scored another run in the top of the ninth inning when Doscher doubled to bring home Hornung, increasing the lead to 5–3. Goldsmith returned to pitch the bottom of the inning. He gave up three hits and when he threw to Barnes on an attempted force play, the second baseman made "a palpable muff," allowing two runs to score and tie the game. Stars right fielder Denny Mack managed a base hit, and because of errors by Goldsmith and

Powers, was able to cross home plate to get the win for Syracuse. The *Free Press* continued:

> The audience for some minutes previously commenced to leave the grounds, expressing in language, not to be mistaken, their supreme disgust at the manner in which the home team had allowed themselves to be bamboozled out of a game which, had Goldsmith continued as he began, would in all probability have resulted in their favor by 4 to 0. If the managers allow games to be run as this one was, and as others have been during the season, they need not expect the public to assist them in paying the salaries and expenses incident to keeping up a first-class nine. The funeral is theirs, however, not ours. Some time ago, and indeed, very recently, the management complained of the meagre patronage the club received from the citizens. Two or three more games like that of yesterday, and the managers, directors, players and umpire will have the entire seating accommodation and grounds for their exclusive benefit. The public is not so blind to deception as many individuals think and cannot be imposed upon with impunity.[16]

It was clear that both newspapers, even the *Advertiser*, where Tecumsehs director and former secretary Harry Gorman was local editor and reporter, agreed there was a distinct odor to what had transpired that day in Tecumseh Park. The *Advertiser* minced no words after the London club lost again to the Stars the next day, this time by a score of 6–3. Goldsmith did not play at all, and Doscher pitched. It said:

> General indignation as expressed through the city yesterday at the loss of Tuesday's game [the first match] to the Stars, and all sorts of reasons were advanced, and insinuations made to account for the unexpected defeat of the Tecumsehs. The universal opinion is that base ball received its death blow in London on the Tecumseh grounds last Tuesday, and that it will be futile to attempt to resuscitate the game here for years to come.... At present confidence in the nine is completely gone; the team is completely demoralized by the sudden defection of its pitcher, and it cannot hope to win games in its present condition. There seems to be but one of two courses left to adopt, a thorough reconstruction or complete disbandment.[17]

The situation was serious. Gorman wouldn't have allowed that report to appear in his paper unless he was profoundly upset, perhaps even angry.

A special meeting of the Tecumseh club was called for July 13, at which time a motion to disband was introduced by directors unwilling to pay out another $2,000 in expenses they faced in the next month. Other directors and some followers of the club preferred to see it reorganized, even though they were disgusted at what they had witnessed. It was suggested that the players would do better under another manager "who understands human nature better than the present incumbent."[18]

12. The Dream Dies

Just as London was reeling at the state of affairs with its ball club, Jim Devlin showed up at Tecumseh Park "showing what he could do with the ball when he wanted to."[19] Devlin, still hoping to persuade the National League to overturn its lifetime expulsion of him for selling out to gamblers, wanted to play ball. His timing couldn't have been worse, as London was preoccupied with wondering whether Goldsmith and his teammates had thrown a game just two days earlier. In the minds of many citizens, the Tecumsehs had become tainted. The sudden appearance of a former Louisville player who had admitted to throwing games for gamblers did nothing to dispel those concerns.

Goldsmith was back as pitcher for two games against the Manchesters, an exhibition 4–2 win on July 12 and a championship match the next day. In the latter game, especially, he pitched "with his old effect." It was reported that several dazzling fielding plays were made by Barnes, Burke, Doscher, and Hall, as the Tecumsehs won, 4–0.[20]

That same night, a large crowd attended a special meeting of the Tecumseh Base Ball Club at the Tecumseh House Hotel. President Jake Englehart turned the chair over to vice-president J. W. Jones so the busy refiner could speak.

> Mr. Englehart informed the meeting that owing to recent occurrences, resulting in the loss of confidence in the Tecumseh club, it had become necessary to call in their friends for consultation. The question to consider was, whether the citizens desired to support the club, and if they were satisfied with it as at present organized. Considerable conversation followed and numerous questions were asked, from which it was elicited that the support given to the club by the citizens was not sufficient to enable it to continue through the season without involving the stockholders in considerable loss. The recent disasters had destroyed the attendance and unless the citizens would renew their patronage it would be impossible to go on. The financial statement showed that some fifteen hundred dollars remained against the fitting up of the grounds, and that this year's business, up to the 15th of July, had resulted in a loss of something over two hundred dollars. In answer to questions from several present, the Directors of the club, individually and collectively, assured the meeting that there was not the slightest ground for crediting the rumors that the Star game on the 9th had been sold. Searching inquiry had been made and the trouble was traced to the fact that Goldsmith was really suffering from severe pains in the region of the heart. Medical advice had been obtained and remedies applied which it was believed would prevent a recurrence of the attacks to which he had been subject of late. The effective way in which he pitched during the two Manchester games encouraged the belief that there would be no further difficulty from that source.
>
> All present expressed their satisfaction at hearing the reports as to crooked play were unfounded, and the strongest desire was manifested to place the club in such a position that no loss would occur in carrying it through the season. Mr. Englehart intimated that the calls upon his time in relation to his own business

were such that he could not discharge the duties of President as efficiently as he would wish to see them done, and he intended to resign. This was met by a decided negative from the meeting. It was then moved by Mr. W. R. Meredith, M.P.P. [Member of Provincial Parliament for London], seconded by Col. [John] Walker, that it is desirable to continue the Tecumseh club, and that steps be taken to secure the stockholders against loss, on the understanding that Mr. Englehart retains the presidency. The resolution was passed without dissent.[21]

The meeting established a "strong and influential committee" to raise funds through subscriptions to the team. The group was off to a fine start, as $500 was committed then and there. It was "confidently asserted" that $2,000 could be raised in a week. In the meantime, the *Advertiser* urged Londoners to show support for the team by turning up at the ballpark and by encouraging directors to continue. Directors met after the public meeting and decided to eliminate the 11th member of the team to cut expenses. That move forced the retirement of Tommy Smith. Arrangements were to be made to play some upcoming games against American opponents in the Ontario communities of Hamilton, Guelph and Woodstock in a bid to attract additional game receipts.

> The attention of the Tecumseh directors was called at their meeting on Saturday to certain rumors current concerning a change in the management, and to the fitness of sundry club officials for their positions. It was ascertained that the rumors referred to originated among some of the players, and the Directors desire to have it understood distinctly that they are thoroughly satisfied with the club manager; have not now and never had the slightest intention of making a change, and that the fullest confidence is reposed in him. They look to the players hereafter to attend strictly and solely to the duties they are paid to perform.[22]

Internal strife and complaints about the style of Tecumsehs captain and manager Ross Barnes had become known, but the directors weren't about to change things at this critical juncture.

The problems in London caught the attention of the *New York Times*. The paper was not known for paying much attention to baseball, beyond carrying some scores. But there on the front page of its July 15 edition was a brief account, headlined: "The Tecumseh Base Ball Club." It said the stockholders had met and had discussed "recent troubles.... The club was shown to stand well financially, and satisfactory evidence being given that the suspicion of crooked play was entirely unfounded, it was unanimously resolved to continue it. No changes were made in the players or the Board of Directors."[23] Boosters of the Tecumsehs who said the team could put the city of London on the map would have been pleased to see recognition in the *Times*. It is doubtful anything short of a catastrophe or natural disaster could have catapulted the

12. The Dream Dies

Canadian city of less than 20,000 souls onto the front page of that august journal.

In coming days, it was reported in the local papers that Jim Devlin had become the pitcher for the Atlantics, London's premier amateur nine from whose ranks the Tecumsehs often drew replacement players. It was also noted that Tommy Smith wasn't unemployed for long. He quickly joined the Syracuse Stars to play outfield.[24] The Tecumsehs entertained Lowell for two exhibition games, winning the first, 2–1, and the second, 13–0, as London bats pounded Lowell pitcher Curry Foley. The Tecumsehs played Worcester in Woodstock on July before a crowd of nearly 1,000 and won, 7–0. In London for a championship game, Worcester was again defeated, this time by a score of 11–6, putting the Tecumsehs temporarily in first place in the race for the pennant, just ahead of Buffalo.[25] The winning streak continued for London as it downed the Cleveland Forest Citys, 5–3, and Springfield, 3–2, both in exhibition games, before embarking on a short road trip.

On August 6 in Troy, the Tecumsehs defeated the Haymakers, 6–0, relying heavily on outstanding pitching and hitting by Goldsmith. The following day, in a second exhibition match, they won again, 12–4, as Doscher pitched several innings. It was learned that Manchester had disbanded, a development that had no impact on the standings of the top three clubs, Buffalo, London, and Syracuse. Just a few days earlier, Binghamton had suffered the same fate. Concerns about the viability of professional teams was not restricted to the International Association, however. Many teams were struggling as the business recession lingered. In the same edition of the *Advertiser*, it was noted that the National League was taking steps to cut costs in a bid to achieve profitability. A League meeting to be held in Providence would consider a "permanent schedule of salaries" for players on League teams. Pitchers would earn $1,200, catchers $1,000, first basemen $700, second basemen $800, third basemen $900, shortstops $700, outfielders $600 and substitutes $500.[26] This determination of player worth was an interesting exercise and likely sent tongues wagging. It also proved divisive, and some players would have seen it as insulting. But it was another example of how the League was determined to control the game and contain its costs.

Tommy Smith, the just-released outfielder of the Tecumsehs, was in uniform for the Stars in an August 9 exhibition game in Syracuse that London lost, 3–1. In another exhibition, London fell, 2–1, to Oswego before returning home to face Rochester.

At its August 10 meeting in Providence, the National League opted against imposing strict salary caps on players, a contentious issue on which consensus could not be reached among delegates. But it did freeze total salaries paid by each club in 1879 at the 1878 level. In an announcement after closed-door deliberations, League president William Hulbert said he believed his organization's efforts "have been appreciated and approved, and that all the lovers of pure and manly sports will concede that its efforts have been directed toward the elevation of the game." He went on:

> It is a part of the experience of the League clubs for the season of 1878 that the business depression has so far affected the receipts that a loss is already assured. At the same time it is apparent that under the present system the loss must fall on the associations from whom the players receive the money earned and much more. The League declines to continue business on this principle, and takes this time to announce to players that for 1879 the aggregate salaries paid by each club must not exceed the sum which the experience of this year has shown can be earned. It has not, however, after discussion, seemed wise at this time to attempt any agreement as to what the association shall pay any or all of the men in its employ. In the line of reduction of expense within probable income of the League, the League has ... entered into an agreement which binds its members to make the contract season for 1879 six months long.... It is expected by thus giving the player fully half a year for the pursuit of any trade or business which he may have he will be enabled to devote the other half to play at less cost to the club.[27]

Hulbert said clubs were barred from paying monetary advances during the winter season because "the practice has in the past encouraged idleness and discouraged some players from following such business or trade as they were fitted for." It was clear the National League was turning the screws on players even more in its pursuit of elusive profit. Particularly galling for players was the assertion that they should find some other line of work to tide them over in the off-season between October 1 and March 31.

London's third public holiday, Civic Holiday, August 12, was looked forward to with some apprehension. The Tecumsehs had lost the Victoria Day and Dominion Day games to Buffalo. Another New York team, Rochester, would be the guest for this one. Spectators were soon put at ease, however. The Tecumsehs' bats were booming and they scored four runs in the first inning, then two more in the second as the Rochesters were held scoreless by Goldsmith. Rochester replaced its pitcher, Burkalow, with Sullivan, but it made no difference. London scored three more runs in the seventh inning. Rochester scored twice in the ninth for a final score of 9–2 for London. The umpire was Jim Devlin, who earlier on the grounds that day had pitched for the Atlantics and led them to a 5–2 victory over the Woodstock Actives. In the Tecumsehs–Rochester game, Devlin's work as umpire drew praise, it being noted, "he is at home at that position. Calm and collected, he keeps an eye on all points that are played."[28]

12. The Dream Dies

The Tecumsehs played Rochester again the next day in Hamilton and lost, 10–6, as Goldsmith gave up 16 hits, and everything London batters hit found the hands (few wore gloves then) of the opposition. As the team prepared for a short road trip, J. A. Williams, secretary of the International Association, announced that William Craver, expelled by the National League for his part in the Louisville scandal, would be allowed to play in the Association. The secretary said Louisville failed to provide a copy of the charges against Craver when asked. Craver, Williams said, had proven his innocence in a hearing before the judiciary committee and was thus entitled to play.[29] The decision of the International Association must have angered League president Hulbert, who had vowed that as long as he was alive, he wouldn't let Craver, Devlin, and the other two crooked Grays ever play again. Yet again, the International Association was asserting itself, demonstrating it was not subservient in any way to the League. Rival leagues can disagree. Minor ones submit.

The Tecumseh trip through New York state was not successful on the field, although none of the games counted for the championship. The Tecumsehs lost on August 14 in Hornellsville by a score of 13–2, then came up short, 15–10, in Buffalo two days later. That latter pasting prompted the *Advertiser* to reprint an item from the *Cincinnati Enquirer* about games played in Buffalo, perhaps in a bid to soften the blow of that particular loss: "People have ceased to take an interest in reports of games played on their own grounds, as it is a foregone conclusion that the umpire will see that the visitors do not win."[30] The *Advertiser* added: "The Rochesters claim to have been swindled out of their last game at Buffalo by Nicholls, the umpire." Back home, on August 19–20, London again disappointed their supporters as they lost, 5–0 and 6–1, to Utica, both games counting toward the championship. The Tecumsehs then took a steamer across Lake Erie to Cleveland, where, on August 21, they lost to the Forest Citys by an 11–8 score. The following day, the visitors from Canada turned the tables on Cleveland with a 12–4 victory. It marked Goldsmith's 48th win—his last as a Tecumseh.

Devlin was pitching for the Atlantics, and Bob Emslie had made way for him by moving to the outfield. After a game in Woodstock before a large crowd, the Atlantics defeated the hometown Actives 3–2. "The Atlantics played a beautiful game, Devlin and Thompson working together like professionals," it was observed in a sly reference to Devlin's past.[31] The Atlantics were well on their way to winning their fourth Canadian amateur baseball championship pennant.

Things were not rosy for the big club in London. While the Tecumsehs were still in Cleveland, the *London Free Press* carried this account:

> A meeting of the stockholders of the Tecumseh Base Ball Club and friends of the team was held at the Tecumseh House last night for the purpose of considering matters of importance in connection with the association. Quite a large number were present. It was shown (to those who were not previously aware of the fact) that the loss of the two games played with the Uticas here this week completely excluded them from any chance in the race for the pennant, and the debt being quite as heavy [*sic*] as the directors wished at the present time to bear out of their own pockets, it was resolved to give the players their release on Saturday next, when they will be paid their salaries in full, and be at liberty to offer their services to other clubs, if they feel so disposed. It is the intention to pay off all liabilities and wind up the affairs of the club in good shape. The debts aggregate, it is reported, some $2,200. The chances are that a club composed of some of the present team, with four or five of the positions filled with amateurs, will be organized at once and finish the two championship games with the Springfields. This is to be done that the latter nine may not be the sufferers by the disbandment of the Tecumsehs.[32]

The Tecumsehs were not alone in their financial problems. On August 22, it was reported that the Hornells had disbanded because of money woes and the loss of their manager. That brought to five the number of teams that had signed on for the championship race only to collapse: Allegheny, Lynn (which had moved to Worcester), Binghamton, Manchester, and Hornellsville. At the end of the season, Rochester did the same.

As the Tecumsehs paid off their players on August 24 and reorganized, the *Advertiser* took time to review the record of the team to that date. It noted that 43 games had been played for the championship and the Tecumsehs had won 27 of them, lost 14, forfeited one, and played another to a draw. In their victories, they had averaged six runs a game. In 10 of the wins, their opposition had been unable to score a run, while the Tecumsehs were held off the score sheet only twice.

> Were it not for the fact that the majority of the defeats inflicted upon the Tecumsehs were due to gross carelessness and an ill-disguised feeling of indifference on the part of some of the players, the record would not be a discreditable one. It may be that the public expected too much from the Tecumsehs, and hence were doomed to disappointment, but the general impression left on the minds of the people is that the Tecumsehs lost games, not because their opponents were too strong for them, but because they did not throw their united strength into the contest as they ought to have done.[33]

In Buffalo, the Bisons were enjoying a good August. They were still vying for first place in the Association. In addition they had defeated four National League teams: Milwaukee, 4–3; Cincinnati, twice, 7–1 and 8–2; Chicago, 3–2; and Indianapolis, 6–3.[34] Late in the month, Dutch Hornung, freshly released from London, signed on with the team. The *Buffalo Courier* congratulated its team on the "disbandment" of the Tecumsehs, a move that would have improved Buffalo's record by removing one of its losses. But the *Advertiser* was quick to jump on that claim. "The *Courier* should know that the Tecumsehs have not disbanded; they have merely dispensed with the services of a number of its players whose places will be filled by others, and the two games with the Springfields necessary to complete its quota of championship games will be played in due time."[35] The paper took the occasion to review the Tecumseh record of 1878 and found that the club had played 72 games against all comers, winning 44 of them. It noted, surprisingly, that this was a better record than the previous year, despite its failure to retain the pennant. The winning percentage in 1878 was 61 percent. In 1877, by comparison, 80 games had been played, with 47 wins recorded.[36] The winning percentage in its successful championship year was just under 59 percent.

By early September, it was reported that Phil Powers was being wooed by Chicago, and that Fred Goldsmith was pitching for Springfield.[37] In Springfield, Goldsmith shared the pitcher's box with Larry Corcoran, the youngster who was released the previous season by Buffalo and whom he had faced in exhibition games. As the month went on, the race between Buffalo and Syracuse for the International Association pennant remained extremely tight. The Tecumsehs were in third place, just ahead of Utica. Meanwhile, in the National League, Boston had a lock on the 1878 championship.

In London, the Atlantics won their fourth consecutive amateur Canadian championship without losing a game, other than two exhibitions against the Tecumsehs and two against the Forest Citys of Cleveland.[38] The Tecumsehs continued to say they were willing to play Springfield if satisfactory arrangements could be made; and the *Advertiser* continually corrected reports from other papers saying the team had disbanded. But the two outstanding championship games with Springfield were never played, the teams unable to make suitable arrangements.[39]

On October 8, a game between Utica and Buffalo marked the end of the race for the IA championship, with the Bisons claiming the pennant. The *Syracuse Courier* disagreed and printed standings that appeared to establish the Stars as champions, with 27 wins and nine losses, followed a game back by Buffalo with 26 wins and ten losses. The Tecumsehs were third, with 23 wins and 11 losses, just ahead of Utica with its 22 wins and 14 losses.[40] The closeness of the race between Buffalo and Syracuse was later adjusted to show Buffalo with 32 wins and 12 losses for a winning percentage of .727. Syracuse was accorded 27 wins and ten losses for a winning percentage of .729. But under the rules of the day, the total number of wins determined the winner, even though modern reference books consider Syracuse the winner because of the better winning percentage.[41] Likewise, London edged out Utica for third place, even though its winning percentage was .643, less than the .667 for Utica. At the time, however, no pennant winner was announced by the International Association, which chose to let its judiciary committee study the records and report its findings.

The Buffalo–Syracuse rivalry was intense, and not unlike the longer-standing one between London and Guelph. One game between the two New York teams that September was included in *Inventing Baseball: The 100 Greatest Games of the Nineteenth Century*, published by the Nineteenth Century Committee of the Society for American Baseball Research. The game itself, on September 14, was nothing remarkable. Buffalo scored early and often to romp to a 9–1 win. Rather, it was noteworthy because of its place in the bigger picture of baseball at the time. It pitted the two most successful non–League teams against each other, and everyone present felt it was a precursor to determining the outcome of the Association championship. "In a larger sense, the game symbolized the 'last hurrah' of the old regime, under which players were in control of the league, local umpires made calls that benefitted local teams, and teams interpreted the rules for themselves."[42]

The International Association had the same approach to baseball as the old National Association, with players having a say in important decisions. They also shared cheap entry fees, loose scheduling, poor business practices, and instability among teams, although the IA easily rivaled the tightly controlled National League in terms of the quality of players and teams.[43] In the Buffalo-Syracuse contest were many players who had long careers ahead of them that included service in the National League. Future hall of famer Pud Galvin and all-stars Dutch Horning, Chick Fulmer, and Davy Force were on the Buffalo side, while curveball specialist Harry McCormick and outstanding second baseman Jack Farrell appeared for the Stars. McCormick had learned the pitch from Candy Cummings and Fred Goldsmith and was becoming a top pitcher in his own right. Even after the game and the season ended, Buffalo and Syracuse fought about their records.

Buffalo had attracted widespread attention because of its winning ways and its dominant pitcher. The team's overall record was 81 wins, 32 losses, and three ties. Galvin had amassed 72 wins, 25 losses, and three ties. He recorded 17 shutouts and won ten games against National League teams, including at least one against each NL club, losing five against them. Galvin threw at least 895 innings that year, it has been estimated—an impressive showing.[44] Better times were yet to come for "the Little Steam Engine."

In London, it was reported that Ross Barnes had signed a deal for $400 a month with the League's Cincinnati Red Stockings for 1879. Phil Powers would play for Springfield, where his old battery mate Fred Goldsmith had signed on.[45] Goldsmith was coming off a season in London where he had pitched 76 games, winning 48 and losing 26. He had pitched 682 innings, leading his team to its third straight Canadian championship.[46] In November, as the former members of the Tecumsehs spoke to teams about the following year, it was announced that longtime club secretary Harry Gorman was also leaving town. An employee of the *Advertiser* since its first edition in 1863, Gorman was praised for his dedication to his craft and his duties as compositor, foreman, reporter, and editor. Staff of the paper presented him with a book, a gold pen and their best wishes on his new challenge.[47] Gorman and journalist George Eyvel, of the *Toronto Globe*, had purchased the weekly *Sarnia Observer* newspaper, about 60 miles west of London. Gorman, who preferred to be known as Henry Gorman in Sarnia, moved there and stayed with the paper until 1917, after converting it to daily publication in 1895. In 1898, he was named police magistrate, a post in which he adjudicated lesser criminal and other offences. He died in 1928 at the age of 90.[48]

The year 1878 had been a tumultuous one for professional baseball in London. The Tecumsehs lost their fans, their players, the Association pennant, and a pioneer whose love of baseball and recruiting efforts had taken a small Canadian city to the top ranks of the game.

The loss of its first championship team was also a blow to the International Association, but far worse was yet to come.

13

Moving On

The National League had struggled through another season in 1878, beset by flagging attendance and money troubles because teams continued to steal players by providing them financial inducements. The buying of talent was an act of desperation by clubs anxious to attract and keep fans during tough economic times. Their financial prospects had actually worsened following the League decision to ban outside teams from League parks—a move compounded by the International Association's reaction to do unto the League as the League had done unto it. With only six members, the National League was a small, exclusive club. Its teams had plenty of open dates and large ballparks, but only a limited number of opportunities to play outside clubs to help them pay their bills. No wonder attendance at their parks was down. Again, the only team to turn a profit was Chicago.[1] Two League members were in trouble: Indianapolis folded, its owner embroiled in financial troubles so deep that he chose to flee the state; Milwaukee was expelled for failing to meet its financial obligations.[2]

The League was left with four teams, and again, president William Hulbert turned his eyes eastward, looking to expand. The same ruthless man who stole the "Big Four" players from Boston for his 1876 White Stockings, then scooped up three from Cincinnati in 1877 when that franchise faltered, was again at work. Hulbert persuaded the top two teams of the International Association, Buffalo and Syracuse, to join the League, a move formally approved at the League's meeting on December 4 in Cleveland. The new Cleveland Blues club was also accepted, and soon afterward, the Troy Trojans, champions of the New York State Association, applied and were added. This brought the National League to eight teams.[3] Troy had a population of about 55,000, and Syracuse about 50,000, both well below the 75,000 threshold set by the League, a situation it was now willing to overlook. All newcomers were required to charge 50 cents admission, and their continued interaction with non–League teams was sharply curtailed.

13. Moving On

For the International Association, the loss of its two most successful teams was a serious blow. It had already lost London, its third-place franchise, to collapse, with no prospect of a return. Now that the National League could boast eight teams, it could schedule more games among its members. This reduced the need to play outside teams, so the League devised a schedule of 84 games. The impact was far-reaching. "Hulbert's expansion cut the opportunities for talented players on IA teams and independent clubs to match their skills on the playing field against their League counterparts," baseball historian David Nemec has noted. "The consequence was that in 1879, for the first time, playing in the League became a status symbol.... It effectively killed the IA as a worthy rival."[4]

As delegates gathered in Utica for the annual meeting of the International Association on February 18, 1879, they may have had a sense of foreboding at the moves being taken by the League. At the outset of the three-day gathering, its judiciary committee faced the knotty task of determining the Association champions. At one point, the notion was promoted that it should be Utica, because of the departure of Buffalo and Syracuse and the late-season troubles of London, which discharged its professionals. After hours of debate, Buffalo was awarded the pennant, with Syracuse second and Utica third, the latter decision rendered because of the loss of the London franchise.[5] The organization renamed itself the National Base-Ball Association, to reflect the loss of Canadian participation. L. J. Powers, of Springfield, was named president. In all, nine clubs indicated they planned to compete for the NBBA pennant in 1879: Utica, Manchester, the Washington Nationals, New Bedford, Holyoke, Worcester, Springfield, and two different clubs from Albany. One from the capital of New York state called itself Albany, while the other, based immediately across the Hudson River, was the Capital City club.[6] Both were located a mere seven miles from Troy, the newly minted member of the National League.

Henry Chadwick at the *Clipper* had never shared Hulbert's vision of tight control of the game by a small group of businessmen. A populist, he looked ahead to the 1879 Association season in the paper's March 2 edition. Chadwick was anxious for it to succeed. Despite its challenges, he declared, "there has never been a better opportunity" to put the Association "on a permanent foundation." It was the only "truly national professional association," he argued, whereas only wealthy stock companies could enter the League. He worried, however, that if the Association did not succeed, its cooperative clubs would face a "chaotic condition." There were still plenty of them in smaller industrial cities, and he feared they might be driven to questionable practices such as showboating and falling under the control of gamblers, thereby succumbing to "the very evils the League ... aims to put a stop to." He acknowledged that organizing teams on a stock company basis was likely the best route to take for their survival. He also urged the Association to retain liberal admission requirements, unlike its rival. He said Association teams couldn't be overly selective about their opponents and should be willing to play unaffiliated clubs, unlike the National League.[7]

The *Clipper* awarded gold medals to the players from the 1878 International Association season who Chadwick felt were best at their positions. Three of them were Tecumsehs: Ross Barnes at second base, Herman Doscher at third, and Dutch Hornung in left field. Three members of Buffalo—Steve Libby at first, Davy Force at shortstop, and Bill McGunnigle, right fielder—were also recognized, along with pitcher Harry McCormick and his catcher, Jerry Dorgan, from Syracuse.[8]

Shortly before Christmas, it was reported that Fred Goldsmith was confined to bed in Springfield, Massachusetts, "with an abscess on his left side, which is doubtless the outcome of the trouble with his side he so often complained [about] last season." His doctor was optimistic of a full recovery and said he expected his patient would again be able to pitch effectively.[9] Goldsmith was entitled to some rest. He had thrown 903 innings in the previous season, 682 for the Tecumsehs and 221 for the Springfields, recording 18 shutouts in 101 games.[10] The problem with his side was aggravated by an off-season injury. Goldsmith had been working in a livery stable and hurt his left side when he tried to stop a runaway horse and buggy. As he did so, the buggy overturned on him.

While recovering, Goldsmith was joined by the London girl he had married in 1877 but who had remained behind in Canada. Rowena Rook, two years younger than Goldsmith, was finishing her musical education with plans to become a concert pianist. Her father, like Goldsmith's father, Ransom, disliked baseball. Rowena's father gave his blessings to the marriage only if his daughter continued her studies at the conservatory. "Rowie," as she was known, had been studying in France that fall of 1878 when Goldsmith signed with Springfield.[11]

Other members of the Tecumsehs were seeking work for the upcoming season, when Goldsmith agreed to return to Springfield, where he and Larry Corcoran would share pitching duties. Joining them was Goldsmith's old battery mate, Phil Powers. The catcher, known as Grandmother, or Grandma, because of his clean living, retained a similar connection to London as Goldsmith. He had dated a girl named Mary during his years in London, and they had married. The couple often returned to her hometown to visit family. In 1882, Powers became player-manager for a revived Tecumsehs team, but it lost money and soon disbanded. He then joined Cincinnati, where, within weeks, he broke his wrist in a collision at home plate and missed most of the rest of the season. His Red Stockings managed without him and won the inaugural pennant of the American Association. Powers stayed with Cincinnati for three more seasons before moving to Baltimore. In Baltimore, he played only nine games, but during that time was reunited with former London pitchers Bob Emslie and Billy Mountjoy. At the end of that 1885 season, Powers retired. He became a regular umpire in the National League from 1886 to 1891, taking time off in 1888 to return yet again to London as player-manager for the local entry in the International Baseball League. He and Mary and their four daughters eventually moved to New York City, where he became a messenger for the Manhattan Bureau of Buildings. He died there of pneumonia in 1914.[12]

National League teams picked up many of the Tecumsehs players for 1879. Joe Hornung signed to play left field for Buffalo, where he had impressed the club with his contributions at the tail end of the 1878 season. The Buffalo championship-winning roster was kept largely intact. Meanwhile, Ross Barnes, Mike Burke, and former Tecumsehs John Magner signed with Cincinnati. Herm Doscher went with Chicago and then moved to Troy, where another former London player, Al Hall, was the center fielder. The ease with which most Tecumsehs found new positions attested to their reputations within the baseball community. They were among the more than 300 players who signed contracts with League and Association teams for the 1879 season.[13]

Henry Chadwick's hopes for the former International Association might have been borne out with a successful third season. But it proved to be a miserable affair, characterized by team instability, treachery, thrown games, and infiltration by gamblers. The new Capital City club was a particular problem. It seemed to be well-financed, having come up with $4,000 to secure a field, and paying three of its players $1,500 each. But the team played poorly, committing countless errors, and its members drank openly and played poker instead of practicing. They didn't win a single game at home and their support from fans began to dwindle.

It was soon discovered that a scheme had been hatched to move the team west to Rochester. By May, local supporters were fed up, and the team released its players to Rochester, where they reconstituted themselves as the Hop Bitters. The name was derived from its sponsor, the Hop Bitters Company, producer of a hop-based potion touted as a medical cure-all. This drew criticism in their new home and elsewhere for promoting a commercial product rather than a city. Meanwhile, back in Albany, an upset member of the city council went so far as to contact the judiciary committee of the Association to file charges of "crooked play" against five men who had become members of the Hop Bitters.

Meanwhile, the Manchester club was suspected of being controlled by gamblers and had become unpopular with the locals. It drew as few as 100 spectators to its home games. Manchester was forced to play on the road to make money, but the team finally collapsed. Utica, the Hop Bitters in Rochester, and Springfield also failed. Disbandment of the latter freed Goldsmith, Powers, and Corcoran to move on. Teams and crowds demonstrated poor, sometimes unruly, behavior throughout the forgettable 1879 season. Ultimately, Albany won the NBBA championship. On its roster were several players who went on to lengthy and successful professional careers, including Tommy Burns, Lipman Pike, and Ned Hanlon.[14]

For 1879, the National League returned to eight teams, the first time since its debut in 1876. A rebuilt Chicago team, in which Albert Goodwill Spalding had invested, enjoyed a strong start, winning three games at home in succession against League newcomers Syracuse and Troy. Cap Anson, the first baseman, was named manager, beginning nearly two decades in that post. Chicago held onto first place, with Providence just behind and Boston a bit further back, until August, when Anson was sidelined with a liver ailment that ended his season. The White Stockings began to falter, and Providence surged, fending off Boston to capture the pennant. Buffalo finished third, with a record of 46 wins and 32 losses, a hair ahead of Chicago by virtue of having one fewer loss. It was a respectable finish for the Bisons, an organization that had turned professional barely two years earlier. Placing seventh was Syracuse, with 22 wins and 48 losses, ahead of cellar-dweller Troy, which won 19 games and lost 56. In early September, facing bankruptcy, Syracuse disbanded after its final game.[15]

On September 17, Fred Goldsmith pitched for Troy after the breakup of Springfield, to record his first win in the National League. It was a 5–4 victory over Chicago, a club to which he was no stranger. The White Stockings remembered him well from their exhibition games against the Tecumsehs and still didn't like losing to him. So, after the season ended, Chicago offered him a contract for 1880. While in Springfield, Goldsmith pitched 327 innings and recorded 26 wins against nine losses.[16] For Troy, he pitched 63 innings in eight League games, winning one more game and losing four.[17]

The National League took a dramatic step on September 29, 1879, that changed baseball with a move that would last nearly a century. The "reserve clause" was adopted that allowed every team to designate as many as five of its players as "reserved" to play for it again the following year. Club owners wanted to protect their best players and keep them from being wooed away by higher salaries elsewhere. For the owners, it was a cost-containment measure, because the League's first four seasons had all been money losers. For players, being reserved was seen at first as flattery and job security—until they realized it reduced their opportunities to seek higher pay from other clubs and led to a reduction in salaries.[18] Ultimately, the "reserve clause" brought some financial stability to the League, but it also generated much resentment, leading to the establishment of rival leagues. Chicago's announcement on October 2 that it had signed Troy's Fred Goldsmith for the 1880 season prompted Troy to protest that the White Stockings had already violated the new "reserve clause" rule.[19] If so, it certainly wasn't the first time Chicago czar and National League president William Hulbert had acted as though rules were made for other people. Yet again, he got away with it.

The annual meeting of the National Base-Ball Association held in New York City on February 18–19, 1880, must have been a gloomy affair. Only four clubs were present: Albany, the Nationals of Washington, Jersey City, and Baltimore. Albany, the Nationals, and Baltimore signed up for the pennant race. Seventeen other clubs opted to become affiliate members. Several of them, particularly Washington and Albany, played exhibition games with League clubs and fared reasonably well. The Nationals played a dozen games before Opening Day, winning four and tying one. Albany played seven, winning four and losing three. Albany struggled to repeat its winning ways from its 1879 campaign, despite such standout players as Lipman Pike, Jimmy Say, and Mike Dorgan. The club played poorly, and it wasn't long before the local press suggested they should either win or disband. For its part, Baltimore disbanded in June, followed a month later by Albany. The Nationals club, the only team left in the championship race, was awarded the pennant. The Association, an organization that had challenged the National League as a rival for baseball supremacy, was dead. As historian David Pietrusza put it:

> Basically, the International Association and the National Base-Ball Association were ultimately unsuited to competition with the more-aggressive, better organized, larger-population-based National League. It would not be long before others were willing to take up the cudgel against William Hulbert's powerful combine.[20]

Another observer, Ted Vincent, has opined that the folding of professional franchises in smaller markets by 1880 and 1881 meant "the number of teams outside the League playing a regular schedule of games could be counted on one hand. Hundreds of players had been driven back to the factories, the mills, or pool halls whence they came."[21]

For the 1880 season, National League clubs began inserting the "reserve clause" in player contracts. Until 1883, five players on each team would see such a clause, after which it was hiked to 11, and eventually everyone on the roster. The schedule was again set at 84 games, allowing each of the eight teams (Worcester had replaced Syracuse) to meet each other 12 times. Buffalo was back, but began the season without Pud Galvin. He had been lured away by the San Francisco Athletics of the California League, who had seen him pitch when a "picked nine" of eastern players toured California late the previous year. In May, Buffalo urged Galvin to return and advanced him $300 to do so. He jumped at the chance, but the Athletics insisted he honor his contract with them. Galvin used an assumed name to elude the authorities the Athletics had contacted in a bid to stop his flight back east, and he rejoined the Bisons for their May 22 game in Cincinnati.[22]

Providence was not the powerhouse it had been in 1879, a factor clearly tied to the "reserve clause." The Grays had placed George Wright, its shortstop and manager, on its reserve list. But Wright unexpectedly opted to retire from the game to grow the sporting goods company he had established in Boston. When he left, Providence was considerably weakened, although it managed a second-place finish in the League. Chicago was the fairytale team of the season, primarily for two basic reasons: hitting and pitching. Team captain Cap Anson was back and healthy after the liver ailment that shortened his previous season, and he batted .337. Three other White Stockings were among the League's top five hitters for 1880. Center fielder George Gore, the overall leader, batted .360, while left fielder Abner Dalrymple batted .330 and shortstop Tom Burns .309.

Pitchers Fred Goldsmith and Larry Corcoran became the League's first pitching rotation (although they had teamed up earlier, in Springfield). Anson, a strict disciplinarian, worked them hard. Corcoran recorded 43 wins, while Goldsmith tallied 21. The latter accomplishment was particularly impressive because Goldsmith notched those wins in only 24 appearances for a League-leading winning percentage of .875. The big right-hander came down with pneumonia in mid–July and was bedridden at his family's home in New Haven.[23] Luckily, he recovered from the same ailment that had claimed the life of his Tecumsehs teammate Ed Somerville in 1877, but he did not return to the lineup until early September. He was no longer pitching to his old friend Phil Powers, who spent part of the 1880 season in Boston. Instead, Goldsmith was still getting used to Frank "Silver" Flint, a hard-drinking but reliable receiver in his second year with the White Stockings. Goldsmith's .875 winning percentage was not topped by any pitcher earning 20 or more victories until 1951. Both Corcoran and Goldsmith were considered good fielders and often took the field in games when the other man pitched, Goldsmith often replacing Anson at first. Anson also liked the fact that Goldsmith was not inclined to party and drink like his catcher Silver Flint and some of the others. When future evangelist Billy Sunday joined the team, Anson picked Goldsmith as the newcomer's roommate.[24] That same 1880 season, Corcoran recorded one of the three no-hitters he pitched in his career.

Chicago was a baseball juggernaut: On July 8, the White Stockings won their 21st consecutive game, defeating Providence, thereby boosting their record to 35 wins against three losses. The impressive winning streak wasn't matched until 1916 by the New York Giants. Second-place Providence was far behind. On September 15, Chicago clinched the National League pennant, its record then standing at 59 wins and 13 losses. Goldsmith had easily made the transition to the National League and played a key role on its best team, although there is some evidence of friction with his new manager. Of Goldsmith, the hard-nosed Cap Anson later said in his autobiography, *A Ball Player's Career*:

> Fred Goldsmith ... was a great big, over-grown, good-natured boy, who was always just a-going to do things that he never did.... He was the possessor of a great slow ball and was always cool and good natured. As a batsman he was only fair, and as a fielder decidedly careless. When it came to backing up a player "Goldy" was never to be relied upon, and after the play was over and he was asked why he had not done so, he would reply: "Oh, I'd a-bin thar ef I'd bin needed." But in spite of this the fact remains that he was rarely on hand when he was needed, and many an overthrown ball found its way into the field that would have been stopped had he been backing up the baseman in the way that he should have done.[25]

Anson obviously didn't care for Goldsmith's work ethic and was determined to push the big man and the diminutive Corcoran alike. The tandem of Corcoran and Goldsmith again helped Chicago win League pennants in 1881 and 1882 when Goldsmith recorded 24 and 28 wins, respectively. Corcoran had 31 and 27 wins in those two years. In 1883, Chicago finished second behind Boston as Corcoran won 34 games and Goldsmith earned 25. Both Corcoran and Goldsmith complained that Anson was too demanding and was abusing their arms, often asking them to perform in back-to-back games. They saw plenty of action and by the end of the 1884 season the twosome had produced 213 wins for the White Stockings in their four years with the club. Both men were suffering from sore arms in 1884 when Chicago finished in a tie for fourth. The 130-pound Corcoran fought through pain to record 35 wins, but the 200-pound-plus Goldsmith, who was three years older, faltered. He registered only nine wins against 11 losses. Never a slouch with the bat, despite his panning by Anson, Goldsmith showed some unexpected power in the hitting department, as if to compensate for his poor pitching. In late May, he drove a ball over the left-field fence in Buffalo for the second home run of his career. Goldsmith was as surprised as anyone and laughed his way around the bases, it was said. Two innings later, he repeated the feat. This time, he collapsed at the plate, convulsed by laughter. Only after pleading by Anson and his teammates did get up and stagger around the bases for his third career round-tripper. By June, however, Goldsmith seemed to have lost interest in his game, and Chicago papers complained he had grown "fat and lazy."[26] Anson traded him to Baltimore in late July after a 13–6 Chicago loss in Cleveland. In Baltimore, Goldsmith picked up three more wins. For 1884, pitchers were allowed to throw overhand, as the rule was eliminated that had limited them to an underhand or sidearm delivery. Goldsmith tried the new technique but found it painful and reverted to his tried-and-true underhand method with which he had achieved so much success. "His arm was gone when he left us, and if he played ball any afterward, it was only in desultory fashion," Anson said in his memoir in which he was critical of other players and managers.

Unable to find a team willing to hire him for 1885, Goldsmith retired. He was 29 and had been a professional for 11 seasons. His arm was done and so was his time in the sun. His last professional game was September 10, 1884, a home game in Baltimore against St. Louis which he lost, 8–3. Overall, his six-year career in the National League saw him win 112 games and lose 68.[27] In the two years before that with London, in the Association, he won another 95 games and lost 49. Of those wins, 41 were against Association rivals playing for the championship. And in 1876, his first season in London, he was credited with another 45 wins against all comers as the Tecumsehs became Canadian champions.[28]

Like other players of the time, Goldsmith tried umpiring once his playing days were over. In 1885, he officiated in the Canadian League and the following season advanced to the National League. In 1888 and 1889, he umpired for the American Association. His work in the Association as a staff umpire was not without controversy, however. On June 24, 1889, Goldsmith failed to appear for a game in Brooklyn between the hometown Bridegrooms and the Columbus Solons. The home team chose a man named Bill Paasch to act as umpire, over the objections of the visitors, who refused to take the field when Paasch called for the game to start. The substitute arbiter declared a forfeit in favor of the home team, but Columbus launched a loud argument that Paasch had no authority to take such a step. Columbus eventually relented and played the game, handing Brooklyn a 13–7 defeat. Brooklyn reported the outcome to the Association as a split doubleheader, because it claimed the first game was intended as a replacement for a rained-out game. Several weeks later, directors of the Association accepted the Brooklyn position, a decision which proved helpful in the pennant race that the Bridegrooms were to win.

Goldsmith may have wished he hadn't shown up for another game in Brooklyn, about two months later. Before a crowd of 15,000, he umpired a September 7 contest when the visitors were the St. Louis Browns. It was the first game of a three-game series that was widely expected to determine the pennant. Trailing 2–1 in the sixth inning, the visitors scored two runs to take the lead. As soon as they got ahead, St. Louis complained to Goldsmith that it was too dark to continue. When he declined to halt the game, the Browns began huddling in conference to kill time and let the darkness gather. St. Louis owner Chris Von der Ahe slipped out of the park to a nearby store where he bought candles, lit them, and arranged them around his team's bench to resemble footlights. This gambit drew a barrage of beer steins from the hometown fans, knocking over some of the candles, which set fire to papers beside the grandstand. A dangerous situation was averted when the blaze was quickly doused. But the crowd was now fired up and anxious to see the game continue, hoping the Bridegrooms could come back.

Despite the poor light, Tommy McCarthy, a Browns outfielder, was seen dunking the game ball in a water bucket to make it water-logged before Brooklyn took its last turn at bat, then trailing, 4–2. The leadoff batter reached first base when the St. Louis catcher failed to catch a third strike and complained bitterly to Goldsmith that he was unable to see the ball. As he did so, the runner alertly stole second base. This caught the attention of the catcher, who fired the ball there. Goldsmith called the runner safe, prompting another furious argument. St. Louis manager Charlie Comiskey loudly insisted it was too dark to play and ordered his Browns off the field. Goldsmith declared a forfeit. More beer steins rained down on the visitors as they left the field, and the Browns later needed a police escort for their safety. More than two weeks later, Association directors ruled that the visitors had been correct to leave the field and the final score would be recorded as 4–2 for St. Louis. Goldsmith was dismissed—or resigned (depending on the source)—ending his career as an umpire.[29]

Buffalo remained in the National League until the end of the 1885 season, when it folded because of poor attendance and lost several of its best players to Detroit. During their seven years in the League, the Bisons finished as high as third, but did no better than seventh a couple of times. Troy was expelled late in 1882, along with Worcester, also because of poor attendance. After a four-year hiatus, Buffalo reappeared in 1890 with the brand-new Players' League, yet another rebel league spawned by dissatisfaction with the National League. The Bisons featured a promising young catcher named Connie Mack, who had spent the previous four seasons with the Washington Nationals in the National League. Like many players who jumped to the Players' League, Mack was bitterly opposed to the salary cap and the "reserve clause" of the League.

The new professional loop of eight teams was owned and operated by players who came from the National League. It had its origins in the Brotherhood of Professional Baseball Players, a union for players founded in 1885. Rather than strike to express their grievances with the League and its reserve system, the Brotherhood opted to form a rival league after finding enough investors. For his part, Mack invested his savings of $500 in the Bisons and caught 123 games for them that season. James "Deacon" White joined the team as first baseman and playing manager. Another player whose nickname reflected his clean-living ways, White had begun his professional career in 1871 with the Cleveland Forest Citys for the inaugural year of the National Association. His 1890 season with the Bisons would be his last, however. Buffalo struggled through 122 games and finished eighth in the eight-team loop, ending the year in desperate financial straits. The Players' League also collapsed after its single season of existence.[30] Despite its short life, a committee chaired by Major League Baseball Commissioner William D. Eckert declared in 1968 that the Players' League should be considered a "major" league, so its statistics and those of its players could be counted in official major league baseball records.[31]

An earlier rival for the National League arrived on the scene in 1882, the same year its president, William Hulbert, died of a heart attack at age 49. The American Association had its roots in the expulsion of Cincinnati by Hulbert in late 1880 for allowing its ballpark to be used on Sundays and for selling beer from a concession on its grounds. Hulbert had replaced Cincinnati with Detroit. By September 1881, Cincinnati and Philadelphia baseball interests had decided that professional baseball must include their cities, and they found like-minded support in St. Louis, Baltimore, Louisville, and Pittsburgh.

In Pittsburgh, Denny McKnight was anxious to get Allegheny City back into the upper echelons of baseball. So, too, were other teams and their officials who had been members of the International Association. Late that year, the

American Association was born, a six-team loop whose members were all backed by beer or liquor money, prompting its nickname, the "Beer and Whiskey League."[32] The founding teams were the Pittsburgh Alleghenys, Cincinnati Red Stockings, Philadelphia Athletics, Baltimore Orioles, Louisville Eclipse, and St. Louis Browns.

As well as playing games on Sundays and selling beer to fans, the rebel league allowed its members to charge as little as 25 cents for admission, in a bid to attract a working-class crowd. The National League still required its teams to charge 50 cents for admission, in its continued effort to keep the riffraff out of its parks and make more money for the owners. Playing a key role in the new organization was McKnight, who was elected its president. For secretary-treasurer, J. A. Williams, the longtime ball enthusiast from Columbus, was chosen. He had held the same post with the International Association.

In many ways, the AA was a revival of the old IA in its desire to challenge the older organization and bring top-flight baseball to communities the League had shunned, expelled, overlooked, or generally deemed unworthy. The new organization adopted rules that varied slightly from the League and placed no restriction on the minimum population for member cities. Unlike the International Association launch during a recession, the new organization debuted in a time of economic recovery and, backed by several brewers, it would last ten seasons.[33]

Its inaugural 1882 campaign saw the American Association accomplish something never before done by a major or minor league team: It ended its first season with the same teams that started the season. No team was disbanded, transferred, or expelled. More importantly, it was a "sparkling success" at the box office.[34] All six teams made money, and they drew more fans to their ballparks than the League and its eight teams.[35] At the end of the season, the AA voted to add two more clubs: Columbus and the New York Metropolitans. National League owners had originally adopted the same attitude of superiority toward the upstart AA as they had with the IA, but became less antagonistic as they witnessed its success and began worrying about the threat posed by this new rival.

In 1884, the League and the AA found a way to work together just as the League learned yet another challenger was on the horizon—one that steadfastly opposed the "reserve clause." The American Association agreed with the League to add four more teams to make it more difficult for the newcomer, the Union Association, to get established. The League and American Association had signed what was known as the "National Agreement" late in 1883, under which the senior League granted major league status to the AA.[36] Both organizations agreed that as many as 14 players could be reserved for the following season by their teams. They also promised not to encroach on each other's geographic territory, among other measures. The Union Association fielded a dozen clubs for its 1884 season, including some from smaller centers like Altoona, Pennsylvania, Wilmington, Delaware, and Kansas City, as well as entirely new nines in Cincinnati, Boston, and Philadelphia.

With so many professional games played that year, and three leagues fielding 34 teams at one time or another, everyone suffered at the gate. But the hastily assembled and unstable Union Association felt it most and expired after a single season. Yet again, like the American Association and the Players' League of 1890, it is considered a major league, and statistics for its players are considered in the records of major league baseball. Otherwise, strange blanks would appear in player records. This is unlike the treatment accorded the International Association, where the contributions of players like Joe Hornung, Fred Goldsmith, Phil Powers, and others have been largely ignored. Anyone researching their records in baseball's major reference works would think those three Tecumsehs didn't play at all in 1876 and 1877, and for only a handful of games at the tail end of the 1878 season, when they joined League teams. It takes some digging even to find them recorded under a "minor" league category. The same applies for Hall of Famer Pud Galvin, whose 1877 and 1878 seasons in the International Association also do not qualify as "major league" service. Many other top-flight ballplayers of the era have suffered the same fate because they chose to play in the International Association.

Were he alive to see it, William Hulbert would only smile at how baseball history has treated those professional baseball players who dared to ply their trade outside his National League.

Hulbert's handiwork survives.

14
After the Glory Days

By the late 1870s, with their foray into the top ranks of professional baseball behind them, Jake Englehart, the deep pockets and president of the London Tecumsehs, and George Sleeman, the owner of the Guelph Maple Leafs, were able to turn their considerable energies back to business. Englehart created a refining empire and dabbled in politics, while Sleeman grew his brewery and pursued a political career. And, coincidentally, both men became pivotal figures in railways.

By 1878, competition from U.S. refiners, whose prices had dipped, hurt the exports for Canadian refiners, so they focused their efforts on the domestic market. This wasn't a deterrent to Englehart, who, with partner Isaac Guggenheim, established the Silver Star refinery in Petrolia. The largest and most modern in the country, it was able to undercut the prices of its competitors. Petrolia had attracted the pair with the promise of waiving property taxes for five years, and it extended the perk for each of their subsequent expansions.[1] Englehart's refinery continued operating in London until a lightning strike in 1883 destroyed most of it. By then, he had relocated his head office to Petrolia and decided not to rebuild in London.

The dozen oil refiners in London had asked the city council to build a pipeline from Petrolia to London to reduce their costs for rail transportation. But city hall balked at putting up $20,000 for the venture. Local politicians had tired of neighbor complaints about the pervasive unpleasant smell from the refinery district in the east end of the city. The fire brigade was kept busy responding to explosions and fires. When the city decided not to accommodate the fledgling oil industry, others followed Englehart's lead and moved 45 miles west to Petrolia.

In 1880, while most of them were still based in London, 19 oilmen decided consolidation was needed for the survival of the industry, so they established the Imperial Oil Company. It was organized as a joint-stock com-

Oil is still being pumped from the fields of Petrolia that were discovered more than 150 years ago. Canada's original oil patch provided wealth for Jake Englehart, who dipped into his pockets to help finance the London Tecumsehs (author's collection).

pany and had a capitalized value of $500,000. With Englehart as vice-president and the company's largest single shareholder, Imperial began acquiring and absorbing competing refiners, the same way John D. Rockefeller and his Standard Oil Company was gobbling up competitors in the United States. The emergence of Imperial Oil as the country's dominant refiner brought much-needed stability to Canada's oil industry.[2] Petrolia began to boom, becoming one of the richest towns in the country. Under Englehart's leadership, Imperial continued to expand and by 1893 it had branch offices across Canada from Halifax to Victoria. Four years later, 8,000 wells were operating in Petrolia, and Imperial was the leading refiner.[3]

It faced a daunting challenge, however. Standard Oil and related firms had moved into the Canadian market by the 1890s, and in 1897, one of them bought a refinery at Sarnia, west of Petrolia along the St. Clair River. Imperial Oil warily watched the moves by its deep-pocketed competitor from south of the border and realized it couldn't compete any longer as Standard entered Imperial markets. The Canadian firm needed large amounts of capital it didn't have. Englehart and his fellow directors reluctantly authorized the sale of 75 percent of its stock to Standard in 1898. It wasn't long before the refining industry withered in Petrolia and relocated to Sarnia.

Jake Englehart met and married Charlotte Eleanor Thompson, the daughter of a farmer from nearby Middlesex County, late in 1891. He was 44, and a millionaire several times over. A dark-haired beauty, "Minnie" was 28, and her sister was married to a Petrolia lawyer who shared Englehart's conservative political views. The couple married in Christ Church, an Anglican congregation in Petrolia. Englehart, a Jew, converted to the Church of England and proved to be a generous benefactor to the church and to the community. For his new wife, he built a fine, red brick, turreted Victorian mansion featuring stained glass, Florentine tile fireplaces, and carved oak staircases and paneling. They called their home Glenview. During their honeymoon in Scotland, the newlyweds discovered they both liked golf, so Englehart added a nine-hole golf course to their sprawling property along Bear Creek.

After baseball, Jake Englehart founded what became one of Canada's largest oil companies and in later years opened up a railway into the northern reaches of the province at the request of the leader of Ontario. He was a generous benefactor, particularly in Petrolia, in the heart of Canada's original oil patch (Glenbow Museum Archives, IP-26-1c).

Englehart held positions on the boards of financial institutions in Petrolia, London and elsewhere as he expanded his refinery operations. The Engleharts were among the leading citizens of the bustling community. Charlotte died suddenly in late 1908 during pregnancy, at age 45. In her will, she gave Glenview, then valued at $50,000, to the town of Petrolia for a much-needed hospital. A devastated Jake was allowed to stay in their home as long as he wanted, but his business interests had been drawing him increasingly to Toronto. He tackled the conversion of Glenview to a 13-bed hospital with his characteristic energy, sparing little expense. Upon his own death, he left money for the addition of two wings and equipment for a maternity ward and x-ray equipment. It was later estimated Englehart put $200,000 into the hospital and its grounds.[4] He endowed it with 400 shares of Imperial Oil to provide a steady source of funds into the future. Today, Charlotte Eleanor Englehart Hospital continues to provide health care to residents of Petrolia and area as part of the Sarnia-based Bluewater Health network.[5] The golf course, Heritage Heights, has been expanded to 18 holes, and nearby is Englehart Park, a municipal green space equipped for skateboarding and other activities for youngsters.

Charlotte and Jake Englehart were committed members of Christ Church, and Jake donated 11 imported bells to the church in her memory. A bronze plaque on a wall inside the church acknowledges the gift of the massive bells, which weigh over five tons and still call parishioners to Sunday service. The bells and plaque survived a 1957 fire that destroyed the original church.

During their years in Petrolia, Englehart was involved in Conservative politics and became president of the Liberal–Conservative Association of Lambton County. He helped elect W. J. Hanna, a friend and Imperial Oil director, to the Ontario Legislature in 1905. That year, the Conservative Party of James Whitney swept to power, toppling the Liberal Party, which had been struggling to push a railway line into the Northern Ontario bush to help settle the area and exploit its timber resources and newly discovered deposits of silver and gold. Hanna persuaded Whitney to appoint his friend Englehart to the publicly owned Temiskaming and Northern Ontario Railway Commission in 1905 and as its chairman in 1906.

As head of the rail line, Englehart often took Charlotte north as he oversaw the work. He was paid of a salary of $5,000 for what was supposed to be a part-time post, but he put in long hours and gave away most of his pay to needy settlers. He acted as general manager as he continued to push the railway toward the far-northern settlement of Cochrane, 140 miles north through rugged country from New Liskeard. After Charlotte died, Englehart pushed himself and the railway even harder.[6] In the rough environs of the north, he presented an odd sight for the miners, lumbermen, and farmers he met in his extensive travels. Englehart seemed so European in manner and dress. Reserved and formal, with impeccable tailoring, high starched collar, a goatee, and pince-nez glasses with a large black ribbon, he soon earned the respect of those he

14. After the Glory Days

met once they saw his ability to get results. Before long, a community was named after him that was a key operational point on the T&NO.

In 1911, the worst forest fire ever to strike Northern Ontario leveled the town of Porcupine, and Englehart used the railway to help evacuate hundreds of fire refugees to safety in the south. He organized relief trains and spent his own money to buy food for people who had lost everything but the clothes on their backs. More than 70 of Porcupine's 3,000 residents either burned to death or drowned as they jumped into Porcupine Lake to escape wind-blown flames. At the T&NO station in newly named Englehart, the railway chairman posted this sign: "No one need pass here hungry, J. L. Englehart." He dipped into his own deep pockets to live up to those words.[7]

In Toronto, Englehart lived in a hotel, as he had done for most of his life, with the exception of his time with Minnie in Petrolia. After the First

In Petrolia, Jake and Charlotte Englehart were among the wealthiest of its citizens and pillars of the petroleum establishment. When Charlotte died, Englehart turned their mansion and property over to the town, along with oil company shares to keep it operating. To this day, the Charlotte Eleanor Englehart Hospital continues to treat patients from across Canada's original oil patch (author's collection).

Jake and Charlotte Englehart's final resting place on a knoll in a cemetery just west of Petrolia. An American who played a key role in Canadian baseball and in the country's petroleum industry, virtually nothing was said upon his death about his involvement with the Tecumsehs (author's collection).

World War, an aging Englehart began to curtail his activities. His death on April 6, 1921, at age 78 prompted obituaries in major newspapers saluting the petroleum pioneer, benefactor, and railway man who had done so much for his adopted country. His funeral in Toronto drew large numbers of political and business leaders. He was buried alongside his beloved Minnie in a granite family vault perched on a grassy knoll in Hillsdale Cemetery just west of Petrolia. His estate was valued at $3.5 million, and he distributed it widely to nieces, nephews, and other members of his and Charlotte's family. He also provided additional support for the Petrolia hospital and donations to several more in Toronto. Hospitals along the rail line he pushed into Northern Ontario were also provided for. And he left $7,500 for Christ Church in Petrolia.[8]

In all the many words said and printed about him upon his passing, none were about his key role in propelling London's Tecumseh baseball team to the top of the baseball world for several memorable years—not even in the London papers.

Another key figure in the Tecumsehs met a much less celebrated end. On June 9, 1882, John Brown, the city treasurer since 1852, was found dead. The longtime supporter and founding president of the Tecumsehs in 1868 had shot himself. His death came as a complete surprise and was the talk of the city. An investigation turned up some significant discrepancies in the city's accounting records. Since at least 1863, there had been rumors of irregularities, thought to have been corrected when it was discovered that a tax collector had failed to remit everything he had collected. The probe after his death eventually concluded that nearly $70,000 was missing from city accounts, a huge amount for the day.[9]

In Guelph, George Sleeman continued to manage baseball teams, most of them amateur nines. In 1885, however, he was elected president of the newly established Canadian Professional League. He quickly ran afoul of its members when he hired George Washington Bradley, the much-traveled American who had pitched for Chicago and against Guelph and London in exhibition games in 1877. Bradley had been blacklisted by the National League and American Association for jumping to the rebel Union Association in 1884 and was looking to extend his career. But Toronto and Hamilton wanted nothing to do with him and they abandoned the Canadian loop for the New York-based International League. Their departure left only Guelph and London in the Canadian League, and Sleeman in a mood to sue. So he did, but his lawsuit went nowhere.

In 1886, Sleeman revived the Maple Leafs and, without much competition in Ontario, sent the team on a 60-game tour of Canada and the United States. They won 41 of those games and briefly reignited baseball fever in Guelph that year. A crowd of 6,000 welcomed the team home at the train station.[10] That was Sleeman's last hurrah, and he withdrew from managing baseball and restricted his role in future to that of fan and supporter.

From 1892 to 1894, a brief return of baseball fever broke out as a semi-professional team organized by new directors won the Canadian championship followed by yet another decline in interest.[11] Sleeman became heavily involved in local politics, becoming Guelph's first mayor when it became a city in 1880. He was re-elected in 1881 and 1882 and again in 1905 and 1906. Between his terms, he became enamored with the concept of electric street railways. He incorporated the Guelph Street Railway in 1894 and was granted the exclusive contract by the city to carry freight and passengers within the city limits. In exchange, Sleeman promised to extend new lines continually throughout the city over a 20-year period. On June 20, 1895, he drove the "first spike" for the system on Waterloo Street in front of his fine stone home. His railway consistently lost money, however, and by 1903 it was in receivership with banks demanding $100,000 from him. His dream of putting his city on rails had been costly to the brewer, personally. The banks seized the operation and also his Sleeman's Silver Creek Brewery. They soon regretted the latter move and sold the brewery back to Sleeman in 1906. Meanwhile, the city decided to continue the rail service and transformed it into the municipally operated Guelph Radial Railway Company. As a result, streetcar service in the city continued until 1939.[12]

In his later years, Sleeman was active in various lodges and service clubs in Guelph and indulged in coin collecting, amassing a valuable collection of coins and medals. He was president and director of a fire insurance company, promoter of the Guelph Opera House and a noted marksman. The aging entrepreneur continued to promote his city at every opportunity. He particularly liked to talk about his days with the Maple Leafs, the Canadian champions and among the best in North America, who had succeeded in putting his city on the map and getting publicity for it in major newspapers. He himself made front-page news in the December 15, 1926, edition of the *Toronto Mail and Empire*:

TALKS OF BASEBALL WHILE UNDER THE KNIFE

Guelph Ex-Mayor, 85 Years Old, Refuses to Take Ether for Operation
Special to The Mail and Empire.

Guelph, Dec. 14–Admitted to the General Hospital suffering from a serious internal complaint, George Sleeman, ex-mayor of Guelph, builder of the local street railway and the man who promoted baseball in this city in the days of the famous Maple Leafs, underwent a remarkable operation today when, disdaining the use of ether, he went through the ordeal of having the trouble remedied with the aid of a local anaesthetic.

Mr. Sleeman, who is over 85 years of age, conversed freely with Dr. H. O. Howitt, who performed the critical operation, and the attending nurses during the hour he was on the operating table, reminiscing of the early days of baseball in Guelph and relating anecdotes in connection with the old Maple Leafs, who were at one time amateur baseball champions of the world.

His condition is reported as favorable, and unless complications set in it is fully expected he will recover.[13]

Sleeman didn't. The following day he was dead. His passing was widely noted in the newspapers. The *Guelph Mercury* carried a prominent story about the loss of the "prominent pioneer businessman," and in an editorial noted that Sleeman was "continually aggressive in everything he believed was for the betterment of the city." The newspaper highlighted his love of sport, particularly baseball, and his time with the Maple Leafs.

Mr. Sleeman won fame for his management of the famous champion Maple Leaf baseball team, at a time when that game was in its infancy on the whole continent of America. This team defeated the best of the United States teams of the period and brought Guelph much desirable publicity. Until the very end of his life, Mr. Sleeman retained his interest in all sports and in baseball particularly. It is worthy of note that in his last conscious moments his thoughts were about some of the men who were players on that famous baseball team, and in making comparisons between the playing abilities of its different members. Mr. Sleeman was a good citizen of Guelph, his counsel and advice being always of value.[14]

The flag at Guelph city hall was flown at half-staff out of respect for the five-time mayor, one of the most tireless boosters the city had ever seen.

Albert Goodwill Spalding, of the Chicago White Stockings, paid a visit to Toronto in late January 1886, primarily to promote his growing line of sporting goods. He was squired around town and shown the sites by officers of the Toronto Baseball Association. At one point, he was persuaded to ride a toboggan down a slope in Rosedale Park. In the evening, he attended the theatre, finding time to speak to a reporter with the *Toronto Mail* newspaper. He was asked about the National League, whose Buffalo and Providence franchises had gone bankrupt just days before, with Washington added to bring the League to seven teams. An opening existed for an eighth club, and Spalding suggested Toronto should consider an application.[15] The report specifically noted he did so "laughingly," but the idea took on a life of its own.

At the time, Toronto was considering the Canadian League of which Sleeman was president, but instead turned its eyes toward joining teams from the New York State League to form the International League in early 1886. Hamilton also joined the new league, leaving Guelph and London in the Canadian loop.[16] Toronto did submit an application to the National League, but the *Mail* observed a few days later that it wasn't being taken seriously. The newspaper dismissed the notion of Toronto playing in any American-based league.[17] Nothing came from the Toronto notion, and the League found its eighth team in the Kansas City Cowboys.

The Pittsburgh Alleghenys, founding members of the American Association in 1882, struggled in the new organization, of which their Denny McKnight was president. The 1883 season was dreadful, as the Alleghenys won only 31 games against 67 losses. They finished seventh in the eight-team AA. McKnight was uncomfortable in his sometimes conflicting roles as team owner and league president, a situation that never seemed to bother Chicago's William Hulbert in the National League. McKnight resigned and tried to sell the team. When that bid fell through in 1884, he stayed with the club and also acted as field manager for a brief stint as the Alleghenys won only 30 games to finish 11th out of 13 clubs. He turned the club presidency over to E. E.

Converse, assumed the role of secretary, and tried to gain entry into the National League for its 1885 season. In that effort, McKnight also failed.

Things appeared to be on the upswing when Pud Galvin agreed to rejoin the Alleghenys for their 1886 campaign. Buffalo sold him to the Pittsburgh club for a reported $2,500, a princely sum at the time, and allowed him to keep $700 of the purchase price. He was signed to a contract of $3,000, making him the highest-paid player in baseball for a time.[18] His Buffalo club had collapsed at the end of 1885, when, to save money, the Bisons had made him manager for 24 games.

Galvin remembered his time with the earlier Allegheny club fondly. Another pre-season signing created big trouble, however. Allegheny hired second baseman Sam Barkley while he was under contract with Baltimore's AA club. The Orioles protested the move, but Association president McKnight took no action, missed meetings, and generally failed to provide the leadership expected of him. Barkley stayed with the Alleghenys, but McKnight lost his job. Club owners were angry at their ineffective president and in March 1886 ousted him by a seven-to-one vote. After that season, the National League finally accepted Pittsburgh as a member. By then, McKnight had moved to New Mexico to oversee a land and cattle company. His involvement in baseball was over after playing such a key role in establishing two different professional leagues. McKnight eventually returned to Pittsburgh, where he became heavily involved in business circles. He died in 1900 at the age of 53.[19]

Galvin's return to the Alleghenys for 1886 produced immediate benefits. He won 29 games and helped his team to a second-place finish, with 80 wins. Galvin, at five-foot-eight, by then had ballooned to 200 pounds and picked up the nickname "The Little Steam Engine," for the huffing and puffing that had become part of his performance. The durable workhorse is credited with becoming the first pitcher in major league baseball to record 300 wins, on October 5, 1888, when he defeated the Washington Nationals, 5–1, on a four-hitter.[20] Had he been credited with the 40 wins he collected in his two seasons in the International Association with Allegheny and Buffalo, his achievement would have come two years earlier. In 1890, Galvin jumped to the Pittsburgh Burghers of the upstart Players' League and won 12 games for them. He returned to the Alleghenys for 1891 under the general amnesty granted players who returned to their former teams.

For 1891, the signing of another player created problems but left a legacy. Infielder Louis Bierbauer had jumped from the Philadelphia Athletics of the American Association to the Philadelphia Quakers of the Players' League for the 1890 season. In 1891, the Athletics failed to field a team in the AA, so the

As the Buffalo Bisons faltered in the 1885 season for lack of fan support, Pud Galvin returned to Pittsburgh to play for the Alleghenys. He pitched for the earlier version of the team that lost the International Association pennant to the London Tecumsehs in 1877. In 1888, he recorded his 300th win, a feat which would have come two years earlier if his years in the IA had been recognized (National Baseball Hall of Fame Library, Cooperstown, N.Y. Pud Galvin 1599-663_FL_PD).

Association itself claimed the rights to all Athletics who had jumped to the Players' League. Through some sort of clerical error, Bierbauer's name did not appear on the AA's reserve list. Allegheny club president J. Palmer O'Neil spotted the omission and signed Bierbauer for 1891. The Association was upset at this pickup by the League team, and the matter was submitted to arbitration, where Allegheny claimed Bierbauer was a free agent and they could sign him. The AA representative at the arbitration hearing lost his cool at one point, shouting: "The action of the Pittsburgh club is piratical!" The ruling came down in favor of Allegheny, who were allowed to keep Bierbauer. And from then on, their team gradually became known as the Pittsburgh Pirates.[21]

Galvin, his abilities beginning to decline, won 14 games that season and five in 1892, before being traded to his hometown St. Louis Browns, where he registered five more wins before retiring at age 35. In his fifteen seasons in the National Association, National League, American Association, and Players League, he had recorded a total of 365 career wins in nearly 6,000 innings pitched. On top of that were his 12 1877 wins for Allegheny in the International Association, and 28 more with Buffalo's IA club of 1878. No other pitcher of his day was as successful as Pud Galvin.

Galvin attempted a comeback with Buffalo in the Eastern League in 1894, but he pitched poorly, his weight now up to 250 pounds. He had a brief stint umpiring in the National League in 1895, but didn't enjoy it. He became a saloon owner, contractor, and pipe-layer in Pittsburgh. Galvin had earned plenty of money during his lifetime, especially while pitching, but had difficulty holding onto it. By 1900, he and his wife, Bridget, and their six surviving children (of 11 that had been born) were living in poverty. In 1902, at the age of 45, Galvin died of chronic stomach inflammation or gastritis. Friends concerned about the welfare of the family he left behind held a fundraising event for his widow and children. The durable Galvin, one of the early game's most successful pitchers, was then largely forgotten for decades. His accomplishments and fate caught the attention of Buffalo baseball historian Joe Overfield, a member of the Society for American Baseball Research, who told a new generation about Galvin's winning record. Overfield showed that the hard-working pitcher deserved a better fate. In 1965, that was addressed when Galvin was inducted into the National Baseball Hall of Fame for the following reasons:

> James Francis "Pud" Galvin was baseball's first 300-game winner. Short and stocky, "The Little Steam Engine" was a tireless worker with a hard fastball and a deceptive pick-off move. Called "the speediest pitcher in his profession," Galvin pitched for 15 seasons, earning 20 or more victories ten times, and twice topping

the 40-win mark. When he retired in 1892, he was the all-time major league leader in wins, innings pitched, games started, games completed, and shutouts. His nickname "Pud" referred to his pitching ability, which turned opposing batters into "pudding."[22]

In London, baseball continued after the Tecumsehs with some teams adopting the famous name in the decades that followed. After the abortive attempt to get a new Canadian Professional League under way in 1886 with George Sleeman and the Maple Leafs, London entered the International League in 1888 with Phil Powers as manager. Toronto and Hamilton were already in the loop founded in 1886 with a renaming of the New York State League. The new Tecumseh players, many imported from south of the border, proved to be more accomplished at drinking than playing baseball. Player turnover was excessive, and the team finished the season with only three of the 14 players with which it started the season. The *London Free Press* disapproved of the nocturnal habits of these Tecumsehs, saying: "Men who carouse at night are not fit to play good ball during the afternoon and the sooner one or two players realize the truth of this, the better for themselves individually and the team collectively."[23] The Temperance movement was strong in London at the time. The Tecumsehs finished fifth in the International League that season, and Syracuse won the pennant. The loop collapsed in 1890 because of poor attendance.

Other professional teams were established in London, bearing the names the Tecumsehs, the Cockneys, and the Alerts. Yet another Canadian League operated for a brief time in 1899, and London did well in it until the league collapsed. From 1919 to 1925, London played in the Michigan–Ontario League, winning its pennant in 1920, 1921, and 1922. In 1940, the Pittsburgh Pirates established a farm club in the city. It played in the PONY (Pennsylvania, Ontario, New York) League for two seasons. A London Army team won the Canadian Sandlot Congress title in 1943 and 1944, and after the war, renamed as the London Majors, won the World Sandlot title in 1948.[24] The Majors continue to play baseball to this day in the Intercounty Baseball League against such rivals as Guelph, Toronto, and Brantford.

Professional baseball returned to London in 1989 after a hiatus of 48 years when the Detroit Tigers established the London Tigers as a AA-class affiliate in the city, which had grown to a population of about 300,000. In its second season in the loop, the Tigers captured the Eastern Association pennant before large and appreciative crowds. Hopes that the professional game was back in town to stay were soon dashed. Attendance declined, and after the 1993 season, the franchise moved to Trenton, New Jersey. The independent

Frontier League arrived in 1999 with the London Werewolves. Despite the innovative marketing and brash promotion of fun-loving owner John Kuhn, the team struggled to attract crowds large enough to survive and it moved to Canton, Ohio, after its third season. The London Monarchs of the Canadian Baseball League appeared in 2001, but the league collapsed before finishing the season. Another Frontier League team, the Rippers, showed up for the 2012 season. The team became mired in controversy over its choice of name and logo, which critics said celebrated notorious murderer Jack the Ripper. Women's groups were outraged and the issue drew widespread media attention, some calling the name and logo inspired, others considering it the height of poor taste. Team owners from Michigan proved insensitive and seemed to revel in the controversy as good for business. They guessed wrong. The team drew poorly and collapsed in July.[25]

Throughout the ups and downs of professional baseball in London, one thing remained constant: the home park. It is a survivor. Tecumseh Park, acquired by china merchant W. J. Reid for the Tecumsehs in 1877, has had a long history linked to the game. The park has seen other uses over the years. In 1892, as interest in bicycling swept London, Reid established a racetrack within the park. The brick-dust track measured a third of a mile long and attracted professional and amateur races for years. The London Bicycle Club arranged the showing of the first moving picture at the park in 1895. In 1883, the Thames River flooded and destroyed the original grandstands and prompted the relocation of the home plate from today's left field to the west side of the playing field in front of new grandstands erected there. The move provided spectators a view of downtown beyond the outfield fence and took the afternoon sun out of the eyes of batters. Football games, equestrian events, political rallies, and boxing matches have all been held in the park over the years. Future Pittsburgh star catcher George "Mooney" Gibson, a London native, played his early ball at the park. Other stars, including Detroit second baseman Charlie Gehringer and the outfielder Ty Cobb, played in exhibition games, the latter remarking that it was a fine facility.[26] In the 1930s, interest in baseball and the park was in decline, and it was widely feared the tired old park, still in private hands, would be razed. A Tecumseh Park "booster day" was held on June 27, 1936, featuring a baseball game between Stratford and London that raised funds to save the park. One of the guests of honor was aging Fred Goldsmith, who made the trip from Michigan. The other was Bob Emslie, the former hurler for the Atlantics and Baltimore of the American Association and longtime National League umpire, who came from nearby St. Thomas. "It was like the old baseball days in London to see the grandstand packed," the *Free Press* reported.

14. After the Glory Days

Tecumseh Park was renamed Labatt Memorial Park in the 1930s. London has been the home for several professional teams for short periods of time. Amateur contests against Guelph continue to this day. This is an evening game between the London Majors and Guelph Royals of the Intercounty League in 2013 (author's collection).

The success of the day will save Tecumseh Park for this year, but this does not solve the problem of the future. Anyone who was at the game on Saturday must have been thoroughly convinced of the necessity of retaining the park as a centre for athletics in London. It is ideally and centrally located and could, without a great expenditure, be converted into the best athletic field for all sports in Canada. One hesitates in these days of financial stress, as far as taxpayers are concerned, to urge that the city should purchase the property. What an opportunity for some philanthropically-minded citizen to do something worth while for London! However, if none is in sight then the citizens will have to consider seriously the question of purchase of these historic grounds. It would be a calamity if they were lost to London.[27]

Members of the Labatt family, whose brewery in London dated back to 1847, may have seen this appeal by the newspaper. The family purchased the property and donated it to the city of London, along with $10,000 for improvements. The property was renamed John Labatt Memorial Park and it appeared that the venerable park was assured a bright future. Mere months later, a devastating spring flood ravaged London and swept away the old grandstand. Without hesitating, perhaps because of the outpouring of public support, or merely to appease the Labatts, the city immediately rebuilt the grandstand and bleacher seats. About the same time, a clubhouse was built that would later become the home for the London Majors.[28]

Labatt Park, as it is generally known, was honored in 1990 as the best natural grass baseball park in North America, winning the Beam Clay Baseball Diamond of the Year award. The contest, sponsored by a distributor of infield materials, was open to all professional baseball parks and was judged by four major league groundskeepers. At the time, Detroit's affiliate, the AA Tigers, were calling it home.[29] In 1994, Labatt Park was granted a historic designation under the Ontario Heritage Act.

As its professional tenants arrived and departed over the years, the park continued to be home for the London Majors and for local minor baseball

In the 1870s, baseball games between the London Tecumsehs and Guelph Maple Leafs attracted as many as 8,000–10,000 fans. These days, games in the Intercounty League between the two cities attract about 500 spectators to the park originally built for the Tecumsehs (author's collection).

14. After the Glory Days

Built as Tecumseh Park, and renamed Labatt Memorial Park in the 1930s when stands were rebuilt following a flood, the park lays claim to being the oldest baseball grounds in the world, as the sign attests. Baseball has a long tradition in London, but professional clubs have had difficulty developing longstanding fan support. The park is used heavily by minor and university baseball clubs (author's collection).

organizations, never failing to impress out-of-town visitors who see it for the first time. Its reputation as a historic gem helped it win a Baseball Canada contest in 2011 as "Canada's Favourite Ballpark." More than 40 ballparks from across the country competed for the honors in online voting.[30]

Controversy raged for a time about whether Labatt Park is the oldest baseball park in North America, if not the world. A rather modest community ball diamond called Fuller Field, located in Clinton, Massachusetts, was entered in the Guinness Book of World Records in 2007 as the "world's oldest continuously used baseball diamond/field." Baseball has been played there since 1878, it was noted. A year later, after Guinness learned Tecumseh/Labatt Park has been the home of baseball since 1877, the entry was changed to London for its 2009 edition. Clinton, a community of 13,500 just north of Worcester, kicked up a fuss, and the notation was changed back to Fuller Field. Clinton historian A. J. Bastarache insisted the diamond in Clinton was older. He argued that the diamond in London had been moved " a significant distance away" from its original location following an 1883 flood. Pressing his case, Bastarache argued: "Saying Labatt is the oldest is like saying the new Yankee Stadium being built next to the one built in 1923 is the same field." Bastarache said Guinness assured him Fuller Field would retain the title of "oldest diamond" and that would not change.[31] Bastarache's version of the facts about London is interesting, but perhaps understandable from Clinton's booster, whose book about the community's history was immodestly titled *An Extraordinary Town*. The fact is that the diamond in London has remained in the same place; only the location of home plate was moved. Regardless, the Guinness entry now reads: "The oldest baseball diamond is Fuller Field in Clinton, Massachusetts, USA, which has been proved to have hosted baseball from 1878 to the present day."[32] So Clinton claims the oldest baseball *diamond,* while London claims it has the oldest *field*.

At 5,200-seat Labatt Park today, the large scoreboard with a city skyline as backdrop proclaims to spectators that they are in the "World's Oldest Baseball Grounds."

15

Pitching the Pitch

In the years he played for Chicago, Fred Goldsmith kept his home in London so Rowena could be near her family while he was on the road, living the life of a big-league pitcher. They bought a fine house on King Street just east of downtown. During the 1884 season, Goldsmith's complaints about soreness in his arm and his poor pitching suggested that as he turned 28, his career was nearing its end. Chicago manager Cap Anson traded him to Baltimore of the American Association after a loss to Cleveland in late July. Back home, Rowena likely saw this report in the *London Advertiser* a few days later: "Fred Goldsmith has received his release from the Chicagos, and will finish the season with the Baltimores. Goldsmith and Anson have not got on well together of late, and the release was anxiously hoped for by Fred."[1] He won three more games with the Orioles to add to the nine earned in Chicago. His efforts to find a new team met with no success. The collapse of the Union Association after its only season in 1884 meant players from its 12 teams had flooded the market for 1885, and Goldsmith, with his old-fashioned delivery and sore arm, found no takers.

He returned to London, where there was some talk that for 1885 he would pitch for London's entry in the new Canadian Professional League being organized by George Sleeman. But with his arm still troubling him, he opted instead to become an umpire. Goldsmith's work behind the plate drew praise, including from the *Toronto Globe*, which on June 30 termed him "the most satisfactory umpire in the league." Following a late August game in Toronto, the same paper reported: "it was impossible to find a flaw in one of his decisions. He says what he has to say and in a tone which bodes no good to the foolhardy player who would dare to question the correctness of his judgment."[2]

Sometime in 1885, Goldsmith opened the F. E. Goldsmith Saloon in the Mansion House Hotel at 62 Dundas Street in downtown London. The move was unexpected for a teetotaler, but despite his well-known name on the door,

After leaving London, Fred Goldsmith spent time with Springfield and then Troy. For 1880, he was signed by the Chicago White Stockings, who remembered how hard he had been to hit when they played London. Goldsmith, back right, was teamed up with Larry Corcoran, front right, in what became the first pitching rotation in the League (National Baseball Hall of Fame Library, Cooperstown, New York, Chicago White Stockings 1880_598-88_PD).

the venture failed within a few months. By February 1886, it was reported that the fledgling barkeeper had reached a "compromise" with his creditors, who were willing to accept 40 cents on each $1 they were owed.[3] Poor patronage was blamed for Goldsmith's lack of success in a city where the Temperance movement was growing.

During the off-season, it was reported he had been offered an umpiring position in the National League.[4] Goldsmith took the job and, in late May, he was also tending bar at the clubhouse adjacent to the ball grounds of the Detroit Wolverines, who were playing their second season in the National League.[5] Reviews of his work as an umpire in the National League were not as positive as they had been in Toronto, and after the 1886 season, the League did not invite him back.

The Goldsmiths moved to the rural crossroads community of Clawson, Michigan, just north of Detroit, to open a general store, and Goldsmith

Fred Goldsmith won 21 games for Chicago in 1880, 24 games in 1881, 28 in 1882, 25 in 1883 and 12 in 1884 before he was traded to Baltimore. He didn't get on well with playing manager Cap Anson, top, who considered him too easy-going (National Baseball Hall of Fame Library, Cooperstown, New York, Chicago White Stockings 1881_3112-81_PD).

became postmaster. It is unclear exactly when the move took place or why the hamlet, 120 miles southwest of London, was chosen by the couple. There, they raised four boys and two girls; after a dozen years, the Goldsmiths moved to Detroit, where Fred worked as a streetcar repairman and salesman. Rowie and Fred drifted apart, however, and they divorced about 1910.

After leaving Rowena, with whom he managed to stay on friendly terms, Goldsmith moved to the Detroit suburb of Birmingham for a job with the Detroit United Railway, the street railway system. He met a much younger woman named Ida Wilshire, a secretary at the public library, and they married in 1911. She was another Canadian girl, a widow originally from Windsor, Ontario, just across the Detroit River. The couple had two daughters during their 15 years in Birmingham. Not long after the girls graduated from school, Ida contracted polio, was institutionalized, and died prematurely, leaving Goldsmith alone in his 70s. Concern for her father prompted Phyllis Castle, Goldsmith's oldest daughter from his second marriage, to insist he move in with her family about 30 miles away, near the town of Ortonville. The old ballplayer settled in and indulged his love for fishing, gardening, carpentry, oil painting, and following the Detroit Tigers on radio.[6]

Fred Goldsmith remained a competitor at heart and proud of his contribution to baseball. Publicity that surrounded an old-timers game in 1896, where Candy Cummings made an appearance, got under Goldsmith's skin. Cummings was being credited with inventing the curveball pitch, and Goldsmith resented it. At the time, he was still attending Tigers games at Briggs Stadium and during one such visit he told a reporter that Cummings hadn't invented the curve at all. Goldsmith insisted that Charles Hamilton (Ham) Avery, a pitcher at Yale University, had thrown and demonstrated the first curve. Cummings, Goldsmith said, was certainly not throwing curves when he saw him pitch for the Atlantics in 1869. The July 1898 edition of *Sporting Life* picked up the story told in Detroit two years earlier by Goldsmith.

> I was a boy in New Haven when I first saw Professor "Ham" Avery pitch a curve. I watched him with open eyes and mouth, and we could scarcely believe it. He was a professor in philosophy at Yale and was pitcher and captain of the team. He demonstrated it, using three poles at Hamilton Park, and afterwards went to New York, where he showed it on the old Capitoline Grounds, I believe they were called.... I learned it at New Haven, and used the ball in the famous Lynn tournament in 1874. I do not believe Cummings used the ball before I did.[7]

Goldsmith clearly credited Avery as the first curveballer, completely dismissing Cummings and his story. He made no claim about inventing it himself, but that would change with the advance of years. In the near term, Goldsmith's assertion produced contradictions from several old-timers. Henry Chadwick, formerly of the *Brooklyn Eagle* and the *Clipper*, and now editing Spalding's *Base Ball Guide*, wrote to *Sporting Life* to say he saw Cummings throw a curve in 1866, before Avery showed up at Yale. Cummings himself weighed in, writing that it was he who taught the pitch to Avery.[8]

15. Pitching the Pitch

Back in London for the Old Boys Reunion of 1903, Goldsmith reminisced at length about the Tecumsehs, the Maple Leafs, London manager Harry Gorman, and his old catcher, Phil Powers. The only thing he had to say on the subject of pitching, however, as noted by the *Advertiser*, was that "he was of the opinion that pitchers today do not know any more about the game than they did a quarter of a century ago."[9] One would have thought he might have mentioned his pioneering use of the curve. In 1906, the Grand Rapids Press found Goldsmith tending bar in Albuquerque, New Mexico. This time, he said he learned the curve from Ham Avery and used it soon afterward at a tournament in Lynn.[10] Again, he attributed the pitch to Avery, but now added the detail that he had learned it from the Yale player.

Cummings didn't appreciate Goldsmith's repeated claim when he learned of it, and wanted to set the record straight. In 1908, for *Baseball* magazine, Cummings penned an article with the title: "How I Pitched the First Curve." Cummings insisted he had taught the curve to Avery. At the time, Cummings already enjoyed support for the invention from Albert Goodwill Spalding, *The Sporting News* founder Alfred H. Spink, and other prominent figures in the game. Cummings's story was that as a boy of 14, in 1863, he was playing on a Brooklyn beach when he discovered the curve while throwing clamshells into the ocean. With experimentation, he said, he was able to make a baseball travel in an arc. Cummings said he debuted the curve in an 1867 game between his Brooklyn Stars team and Harvard College.[11]

In 1924, the same year his rival Cummings died, Goldsmith said he took part in a public demonstration of his deceptive pitch as a young man. A few months later, he provided additional details to a reporter from the *Chicago Tribune*. Goldsmith said that Avery, a Yale philosophy professor and pitcher for its team, helped him develop the curve, but no one believed such a pitch was possible.

> They laughed it off as an "optical illusion." Of all the sportswriters who covered the game, "Pop" Chadwick of the *Brooklyn Eagle* was the only one who really believed in the curve. Pop refused to be laughed off. He arranged for me to go to New York and I demonstrated to a huge crowd in the old Capitoline grounds he was right. This was in 1868 when I was 14 years old [born in 1848, he actually turned 14 on October 18, 1862]. Three posts were set in a straight line. I stood on one side of an end post and threw the ball so that it curled around the far side of the center post back by the near side of the third post. The fans of those days were dumbfounded but they had to accept the evidence of their eyes.[12]

This was the first public telling of a curveball demonstration that took place before a large number of witnesses. In this version, Henry Chadwick had arranged the experiment and was among those on hand to see it, according to Goldsmith. But Chadwick in his 1898 letter to *Sporting Life* had already credited Cummings with throwing the pitch as far back as 1866 (Chadwick had died in 1908, so he couldn't clarify matters).

Three years later, Goldsmith added some important embroidery to his tale. During a 1927 visit to London, he sat down with *London Advertiser* writer E. J. Carty to recall his glory days in London, now insisting he was the first to throw the curve. Carty began his account with a factual error as he shared Goldsmith's lengthy claim from that year, to which he had added entirely new twists:

> Fifty-five years ago, or in 1872, there was not a real baseball league in America. [Players in the second year of the National Association would have been surprised at that.] Certain teams went from place to place to play but they were free agents. Every small town had its favorite team, and New Haven, Conn., where Fred Goldsmith was born, was no different from the rest. Mr. Goldsmith was playing with a corner lot team, and he made quite a name for himself as a pitcher. He was hard to hit, and there was much talk in regard to how we was able to throw a ball that "ducked" the bat that swung at it. Now this mode of pitching had not merely happened to Goldsmith. He accords a fellow pitcher named Fred Hall, of New Haven, the credit for having given him the idea of the curved ball.
>
> One day Hall told Goldsmith that he could pitch a ball so that it would fly off a bat, and thus could not be knocked any distance. Hall explained that he had discovered that by twisting the ball with his fingers, as it left his hand, it spun as it sped onward and that thus it could not be safely hit.
>
> Goldsmith listened and then tried the twist himself. To his amazement he found that he could pitch the ball so that it would swing away from the batter and back toward the catcher. This was the simplest of all curves—the out-curve. Subsequently he was able to make the ball curve in or out and up or down as he chose.
>
> The stunt was brand new, and it baffled the batters of opposing teams. No one else could pitch like Goldsmith, and soon letters were written to the local papers discussing the innovation. Hamilton Avery, a friend of Goldsmith, and afterwards a pitcher for Yale College, claimed the curved ball was impossible. He quoted aeronautics, physics, and engineering to prove the fallacy of Goldsmith's claim, and the fans took sides with vengeance.
>
> Finally, two sporting writers, Todd Coles, of the *Mirror of Sports*, New York, and Pop Chadwick, of the *Brooklyn Eagle*, arranged a demonstration and invited Fred Goldsmith to go to New York and show his wares. This was in 1872, and the test took place on what were known as the Capitoline Grounds. Goldsmith was then a little more than 15 years old.
>
> Pitching was a peculiar art in those days. The pitcher was not allowed to "wind up." The ball had to be delivered from the thigh above the knee. It was only 45 feet from the pitcher's box to the home base. But Goldsmith was not tried out in a game. With thousands of people looking on, three stakes were

driven in the ground. Goldsmith was asked to pitch a ball so that it would cut the top of the first stake, curve around the second one and curve back to the third one. He did the trick and was given full credit for it. Immediately pitchers everywhere were studying the curved ball, and the out-curve was soon fairly common.[13]

In this version, Ham Avery was depicted as a skeptic, rather than as an inventor. Goldsmith had to show Avery that a curve was possible. And this public demonstration occurred in 1872, not 1866. Like fine wine, the story of Goldsmith, now 71, was improving with age.

The Sporting News decided in late 1931 to review the evolution of pitching over the years. In the second part of its three-part series, it considered the curveball. Among those pictured as "some masters of the curveball art" were Goldsmith and Larry Corcoran, the duo who had shared pitching duties in Springfield and Chicago.[14] Upon seeing the article, Goldsmith decided to write about his curveball experiences for the same publication. In his subsequent piece that was published, he described his curveball demonstration from 1870 (no longer 1868 or 1872) and stated that he had printed proof of it. Goldsmith said the *Yale College Journal* carried a story in 1870 because of "a freak delivery I had acquired in my endeavor to get as much revolutionary motion on the ball as possible, thinking it would be more baffling to the batter." The *Journal*, he said, discussed whether a ball could be made to arc. Goldsmith wrote that the controversy prompted Henry Chadwick to conduct the test at the Capitoline Grounds in August 1870 before a "large crowd of spectators." Goldsmith then quoted from an article he said Chadwick wrote for the *Brooklyn Eagle* describing the event. It was dated August 17, 1870:

> Fred Goldsmith has won fame by developing a ball that twisted, proving to countless skeptics that a sphere could cheat natural laws. Yesterday at the Capitoline Grounds, a large crowd assembled and cheered lustily as a youth from New Haven, Connecticut, named Fred Goldsmith, demonstrated to the satisfaction of all that a baseball could be so manipulated and controlled by throwing it from one given point to another as to make a pronounced arc in space. The test was made by drawing a chalkline on the ground a distance of 45 feet from one extremity to the other. An eight-foot pole was driven in an upright position at each end. Another pole was set in the same manner half-way between the two end poles, planted directly upon the line. Now, everything was set for the test. Goldsmith was placed on the left side of the chalkline near the end pole facing the pole at the other end. The purpose of this was that the ball delivered from the thrower's hand was to cross the line, and circle the center pole and return to the same side of the line from which it was thrown, before reaching the far pole. This feat was successfully accomplished six or eight times and that which had up to this point been considered an optical illusion and against all rules of philosophy was now an established fact. Henry Chadwick, Editor.[15]

Goldsmith suddenly had what appeared to be proof of his achievement. His claim to curveball paternity came many years after the fact. His evidence was also arriving late in the day, for reasons unknown. He would carry the article with him wherever he went.

Goldsmith seldom turned down an excuse to return to London and talk baseball, so he readily agreed to join other veteran players at the "booster day" held for Tecumseh Park in 1936. The place was falling into disrepair, and the fundraiser to help renovate it attracted thousands of fans. Among the honored guests were Goldsmith and Bob Emslie, former pitcher for the London Atlantics, Baltimore Orioles, and longtime National League umpire. At the event, Goldie was saluted as originator of the curveball.[16] Two years later, Goldsmith returned for the London Old Boys Reunion and was again credited with inventing the pitch and for bringing baseball glory to the city. He received a great hand from 1,200 spectators on hand for a benefit ball game.[17] As was his habit, he showed the *Eagle* news item as proof of his 1870 demonstration. It would be Goldsmith's last visit to the city in which he had been hailed as a hero as a much younger man and where he was still highly regarded.

His continued trips to Briggs Stadium in his hunt for recognition paid dividends in 1937. On June 6, the visiting Yankees brought with them New York sportswriters who picked up on Goldsmith's claim and accepted it as fact once they saw his newspaper clipping. The only doubter, ironically, was Ed Hughes of the *Brooklyn Eagle*. He had trouble swallowing this assertion made so many years after Cummings had been accepted as the first curveballer. The stories filed by the reporters that day led to an invitation for Goldsmith to appear on the *Ripley's Believe It or Not!* radio show in New York. On the program, aired in October, Goldsmith told host Robert Ripley: "I threw the first curveball, and nobody believed I could do it. Here's a newspaper clipping telling about it."[18] That was good enough for Ripley. While in the city, the old hurler was interviewed by several newspapers and he amended his story yet again. He said he had taught the pitch to Hamilton Avery. Goldsmith's recitation had come full circle from his first telling in 1898, when he credited Avery with teaching it to him.[19]

Researcher David Arcidiacono has highlighted inconsistencies and factual errors in Goldsmith's several versions of his story about inventing and demonstrating the curveball. He noted that Candy Cummings never played for the Atlantics, much less in 1869 when Goldsmith said he saw Cummings pitch for the club. Hamilton Avery was a student at Yale, not a professor. The Cincinnati native didn't begin his studies there until 1871, and didn't join its ball team until two years later. Arcidiacono's dogged research found that Goldsmith did not appear in an 1874 tournament in Lynn; he did the following year, but did not pitch. The *Yale College Journal* cited by Goldsmith never existed. Further, Goldsmith had changed his story substantially after saying in 1906 he learned the curve from Avery. And it wasn't until six months after Cummings died in 1924 that Goldsmith spoke of his own demonstration at the Capitoline Grounds. Seven more years passed before Goldsmith began showing around the clipping from the *Eagle* to buttress his claim. Yet that particular article cannot be located by modern-day researchers, including the highly motivated Arcidiacono. Digital and manual searches of the archives of the newspaper have failed to find it. In fact, none of the newspapers in Brooklyn, which followed baseball closely at the time, had any accounts of such a demonstration in 1870. The only references to baseball in the August 17, 1870, edition of the *Eagle* were about the New York Mutuals defeating Cleveland, and an item about an upcoming picnic hosted by the Brooklyn Atlantics. Arcidiacono discovered that a remarkably similar curveball test occurred in Cincinnati in 1877, featuring pitchers Bobby Mitchell and Tommy Bond. The researcher concluded: "The simple fact that there was even the need for a test in 1877 seems to suggest that no definitive demonstration had occurred previously."[20]

Fred Goldsmith moved to Michigan after baseball and raised two families. He attended Detroit Tigers games and was often the guest of honor at baseball reunions back in London. In his twilight years, he insisted he had invented the curve ball pitch. He died two days before *The Sporting News* carried a story about his claim in 1939. This is a self-portrait (John R. Castle, Jr.).

Arcidiacono could find no reference to Goldsmith's demonstration in any of the three Yale publications that existed in the early 1870s. Yet he found references to the "curved pitching" of both Avery and Cummings. The historian, who conducted the most comprehensive study of Goldsmith and his claim to date, conceded that all he was able to prove was there was no demonstration of the curveball by a 14-year-old Goldsmith in Brooklyn in 1870. The pitcher may have demonstrated it elsewhere at some other time, but even so, Arcidiacono concluded, any such demonstration would not necessarily prove Goldsmith was the first to throw it. It is possible, he suggested, that the demonstration story was "completely fabricated."

In his twilight years, Goldsmith enjoyed recalling his days as one of the top pitchers in baseball. He described his clipping from the *Brooklyn Eagle* as his "most prized possession," adding, "the most fun I get now is sitting and remembering what I used to do."[21] Perhaps, in the warm glow of happy memories from so long ago, he had confused some of his details. The clipping remains a mystery.

Goldsmith turned 80 in 1936 and was still determined to get the recognition he felt he was due. The National Baseball Hall of Fame was set to open in 1939 on what was touted as the 100th anniversary of the invention of baseball in Cooperstown, New York. For several years in advance, as plans for the baseball shrine were being formulated, there was debate in baseball circles about which players should be honored there.

Cooperstown had been selected because of the story that baseball was invented in the village in 1839, according to an eyewitness. Abner Graves, an aging mining engineer from Denver, first told the story in 1905, and it was readily accepted by those anxious for proof that the game was a purely American invention. In Graves's story, Abner Doubleday, who later became a Civil War hero, devised it on the spot. The tale received a significant push from Albert Goodwill Spalding—even though it had failed to withstand even minimal historical scrutiny—and eventually found its way into American folklore and school textbooks. Graves had embellished his tale, told for the first time 66 years after it supposedly took place. In his retelling, he graduated from witness to active participant in that seminal game. His story, evidence suggests, was most likely adapted from another story about an early game of baseball played elsewhere, or merely inspired by it.[22] To this day, however, many Americans still believe baseball's creation myth to be true.

As early as 1935, baseball was soliciting the names of the first players to elect into the Hall of Fame in 1936, three years before it opened. A 78-member committee of old-timers had been established to select players from before 1900, and Goldsmith found himself on the committee. He was provided a list of players for whom he could vote and was pleased to see his name on it.

15. *Pitching the Pitch*   231

Goldsmith placed his vote for right-handed pitcher Charley "Old Hoss" Radbourn, who had won 309 games with Providence and Boston.[23] In 1939, it was announced that that year's inductees would include Radbourn, Candy Cummings, and two former White Stockings with whom he had clashed: Cap Anson and Albert Goodwill Spalding. Cummings was elected in the "executive" category, but it would be noted on his plaque in the hall that he "pitched first curve ball in baseball history. Invented curve as amateur ace of Brooklyn Stars in 1867."[24]

Goldsmith had been feeling unwell ever since he returned from the 1938 London Old Boys Reunion and had moved from Ortonville to Berkley, Michigan, into the home of another daughter, Ellen Stieler. Her place was close to a hospital, and Goldsmith didn't venture far from his bed. He was weak, and his doctor said he was suffering from heart failure and should be kept comfortable. Frail and failing, he continued to listen to ball games on the radio and read the sports sections.[25] He became decidedly uncomfortable in early 1939 when he learned Cummings was to be inducted into the Hall of Fame—and credited with inventing the curve. He was agitated further when he read a review of the new movie, *A Century of Baseball*, which made the same assertion about Cummings. Concerned about the terrible impact this was having on her father, Ellen contacted *The Sporting News* to say he was upset he wasn't acknowledged in any way. In March, Goldsmith was interviewed by its writer E. G. Brands. The resulting article appeared in its March 30 edition headlined: "Hurler for Anson Fighting to the End for Honor of Pitching the First Curve."

> Lying in a critical condition at his home in Berkley, Mich., is Fred E. Goldsmith, one of the oldest living players who disputes the claims advanced in behalf of Arthur Cummings as the first to throw a curve ball. Deacon White, 91, probably is the oldest. Ill for years and bed-ridden for weeks, Goldsmith recently took a turn for the worse, after reading a review of a movie that gave Cummings credit for the first curve.
>
> Goldsmith for years maintained that the honor should have been his and the official recognition given Cummings for the centennial celebration noticeably caused him keen chagrin. It is said he brooded over the disappointment so much that it brought a relapse.... Little hope is now held for his recovery.[26]

Goldsmith never saw the article. He died two days before it appeared. He was 82. The *Detroit News* reported his passing this way: "Fred Goldsmith died at his home in Berkley, Mich., last night, firmly believing that he belonged in the Base Ball's Hall of Fame as inventor of the curve ball."[27] The *News* noted the controversy about the first to hurl the pitch, saying the Hall of Fame had resolved the question in favor of Cummings. The *Detroit Free Press* also reported how upset Goldsmith had become at the recognition accorded Cummings. It repeated his assertion that he had pitched the curve before Cummings and added that Goldsmith had taught it to Hamilton Avery. The *Free Press* said publication of Goldsmith's claim in *The Sporting News* was imminent. "However, *The Sporting News* article will be too late to bring any stimulating cheer to the ailing baseball veteran. He died firm in his conviction that he was the curve's originator but sorely disappointed that baseball did not officially recognize his claims."[28]

Nearly six weeks later, *The Sporting News* assessed the six new Hall of Famers for 1939 and raised its editorial eyebrows about one of them. "There can be no doubt but that five of them belong there. Whether the sixth should be selected over some others, who have been mentioned, depends upon the premise on which Cummings was included." It continued:

> However, many are at a loss to account for the selection of Cummings over others whose records in the game are more impressive, even though his inclusion is based on the claim that he was the first curve-ball pitcher. So far as documentary proof is concerned, the distinction of being the first to perfect the curve seems to be shared equally by Fred E. Goldsmith and Cummings and no conclusive evidence has yet been produced to show that one preceded the other. Cummings' career antedates that of Goldsmith, but Goldsmith served longer in organized ball.[29]

In June, to mark the 100th anniversary of baseball (based on the Cooperstown myth), *The Sporting News* carried images of Cummings and Goldsmith side-by-side under the headline "Co-Originators of the Curve Ball." The brief item noted the controversy surrounding the two hurlers and suggested it may never be known which of the two men had been the first to throw the revolutionary pitch in a game.[30]

Goldsmith's pallbearers were members of the Old Time Ball Players Association, and he was buried in Berkley's Roseland Park Cemetery next to his first wife, Rowena, who died the previous year. There is no marker to show his final resting place.[31]

Four years after he died, Goldsmith's claim received a boost from legendary baseball manager Connie Mack. During a visit to London during a war bond campaign, Mack gave a brief speech at newly named Labatt Park. It was his first visit to London, but he knew the city was famous for its baseball exploits. "I realize you have had baseball greats in London," the Philadelphia Athletics manager said. "There was Fred Goldsmith, the first man to pitch a curve ball. I remember batting against him."[32] Mack didn't provide details, however. Goldsmith's career ended in 1884 and Mack didn't debut as a professional until 1886 with Washington of the National League. So it is hard to know when Mack would have faced Goldsmith and his curve.

The controversy did not die with Goldsmith. Many years later, his grandson, John R. Castle, Jr., took up his cause. Born in 1935, Castle was a youngster when his grandfather moved into the Castle home near Ortonville. He recalled his mother, Phyllis, noting how heartbroken Goldsmith was at the lack of recognition for his invention. "'I'll make it right, Daddy,'" he said Phyllis promised her father on his deathbed. "'I promise you'll get credit for your curveball.'"[33] John Castle made it his mission in later life to highlight his grandfather's accomplishments and get the attention that had eluded him. Castle recalled fondly the time he spent bonding with his grandfather and learning from him about baseball, fishing, feeding the chickens, and gardening. Castle began to conduct research into Goldsmith's career in about 1990, but had to set it aside for about a decade as he went through rehabilitation at his home in Colorado after a serious car accident. "I decided that his complete baseball history should be told," he wrote, acknowledging it would take much effort to uncover the statistics for Goldsmith. He set out to document every amateur and professional game in which Goldsmith pitched, finding box scores and newspaper articles in libraries, universities, historical societies, private collections, the Library of Congress, and the National Baseball Hall of Fame.

The product of his labors was a self-published book in 2010 that he distributed widely. It had a cumbersome title that left no doubt he was advocating for his grandfather: *Goldie's Curve Ball: How Fred E. Goldsmith Invented, Demonstrated, Mastered, & Championed the Curve Ball*. In it, Castle painstakingly documented Goldsmith's record, game by game, season by season, since his debut for Bridgeport in 1874, at age 18. That year, Goldie won two of the club's ten games without a loss. The following year with Bridgeport, he won ten games and lost three before turning professional in October, playing shortstop in a single game for New Haven. Goldsmith, Castle found, played in 13 games for New Haven to start the 1876 season, pitching in five contests and winning all of them. He joined the Tecumsehs on May 24 and went on to win 41 games, 11 of them shutouts, with five losses. In 1877, the year London was a founding member of the International Association and won its pennant, Goldsmith won 47 games, including six shutouts, and he lost 23. For 1878, he won 48, 14 of them shutouts, and lost 26. Joining Springfield on August 29, he recorded another 11 victories, four of them shutouts, with 11 losses. The following year with Springfield, Goldsmith won 26 games, four of them shutouts, as he lost nine and tied one. In five seasons spent with New Haven, London, and Springfield, he had amassed 183 victories.

Goldsmith joined Troy to finish the 1879 season, playing in the National League for the first time. With Troy, he won five games, lost four, and tied one.[34] Three of those wins were against Albany of the International Association, so the major league record book ignores them and acknowledges only two of his five wins. By the time he ended his career late in 1884, Goldsmith had recorded another 110 National League wins. In his entire professional career, Castle figured Goldsmith won 296 games and lost 137 for a winning percentage of .684.[35] Tweaking that number slightly to add a Tecumseh win against Cleveland missed by Castle and to align it with his "major league" record, Goldsmith recorded a total of 295 wins as a professional. Castle noted his grandfather had eight seasons in which he won at least 20 games.

Castle was thrilled when the 1877 Tecumsehs were inducted into the London Sports Hall of Fame in 2009. At age 74, he joined the salute to the team for which his grandfather had been a vital cog. *London Free Press* reporter Ryan Pyette interviewed Castle about his campaign to get recognition for Fred Goldsmith. When Pyette suggested the next induction for Goldsmith should be at Cooperstown, Castle agreed that was "appropriate."[36]

In the end, however, does it really matter whether Cummings or Goldsmith invented the curve pitch? Barring solid, verifiable evidence, trying to anoint its inventor based on memories is about as wise as trying to anoint one person as the inventor of baseball. We have seen the historical folly of that (sorry, Abner).

Both players were pioneers—Cummings with less proof of making that first revolutionary pitch than did Goldsmith with his *Eagle* clipping of dubious authenticity. Yet Cummings is in the National Baseball Hall of Fame based on his uncorroborated claim, for which he found important supporters. During his four years in the National Association and two more in the National League, Cummings recorded 145 wins against 94 losses. Yet one would be hard-pressed to suggest Cummings should be removed from the Hall of Fame.

A better course would be to add Fred Goldsmith, who had twice as many victories as Cummings, recording fully 183 of them in the five years before he joined the National League. In the League, where his skills began to decline, he added another 112 wins. That gave him a career grand total of 295, a mere five shy of the generally celebrated 300-win mark. Aside from failing to get proper recognition for his curveball, his full pitching record as a professional has been overlooked because he played in the one league that William Hulbert and baseball historians considered to be unworthy.

It would, indeed, be appropriate for Fred Goldsmith to join Candy Cummings and the others in Cooperstown.

Epilogue

Few Canadians fully understand the deep connection their country has to the game of baseball. The roots date back to at least 1838, when a game resembling baseball was played just east of London in Southwestern Ontario. An account of that rather crude game was published many years later.[1] That was not the first game of baseball; rather, it is considered the first "recorded" game, albeit nearly 50 years after the fact. Canadians are also likely unaware of the baseball powerhouses that Guelph and London became in the 1870s as they competed against each other and newly industrialized cities large and small in eastern North America that had embraced the game. Toronto, the home of today's Blue Jays, was surprisingly slow to discover the game and play it at the same level as the much smaller centers of London and Guelph.

The story of the Tecumsehs reflects an era in history and in the evolution of baseball when anything seemed possible. Cities competed for newcomers, and their manufacturers vied for new markets as rail connections steadily expanded and improved. Baseball provided another outlet for that competitive drive, and rivalries became fierce and entrenched. London, with 18,000 inhabitants, and Guelph, with 8,000, could be equals on the diamond if their teams were good enough. Population didn't matter. Likewise, the ball field was where the small Canadian communities could engage much larger American cities with which they would otherwise have no connection whatsoever. The two Canadian cities found themselves mentioned in faraway journals like the *New York Times*, not for the accomplishments of industry, nor due to some natural disaster or human tragedy, but for baseball. To reach the top echelon of play, the Tecumsehs and Maple Leafs found it necessary to hire American players, but they retained a core of Canadians able to play the game at the highest level, who later joined teams in other professional leagues, or umpired in them, into the 1880s and beyond.

Small businessmen, merchants, and local politicians all engaged in the local boosterism that characterized the age. Many of those involved in baseball went on to careers in another competitive field: politics. George Sleeman became mayor of Guelph, for instance. Jake Englehart worked his talents behind the scenes and earned the trust and respect of the premier of Ontario, who called upon him to complete a difficult rail line.

Baseball and politics often appealed to similar personalities. Other little-known connections exist between baseball and Canadian politicians. For instance, Lester B. Pearson, prime minister of Canada in the 1960s, was an accomplished player as a young man. In 1919, at age 22, Pearson played third base for the semi-professional Guelph Maple Leafs. He realized the game didn't provide the sort of career he was looking for and decided to move on. In later life, as a diplomat, Pearson enjoyed telling other diplomats he was the only one among them who had ever been paid to play baseball.[2] When he trotted out that icebreaker, it is likely his American colleagues were most surprised of all. In his honor, the annual game held many years later between the Montreal Expos and the Toronto Blue Jays was named the Pearson Cup. With the demise of the Expos, the cup now rests in the Canadian Baseball Hall of Fame in St. Marys, Ontario.

Charles Trudeau, wealthy father of future Prime Minister Pierre Elliot Trudeau, was a member of the ownership group for the Triple-A Montreal Royals. In 1935, he attended spring training for the club in Florida. There, he contracted pneumonia and died. His son, Pierre, was a teenager and keenly felt the loss of his father. In 1982, at the All-Star game for Major League Baseball held in Montreal, toward the end of his time as prime minister, Trudeau said: "If my father had his choice, he would have preferred me to be an all-star player than to be here as an invited guest."[3] The Royals became an affiliate of Brooklyn, and in 1946, Jackie Robinson starred for them on his way to breaking the major league color barrier the next year with the Dodgers.

The first-ever black player in organized professional baseball debuted against the London Tecumsehs in 1878. Pitcher Bud Fowler was brought in to play for Lynn, Massachusetts, and his Live Oaks were leading, 3–0, when London players walked off the field, upset at the umpiring. Lynn was awarded a forfeit. Fowler's appearance in the game was largely forgotten, and for years, catcher Moses Fleetwood Walker was hailed as the first black professional as a member of the 1884 Toledo team in the American Association. Fowler, born John Jackson, bounced around baseball for a long time and appeared in the uniform for two semi-professional teams north of the border, the Guelph Maple Leafs (twice) and the Petrolia Imperials.[4]

Players like Fowler, and cities such as London, Guelph, Albany, Rochester,

Utica, Binghamton, Manchester, Lowell, Lynn, and even tiny Hornellsville made their mark in baseball at a time when the game was maturing into a business. But because they competed in the International Association, a worthy successor to the player-centered National Association, their accomplishments and those of the men on their rosters are not well known or appreciated today. In 1882, many of the same men who launched the IA five years earlier established the American Association—and for many of the same reasons. In 1884, the Union Association was created to challenge the National League and its monopolistic ways. The Players' League of 1890 had its origin in similar complaints about the older league and its reserve clause. The latter two rebel leagues each lasted a single season, yet Major League Baseball decided that all three organizations are worthy of "major league" status. Baseball's first professional league, the National Association, is also considered a major. Only the International Association, which operated from 1877 to 1880, has been denied such status. It enjoyed two solid seasons while the National League struggled and nearly collapsed. The IA's third year was difficult, however, because of the damage inflicted when the League took three of its teams. Its fourth campaign saw it wither and die.

A search for players and their records in sources like Baseball-reference.com or baseball bibles such as *Total Baseball* or *The Great Encyclopedia of 19th Century Major League Baseball* makes it difficult to see a full picture of the early days of stars such as Hall of Famers Pud Galvin, Dan Brouthers and Candy Cummings, or Joe Hornung, Fred Goldsmith, and others. Or the full record of players who spent a season or two playing with Association teams, like Tecumsehs Ross Barnes and Juice Latham, or pitcher Lip Pike, first baseman Tim Murnane, catcher Jerry Dorgan, and many others. One has to dig into "minor league" classifications, where they exist, to fill in the blanks that appear in their official records.

Galvin, the first 300-game winner in major league baseball, achieved that status with a victory in October 1888, traditional sources indicate. But this didn't take into account the 40 wins he amassed in his time with Allegheny and Buffalo in the International Association. Credited with 365 wins, not including those 40, he is listed as the fifth-most successful pitcher of all time. Had those IA wins been added, he would jump to third, a mere 12 victories behind legendary Walter Johnson, and vaulting past Christy Mathewson and Grover Cleveland Alexander, both of whom recorded 373 wins. Adding his numbers from the International Association, Galvin's performance becomes even more impressive. Likewise, Fred Goldsmith's career record would be even more remarkable had he been credited with the 183 wins he earned while in the International Association, bringing him to five short of 300. As a contemporary of Galvin, Goldsmith still deserves consideration for Hall of Fame honors as a successful pioneer.

The men behind the London Tecumsehs and Guelph Maple Leafs were successful in baseball, but even more so in their off-field endeavors. Imperial Oil, the firm established in 1880 by Jake Englehart and 15 other refiners, is one of the largest companies in Canada today. Imperial Oil is the largest oil refiner and a major producer of oil and natural gas, a key petrochemical producer, and a leading retailer of gasoline, under the Esso and Mobil brand names.[5]

George Sleeman's Silver Creek Brewery was turned over to family members after his death, but in 1933 the firm was caught smuggling Prohibition-era beer into Detroit by U.S. authorities, and the family had to sell the business to pay taxes owing. A second brewery, Spring Bank Brewery, was also sold about the same time, ending the Sleeman family connection to brewing. In 1985, however, John W. Sleeman, a great-grandson of George Sleeman, re-established the Sleeman Brewing and Malting Company and soon began brewing Sleeman Cream Ale. The company found immediate success by using a 100-year-old recipe from George Sleeman for its brew. By 1992 the company, which had expanded into the Ontario market, shipped its first beer to Detroit—this time, legally. Sapporo Breweries of Japan acquired Sleeman

Pud Galvin became the first pitcher to record 300 wins in his career. But because he played with two teams in the International Association early in his career, 40 more wins were not counted because historians insist the IA was not a major league (National Baseball Hall of Fame Library, Cooperstown, New York. Pud Galvin 1882_24-40_HS_PD).

Breweries for $400 million in 2006, and John W. Sleeman was kept on to run the Guelph operation.[6] Today, the city's fine downtown sports and entertainment center is known as the Sleeman Centre. So the Sleeman name can still be found in Ontario today, just as the Englehart name survives on a hospital and park in Petrolia and as a community in Northern Ontario.

There are few tangible reminders of the International Association today. Perhaps the most celebrated is Labatt Park, originally created on flood-prone river flats as Tecumseh Park in 1877 for the London team. It was built specifically to help launch the club into the Association, where it won the pennant that same year. The London field has a sister, of sorts, in historic Wrigley Field in Chicago. The latter park was built in 1914 as Weeghman Park, home for the Chicago Whales of the short-lived Federal League. That league, too, like the upstart American League that debuted in 1900, has been accorded major league status, and players get full credit for their statistics in the two years the Federal League existed.

To this day, there is only one league still relegated to minor league status even though it attracted some of the top professionals of its day and nearly toppled the National League: The International Association.

Inferior status for it was insisted upon by National League kingpin William Hulbert and by his league. Such a designation has been perpetuated by Major League Baseball and latter-day historians. The Association never considered itself subordinate or second-rate in any way, and neither did its players. The fact that such discrimination continues to this day is a mystery, and untenable.

In every way, the record shows, the International Association was a worthy contender at a pivotal time in baseball history and deserving of status as a major league. And as winners of its first pennant, the London Tecumsehs of 1877 can be considered Canada's first major league champions.

Chapter Notes

Chapter 1

1. Hugh M. Grant, "The 'Mysterious' Jacob L. Englehart and the Early Ontario Petroleum Industry," *Ontario History* LXXXV, no. 1 (March 1993).
2. "Oil Springs Boom and Bust," Oil Museum of Canada, accessed April 22, 2013 www.lclmg.org/lclmg/Museums/OilMuseumof Canada/BlackGold2/OilHeritage/OilSprings/tabid/208/Default.aspx.
3. Bill Gladstone, *A History of the Jewish Community of London Ontario from the 1850s to the Present Day* (Toronto: Then and Now Books, 2011), 17.
4. Hugh Grant and Henry Thille, "Tariffs, Strategy and Structure: Competition and Collusion in the Ontario Petroleum Industry, 1870–1880," *The Journal of Economic History* 61, no. 2 (June 2001), 391.
5. "Petroleum: The Oil Field of Canada West," *New York Times*, April 2, 1866, 8.
6. Gary Regan and Mardee Haidin Regan, *The Book of Bourbon and Other Fine American Whiskeys* (London: Mixellany Books, 2009), 40, 41.
7. "History of Spirits in America," the Distilled Spirits Council of the United States, accessed May 6, 2013, http://www.discus.org/heritage/spirits.
8. Ibid.
9. "Distilled Spirits," *Cyclopedia of Political Science* 1, entry 375. Library of Economics and Liberty, accessed January 6, 2013, http://www.econlib.org/library/YPDBooks/Lalor/llCy375.html.
10. Ibid.
11. "The Liquor Frauds," *The New York Times*, December 29, 1866, 4.
12. Ibid.
13. *The Straits Times* of Singapore (Nov. 15, 1922), 13; accessed January 8, 2013, http://newspapers.nl.sg/Digitised/Article/straitstimes19221115.2.86.aspx.
14. R. G. Dun Collection, Canada, Volume 19, 13, quoted in Grant, "The 'Mysterious' Jacob L. Englehart and the Early Ontario Petroleum Industry," 68.
15. R. G. Dun Collection, New York City, Volume 348, 900, quoted in Grant, "The 'Mysterious' Jacob L. Englehart and the Early Ontario Petroleum Industry," 69.
16. Charles Whipp and Ed Phelps, *Petrolia: 1866–1966* (Petrolia, ON: *Petrolia Advertiser-Topic* and Petrolia Centennial Committee, 1966), 10.
17. *Monetary Times* 5, August 14, 1871, 85; *Monetary Times* 5, May 3, 1872, 864; *Monetary Times* 6, October 18, 1872, 308; R. G. Dun Collection Canada, Volume 25, 246, as quoted in Grant, "The Mysterious Jacob L. Englehart and the Early Ontario Petroleum Industry," 70.
18. Grant and Thille, "Tariffs, Strategy and Structure: Competition and Collusion in the Ontario Petroleum Industry, 1870–1880," fn 392.
19. The connection between the Sonneborns, Englehart, and Carbon Oil are laid out in a court case brought by a bank that claimed that when Jonas Sonneborn went bankrupt in 1874, he hid his assets to avoid repaying the bank a line of credit of 300,000 Reichsmarks. Among the lawyers involved was J. Albert Englehart, brother of Jacob. See Deutsche National Bank vs. Jonas Sonneborn and others, Supreme Court of New York, Evening Post Steam Presses (New York: 1879), 50, 51, accessed November 6, 2013, https://play.google.com/books/reader?id=4emNTdE_QJY C&printsec=frontcover&authuser=O&hl=en &pg=GBS.RA1-PA54.

20. R. G. Dun Collection, New York, Volume 348, 900 ff, quoted in Grant, "The 'Mysterious' Jacob L. Englehart," 71.
21. "Crimean War," Library and Archives Canada, accessed December 4, 2012, http//www.collectionscanada.gc.ca/confederation/023001–3010.18-e.html.
22. Frederick H. Armstrong, *The Forest City: An Illustrated History of London, Canada* (London, ON: Windsor Publications, 1986), 86.
23. "Canadian Trade with the United States," in The History of American Business, accessed November 5, 2013, http://historybusiness.org/2371-canadian-trade-with-the-united-states.html.
24. Armstrong, 99.
25. Fred Landon, "Some Effects of the American Civil War on Canadian Agriculture," *Agricultural History* 7, no. 4 (October 1933), 165–168.
26. "Conspiracy in Canada," Central Intelligence Agency, accessed Nov. 5, 2013, https://www.cia.gov/library/publications/additional-publications/civil-war/37.html.
27. *The Carty Chronicles of Landmarks and Londoners*, ed. Catherine B. McEwen (London, ON: London and Middlesex Historical Society, 2005), 80, 81.
28. P. G. T. Beauregard, General, accessed November 13, 2013, www.civilwar.org/education/history/biographies/p-g-t-beauregard.html.
29. The *Carty Chronicles of Landmarks and Londoners*, 79, 80.
30. Clement Vallandigham, Ohio History Central, accessed November 13, 2013, www.ohiohistorycentral.org/w/Clement_Vallandigham.
31. Daniel J. Brock, *Fragments from the Forks: London Ontario's Legacy* (London, ON: London and Middlesex Historical Society, 2011), 66.
32. "Fugitive Slave Chapel is Steeped Deep in History," *London Advertiser*, May 8, 1926. This article about a chapel established in London by runaway slaves also dealt with memories of old-timers about the impact of the Civil War on the city. Writer E. J. Carty recalled talking to elderly druggist William Edge about his recollections. Edge had moved to London from New York City, and his obituary in 1918 called him "one of London's most highly esteemed citizens." Carty recalled Edge telling him that smoke from the battlefield in Gettysburg hung "heavily" over the city, obscuring the sun. Copies of the *London Free Press* from early July 1863 do not exist, so a primary source cannot be found. At that time, the *Free Press* was the only newspaper in the city. The rival *London Advertiser* was first published in October 1863.
33. "The Old Tecumseh House," *London Free Press*, September 16, 1929.
34. "Conspiracy in Canada," Central Intelligence Agency.
35. Ibid.
36. "Depot of Prisoners of War on Johnson's Island," accessed Nov. 6, 2013, http://www.johnsonsisland.org/history/war.htm.
37. William Ryczek, *Blackguards and Red Stockings: A History of Baseball's National Association 1871–1875* (Wallingford, CT: Colebrook Press, 1992), 6.
38. Armstrong, *The Forest City*, 17–22.
39. Ibid., 99–101.

Chapter 2

1. John Thorn, *Baseball in the Garden of Eden* (New York: Simon & Schuster, 2011), 57. Thorn quotes Peter A. Piccione, "Batting the Ball," in *College of Charleston Magazine* 7, no. 1, Spring/Summer 2003, 36, for a reference to game called seker-hemat, which translates as "batting the ball."
2. "New Discovery by SABR member David Block confirms baseball was played by royalty in England in 1700s," Society for American Baseball Research, accessed Nov. 12, 2013, www.sabr.org/latest/new-discovery-sabr-member-david-block-confirms-baseball-was-played-royalty-england-1700s.
3. David Block, *Baseball Before We Knew It* (Lincoln, NE: University of Nebraska Press, 2005), 178–79.
4. Jane Austen, *Northanger Abbey* (London: Simms and M'Intyre, 1853), 6, quoted in Thorn, *Baseball in the Garden of Eden*, ix.
5. Block, *Baseball Before We Knew It*, 24.
6. Ibid., 87–88.
7. Monica Nucciarone, *Alexander Cartwright: The Life Behind the Baseball Legend* (Lincoln, NE: University of Nebraska Press, 2009), 178.
8. Ibid., 229.
9. "Bud Selig Thinks Abner Graves Invented Baseball. Of Course He Does," Deadspin, accessed November 20, 2013, http://deadspin.com/5684393/bud-selig-thinks-abner-graves-invented-baseball-of-course-he-does?skyline=true&s=i.
10. *Spalding's Official Base Ball Guide, 1903*

(New York: American Sports Publishing, 1903), 7.

11. "Baseball at Delmonico's," *New York Times*, April 9, 1889, 5, quoted in Thorn, *Baseball in the Garden of Eden*, 235.

12. A. G. Spalding, "The Origin of the Game of Base Ball," *Akron Beacon Journal*, April 1, 1905, 6.

13. "Abner Doubleday Invented Base Ball," *Akron Beacon Journal*, April 4, 1905, 5.

14. Albert G. Spalding, *America's National Pastime* (New York: American Sports Publishing, 1911), 19.

15. Robert Elias, *The Empire Strikes Out: How Baseball Sold U.S. Foreign Policy and Promoted the American Way Abroad* (New York: The New Press, 2010), 283.

16. Alfred H. Spink, *The National Game*, 2nd ed. (St. Louis: The National Game, 1911), 54, quoted in Block, *Baseball Before We Knew It*, 17.

17. "Denver Man Played First Baseball Game in History of Sport, *Denver Post*, May 9, 1912, 3.

18. "Denver Invalid, 90, Shoots Wife," *Denver Post*, June 17, 1924, 1; and "Abner Graves, Who Killed Wife, Left Estate of $10,000," *Denver Post*, February 17, 1927.

19. "Very Like Base Ball. A Game of the Long-ago Which Closely Resembled Our Present National Game," *Sporting Life*, May 5, 1886, 5.

20. Brian Martin, *Baseball's Creation Myth: Adam Ford, Abner Graves and the Cooperstown Story* (Jefferson, NC: McFarland, 2013). This is the first telling of the likely connection between Ford and Graves.

21. Robert Knight Barney, a former president of the North American Society for Sport History and a long-time editorial board member of *NINE: A Journal of Baseball History and Social Policy Perspectives*, with researcher Nancy Bouchier probed the Ford story and are convinced it is valid. Their paper, "A Critical Examination of a Source on Early Ontario Baseball: The Reminiscence of Adam E. Ford," appeared in *Journal of Sport History* 15, no. 1 (Spring 1988), 76.

22. Thorn, *Baseball in the Garden of Eden*, 43.

23. Robert Knight Barney, "Whose National Pastime? Baseball in Canadian Popular Culture," *The Beaver Bites Back?: American Popular Culture in Canada*, edited by David H. Flaherty and Frank E. Manning (Montreal: McGill-Queen's University Press, 1993), 154.

24. William Humber, "Cheering for the Home Team: Baseball and Town Life in Nineteenth Century Ontario, 1854–1869," a paper presented at the Fifth Canadian Symposium on the History of Sport and Physical Education, University of Toronto, August 26–29, 1982, 62.

25. "Ball Play," *New York Clipper*, September 27, 1856. (Page 516 in Fulton Collection.)

26. George Railton, *Railton's Directory for the City of London, C.W., 1856–1857* (London, Canada West: George Railton, Notary Public, 1856), 25.

27. "London Base Ball Club," advertisement, *London Free Press*, May 1, 1856; and "London Ball Club," *London Free Press*, May 5, 1856.

28. William Humber, *Diamonds of the North: A Concise History of Baseball in Canada* (Toronto: Oxford University Press, 1995), 23–24.

29. *Buffalo Daily Courier* of August 31 and October 1, 1860, as quoted in William Humber, "The Lost Canadian Game of the Two-worded Baseball," an unpublished paper. The former account notes the Canadian team "is still in its infancy, having played but a short time under the Rules and Regulations of the National Association of Ball Players." In the latter report, the Young Canadians were erroneously identified as a Toronto team, but the roster is the same as in the earlier account.

30. Joseph Overfield, "Baseball in Buffalo Before the Civil War," from *Niagara Frontier* (Summer 1964), 103, quoted in Peter Morris, *Base Ball Pioneers, 1850–1870: The Clubs and Players Who Spread the Sport Nationwide* (Jefferson, NC: McFarland, 2012), 103.

31. Humber, *Diamonds of the North*, 25.

32. Ibid., 64.

33. *New York Clipper*, September 10, 1864, quoted in Humber, 65.

34. *New York Clipper*, October 1, 1864, quoted in Humber, 66.

35. "The B. B. Match at Detroit," *London Free Press*, August 23, 1867; and Humber, *Diamonds of the North*, 28.

36. Alexander J. Young, *Beyond Heroes: A Sport History of Nova Scotia* (Hantsport, N.S.: Lancelot Press, 1988), 95, quoted in Don Morrow, Mary Keyes, Wayne Simpson, Frank Cosentino, Ron Lappage, *A Concise History of Sport in Canada* (Toronto: University of Toronto Press, 1989), 111.

37. "Base Ball," *Guelph Mercury*, June 16, 1868.

38. "The International Base Ball Match," *London Free Press*, June 18, 1868.

39. "Base Ball Match," *Guelph Mercury*, August 5, 1868.

40. David L. Bernard, "The Guelph Maple Leafs: A Cultural Indicator of Southern Ontario," *Ontario History* 84, no. 3 (September 1992), 214.

41. Leo A. Johnson, *History of Guelph, 1827–1927* (Guelph, ON: Guelph Historical Society, 1977), 254.

42. Ibid., 212–13, 256.

43. The date 1861 appears in *Historic Guelph: The Royal City* (Guelph, ON: Guelph Historical Society, 1988); and in Sleeman's own account in the Higinbotham Scrapbook, Number Three, undated newspaper clipping, Guelph Public Library, as quoted in Leo A. Johnson, *History of Guelph, 1827–1927* (Guelph, ON: Guelph Historical Society, 1877), 330. Among other places, the 1863 date appears in David L. Bernard, "The Guelph Maple Leafs: A Cultural Indicator of Southern Ontario."

44. A good overview of the early days of baseball in Guelph can be found in the Sleeman Collection, Archives, and Special Collections at the McLaughlin Library at the University of Guelph, particularly in a lengthy article from the *Guelph Mercury*, not dated, but believed to be from 1916, based on a reference to George Sleeman, aged 75, who was interviewed for the article.

45. "Baseball Was Started in Guelph in 1861—That Was the Real Beginning of Maple Leafs," *Guelph Mercury*, unknown date, 1916, held in Sleeman Collection, Archives and Special Collections, McLaughlin Library, University of Guelph, Ontario.

46. "Praising Famous Men: The Story of George Sleeman and the Guelph Maple Leafs," paper presented by William Humber, Canadian baseball historian, to Nineteenth Century Baseball Conference, Society for American Baseball Research, Cooperstown, New York, April 20, 2013.

47. Alan Metcalfe, *Canada Learns to Play: The Emergence of Organized Sport, 1807–1914* (Toronto, ON: Oxford University Press, 1987), 90, quoted in David L. Bernard, "The Guelph Maple Leafs: A Cultural Indicator of Southern Ontario," 214.

48. "The Early Days: The Silver Creek Brewery," Archival and Special Collections, University of Guelph Library, accessed December 8, 2013, http://www.lib.uoguelph.ca/resources/archival_&_special_collections/th e_collections/sleeman/brewing_history/silver creek_breweries.cfm.

49. Leo A. Johnson, *History of Guelph, 1827–1927* (Guelph, ON: Guelph Historical Society, 1977), 330.

Chapter 3

1. Maple Leaf team ledger maintained by George Sleeman for 1874, located in the Sleeman Collection, Archives and Special Collections, McLaughlin Library, University of Guelph, Ontario.

2. "Baseball Was Started in Guelph in 1861—That Was the Real Beginning of Maple Leafs," *Guelph Mercury*, unknown date, 1916; held in Sleeman Collection, Archives and Special Collections, McLaughlin Library, University of Guelph, Ontario. The article is of particular value, despite its lack of date, because it indicates that the information it contains came from Sleeman and William Sunley, the original Maple Leaf player who pitched until 1874. At the time of the article, Sleeman was 75 and Sunley 76. They were interviewed by the *Mercury* reporter at Sleeman's house for two hours, it reports.

3. "Base Ball Tournament," *Guelph Mercury*, July 6, 1874, 1.

4. Paul Batesel, *Players and Teams of the National Association, 1871–1875* (Jefferson, NC: McFarland, 2012), 31.

5. "Watertown Tournament," *Guelph Mercury*, July 8, 1874.

6. "Watertown Tournament," *Guelph Mercury*, July 9, 1874, 1.

7. Leo A. Johnson, *History of Guelph, 1827–1927* (Guelph, ON: Guelph Historical Society, 1977), 330; quoting Higinbotham Scrapbook Number Three, Guelph Public Library, from an undated newspaper clipping.

8. *Historic Guelph: The Royal City* (Guelph, ON: Guelph Historical Society, 1988), 50; quoting an unattributed newspaper clipping, Sleeman Collection.

9. *Harpers Weekly*, September 12, 1874, 761–62.

10. "Praising Famous Men: The Story of George Sleeman; and the Guelph Maple Leafs," paper presented by William Humber to the Nineteenth Century Baseball Conference of the Society for American Baseball Research, Cooperstown, New York, April 20, 2013, 73.

11. "Base Ball," *Guelph Mercury*, July 16, 1874, 1.

12. Sleeman's ledger for August 5 and 6, for instance, showed payments of $40 apiece to Jones, Keerl, Maddock, Billy and Tom Smith, Myers, Spence, Colson, and Sunley. These were aside from itemized expenses for the players; Sleeman Collection.
13. "Guelph Maple Leaf Base Ball Club," April 8, 1875 newspaper account entitled "Special to the Liberal," Sleeman Collection.
14. "Panic of 1873," National History Education Clearinghouse, accessed December, 25, 2013, http://teachinghistory.org/history-content/beyond-the-textbook/24579.
15. L. N. Bronson, "Colleagues Bid Farewell to Editor Gorman: 1878 Presentation Addresses Recalls Newspapermen of the Past," *London Free Press,* Feb. 15, 1964.
16. William Humber, *Cheering for the Home Team* (Erin, ON: Boston Mills Press, 1983), 32.
17. "Cricket on Lake Horn—the Town vs. the Garrison," *London Free Press,* February 20, 1862.
18. "The First Match," *London Free Press,* August 24, 1867.
19. "Interesting Base Ball Match," *London Free Press,* September 7, 1867.
20. "Base Ball," *London Free Press,* September 17, 1867.
21. Humber, *Cheering for the Home Team,* 32.
22. Les Bronson, veteran newspaperman and local historian, from his speech, "The History of Baseball in London," delivered February 15, 1972 to the London and Middlesex Historical Society, found in Regional Room Archives, D. B. Weldon Library, Western University, London, Ontario.
23. An excellent account of the life of Tecumseh. His vision and his alliance with the British and special relationship with General Isaac Brock can be found in a book by James Laxer, *Tecumseh and Brock: The War of 1812* (Toronto, ON: House of Anansi Press, 2012).
24. *London Old Boys Souvenir Program, 1903* (London, ON: London Old Boys Reunion, 1903), 20.
25. L. N. Bronson, "Three Tecumsehs Made All-Star Baseball Team in 1872," *London Free Press,* June 17, 1972, 40.
26. "Base Ball. The Re-Organized Tecumsehs—Election of Officers," *London Advertiser,* July 29, 1873.
27. "The Knowlton Cup," *London Free Press,* August 14, 1873.
28. *Bryce's Base Ball Guide for 1876* (London, ON: William Bryce, 1876), 10.

29. "The Governor-General," *London Free Press,* August 28, 1874.
30. Les Bronson speech, "The History of Baseball in London."
31. Bronson, "Three Tecumsehs Made All-Star Baseball Team in 1872."
32. "Tecumsehs and Maple Leaf," *London Free Press,* May 25, 1875.
33. "The Ball Field," *London Free Press,* August 4, 1875.
34. "Ball and Bat. Exciting Match at Guelph Yesterday," *London Free Press,* August 17, 1875.
35. "Base Ball. A Sad Disappointment," *London Advertiser,* August 19, 1875.
36. "The Match between the Maple Leafs and Tecumsehs a Grand Fizzle," *London Free Press,* August 19, 1875.
37. *Bryce's Base Ball Guide for 1876,* 11.
38. Ibid.
39. Batesel, *Players and Teams of the National Association, 1871–1875,* 164.
40. "Ball Players Arrested," London Advertiser, September 24, 1875; New Haven Register, September 14, 1875; and New York Clipper, October 2, 1875, quoted in William J. Ryczek, *Blackguards and Red Stockings: A History of Baseball's National Association, 1871–1875* (Wallingford, CT: Colebrook Press, 1992), 195, 196.
41. *Bryce's Base Ball Guide for 1876,* 11.
42. "Diamond Field Notes," *London Free Press,* September, 17, 1875.
43. *London Free Press* and *London Advertiser* accounts of the Michigan tour, September 23, 24, 1875.
44. "The Ball Field," *London Advertiser,* September 7, 1875, 1.
45. "The Ball Field," *London Advertiser,* September 25, 1875.

Chapter 4

1. "Base Ball," *London Free Press,* January 3, 1876.
2. Lee Allen, "Baseball's Immortal Red Stockings," *Bulletin of the Historical and Philosophical Society of Ohio* 19 (1961), 191–94, quoted in John Thorn, *Baseball in the Garden of Eden: The Secret History of the Early Game* (New York: Simon and Schuster, 2011), 143.
3. David Pietrusza, *Major Leagues: The Formation, Sometimes Absorption and Mostly Inevitable Demise of 18 Professional Baseball Organizations, 1871 to Present* (Jefferson, NC: McFarland, 1991), 21.

4. Ibid., 20.
5. William J. Ryczek, *Blackguards and Red Stockings: A History of the National Association 1871–1875* (Wallingford, CT: Colebrook Press, 1992), 14.
6. Ted Vincent, *Mudville's Revenge: The Rise and Fall of American Sport* (Lincoln, NB: University of Nebraska Press, 1981), 33.
7. Paul Batesel, *Players and Teams of the National Association, 1871–1875* (Jefferson, NC: McFarland, 2012), 12.
8. Ibid., 8.
9. Ibid., 9.
10. Vincent, *Mudville's Revenge*, 135.
11. Michael Haupert, "William Hulbert," Society for American Baseball Research Bio-Project, accessed January 11, 2014, http://sabr.org/bioproj/person/d1d420b3.
12. Ibid., 3.
13. Pietrusza, *Major Leagues*, 25.
14. Joseph M. Overfield, *"David W. Force,"* *Nineteenth Century Stars* (Phoenix: Society for American Baseball Research, 2012), 94.
15. Glenn Dickey, *The History of National League Baseball* (Briarcliff Manor, NY: Stein and Day, 1979), 5.
16. Pietrusza, *Major Leagues*, 28.
17. Vincent, *Mudville's Revenge*, 136.
18. Haupert, "William Hulbert," 5; Pietrusza, *Major Leagues*, 27.
19. "A New League," *New York Clipper*, February 12, 1876.
20. Pietrusza, *Major Leagues*, 31.
21. Ryczek, *Blackguards and Red Stockings*, 227.
22. "Base Ball: Convention of Canadian Clubs at Toronto," *London Advertiser*, April 8, 1876.
23. *Bryce's Base Ball Guide 1876* (London, ON: William Bryce, 1876).
24. "DeWitt's Base-Ball Guide," Baseball-reference.com, accessed January 15, 2014, www.baseball-reference.com/bullpen/DeWitt%27s_Base-Ball_Guide and www.baseball-reference.com/bullpen/Beadle%27s_Dime_Base_Ball_Player.
25. "Base Ball," *London Advertiser*, April 17, 1876.
26. Les Bronson, "History of Baseball in London," a paper delivered by the newspaperman and historian to the London and Middlesex Historical Society, February 17, 1972, 19.
27. Batesel, *Players and Teams of the National Association, 1871–1875*, 82.
28. "The Ball Field," *London Advertiser*, May 5, 1876.
29. Bronson, "History of Baseball in London," 19.
30. "The Ball Field," *London Advertiser*, May 17, 1876.
31. Batesel, *Players and Teams*, 163.
32. "The Ball Field," *London Advertiser*, May 18, 1876.
33. "The Ball Field," *London Advertiser*, May 20, 1876.

Chapter 5

1. See Nancy Bouchier and Robert Barney, "A Critical Examination of a Source on Early Ontario Baseball: The Reminiscence of Adam E. Ford," *Journal of Sport History* (Spring 1988).
2. "The Ball Field," *London Advertiser*, May 23, 1876.
3. "The Game in London," *Guelph Mercury*, May 25, 1876.
4. "The Ball Field. A Grand Game for the Championship," *London Advertiser*, May 25, 1876.
5. Ibid.
6. "The Ball Field," *London Advertiser*, May 26, 1876.
7. "The Ball Field," *London Advertiser*, May 27, 1876.
8. "The Ball Field," *London Advertiser*, June 19, 1876.
9. "The Ball Field. A Notable Victory for the Tecumsehs," *London Advertiser*, June 27, 1876.
10. Ibid.
11. "The Ball Field," *London Advertiser*, July 4, 1876.
12. "The Ball Field," *London Advertiser*, July 10, 1876.
13. "The Ball Field," *London Advertiser*, July 20, 1876.
14. "Championship Game," *London Advertiser*, July 21, 1876.
15. The *Guelph Mercury* as quoted in "The Ball Field," *London Advertiser*, July 23, 1876.
16. *Kingston News*, quoted in "The Ball Field," *London Advertiser*, August 7, 1876.
17. "The Trip to London Yesterday," *Guelph Mercury*, August 10, 1876.
18. "Our Day," *London Advertiser*, August 10, 1876.
19. "The Trip to London Yesterday," *Guelph Mercury*, August 10, 1876.
20. "The Great Game," *London Advertiser*, August 29, 1876.

21. "Outdoor Sports," *London Advertiser,* August 30, 1876.
22. "Yesterday's Game: The Tecumsehs Play a Poor Game," *London Advertiser,* August 31, 1876.
23. "Outdoor Sports," *London Advertiser,* September 2, 1876.
24. "Base Ball Field," *Guelph Mercury,* August 12, 1876.
25. "Outdoor Sports," *London Advertiser,* September 5, 1876.
26. "Outdoor Sports," *London Advertiser,* September 6, 1876.
27. "Outdoor Sports," *London Advertiser,* September 11, 1876.
28. "Outdoor Sports: More of It," *London Advertiser,* September 13, 1876.
29. Ibid.
30. Letter to George Sleeman from Harry Gorman, dated September 20, 1876, in Sleeman Collection of documents, University of Guelph Library, Guelph, Ontario.
31. Outdoor Sports," *London Advertiser,* September 20, 1876.
32. "The Ball Field," *London Advertiser,* September 30, 1876.
33. "The Canadian Championship," *New York Clipper,* October 7, 1876.
34. "Base Ball," *London Advertiser,* October 9, 1876.
35. "Base Ball," *London Advertiser,* October 11, 1876.
36. "The Championship of Canada," *New York Clipper,* October 14, 1876.

Chapter 6

1. "The Ball Field," *London Advertiser,* April 16, 1877.
2. Ibid.
3. *London Advertiser,* April 17, 1877.
4. "Ball and Bat," *London Free Press,* April 25, 1877.
5. "Ball and Bat," *London Free Press,* May 2, 1877.
6. "Opening the Base Ball Season," *London Advertiser,* April 30, 1877.
7. *Canadian Illustrated News* (July 14, 1877), quoted in Pat Morden, *Putting Down Roots* (St. Catharines, ON: Stonehouse Publications, 1988), 47.
8. *London Advertiser,* April 30 and May 4, 1877.
9. For example: "The Guelph Foreign Legion feel very touchy over comparisons between them and the Tecumsehs," *London Advertiser,* August 4, 1875.
10. Glenn Dickey, *The History of National League Baseball* (Briarcliff Manor, NY: Stein and Day, 1979), 8.
11. Letter from J. S. Price, Alumni Affairs, Lafayette College, Easton, Pennsylvania, to Dan Ginsburg, of Pittsburgh, April 2, 1970, in Harmar D. McKnight file, Library, National Baseball Hall of Fame and Museum, Cooperstown, NY.
12. *Baseball's First Stars,* eds. Frederick Ivor-Campbell, Robert L. Teimann, and Mark Rucker (Cleveland, OH: The Society for American Baseball Research, 1996), 109.
13. "The International Association," *New York Clipper,* January 20, 1877, 339, in bound edition in Library of National Baseball Hall of Fame and Museum, Cooperstown, NY.
14. "Base Ball: The City Clubs Organizing," *London Advertiser,* February 15, 1877.
15. "Base Ball Notes," *London Free Press,* February 15, 1877.
16. "The International Association," *New York Clipper,* January 27, 1877, 346; in bound edition found in Library of National Baseball Hall of Fame and Museum, Cooperstown, NY.
17. Ibid.
18. "The International Association," *New York Clipper,* February 10, 1877, 363; in bound edition of the newspaper, Library, National Baseball Hall of Fame and Museum, Cooperstown, NY.
19. Ted Vincent, *Mudville's Revenge: The Rise and Fall of American Sport* (New York: Seaview Books, 1981), 143.
20. Ibid., 142.
21. "Baseball: Organization of the International Association," *Philadelphia Inquirer,* February 22, 1877, 2.
22. Ryczek, *Blackguards and Red Stockings,* 57.
23. "International Association," *New York Clipper,* March 10, 1877, 394; in bound edition in Library, National Baseball Hall of Fame and Museum, Cooperstown, NY.
24. "The Ball Field," *London Advertiser,* April 20, 1877.
25. Scott Reynolds Nelson, "The Real Great Depression," *Chronicle of Higher Education,* October 17, 2008, accessed March 28, 2013, http://srnels.people.wm.edu/articles/realGrtDepr.html.
26. Elliott J. Gorn, Randy Roberts, and Terry D. Bilhartz, *Constructing the American Past: A Sourcebook of a People's History,* Vol. Two (New York: Pearson, Longman, 2005), 19.

27. Henry Chadwick, editor of the *New York Clipper,* urged National League owners to drop their admission price to 25 cents from 50 cents, "and you must proportionately lower your salaries. One thousand dollars for seven months of such services as a professional ballplayer is called upon to perform, even when he is not indisposed, is amply sufficient," quoted in Dickey.

28. Les Bronson, "History of Baseball in London," a paper based on a speech delivered to the London–Middlesex Historical Society, February 15, 1972, in London, 32.

29. Michael Haupert, "MLB's Annual Salary Leaders, 1874–2012," *Outside the Lines,* Fall 2012, SABR's Business of Baseball Research Committee Newsletter, accessed March 29, 2013, http://sabr.org/research/mlbs-annual-salary-leaders-1874-2012.

30. *London Advertiser,* April 30, 1877.

31. "The Growth of Pittsburgh: Annexation and Population," source: U.S. Census History, accessed February 10, 2013, http://www.brooklineconnection.com/history/Facts?Growth.html.

32. *The Story of Old Allegheny City* (Pittsburgh, PA: Allegheny Centennial Committee, 1941), 20–33.

33. *A Chronological History of Old Allegheny City, Penna,* compiled for the Allegheny City Society (Pittsburgh: Don Kuhl Printing, 1969).

34. *The Story of Old Allegheny City,* 26.

35. John N. Ingham, "Iron and Steel in the Pittsburgh Region: The Domain of Small Business," Business and Economic History, second series, vol. 20, 1991, 108, accessed March 23, 2013, http://www.thebhc.org/publications/BEHprint/v020/p0107-p0116.pdf.

36. Dan Rooney and Carol Peterson, *Allegheny City: A History of Pittsburgh's North Side* (Pittsburgh: University of Pittsburgh Press, 2013), 60.

37. "Oil Springs: Boom and Bust," Oil Museum of Canada, accessed April 22, 2013, www.lclmg.org/lclmg/Museums/OilMuseumofCanada/BlackGold2/OilHeritage/OilSprings/tabid/208/Default.aspx.

38. Hugh Grant and Henry Thille, "Tariffs, Strategy, and Structure: Competition and Collusion in the Ontario Petroleum Industry, 1870–1880," *The Journal of Economic History* 61 no. 2 (June 2001), 397.

Chapter 7

1. "A Hard Road to Travel," *London Advertiser,* June 8, 1877.

2. *Mercantile Agency Reference Book forthe Dominion of Canada,* September 1879 (London, ON: Dun, Wiman and Company, 1879).

3. Letter from Chick Fulmer dated February 12, 1877, to George Sleeman, Sleeman Papers, Archival Collections, University of Guelph Library, Guelph, Ontario.

4. *Baseball's First Stars,* 182.

5. Letter from George Zettlein dated Nov. 16, 1876, to George Sleeman, Sleeman Papers.

6. Letters dated December 14, 29, 1876 and January 8, 1877 from Peter Hotaling to George Sleeman, Sleeman Papers.

7. Letters dated November 16 and December 19, 1876, from Scott Hastings to George Sleeman, Sleeman Papers.

8. Hastings letter to Sleeman, dated February 8, 1877, Sleeman Papers.

9. Postcard from Marshall Quinton, dated March 19, 1877, to George Sleeman, Sleeman Papers.

10. Letter from William Craver, dated February 11, 1877, to George Sleeman, Sleeman Papers.

11. Letter from James A. Devlin dated February 28, 1877, to George Sleeman, Sleeman Papers.

12. Paul Batesel, *Players and Teams of the National Association: 1871–1875* (Jefferson, NC: McFarland, 2012), 45, 49.

13. The Bio Project of SABR: Pud Galvin, by Charles Hausberg, accessed March 29, 2013, http://sabr.org/bioproj/person/38c553ff.

14. "'Gentle Jeems' Jim Galvin: Buffalo's First Superstar," by Joe Overfield, in "Bison Tales," *The Bisongram,* February/March 1993, in Pud Galvin files, Library, National Baseball Hall of Fame and Museum, Cooperstown, NY.

15. Rooney and Peterson, 108, 163.

16. David Nemec, *The Great Encyclopedia of 19th Century Major League Baseball* (New York: Donald I. Fine Books, 1997), 89.

17. *New York Clipper,* January 27, 1877; quoted in The Bio Project of SABR: The League Alliance, by Brock Helander, accessed February 2, 2014, http://sabr.org/bioproj/topic/league-alliance.

18. *New York Clipper,* March 3, 1877; quoted in The Bio Project of SABR: The League Alliance.

19. *New York Times,* December 6, 1877; (Chicago) *InterOcean,* December 6, 1877; *Chicago Tribune,* December 9, 1877; *Milwaukee Daily Sentinel,* December 10, 1877, quoted in The Bio Project of SABR: The League Alliance.

20. "Base Ball. The International Annual

Meeting," *London Advertiser,* February 21, 1878; and *St. Louis Globe-Democrat,* February 24, 1878, quoted in The Bio Project of SABR: The League Alliance.

Chapter 8

1. David Q. Voigt, *American Baseball* (Norman, OK: University of Oklahoma Press, 1966), 77.
2. "William Hulbert," by Michael Haupert, Bio Project of the Society for American Baseball Research, accessed February 5, 2014, http://sabr.org/bioproj/person/d1d42ob3.
3. David Pietrusza, *Major Leagues: The Formation, Sometimes Absorption and Mostly Inevitable Demise of 18 Professional Baseball Organizations, 1871 to Present* (Jefferson, NC: McFarland, 1991), 39.
4. David Q. Voigt, *American Baseball,* 76.
5. Ted Vincent, *Mudville's Revenge: The Rise and Fall of American Sport* (Lincoln, NB: University of Nebraska Press, 1981), 143.
6. "The Sleeman Family," *Guelph Historical Society Publications* 14 no. 2, Sleeman Collection, Archival Collections, University of Guelph Library, Guelph, Ontario.
7. "The International Association," *New York Clipper,* February 10, 1877.
8. "The International Association," *New York Clipper,* March 3, 1877.
9. Charlton's Baseball Chronology: 1877. BaseballLibrary.com, accessed February 6, 2014, http://dev.baseballlibrary.com/chronology/byyear.php?year=1877&previous=yes.
10. Ibid.
11. Ibid.
12. "The Ball Field," *London Advertiser,* May 4, 1877.
13. "The Ball Field," *London Advertiser,* May 8, 1877.
14. "The Ball Field," *London Advertiser,* May 10, 12, 14, 1877.
15. "The Base Ball Field," *Guelph Mercury,* May 11, 1877; and "International Base Ball Championship," *Guelph Mercury,* May 12, 1877.
16. "The Ball Field," *London Advertiser,* May 14, 1877.
17. "Ball and Bat," *London Free Press,* May 18, 1877; and "International Championship," *Guelph Mercury,* May 18, 1877.
18. Hamilton Spectator as quoted in *Guelph Mercury,* May 17, 1877.
19. "The Ball and Bat," *Guelph Mercury,* May 22, 1877.
20. "Base Ball," *London Free Press,* May 25, 1877.
21. "The Ball and Bat," *Guelph Mercury,* May 25, 1877.
22. "The Tecumsehs' Tour," *London Advertiser,* June 1, 1877.
23. "A Foul Tip," *London Advertiser,* June 7, 1877.
24. "A Hard Road to Travel," *London Advertiser,* June 8, 1877.
25. "The Tecumsehs' Tour," *London Advertiser,* June 11, 1877.
26. "The Tecumsehs' Tour," *London Advertiser,* June 12, 1877.
27. John M. Rosenburg, *They Gave Us Baseball: The 12 Extraordinary Men Who Shaped the Major Leagues* (Harrisburg, PA: Stackpole Books, 1989), 24.
28. David Nemec, *The Great Encyclopedia of 19th Century Major League Baseball* (New York: Donald I. Fine Books, 1997).
29. "The Ball Field," *London Advertiser,* June 14, 1877.
30. Charlton's Baseball Chronology, 1877.
31. "Base Ball," *London Advertiser,* June 22, 1877.
32. "The Ball Field," *London Advertiser,* June 26, 1877.
33. "Ball and Bat," *London Free Press,* July 2, 1877.
34. "Base Ball," *London Advertiser,* July 3, 1877.
35. "Ball and Bat," *London Free Press,* July 3, 1877.

Chapter 9

1. Ted Vincent, *Mudville's Revenge: The Rise and Fall of American Sport* (Lincoln, NB: University of Nebraska Press, 1981), 144.
2. "Ball Field," *London Advertiser,* December 8, 1877.
3. *Indianapolis Sentinel,* July 5, 1877, as quoted in "The Ball Field," *London Advertiser,* July 7, 1877.
4. *Columbus Sunday News,* July 8, 1877, as quoted in "The Tecumsehs Out West," *London Advertiser,* July 10, 1877.
5. Columbus State Journal, as quoted in "Base Ball," *London Advertiser,* July 13, 1877.
6. "The Ball Field," *London Advertiser,* July 17, 1877.
7. "The Next Page: The Railroad War," post-gazette.com, the *Pittsburgh Post-Gazette,* accessed March 18, 2013, www.post-gazette.

com/stories/opinion/perspectives/the-next-page-the-railroad-war-4923394/.
  8. Ibid.
  9. "The Great Railroad Strike," Digital History, accessed March 3, 2013, http://www.digitalhistory.uh.edu/disp_textbook.cfm?smtID=2&psid=3189.
  10. "The Railroad Strike of 1877 Historical Marker," ExplorePAhistory.com, accessed March 18, 2013, www.explorepahistory.com/hmarker.hph?markerID=1-A-1C1.
  11. Dan Rooney and Carol Peterson, *Allegheny City: A History of Pittsburgh's North Side* (Pittsburgh: University of Pittsburgh Press, 2013), 82.
  12. "Base Ball Notes," *Guelph Mercury*, July 27, 1877.
  13. Joe Overfield, "'Gentle Jeems' Jim Galvin: Buffalo's First Superstar," "Bisontales" in the (Buffalo) *Bisongram*, February, March, 1993, 26.
  14. *Guelph Mercury*, quoted in "The Ball Field," *London Advertiser*, July 15, 1877.
  15. "Base Ball Notes," *Guelph Mercury*, July 19, 1877.
  16. "Base Ball Notes," *Guelph Mercury*, July 14, 1877.
  17. "The Ball Field," *London Advertiser*, July 20, 1877.
  18. Charlton's Baseball Chronology: 1877," BaseballLibrary.com, accessed February 5, 2014, http://dev.baseballlibrary.com/chronology/byyear.php?year=1877&previous=yes.
  19. "The Old, Old Story," *Guelph Mercury*, August 11, 1877.
  20. "The Ball Field," *London Advertiser*, August 14, 1877.
  21. Charlton's Baseball Chronology: 1877.
  22. "The Holiday," *London Advertiser*, August 16, 1877.
  23. "Origins of the Pitching Rotation," by Frank Vaccaro, *Fall 2011 Baseball Research Journal*, accessed February 23, 2014, http://sabr.org/research/origins/-pitching-rotation.
  24. "Base Ball," *Guelph Mercury*, August 23, 1877.
  25. "Base Ball," *Guelph Mercury*, August 27, 1877.
  26. David Pietrusza, *Major Leagues: The Formation, Sometimes Absorption and Mostly Inevitable Demise of 18 Professional Baseball Organizations, 1871 to Present* (Jefferson, NC: McFarland, 1991), 33.
  27. Ibid., 34–37.
  28. "Ball and Bat," *London Free Press*, August 28, 1877.
  29. "Tecumsehs vs. Maple Leaf," *Guelph Mercury*, August 30, 1877.
  30. "The Ball Field," *London Advertiser*, August 31, 1877.
  31. "The Ball Field," *London Advertiser*, September 3, 1877.
  32. "The Ball Field," *London Advertiser*, September 13, 1877.
  33. "The Ball Field," *London Advertiser*, September 10, 1877.
  34. "Base Ball Notes," *Guelph Mercury*, September 19, 1877.
  35. "The Ball Field," *London Advertiser*, September 17, 1877.
  36. Charlton's Baseball Chronology: 1877.
  37. "The Ball Field," *London Advertiser*, September 17, 1877.
  38. Ibid.
  39. "Base Ball Notes," *Guelph Mercury*, September 20, 1877.
  40. "The Ball Field," *London Advertiser*, September 24, 1877.
  41. Letter dated September 24, 1877, Columbus, Ohio, from J. A. Williams, secretary of the International Base Ball Association, to George Sleeman, Maple Leaf Base Ball Club, Guelph, Ontario, in Sleeman Collection, University of Guelph Library, Guelph, Ontario.
  42. "The Ball Field," *London Advertiser*, September 25–27, 1877.
  43. "Base Ball Notes," *London Free Press*, October 1, 1877.
  44. "Base-Ball," *New York Times*, October 2, 1877, 8.
  45. "Base Ball Notes," *London Free Press*, October 1, 1877.
  46. Ibid.
  47. "The International Championship," *New York Clipper*, October 13, 1877.
  48. "Base Ball," *Guelph Mercury*, October 19, 1877.
  49. "The Champion's Record," *London Free Press*, October 5, 1877.
  50. "The Star Club of Syracuse," *New York Clipper*, October 27, 1877.
  51. Charlton's Baseball Chronology: 1877.
  52. *Chicago Post*, quoted in "Ball Field," *London Advertiser*, November 19, 1877.

Chapter 10

  1. "International Championship," *New York Clipper*, October 20, 1877.
  2. *Syracuse Courier* as quoted in "Base Ball," *London Advertiser*, October 24, 1877.

3. "International Championship," *New York Clipper,* October 27, 1877.
4. "The Allegheny's Claims and Charges," *New York Clipper,* November 3, 1877.
5. Ted Vincent, *Mudville's Revenge: The Rise and Fall of American Sport* (Lincoln, NB: University of Nebraska Press, 1981), 146.
6. David Pietrusza, *Major Leagues: The Formation, Sometimes Absorption and Mostly Inevitable Demise of 18 Professional Baseball Organizations, 1871 to Present* (Jefferson, NC: McFarland, 1991), 48.
7. David Nemec, *The Great Encyclopedia of Nineteenth Century Major League Baseball* (New York: Donald I. Fine Books, 1997), 109.
8. "Ball Field. Meeting of the National League," *London Advertiser,* December 8, 1877.
9. "Base Ball," *London Free Press,* December 8, 1877.
10. Pietrusza, *Major Leagues,* 49.
11. "Base Ball," *London Free Press,* December 8, 1877.
12. John Thorn, *Baseball in the Garden of Eden: The Secret History of the Early Game* (New York: Simon & Schuster, 2011), 154–64.
13. Pietrusza, *Major Leagues,* 49.
14. Vincent, *Mudville's Revenge,* 147.
15. *New York Mercury,* quoted in "The Ball Field," *London Advertiser,* December 17, 1877.
16. Letter from Harry Gorman, secretary of the Tecumseh Base Ball Club, dated December 10, 1877 to H. L. [?] Sprague, of the Buffalo Club, from the collection of late Buffalo baseball historian Joe Overfield, copy provided to author by Canadian baseball historian Bill Humber.
17. Letter from Gorman to Sprague, dated December 17, 1877, Overfield collection, shared by Humber.
18. Pietrusza, *Major Leagues,* 40–41.
19. Letter from Gorman to Sprague, dated January 2, 1878, Overfield collection, shared by Humber.
20. Pietrusza, *Major Leagues,* 49–50.
21. *Boston Herald* as quoted in "Ball Field," *London Advertiser,* January 28, 1878.
22. *New York Mercury,* quoted in "Ball Field," *London Advertiser,* April 1, 1878.
23. "Base Ball: The International Annual Meeting," *London Advertiser,* February 21, 1878.
24. "The Ball Field," *London Advertiser,* March 11, 1878.
25. "Ball Field Notes," *London Advertiser,* March 18, 1878.
26. "Ball Field," *London Advertiser,* March 27, 1878.
27. *Buffalo Express,* quoted in "Base Ball," *London Advertiser,* March 25, 1878.
28. *New York Mercury,* quoted in "Ball Field," *London Advertiser,* April 1, 1878.
29. "The First Great Minor League Club," by Joe Overfield, Society for American Baseball Research Journals Archive, accessed March 5, 2014, http://research.sabr.org/journals/first-great-minor-league-club.
30. Ibid.
31. Nemec, *The Great Encyclopedia,* 110.

Chapter 11

1. "SABR 43: Ross Barnes Selected as Overlooked 19th Century Baseball Legend for 2013," accessed March 6, 2014, http://sabr.org/latest/sabr-43-ross-barnes-selected-overlooked-19th-century-baseball-legend-2013.
2. Charlton's Baseball Chronology, BaseballLibrary.com, accessed March 6, 2014, http://www.baseballlibrary.com/chronology/byyear.php?year=1876.
3. Michael Haupert, "MLB's Annual Salary Leaders 1874–2012," *Society for American Baseball Research,* accessed March 6, 2014, http://sabr.org/research/mlbs-annual-salary-leaders-1874-2012.
4. "Out-Door Sports," *London Advertiser,* November 12, 1878.
5. Robert H. Schaefer, "The Lost Art of Fair-Foul Hitting," *The National Pastime: A Review of Baseball History,* Vol. 20, Society of American Baseball Research, accessed March 6, 2014, http://research.sabr.org/files/SABR-National_Pastime-20.pdf
6. *Nineteenth Century Stars: 2012 Edition,* eds. Robert L. Tiemann and Mark Rucker (Phoenix, AZ: The Society for American Baseball Research, 1989, 2012), 19.
7. David Pietrusza, *Major Leagues: The Formation, Sometimes Absorption and Mostly Inevitable Demise of 18 Professional Baseball Organizations, 1871 to Present* (Jefferson, NC: McFarland, 1991), 43.
8. "Out-Door Sports," *London Advertiser,* April 15, 1878.
9. "Merkle Bonehead Play," Baseball-Reference.com, accessed March 8, 2014, http://www.baseball-reference.com/bullpen/Merkle_Bonehead_Play.
10. "Bob Emslie," by David Cicotello, The BioProject, Society for American Baseball Research, accessed March 6, 2014, http://sabr.org/bioproj/person/d8dafeb2

11. "Out-Door Sports," *London Advertiser*, April 25, 1878.
12. "Out-Door Sports," *London Advertiser*, April 27, 1878.
13. "Out-Door Sports," *London Advertiser*, May 1, 1878.
14. *Buffalo Courier*, quoted in "A Sad Defeat," *London Advertiser*, May 2, 1878.
15. Jeffrey Michael Laing, *Bud Fowler: Baseball's First Black Professional* (Jefferson, NC: McFarland, 2013), 66.
16. *Boston Daily Advertiser*, May 18, 1878, quoted in Laing, *Bud Fowler.*
17. Ibid.
18. Laing, *Bud Fowler*, 275n.
19. *Boston Daily Globe*, May 18, 1878, quoted in Laing, *Bud Fowler*, 67.
20. Laing, *Bud Fowler*, 70–71.
21. Pietrusza, *Major Leagues*, 62.
22. "Out-Door Sports," *London Advertiser*, May 20, 1878.
23. "The Ball and Bat," *Guelph Mercury*, May 17, 1878.
24. "Out-Door Sports," *London Advertiser*, May 22, 1878.
25. "Out-Door Sports," *London Advertiser*, May 24, 1878.
26. "The New Tecumseh Club," *London Free Press*, May 24, 1878.
27. "Ball and Bat. London's Day Off," *London Advertiser*, May 25, 1878.
28. "Out-Door Sports," *London Advertiser*, May 30, 1878.
29. "Out-Door Sports," *London Advertiser*, May 31, 1878.
30. "Out-Door Sports," *London Advertiser*, June 3, 1878.
31. "Out-Door Sports," *London Advertiser*, June 7, 1878.
32. "Base-Ball," *Guelph Mercury*, June 12, 1878.
33. "Out-Door Sports," *London Advertiser*, June 11, 1878.
34. "Base-Ball," *Guelph Mercury*, June 12, 1878.
35. "Out-Door Sports, *London Advertiser*, June 17, 1878.
36. "The Ball and Bat," *Guelph Mercury*, June 19, 1878.

Chapter 12

1. "Out-Door Sports," *London Advertiser*, June 21, 1878.
2. "Ball and Bat," *Guelph Mercury*, June 25, 1878.
3. "Out-Door Sports," *London Advertiser*, June 26, 1878.
4. "Out-Door Sports," *London Advertiser*, June 27, 28, 29, and July 1, 1878.
5. "Base Ball," *London Advertiser*, July 2, 1878.
6. "Base Ball Match," *Guelph Mercury*, July 2, 1878.
7. See, for instance, a report from the *Chicago Tribune*, quoted in the *London Advertiser*, August 22, 1878, in which it complains about the work of Nicholls awarding two runs to Buffalo in a game with the White Stockings: "... it was the most bare-faced case of daylight robbery ever seen in baseball"; and "Farewell to Old-style Ball," by W. Lloyd Johnson, in *Inventing Baseball: The 100 Greatest Games of the Nineteenth Century*, ed. Bill Felber (Phoenix: Society for American Baseball Research, 2013), 110.
8. *Buffalo Express*, quoted in "Out-Door Sports," *London Advertiser*, July 6, 1878.
9. "Out-Door Sports," *London Advertiser*, July 8, 1878.
10. Ibid.
11. "The Ball and Bat," *Guelph Mercury*, July 9, 1878.
12. *Utica Republican*, quoted in "Out-Door Sports," *London Advertiser*, July 9, 1878.
13. "Out-Door Sports," *London Advertiser*, June 7, 21, and 26, 1878.
14. "Out-Door Sports," *London Advertiser*, July 10, 1878.
15. "Base Ball Notes," *London Free Press*, July 10, 1878.
16. Ibid.
17. "Out-Door Sports," *London Advertiser*, July 11, 1878.
18. "The Ball and Bat," *Guelph Mercury*, July 11, 1878.
19. "Out-Door Sports," *London Advertiser*, July 12, 1878.
20. "Out-Door Sports," *London Advertiser*, July 15, 1878.
21. Ibid.
22. Ibid.
23. "The Tecumseh Base Ball Club," *New York Times*, July 15, 1878, 1.
24. "Base Ball Notes," *London Free Press*, July 16, 1878; and "Out-Door Sports," *London Advertiser*, July 17, 1878.
25. "Out-Door Sports," *London Advertiser*, July 22, 1878.
26. "Out-Door Sports," *London Advertiser*, August 8, 1878.
27. "Out-Door Sports," *London Advertiser*, August 13, 1878.

28. "Our Civic Holiday," *London Advertiser*, August 13, 1878.
29. "Out-Door Sports," *London Advertiser*, August 14, 1878.
30. "Out-Door Sports," *London Advertiser*, August 19, 1878.
31. "Out-Door Sports," *London Advertiser*, August 20, 1878.
32. "The Tecumseh Club," *London Free Press*, August 22, 1878.
33. "Out-Door Sports. The Tecumseh Record," *London Advertiser*, August 24, 1878.
34. "Base Ball Notes," *London Free Press*, August 24, 1878.
35. "Out-Door Sports," *London Advertiser*, August 26, 1878.
36. "The Champion's Record," *London Free Press*, October 5, 1877.
37. "Out-Door Sports," *London Advertiser*, September 2, 1878.
38. "Base Ball," *London Advertiser*, October 2, 1878.
39. "Out-Door Sports," *London Advertiser*, October 12, 1878.
40. "Out-Door Sports," *London Advertiser*, October 10, 1878.
41. David Nemec, *The Great Encyclopedia of 19th Century Major League Baseball* (New York: Donald I. Fine Books, 1997), 114.
42. "Farewell to Old-style Ball," by W. Lloyd Johnson, in *Inventing Baseball: The 100 Greatest Games of the 19th Century*, ed. Bill Felber (Phoenix: Society for American Baseball Research, 2013), 112.
43. Ibid., 110.
44. "Pud Galvin," by Charles Hausberg, BioProject of the Society of American Baseball Research, accessed March 16, 2014, http://sabr.org/bioproj/person/38c553ff.
45. "Out-Door Sports," *London Advertiser*, October 19 and 28, 1878.
46. John R. Castle Jr., *Goldie's Curve Ball: How Fred E. "Goldie" Goldsmith Invented, Demonstrated, Mastered & Championed the Curve Ball* (Colorado Springs, CO: Home-Light Publishing, 2010), 99.
47. "Presentation," *London Advertiser*, November 16, 1878.
48. "Henry Gorman, Former Editor, Magistrate, Dies," *Sarnia Observer*, November 14, 1928.

Chapter 13

1. Ted Vincent, *Mudville's Revenge: The Rise and Fall of American Sport* (Lincoln, NB: University of Nebraska Press, 1981), 149.
2. Pietrusza, *Major Leagues*, 40.
3. David Nemec, *The Great Encyclopedia of 19th-Century Major League Baseball* (New York: Donald I. Fine Books, 1997), 121.
4. Ibid.
5. "Base Ball Notes," *London Free Press*, February 21, 1879.
6. Pietrusza, *Major Leagues*, 56.
7. Vincent, *Mudville's Revenge*, 149, 150.
8. *New York Clipper* as quoted in *London Advertiser*, March 3, 1879.
9. "The Diamond Field," *London Advertiser*, December 19, 1878.
10. John R. Castle Jr., *Goldie's Curve Ball: How Fred E. "Goldie" Goldsmith Invented, Demonstrated, Mastered and Championed the Curve Ball* (Colorado Springs, CO: Homelight Publishing, 2010), 111.
11. Ibid., 109.
12. "Phil 'Grandma' Powers," *Major League Baseball Profiles 1871–1900*, ed. David Nemec (Lincoln, NB: University of Nebraska Press, 2011), 271.
13. "The Diamond Field," *London Advertiser*, December 19, 1878.
14. Pietrusza, *Major Leagues*, 56–59.
15. Charlton's Baseball Chronology: 1879, BaseballLibrary.com accessed March 22, 2014, http://dev.baseballlibrary.com/chronology/byyear.php?year=1879.
16. Castle, *Goldie's Curve Ball*, 120.
17. Baseball-reference.com, accessed March 27, 2014, http://www.baseball-reference.com/players/g/goldsfr01.shtml
18. Nemec, *The Great Encyclopedia*, 134.
19. Charlton's Baseball Chronology: 1879.
20. Pietrusza, *Major Leagues*, 60.
21. Vincent, *Mudville's Revenge*, 151.
22. "Pud Galvin," by Charles Hausberg, the BioProject of the Society for American Baseball Research, accessed March 22, 2014, http://sabr.org/bioproj/person/38c553ff.
23. Castle, *Goldie's Curve Ball*, 129.
24. Ibid., 194, 195.
25. Adrian Constantine Anson, *A Ball Player's Career* (Dodo Press UK, reprint of 1900 edition, www.dodopress.co.uk), 95.
26. "Fred Goldsmith," by David Fleitz, the BioProject of the Society for American Baseball Research, accessed March 7, 2014, http://sabr.org/bioproj/person/99c4a5f5.
27. Ibid.
28. Castle, *Goldie's Curve Ball*, 66.
29. David Nemec, *The Beer and Whisky League: The Illustrated History of the American Association—Baseball's Renegade Major League*

(New York: Lyons and Burford, 1994), 174–76.

30. "Connie Mack," by Doug Skipper, the BioProject of the Society for American Baseball Research, accessed March 24, 2014, http://sabr.org/bioproj/person/3462e06e.

31. Frank P. Jozsa Jr., *Major League Baseball Expansions and Relocations: A History, 1876–2008* (Jefferson, NC: McFarland, 2010), 128.

32. Nemec, *The Great Encyclopedia*, 166, 167.

33. Nemec, *The Beer and Whiskey League*, 22.

34. Vincent, *Mudville's Revenge*, G64.

35. Nemec, *The Great Encyclopedia*, 167.

36. "The History of Major League Baseball," by David Q. Voigt, in *Total Baseball: The Ultimate Encyclopedia of Baseball, Third Edition*, eds. John Thorn and Peter Palmer (New York: HarperPerennial, 1993), 13.

Chapter 14

1. Charles Whipp and Edward Phelps, *Petrolia: 1866–1966* (Petrolia, ON: Petrolia Advertiser-Topic and the Petrolia Centennial Committee, 1966), 24.

2. Hugh M. Grant, "The 'Mysterious' Jacob L. Englehart and the Early Ontario Petroleum Industry," *Ontario History: The Quarterly Journal of the Ontario Historical Society*, 85, no. 1 (March 1993), 73.

3. *Petrolia: 1866–1966*, 58.

4. "Petrolia Mourns the Death of Great Benefactor," *Petrolia Advertiser-Topic*, April 7, 1921.

5. Biographies of Jacob Lewis Englehart and Charlotte Eleanor Englehart, author unknown, kept in Lambton Room, Lambton County Public Library, Wyoming, Ontario.

6. Albert Tucker, *Steam into Wilderness: Ontario Northland Railway 1902–1962* (Toronto: Fitzhenry & Whiteside, 1978), 31–32.

7. Ian Sclanders, "The Amazing Jake Englehart," *Imperial Oil Review* (September 8, 1955), 6–7.

8. Notarial Copy of Letters Probate of Will of Jacob Lewis Englehart, late of the Town of Petrolia, deceased. Located in Lambton Room of Lambton County Public Library, Wyoming, Ontario.

9. Frederick H. Armstrong, *The Forest City: An Illustrated History of London, Canada*, (London ON: Windsor Publications, 1986), 150.

10. Lisa Bowes, "George Sleeman and the Brewing of Baseball in Guelph," *Historic Guelph: The Royal City*, 27 (1987–88), 54–55.

11. Leo A. Johnson, *History of Guelph 1827–1927* (Guelph, ON: Guelph Historical Society, 1977), 330–31.

12. "The Life and Death of Trams," *Guelph Daily Mercury*, May 25, 1991, 9.

13. "Talks of Baseball While under Knife," *Toronto Mail and Empire*, December 15, 1926, 1.

14. "Late Geo. Sleeman," *Guelph Mercury*, December 16, 1926.

15. "Baseball. A Visitor from Chicago," *Toronto Mail*, January 22, 1886.

16. "Note and Comment," *Toronto Mail*, February 23, 1886.

17. "Note and Comment," *Toronto Mail*, February 1, 1886.

18. Rich Westcott, *Winningest Pitchers: Baseball's 300-Game Winners* (Philadelphia: Temple University Press, 2002), 6.

19. *Baseball's First Stars*, Frederick Ivor-Campbell, general editor (Cleveland, OH: Society for American Baseball Research, 1996), 109.

20. Westcott, *Winningest Pitchers*, 7.

21. John McCollister, *The Bucs!: The Story of the Pittsburgh Pirates* (Lenexa, KS: Addax Publishing, 1998), 24–31.

22. National Baseball Hall of Fame and Museum: 2012 Yearbook (Lynn, MA: H.O. Zimman, 2012), 80.

23. "Carousing was a problem with 1888 baseball players," Les Bronson, "Looking over Western Ontario," *London Free Press*, August 9, 1988, in which he quoted an undated *Free Press* article from 1888.

24. James Bullbrook, "Home Plate," *London Free Press*, March 28, 1991, 7.

25. Steve Green, "Struggling Rippers Pack It In," *London Free Press*, July 25, 2012.

26. "Reasons for Designation of Labatt Park," prepared by the Local Architectural Heritage Conservation Advisory Committee of London City Council as part of the documentation the City of London that led to naming the park a heritage property on July 1, 1994.

27. "Tecumseh Park," *London Free Press*, June 29, 1936.

28. "Labatt Memorial Park," Canada's Historic Places, accessed April 6, 2014, http://www.historicplaces.ca/en/rep-reg/place-lieu.aspx?id=10078.

29. "Super Turf Tigers' Edge," *London Reporter*, March 8, 1990.

30. "Baseball Canada to Honour Labatt

Park," *Baseball Canada,* August 3, 2012, accessed April 4, 2014, http://www.baseball.ca/eng_news_story.cfm?NewsID=2162.

31. Karen Nugent, "SAFE! Clinton's Fuller Field Baseball Diamond Reclaims Title," *Worcester* (MA) *Telegram and Gazette,* October 15, 2008, accessed April 6, 2014, http://www.telegram.com/article/20081015/NEWS/810150593/1008.

32. Guinness World Records: Oldest Baseball Field Diamond, accessed April 6, 2014, http://www.guinnessworldrecords.com/world-records/3000/oldest-baseball-field-diamond.

Chapter 15

1. "Skill and Muscle," *London Advertiser,* August 4, 1884.
2. "Notes," *Toronto Globe,* August 31, 1885.
3. "London and Precincts," *London Advertiser,* February 9, 1886.
4. "Skill and Muscle," *London Advertiser,* February 19, 1886.
5. "Sporting Notes," *Guelph Mercury,* May 26, 1886.
6. John Castle Jr., *Goldie's Curve Ball: How Fred E. Goldsmith Invented, Demonstrated, Mastered & Championed The Curve Ball* (Colorado Springs, CO: Homelight Publishing, 2010), 191–92.
7. *Sporting Life,* July 16, 1898, quoted in "Fred Goldsmith: A Closer Look," by David Arcidiacono, in *Base Ball: A Journal of the Early Game,* Fall 2012, (Jefferson, NC: McFarland, 2012), 73.
8. *Sporting Life,* August 6 and 20, 1898, quoted in "Fred Goldsmith: A Closer Look," Arcidiacono, 73.
9. "Fred Goldsmith Tells of the Ball Games of 1876–77," *London Advertiser,* August 5, 1903.
10. *Grand Rapids Press,* August 6, 1906, quoted in "Fred Goldsmith: A Closer Look," Arcidiacono, 73.
11. David Fleitz, "Candy Cummings," a BioProject of the Society for American Baseball Research, accessed April 12, 2014, http://sabr.org'bioproj/person/99fabe5f.
12. *Chicago Tribune,* October 2, 1879, quoted in "Fred Goldsmith: A Closer Look," Arcidiacono, 70–71.
13. E. J. Carty, "Fifteen Thousand Cheered First Curved-Ball Pitcher As London Won Big Game," *London Advertiser,* August 20, 1927.
14. *The Sporting News,* December 10, 1931, quoted in "Fred Goldsmith: A Closer Look," Arcidiacono, 71.
15. *The Sporting News,* March 2, 1932.
16. "3,000 Booster Day Fans See London Win," *London Free Press,* June 29, 1936, 21.
17. "Visiting Nine Wins Exhibition," *London Free Press,* August 30, 1938.
18. Castle, *Goldie's Curve Ball,* 206.
19. Undated 1937 newspaper clipping, likely the *New York Journal-American,* in Fred Goldsmith file folder, National Baseball Hall of Fame Library, Cooperstown, New York, quoted in "Fred Goldsmith: A Closer Look," Arcidiacono, 74–75.
20. David Arcidiacono, "Fred Goldsmith: A Closer Look," In *Base Ball: A Journal of the Early Game* (Jefferson, NC: McFarland, Fall 2012), 78.
21. *The Sporting News,* March 30, 1939, 2.
22. Brian Martin, *Baseball's Creation Myth: Adam Ford, Abner Graves and the Cooperstown Story* (Jefferson, NC: McFarland, 2013).
23. Castle, *Goldie's Curve Ball,* 202.
24. Inscription on plaque for Candy Cummings, National Baseball Hall of Fame and Museum, Cooperstown, New York.
25. Castle, *Goldie's Curve Ball,* 215.
26. *The Sporting News,* March 30, 1939, 2.
27. Sam Greene, "Goldsmith Dies Insisting He Invented Curve Ball," *Detroit News,* March 29, 1939.
28. E. L. Warner, Jr., "Historians' Oversight Hastens Star's Death," *Detroit Free Press,* March 29, 1939.
29. "Six Hits and an Error," *The Sporting News,* May 11, 1939, 4.
30. "Co-Originators of the Curve Ball," *The Sporting News,* June 22, 1939, 16.
31. David Fleitz, "Fred Goldsmith," a BioProject of the Society for American Baseball Research, accessed March 17, 2014, http://sabr.org/bioproj/person/99c4a5f5.
32. *London Free Press,* August 12, 1943, quoted in Castle, 220.
33. Castle, *Goldie's Curve Ball,* 12.
34. Ibid., 40–122.
35. Ibid., 189.
36. Ryan Pyette, "Grandson Inspired by Baseball Legend," *London Free Press,* November 6, 2009, D1.

Epilogue

1. Nancy Bouchier and Robert Knight Barney, "A Critical Examination of a Source on

Early Ontario Baseball: The Reminiscence of Adam E. Ford," *Journal of Sport History* (Spring 1988), 78.

2. Andrew Cohen, *Extraordinary Canadians: Lester B. Pearson* (Toronto: Penguin, 2008), 27.

3. William Humber, *Diamonds of the North: A Concise History of Baseball in Canada* (Toronto: Oxford University Press, 1995), 113–14.

4. Jeffrey Michael Laing, *Bud Fowler: Baseball's First Black Professional* (Jefferson, NC: McFarland, 2013), 66–71.

5. Imperial Oil of Canada website, accessed April 20, 2014, http://www.imperialoil.ca/Canada-English/default.aspx.

6. "A Brief Synopsis of The Sleeman Brewing and Malting Co. Ltd. Past and Present. 1995," produced by Sleeman Brewing, and the University of Guelph Archives website, accessed April 20, 2014, http://www.lib.uoguelph.ca/resources/archival_&_special_collections/the_collections/digital_collections/sleeman/brewing_history/the_sleeman_brewery.cfm.

Bibliography

Books

Anson, Adrian Constantine. *A Ball Player's Career.* Illustrated Edition. United Kingdom: Dodo Press reprint of 1900 edition.

Armstrong, Frederick. *The Forest City: An Illustrated History of London, Canada.* London, ON: Windsor Publications, 1986.

Barney, Robert Knight. "Whose National Pastime? Baseball in Canadian Popular Culture." In *The Beaver Bites Back? American Popular Culture in Canada,* edited by David H. Flaherty and Frank E. Manning. Montreal: McGill–Queen's University Press, 1993.

Batesel, Paul. *Players and Teams of the National Association, 1871–1875.* Jefferson, NC: McFarland, 2012.

Block, David. *Baseball Before We Knew It: A Search for the Roots of the Game.* Lincoln, NE: University of Nebraska Press, 2005.

Bremner, Archie. *Illustrated London: City of London, Ontario, Canada. The Pioneer Period and the London of Today.* London, ON: London Printing and Lithographing, 1900.

Brock, Daniel J. *Fragments from the Forks: London Ontario's Legacy.* London, ON: London and Middlesex Historical Society, 2011.

Bryce's Base Ball Guide 1876. London, ON: William Bryce, 1876.

Carnegie, Andrew. *Autobiography of Andrew Carnegie.* London: Constable and Co., 1920. Gutenberg eBook accessed at www.gutenberg.org/files/17976/17976-h/17976-h.htm.

The Carty Chronicles of Landmarks and Londoners, ed. Catherine B. McEwen. London, ON: London and Middlesex Historical Society, 2005.

Castle, John R. Jr. *Goldie's Curve Ball: How Fred E. "Goldie" Goldsmith Invented, Demonstrated, Mastered & Championed the Curve Ball.* Colorado Springs, CO: HomeLight, 2010.

A Chronological History of Old Allegheny City, Penna. Compiled for the Allegheny City Society. Pittsburgh, PA: Don Kuhl Printing, 1969.

Cohen, Andrew. *Extraordinary Canadians: Lester B. Pearson.* Toronto: Penguin, 2008.

Dewey, Donald, and Nicholas Acocella. *The New Biographical History of Baseball.* Chicago: Triumph, 2002.

Dickey, Glenn. *The History of National League Baseball.* Briarcliff Manor, NY: Stein and Day, 1979.

Elias, Robert. *The Empire Strikes Out: How Baseball Sold U.S. Foreign Policy and Promoted the American Way Abroad.* New York: The New Press, 2010.

Felber, Bill, ed. *Inventing Baseball: The 100 Greatest Games of the Nineteenth Century.* Phoenix: Society for American Baseball Research, 2013.

Gladstone, Bill. *A History of the Jewish Community of London Ontario.* Toronto: Now and Then Books, 2011.

Gorn, Elliott J., Randy Roberts, and Terry D. Bilhartz. *Constructing the American*

Past: A Sourcebook of a People's History, Volume Two. New York: Pearson, Longman, 2005.

Humber, William. *Cheering for the Home Team: The Story of Baseball in Canada.* Erin, ON: The Boston Mills Press, 1983.

_____. *Diamonds of the North: A Concise History of Baseball in Canada.* Toronto: Oxford, 1995.

Ivor-Campbell, Frederick, and Mark Rucker, eds. *Baseball's First Stars.* Cleveland: Society for American Baseball Research, 1996.

Johnson, Leo A. *History of Guelph: 1827–1927.* Guelph, ON: Guelph Historical Society, 1977.

Jozsa, Frank P. Jr. *Major League Baseball Expansions and Relocations: A History, 1876–2008.* Jefferson, NC: McFarland, 2010.

Laing, Jeffrey Michael. *Bud Fowler: Baseball's First Black Professional.* Jefferson, NC: McFarland, 2013.

Laxer, James. *Tecumseh and Brock: The War of 1812.* Toronto, ON: House of Anansi Press, 2012.

Levine, Peter. *A. G. Spalding and the Rise of Baseball: The Promise of American Sport.* New York: Oxford, 1985.

Martin, Brian. *Baseball's Creation Myth: Adam Ford, Abner Graves and the Cooperstown Story.* Jefferson, NC: McFarland, 2013.

May, Gary. *Hard Oiler!: The Story of Early Canadians' Quest for Oil at Home and Abroad.* Toronto: Dundurn, 1998.

McCollister, John. *The Bucs!: The Story of the Pittsburgh Pirates.* Lenexa, KS: Addax, 1998.

McGee, Patricia. *The Story of Fairbank Oil: Four Generations of the Family Producing Oil Longer Than Anyone in the World.* Petrolia, ON: Words Unlimited Ink, 2004.

Mercantile Agency Reference Book for the Dominion of Canada, July 1882. Montreal: Dun, Wiman, 1882.

Nemec, David. *The Beer and Whisky League: The Illustrated History of the American Association—Baseball's Renegade Major League.* New York: Lyons and Burford, 1994.

_____. *The Great Encyclopedia of 19th Century Major League Baseball.* New York: Donald I. Fine Books, 1997.

_____. *Major League Baseball Profiles: 1871–1900. Volume 1. The Ballplayers Who Built the Game.* Lincoln: University of Nebraska Press, 2011.

Nucciarone, Monica. *Alexander Cartwright: The Life Behind the Baseball Legend.* Lincoln, NE: University of Nebraska Press, 2009.

Phelps, Edward C.H., Charles B. Whipp, and Lee Pethick, eds. *Petrolia Ontario-Canada: 150 Years 1854–2004.* Petrolia, ON: Van Tyl and Fairbank, 2004.

Pietrusza, David. *Major Leagues: The Formation, Sometimes Absorption, and Mostly Inevitable Demise of 18 Professional Organizations, 1871 to Present.* Jefferson, NC: McFarland, 1991.

Regan, Gary, and Mardee Haidin Regan. *The Book of Bourbon and Other Fine Whiskeys.* London: Mixellany, 2009.

Rooney, Dan and Carol Peterson. *Allegheny City: A History of Pittsburgh's North Side.* Pittsburgh: University of Pittsburgh Press, 2013.

Rosenburg, John M. *They Gave Us Baseball: The 12 Extraordinary Men Who Shaped the Major Leagues.* Harrisburg, PA: Stackpole, 1989.

Ryczek, William J., *Blackguards and Red Stockings: A History of Baseball's National Association 1871–1875.* Jefferson, NC: McFarland, 1992.

Spalding's Official Base Ball Guide, 1903. New York: American Sports Publishing, 1903.

The Story of Old Allegheny City. Compiled by Workers of the Writers' Program of the Works Projects Administration in the Commonwealth of Pennsylvania. Pittsburgh: Allegheny Centennial Committee, 1941.

Thorn, John. *Baseball in the Garden of Eden: The Secret History of the Early Game.* New York: Simon and Schuster, 2011.

Thorn, John and Pete Palmer, eds. *Total Baseball: The Ultimate Encyclopedia of Baseball: Third Edition.* New York: HarperCollins, 1993.

Tiemann, Robert L,. and Mark Rucker, eds.

Nineteenth Century Stars. Phoenix: Society for American Baseball Research, 2012.
Tucker, Albert. *Steam into Wilderness: Ontario Northland Railway 1902–1962.* Toronto: Fitzhenry and Whiteside, 1978.
Vincent, Ted. *Mudville's Revenge: The Rise & Fall of American Sport.* Lincoln, NE: University of Nebraska Press, Bison Book printing, 1994.
Voigt, David Q. *American Baseball.* Norman, OK: University of Oklahoma Press, 1966.
Westcott, Rich. *Winningest Pitchers: Baseball's 300-Game Winners.* Philadelphia: Temple University Press, 2002.
Whipp, Charles and Edward Phelps. *Petrolia: 1866–1966.* Petrolia, ON: Petrolia Advertiser–Topic and Petrolia Centennial Committee, 1966.

Articles

Arcidiacono, David. "Fred Goldsmith: A Closer Look." *Base Ball: A Journal of the Early Game,* Fall 2012.
"Baseball Canada to honor Labatt Park." *Baseball Canada,* August 3, 2012. www.baseball.ca/eng_news_story.cfm?NewsID=2162.
Bernard, David L. "The Guelph Maple Leafs: A Cultural Indicator of Southern Ontario." *Ontario History,* 84, no. 3 (September 1992).
Bouchier, Nancy B., and Robert Knight Barney. "A Critical Examination of a Source on Early Ontario Baseball: The Reminiscence of Adam E. Ford." *Journal of Sport History* 15, no. 1 (Spring 1988).
Bowes, Lisa. "George Sleeman and the Brewing of Baseball in Guelph 1872–1886." *Historic Guelph: The Royal City* 27 (1987–88). Guelph Historical Society.
Bronson, Les. "History of Baseball in London," article derived from speech delivered to the London-Middlesex Historical Society, February 15, 1972.
"Canadian Trade with the United States," in *The History of American Business,* accessed November 5, 2013, http://history-business.org/2371-canadian-trade-with-the-united-states.html.
"Conspiracy in Canada," Central Intelligence Agency, accessed Nov. 5, 2013, https://www.cia.gov/library/publications/additional-publications/civil-war/37.htm.
"Depot of Prisoners of War on Johnson's Island, Ohio," www.johnsonsisland.org.
"Englehart, Jacob Lewis," *Dictionary of Canadian Biography Online,* www.biographi.ca/EN009004-119.01-e.php?id_nbr=8126.
Grant, Hugh H. "The 'Mysterious' Jacob L. Englehart and the Early Ontario Petroleum Industry." *Ontario History* 85, no. 1 (March 1993).
Grant, Hugh M. and Henry Thille. "Tariffs, Strategy, and Structure: Competition and Collusion in the Ontario Petroleum Industry, 1870–1880." *The Journal of Economic History* 61, no. 2 (June 2001).
"The Great Railroad Strike," Digital History, accessed March 3, 2013, http://www.digitalhistory.uh.edu/disp_textbook.cfm?smtID=2&psid=3189.
Guinness World Records: Oldest Baseball Field Diamond, accessed April 6, 2014, http://www.guinnessworldrecords.com/world-records/3000/oldest-baseball-field-diamond.
Haupert, Michael. "MLB's annual salary leaders, 1874–2012." Society for American Baseball Research, Business of Baseball Research newsletter, Fall 2012, accessible at http://sabr.org/research/mlbs-annual-salary-leaders-1874-2012.
"History of Distilled Spirits in America." Distilled Spirits Council of the United States, www.discus.org/heritage/spirits.
Humber, William, "Cheering for the Home Team: Baseball and Town Life in Nineteenth Century Ontario, 1854–1869," a paper presented at the Fifth Canadian Symposium on the History of Sport and Physical Education, University of Toronto, August 26–29, 1982.
Ingham, John N. "Iron and Steel in the Pittsburgh Region: The Domain of Small Business." *Business and Economic History,* Second Series, Volume 20 (1991).
Johnson, W. Lloyd. "Farewell to Old-style Ball." In *Inventing Baseball: The 100 Greatest Games of the 19th Century,* ed-

ited by Bill Felber. Phoenix: Society for American Baseball Research, 2013.

"Labatt Memorial Park." *Canada's Historic Places,* accessed April 6, 2014, http://www.historicplaces.ca/en/rep-reg/placelieu.aspx?id=10078.

Landon, Fred. "Some Effects of the American Civil War on Canadian Agriculture." *Agricultural History* 7, no. 4 (October 1933).

Mann, Alfred N. "Some Petroleum Pioneers of Pittsburgh." Originally published in *Western Pennsylvania Magazine,* Summer 2009, www.heinzhistorycenter.org/uploads/Media/4_MicrosoftWord_Mann_Petroleum_web.pdf.

National Baseball Hall of Fame and Museum: *2012 Yearbook.* Lynn, MA: H. O. Zimman, 2012.

Nelson, Scott Reynolds. "The Real Great Depression." *Chronicle of Higher Education,* October 17, 2008, accessed March 28, 2013, http://srnels.people.wm.edu/articles/realGrtDepr.html

Nugent, Karen, "Clinton's Fuller Field Baseball Diamond Reclaims Title," *Worcester (MA) Telegram & Gazette,* October 15, 2008.

"Oil Springs Boom and Bust," Oil Museum of Canada, accessed April 22, 2013 www.lclmg.org/lclmg/Museums/OilMuseumofCanada/BlackGold2/OilHeritage/OilSprings/tabid/208/Default.aspx.

Overfield, Joseph M. *"David W. Force," Nineteenth Century Stars.* Phoenix: Society for American Baseball Research, 2012.

———. "The First Great Minor League Club." *SABR Baseball Research Journals Archive* online, http://research.sabr.org/journals/first-great-minor-league-club.

———. "'Gentle Jeems' Jim Galvin: Buffalo's First Superstar," *Bisongram,* February/March 1993.

Peterson, Richard. "Pittsburgh Pirates." In *Encyclopedia of Major League Baseball Clubs,* edited by Steven A. Reiss. Westport, CT: Greenwood Press, 2006.

"Phil 'Grandma' Powers." In *Major League Baseball Profiles 1871–1900,* edited by David Nemec. Lincoln, NB: University of Nebraska Press, 2011.

Schaefer, Robert H. "The Lost Art of Fair-Foul Hitting." *The National Pastime: A Review of Baseball History,* no. 19 (1999).

Sclanders, Ian. "The Amazing Jake Englehart." *Imperial Oil Review,* September 8, 1955.

Smith, E. Anne, "Remembering a Grand Hotel," *London CityLife Magazine,* April-May, 2003.

Vaccaro, Frank. "Origins of the Pitching Rotation," Fall 2011 *Baseball Research Journal,* accessed February 23, 2014, http://sabr.org/research/origins/-pitching-rotation.

Voigt, David Q. "The History of Major League Baseball." In *Total Baseball: The Ultimate Encyclopedia of Baseball, Third Edition,* edited by John Thorn and Peter Palmer. New York: HarperPerennial, 1993.

Newspapers

Akron (OH) Beacon Journal
Denver Post
Detroit Free Press
Detroit News
Guelph Mercury
Harper's Weekly
London Advertiser
London Free Press
London Reporter
New York Clipper
New York Times
Petrolia (ON) Advertiser-Topic
Philadelphia Inquirer
Sarnia (ON) Observer
Toronto Globe
Toronto Mail
Toronto Mail and Empire
Worcester (MA) Telegram & Gazette

Online Resources

Baseball-reference.com
Bioproj.sabr.org
Charlton's Baseball Chronology, Baseball-Library.com

Index

Page numbers in ***bold italic*** indicates pages with pictures.

Alaskas of Brooklyn 99, 154
Albany, New York 191
Albany Base Ball Club 194, 195, 234
Alerts 215
Alexander, Grover Cleveland 237
Alleghenys of Pittsburgh 99, 100, 102, 111–113, 118–120, 130–132, 140–144, 146, 147, 154, 156, 157, 163–165, 170–173, 186, 200, 201, 211, 212, 213, 214, 237
American Association 108, 110, 112, 113, 163, 167, 193, 198, 200–202, 209, 211, 212, 214, 215, 221, 237
American League 239
Andrus, C.W. 137
Anson, Adrian Constantine "Cap" 49, 61, 83, 125, 135, 137, 167, 194, 196–198, 221, ***223***, 231
Arcidiacono, David 228–230
Athletics of Philadelphia 41, 49, 60, 61, 63, 65, 107, 116, 121, 201, 212, 214, 232
Auburns of New York 86, 135, 151, 166
Austin, Jane 26
Avery, Charles Hamilton "Ham" 224–230, 232

Bailey (player) 177
Baltimore Orioles 201, 212, 221, 228
Baltimores 193, 195, 198
Barkley, Sam 212
Barnes, Roscoe "Ross" 9, 49, 61, 74, 83, 101, 124, 151, 155, 156, 158, 160, ***161***, 162, 164–169, 171, 172, 175–177, 179, 180, 182, 189, 192, 193, 237
Bastarache, A.J. 219, 220
Beachville, Ontario 2, 30, 32–34, 72
Beadle's Dime Base–Ball Player 67
Beam Clay Diamond of the Year award 218
Beauregard, Brigadier General P.G.T. 19
"Beer and Whiskey League" 201
Bierbauer, Louis 212, 214

Binghamton Crickets 76, 114, 123, 156, 171, 175, 176, 179, 186
Birrell, W.H. 144
Blackburn, Josiah 45
Block, David 2
Blong, Joe 81, 82, 127
Bond, Tommy 122, 136, 229
Bookless, William 36
Boston Red Caps 104, 111, 116, 119, 121, 122, 133, 136, 145, 148, 150, 170, 194
Boston Red Stockings 37, 39, 41, 49, 53, 59–61, 65, 86, 88, 104, 111, 116, 160
Bowmanville, Ontario 6
The Boy's Own Book 26
Bradley, George H. "Foghorn" 41, 81, 104, 119–123, 125–129, 137, 143, 144, 158, 166, 168, 169, 172, 179
Bradley, George Washington 125, 137, 173, 209
Brands, E.G. 231
Brannock, Mike 72
Bridwell, Al 163
Brock, General Isaac 48
Brooklyn Alaskas 99, 154
Brooklyn Atlantics 4, 34, 35, 41, 43, 44, 68, 69, 83, 93, 104, 105, 107, 119, 122, 134, 163, 164, 183–185, 187, 199, 224
Brooklyn Bridegrooms 198, 199
Brooklyn Dodgers 236
Brooklyn Eckfords 49, 107
Brooklyn Stars 225, 231
Brother Jonathan Club of Detroit 34
Brotherhood of Professional Baseball Players 200
Brouthers, Dan 237
Brown (player) 84, 85
Brown, Jim 69, 73
Brown, John 46, 49, 70, 209
Brown, Tom 69
Bryce, William 66, 67
Bryce's Base Ball Guide 50, 53, ***66***, 67

261

Index

Buckeyes of Columbus, Ohio 99, 100, 105, 118, 128, 130, 141, 147
Buffalo Bisons 151, 155, **157**, 158, 165, 169–172, 176–178, 183–187, 190–194, 196, 199, 200, 212, 213, 214, 237
Bulkeley, Morgan 63, 116
Burke, Mike 105, 142, 143, 158, 165, 172, 181, 193
Burns, Ken 7
Burns, Tommy 194, 196

California League 196
Cameron, John 46
Canadian Association of Base Ball Players 34, 65, 67
Canadian Baseball Hall of Fame 236
Canadian Baseball League 216
Canadian Professional League 198, 209, 211, 215, 221
Canadian Sandlot Congress 215
Capital City Club 191, 193
Carnegie, Andrew 102
Cartwright, Alexander Joy, Jr. 26, 27
Carty, E.J. 226
Cass Club of Detroit 76, 84, 112
Castle, John R. 233, 234
Castle, Phyllis 224, 233
Centennial celebrations 101
Chadwick, Henry 27, 28, 63, 64, 67, 88, 89, 96, 97, 118, 144, 146, 155, 191–193, 224–227
Champion City club of Springfield, Ohio 132
Chancellor, John 7
Charlotte Eleanor Englehart Hospital 206, **207**
Chase, Charles E. 136, 137
Chelseas of Brooklyn 41, 99, 123
Chicago Whales 239
Chicago White Stockings 9, 60–62, 74, **75**, 81, 83, 89, 107, 110, 116, 124–126, 129, 137, 148, 151, 160, 161, 162, 167, 170, 172, 186, 187, 190, 193–198, 209, 211, 221, **222**, **223**, 231
Cincinnati Red Stockings 37, 58, 105, 107, 116, 125, 126, 129, 138, 148, 162, 170, 186, 189, 190, 193, 200, 201
Clapp, John 134
Cleveland 221
Cleveland Blues 190
Cleveland Forest Citys 46, 49, 61, 160, 171, 177, 183, 185, 187, 200, 221, 229, 234
Cobb, Ty 216
Coles, Todd 226
Columbus Buckeyes 99, 100, 105, 118, 128, 130, 141, 147, 201
Columbus Solons 198, 199

Comiskey, Charlie 199
Conklin, James 24
Converse, E.E. 212
Cooperstown, New York 8, 27, 29, 30, 230, 232, 234
Corcoran, Larry 135, 157, 158, 187, 192, 194, 196–198, **222**, 227
Craver, William H. "Bill" 110, 111, 113, 115, 136, 137, 148, 178, 185
Creamer, George 112
cricket 2, 22, 24, 26, 32, 46, 50, 51, 139
Crooks, A.P. 121
Cummings, William A. "Candy" 37, 99, 112, 119, 123, 126, 138, 141, 168, 188, 224, 225, 228, 230–232, 234, 237

Dalrymple, Abner 196
Dartmouth, Nova Scotia 2
Dauntless Club of Toronto 44
Denny, Elizabeth 95
Detroit Aetnas 53, 55, 74–76, 78, 86, 88
Detroit Tigers 215, 224, 229
Detroit Wolverines 222
Devlin, James A. 110, 111, 113, 115, 136, 137, 140, 148, 178, 181, 183–185
DeWitt's Base Ball Guide 67
Dinnen, Mike 68, 79, 81, 85, 105, 121, 122, 127, 142, 143, 158, 162, 163, 172
Dixon, C.J. 120, 135, 154, 159
Dolan, Tom 112, 143, 157, 158, 165
Dorgan, Jerry 192, 237
Dorgan, Mike 134, 195
Doscher, John Henry "Herm" 105, 123, 126, 155, 158, 164, 165, 169, 171, 179, 180, 181, 183, 192, 193
Doubleday, Abner 8, 27, 29, 30, 230
Drill Shed Grounds 6
Dunnigan, Joe 162, 172

Eastern League 214
Eastons of Easton, Pennsylvania 41
Eckert, William D. 200
economic collapse of 1873 101
Eggler, Dave 157, 158, 177
Elm Citys of New Haven 54, 83, 233
Ely (player) 85
Elysian Fields, Hoboken, New Jersey 26
Emslie, Bob 50, 76, 163, 164, 185, 193, 216, 228
Englehart, Charlotte Eleanor 205, 206, 207, **208**
Englehart, Hannah 11
Englehart, Jacob "Jake" 4, 11, 12, **13**, 14, 15, 16, 17, 24, 53, 70, 73, 74, 88, 92, 93, 103, 106, 154, 167, 169, 173, 181, 182, 203, 204, **205**, 206, 207, **208**, 236, 238
Englehart, Joel 11

Englehart, Ontario 207, 239
Englehart Park, Petrolia 206
Eries of Erie, Pennsylvania 126, 127, 130, 133
Essex of Buffalo 99
Evers, Johnny 163
Eyvel, George 189

Fairbanks of Chicago 99
Fall River of Massachusetts 141
Farrell, Jack 188
F.E. Goldsmith Saloon 221
Feast, Alfred 36
Federal League 239
Ferguson, Bob 59
the Field (team) 58
Flint, Frank "Silver" 159, 196, 197
Flyaways of New York 41, 43
Foley, Curry 158, 183
Force, Davy 61, 62, 151, 157, 158, 183, 188, 192
Ford, Dr. Adam 30–32
Forest City Base Ball Club of Cleveland 46, 49, 61, 160, 171, 177, 183, 185, 187, 200, 221, 229, 234
Fowler, Bud (John Jackson) 166, 167, 236
Frontier League 216
Fuller Field 219, 220
Fulmer, Chick 107, 112, 113, 142, 143, 157, 158, 165, 188

Galvin, Bridget 214
Galvin, James "Pud" 112, 113, 119, 126, 132, 143, 144, 157, 158, 165, 170, 171, 176, 177, 188, 196, 202, 212, *213*, 214, 215, 237, ***238***
Geer, Billy 54
Gehringer, Charlie 216
Gibson, George "Mooney" 4, 216
Gillean, Tom 4, 51, 69, 73, 79, 105, 122, 125, 137, 138, 178
Gillespie, Patrick 158, 159
Glenview 205, 206
Goldsmith, Fred "Goldie" 4, 8, ***68***, 69, 70, 74, 75, 77, 81–83, ***84***, ***91***, 104, 105, 112, 119–124, 126–130, 133, 135, 137–139, 141–144, 158, 162, 163, 165, 166, 168, 170, 171, 174, 176, 177, 179–181, 183–185, 187–189, 192, 194–199, 202, 216, 221, ***222***, ***223***, 224–228, ***229***, 230, 232–234, 237, 238
Goldsmith, Ransom 192
Goldsmith, Rowena 221–224, 232
Goodman, Jake 112
Gore, George 196
Gorman, Cornelius 45
Gorman, Henry "Harry" 5, 45, 46, 47, 49, 50, 53, 67, 68, 69–72, 73, 83, 86, 88, 94, 96, 98–100, 106, 110, 111, 118, 128, 142, 146, 147, 149, 151–154, 169, 176, 180, 189, 225
Graffen, Mase 81
Graves, Abner 28–31, 230
Great Railroad Strike 1877, 130–132
Guelph Maple Leafs 3, 4, 8, ***23***, 33, 35, 37, 39, 41, ***42***, 43, 50–53, 55–57, 65, 67, 69, 71–74, 77, 79, 83, 84, 85, 87, 88, 89, 90, 93, 94, 99, 100, 105, 106, 109, 111, 117, 118, 120–122, 126, 132–135, 137–139, 141, 144, 146, 154, 155, 158, 159, 167, 168, 170, 174, 175–177, 188, 203, 209–211, 215, 218, 225, 235, 236, 238
Guelph Royals ***217***
Guggenheim, Isaac 14, 203

Hall, Albert "Al" 134, 162, 164–166, 169, 172, 177, 181, 193
Hall, Fred 226
Hall, George 113, 136, 137, 140, 148
Hallinan, Jimmy 129
Hamilton Burlingtons 33
Hamilton Maple Leafs 33, 34, 36
Hamilton Standards 74, 75, 80, 121, 130
Hamilton Young Canadians 33
Hanlon, Ned 194
Harold, Donald 88
Harper, Prime Minister Stephen 1
Harrison, General William Henry 29, 48
Hartford Dark Blues 63, 86, 92, 99, 116, 119, 128, 130, 136, 172
Hastings, Scott 107, 109, 120
Haymakers of Troy 111, 112, 114, 154, 166, 178, 183
Hewer, James 159, 175
Higham, Dick 101
Hines, Captain Thomas Henry 20, 21
Holbert, Bill 112
Holyoke of Massachusetts 154, 191
Hop Bitters of Rochester 193, 194
Hornells of Hornellsville 114, 135, 139, 156, 170, 171, 173, 176, 179, 185, 186
Hornung, Joe "Dutch" 4, 8, 67, 68, 73, 79, 81, 82, ***84***, 85, ***91***, 105, 121–123, 134, 137, 143, 158, 165, 167, 169, 171, 174, 176, 177, 179, 186, 188, 192, 193, 202, 237
Hotaling, Pete 107, 108, 134
Hughes, Ed 228
Hulbert, William 9, 61–64, 83, 111, 114, 116, 125, 126, 129, 137, 140, 145, 148–152, 159, 160, 162, 184, 185, 190, 191, 195, 200, 211, 234, 239
Humber, William 6, 31, 32, 33, 43
Hunter, Billy 69, 77

Indianapolis Blues 148, 170, 186, 190
Ingersoll, Ontario 34, 35, 42

Index

Intercounty Baseball League 215, *217*, *218*
International Association of Professional Base Ball Players 4, 5, 8–10, *98*, 99, 100, 104, 105, 108, 113, 115, 117–119, 121, 124, 126, 130, 133, 134, 138, *140*, 141, 144–148, 150, 152, 153, 155–158, 164–168, 170, 175, 176, 178, 185–189, 191, 200, 202, 211, 215, 233, 234, 237, 238, 239
International Baseball League 193
Iroquois of Markham 168
Ithacas 88

Jersey City 195
Johnson, Walter 237
Johnson's Island 21
Jones, Charley 129
Jones, J.W. 181
Jones, William 40

Kansas City Cowboys 211
Keerl, George 37, 40, 72, 85
Kennedy, Doc 157
Kinsella, W.P. 6
Klu Klux Klan (KKK) 40, 41
Knowdell, Jake 104, 119, 123, 127, 135–137, 144, 162, 163, 170
Knowlton Cup 49
Kuhn, John 216

Labatt Memorial Park *217*, 218, *219*, 220, 232, 239
Lapham, William 72, 73, 77, 82, 158, 159
Latham, George Warren "Juice" 54–58, 68–70, 76, 79, 158, 237
Lawlor, Mike 105
League Alliance 114, 115, 139, 140
Leary, Jack 69, 80
Ledwith, Mike (Buck) 68, 79, 81, 83, 123
Libby, Steve 192
Live Oaks of Lynn, Massachusetts 99, 100, 118, 123, 126, 136, 138, 141, 146, 154, 156, 158, 166, 167, 186, 236
London Atlantics 228
London Base Ball Club 33, 46
London Cockneys 215
London Cricket Club 51
London Majors 215, *217*, 218
London Monarchs 216
London Morning Stars 48, 49
London Rippers 216
London Sports Hall of Fame 234
London Tigers 215
London Werewolves 216
Louisville Base Ball Club 109
Louisville Eclipse 201
Louisville Grays 104, 110, 111, 116, 129, 136, 140, 149, 155

Love, Frank 49
Lowell of Massachusetts 154, 156–158, 166, 183
Luff, Henry 54, 170
Lynch (player) 168
Lynn Live Oaks 99, 100, 118, 123, 126, 136, 138, 141, 146, 154, 156, 158, 166, 167, 186, 236

Mack, Connie 200, 232
Mack, Denny 179
Maddock, Charlie 41, 72, 159
Magner, John 105, 123, 124, 126, 133, 134, 193
Malone, Fergus 101
Manchesters of New Hampshire 99, 100, 118, 119, 123, 133, 134, 156, 166, 180, 183, 186, 191, 194
Mathewson, Christy 237
McCarthy, Tommy 199
McCormick, Harry 120, 122, 124, 169, 188, 192
McCormick, Jim 130, 159
McGunnigle, Bill 158, 170, 192
McGunnity, Billy 118
McKelvey, John 142, 143
McKnight, Harmar Denny 95, 96, 98, 100, 111–114, 118, 131, 141, 147, 167, 201, 211, 212
McKnight, Robert 95
McLean, Hugh 68, 69
McSorley, John "Trick" 158
McVey, Cal 61, 83, 160
Meacham, Lewis 150, 151
Medill, Joseph 129
Meredith, William R. 47, 182
Merkle, Fred 163, 164
"Merkle's Boner" 163
Merritt, William 159
Mills, Abraham G. 28, 29
Milwaukee Cream Citys (a.k.a. Grays) 112, 141, 148, 170, 186, 190
Mitchell, Bobby 229
Moore, Edwin "Ed" 16, 24, 47, 49, 54, 71, 78, 83, 84, 88, 169
Morden, Ralph 47
Morning Stars of London 48, 49
Morris, Peter 1
Mountain, W.F. 67, 77
Mountain City of Altoona, Pennsylvania 99
Mountjoy, Billy 105, 193
Mulkern, P. 169
Murnane, Tim 237
Murphy, Henry 166
Mutuals of Jackson 53, 55, 74–76
Mutuals of New York 59, 60, 63, 86, 107, 110, 112, 116, 136

Myers, Hank 40, 41
Myers, Harry 72, 74

Nassaus of Brooklyn 41
National Association of Professional Base Ball Players 9, 39, 49, 54, 58–62, 65, 100, 101, 104, 105, 109, 112, 116, 148, 160, 237
National Base-Ball Association (NBBA) 191, 194, 195
National Baseball Hall of Fame 8, 9, 99, 112, 214, 230, 233, 234
National League of Professional Base Ball Clubs 4, 5, 9, 28, 41, 62–65, 67, 70, 88, 94, 96–100, 104, 105, 107, 109, 110–117, 119, 121, 125, 126, 129, 136, 137, 140, 145, 147–150, 152, 153, 155, 156, 158, 161, 162–164, 178, 183–185, 187, 188, 190–198, 200, 201, 209, 211, 214, 216, 222, 228, 233, 234, 239
Neff, J. Wayne 138
Nelson, Candy 112, 143
Nemec, David 191
New Bedford, Connecticut 154, 156, 166, 191
New Havens 54
New York Giants 163, 197
New York Knickerbockers 26, 27, 31
New York Metropolitans 201
New York Mutuals 37, 229
New York State League 211
Newberry, John 26
Niagaras of Buffalo 33
Nicholls, C.W. 177, 186
Nichols, Alfred 113, 136, 137, 148
Nichols, J.T. 51, 85
Nineteenth Century Committee of the Society for American Baseball Research 188
Nolan, Ed "The Only" 178
Northanger Abbey 26
Nucciarone, Monica 27

O'Day, Hank 164
O'Neil, J. Palmer 214
Oil Springs, Ontario 11, 12, 15
OK Base Ball club 49
Old Time Ball Players Association 232
Oneida team 41
Oswego, New York 183
Overfield, Joe 214

Paasch, Bill 198, 199
Pearson, Lester B. 236
Pearson Cup 236
Pennsylvania Brown Stockings 99
Pennsylvania Eastons 41
Perrin, Daniel 47
Peters, John 125, 137

Petersville, Ontario 91
Petrolia Imperials 167, 236
Petrolia, Ontario 11, 12, 15, 103, 167, 203–208, 239
Philadelphia Athletics 41, 49, 60, 61, 63, 65, 107, 116, 121, 201, 212, 214, 232
Philadelphia Centennials 104
Philadelphia Nationals 37
Philadelphia Pearls 41
Philadelphia Quakers 212
Pietrusza, David 5, 148, 152, 195
Pike, Lipman "Lip" 194, 195, 237
Pittsburgh Alleghenys 99, 100, 102, 111–113, 118–120, 130–132, 140–144, 146, 147, 154, 156, 157, 163–165, 170–173, 186, 200, 201, 211, 212, 213, 214, 237
Pittsburgh Base Ball Association 95
Pittsburgh Burghers 212, 214, 215
Players' League 113, 200, 202, 212, 237
PONY (Pennsylvania, Ontario, New York) League 215
Powers, L.J. 191
Powers, Phil "Grandmother" 8, 73, 74, 77, 79, 81, 82, *84*, 85, *91*, 104, 105, 119–121, 123, 125–127, 134–137, 139, 142, 143, 145, 158, 165, 169–172, 174, 175, 180, 187, 192–194, 196, 202, 215, 225
Procter, General Henry 48
Prospect Park, Brooklyn 155
Providence (Rhode Island) Grays 148, 170, 194, 196, 197
Pyette, Ryan 234

Quinn, Joe 125
Quinton, Marshall 105, 106, 109, 136, 137, 143, 144, 159, 162, 175, 176

Radbourn, Charley "Old Hoss" 231
Rankin, A.B. 153
Reading of Reading, Pennsylvania 99
Reid, Bill 105, 134, 159
Reid, W.J. 90, 216
Reis, Lawrence 145
Resolutes of Elizabeth, New Jersey 82, 99
Rippers 216
Robinson, Jackie 236
Rochesters of Rochester, New York 41, 99, 100, 118, 133, 135, 154, 155, 157, 163, 166, 171, 172, 183–186
Rockefeller, John D. 204
Rook, Rowena 192
rounders 8, 25, 26, 27, 28
Royal Oaks 6
Ryczek, William 21, 22, 65

St. Lawrence club of Kingston 65, 68, 69, 78, 80

St. Louis Brown Stockings 81, 82, 95, 116, 127, 199, 201, 214
St. Louis Red Stockings 95, 99, 105, 112
San Francisco Athletics 196
San Franciscos of San Francisco 99
Say, Jimmy 195
Say, Louis 119, 138
Seattle Mariners 165
Seattle Seahawks 165
Selig, Bud 27
Selkirk Settlement, Manitoba 2
Seymour, Dorothy 1
Seymour, Harold 1
Shevlin (player) 55, 56, 123
Shuttleworth, Jim 33
Shuttleworth, William 33
Silver Ball Trophy 34, 35, 37, 67, *87*, 121, 144
Silver Creek Brewery 37, *38*
Silver Creeks 69, 83
Sleeman, George 3, 4, *23*, 37, 38, *39*, 40, 41, *42*, 43-45, 50, 52, 65, 67, 69, 71, 74, 79, 83, 85, 86, 93, 94, 98-100, 105-112, 117, 118, 133, 135, 139, 141, 147, 159, 167, 168, 203, 209-211, 215, 221, 236, 238
Sleeman, John W. 37, 238, 239
Sleeman Brewing and Malting 38
Sleeman Centre 239
Sleeman Collection of letters 106, 107
Smith, Billy 41, 72, 106, 121, 126, 138, 159, 174-177
Smith, Harry 129
Smith, Tommy 79, 105, 106, 135, 143, 158, 159, 164, 165, 167, 182, 183
Society for American Baseball Research 214
Somerville, Ed 104, 120, 121, 123, 126, 127, 137, 142, 144, 145, 196
Sonneborn, Jonas 14, 15
Sonneborn, Solomon 14, 16, 17
Southam, Richard 4, 47, 49, 92, 120, 121
Southam, William 45, 47
Spalding, Albert Goodwill 1, 8, 28, 29, 39, 49, 61, 62, 74, 83, 88, 89, 98, 101, 113, 114, 124, 125, 139, 160, *161*, 194, 211, 225, 229-231
Spalding's Official Base Ball Guide 28, 29, 67, 224
Special Base Ball Commission 28, 29
Spence, Harrison 37, 40, 41, 85
Spencer, W. 105, 122, 123
Spink, Alfred H. 225
Sprague (club official) 151, 152
Springfield of Massachusetts 154, 169, 183, 187, 191, 192, 194, 233
Staten Island club of New York 44
Staten Islands 44

Stieler, Ellen 231
Strief, George 130
Sullivan (player) 85, 106, 154, 159, 184
Sullivan, Denny 158
Sullivan, James 84, 120, 122, 135
Sunday, Billy 197
Sunley, William 41
Sutton, Ezra 61
Syracuse Stars 86, 88, 108, 114, 120, 122, 124, *140*, 156, 157, 166, 170, 172, 173, 177-181, 183, 187, 188, 190, 191, 194, 196, 215

Tecumseh (Shawnee leader) 47, 48
Tecumseh Base Ball Association 70
Tecumseh House Hotel *16*, 19, 20, 46, 47, 49, 53, 54, 72, 74, 144, 169
Tecumseh Park 92, 93, 104, 122, *127*, 142, 155, 162, 180, 216, *217*, *219*, 228, 239
Thayer, Fred 118
Thompson (player) 185
Thompson, Charlotte Eleanor 205, 206, 207, *208*
Thorn, John 1, 25
Toronto Base Ball Association 67, 211
Toronto Blue Jays 5, 7-9, 235, 236
town ball 31
Triple-A Montreal Royals 236
Troy Haymakers 111, 112, 114, 154, 166, 178, 183
Troy Trojans 190, 191, 193-195, 233
Trudeau, Charles 236
Trudeau, Pierre Elliott 236
Tuells (player) 77
Tuft, James 166, 167
Tyng, James 118

Unas of Kalamazoo 55
Union Association 112, 202, 209, 221, 237
Utica Base Ball Club 156, 158, 169, 170, 176, 178, 179, 185, 187, 188, 191, 194

Vallandigham, Clement 19-21
Van Burkalow, Isaac 157, 184
Vancouver Canucks 165
Vincent, Ted 63, 98, 99, 117, 150, 195
Voigt, David 117
Von der Ahe, Chris 199

Waite, L.C. 95, 96, 98, 118
Walker, Col. John 182
Walker, Moses Fleetwood 167, 236
Walsh (player) 85, 159
Ward, John Montgomery 158
Washington Nationals 191, 195, 200, 212
Waterman, Fred 105
Waterman, Herman 12

Waterman, Isaac 12
Watertown, New York 40, 41, 42, 43
Watertown Tournament 41, 50
Weaver, Sam 121
Westerns of Keokuk, Iowa 60
Whalen (player) 83, 123
Wheeling Standards 130
White, Hamilton 155
White, James "Deacon" 61, 122, 160, 200
Whitney, Arthur 109
Whitney, J.W. 155, 156, 164
Wigmore, Richard 72
Williams, J.A. 141, 155, 185, 201
Williams, James Miller 11
Williamson, Ned 113, 143, 159
Wilshire, Ida 224

Woodstock Actives 184, 185
Woodstock Excelsiors 69
Woodstock Young Canadians 33–35, 47
Worcesters of Massachusetts 183, 191, 196, 200
Wordsworth, Favel 81, 83, 123
World Sandlot baseball title 215
World Series 7
Wright, George 86, 196
Wright, Harry 160
Wrigley Field 239

Young, Nick 59, 139

Zettlein, George "Charmer" 107, 108
Zorras 32

www.ingramcontent.com/pod-product-compliance
Ingram Content Group UK Ltd.
Pitfield, Milton Keynes, MK11 3LW, UK
UKHW041931140426
5217IPUK00014B/421